EXECUTIVE RESOURCE MANAGEMENT

ROBERT BARNER

EXECUTIVE
RESOURCE
MANAGEMENT

**BUILDING AND RETAINING AN
EXCEPTIONAL LEADERSHIP TEAM**

DAVIES-BLACK PUBLISHING
PALO ALTO, CALIFORNIA

Published by Davies-Black Publishing, an imprint of Consulting Psychologists Press, Inc., 3803 East Bayshore Road, Palo Alto, CA 94303; 800-624-1765.

Special discounts on bulk quantities of Davies-Black books are available to corporations, professional associations, and other organizations. For details, contact the Director of Book Sales at Davies-Black Publishing, an imprint of Consulting Psychologists Press, Inc., 3803 East Bayshore Road, Palo Alto, CA 94303; 650-691-9123; Fax 650-623-9271.

Visit the Davies-Black Publishing website at www.daviesblack.com.

04 03 02 01 00   10 9 8 7 6 5 4 3 2 1
Printed in the United States of America

Library of Congress Cataloging-in-Publication Data
Barner, Robert
    Executive resource management : building and retaining an exceptional leadership team / Robert Barner.
        p. cm.
    Includes bibliographical references (p.) and index.
    ISBN 0-89106-140-1 (hc.)
    1. Executives. 2. Leadership. I. Title.

    HD38.2.B37 2000
    658.4′092—dc21

                                                              99-089257

FIRST EDITION
First printing 2000

CONTENTS

FIGURES

TABLES

Everyone writes for a different reason. First-time writers (bless their naive souls!) write for the incredible fame and fortune their books will surely bring them. Some writers write as a sort of masochistic means of purging the soul. In the thirteenth century these millennial flagellants would have adorned themselves in hair shirts and cat-o'-nine-tails. Today they write. Each time I start to conclude a writing project—in a room surrounded by research notes, sticky-pad reminders, and my ever-present cappuccino machine—I swear to myself that I'll never start another one. To break that promise, a new writing project has to fulfill four critical conditions.

Condition #1: It must help me overcome intellectual frustration. The book you are reading began as all my other writing projects have begun: with the frustration that comes from searching the bookstores and not being able to find what I need in the way of an adequate business resource. In the case of this book, my journey began about two years ago when I was having difficulty finding useful information on the field of executive resource management. The fact is, I wasn't even able to find anything that put a decent, well-encompassing label on the subject I refer to as "executive resource management." What I found instead were either books that focused on the "great man/woman" theory of leadership (here's what it takes to be the best) or texts that centered on one limited aspect of the puzzle, such as the executive selection process or executive development. I found it very frustrating that most of these latter books were written from the perspective of the "holy priests of HR"—that is to say that they were boring, detailed tomes. I didn't feel that they did a good job of highlighting some of the really exciting research and innovations that are forcing us to reexamine the way we think about executive resource management. That line of thinking was dangerous because it led me to consider whether a book on the subject of executive resource management would be useful to senior-level executives and HR leaders such as myself.

Condition #2: The subject must be engaging. The field of executive resource management most certainly is engaging. To me, there are few things more exciting than being a strategist in the game of business—staging the chessboard in such a way that it sets your company far ahead of the competition. In today's business environment, executive capability is the queen's piece on the board. There is no faster way of growing shareholder value while bringing your competitors to their knees than by selecting and developing a winning senior leadership team. As I discuss in the first chapter, when it comes to executive selection, retention, and development, the stakes are shooting up very quickly. The cost associated with hiring an inept senior executive or losing a key player has come to be very high. In *Executive Resource Management* I've tried to arm you with the tools, methods, and strategies you'll need to make executive resource decisions that can support the needs of your company.

Condition #3: The subject area must be continually evolving. I don't enjoy writing about subjects that have been beaten to death in the popular literature. One of the exciting things about the field of executive resource management is that it is changing on a day-to-day basis. In this book I've tried to highlight many of these changes, from the way that the Internet is forcing the hybridization of external search firms, to the use of competitive intelligence in conducting "talent raids" on competitors, to the use of computerized business simulations and action learning to integrate classroom learning with work applications. As you read my book I will be very surprised if you don't encounter a least a few new and innovative ideas that you can add to your management arsenal.

Condition #4: I have to be creating something of substance. The last thing I want to write (or read for that matter) is what I call an "airport read"—that is, a glossy book that, being 90 percent glitter and hype, attempts to substitute the latest jargon for solid research and analysis (perhaps my next book will be on reenvisioning your existing paradigm as a means of reexamining your core competencies). Instead, I want to craft something that doesn't lose its value when you touch down at the other end of your flight—a work that can be repeatedly referred to for help and assistance. If I've done my job properly, each chapter of *Executive Resource Management* should contain detailed guidelines and techniques for putting new ideas into action. Whenever possible, I've also tried to provide charts, tables, and graphic models that help illustrate key concepts.

One final word before I close. I'm a corporate HR executive, not an academic. The concepts and ideas I'll be introducing throughout this book are more than abstract theory. They represent the advice and guidelines I've gathered and applied in over twenty years in the HR field, with experience ranging from succession planning modeling, to executive recruitment and assessment, to organizational and executive development. Given the broad scope of subjects encompassed within this work, I've also attempted to pull in a variety of experts in the field of executive resource management, ranging from senior-level line executives within both large and small companies, to corporate HR leaders, to leading researchers and consultants. As a writer my role has been to attempt to weave together these separate threads of thought into what I hope is an engaging conceptual fabric. If you've purchased this book it is probably because you are part of that invisible learning community. Accordingly, I invite you to contact me with your comments and questions at ibscribe@aol.com. Let's talk.

ACKNOWLEDGMENTS

I think that writing a business book is quite often a team effort. The truth is that behind the singular entity known as "the author," there are a lot of other people who generously contribute their time and energy to the task of making a writing project a success. For me, those people include a number of friends and respected associates. Erica Fitch, a recent graduate of University of Baltimore's M.S. program in industrial and organizational psychology, provided valuable assistance in much of the initial research for this text. My wife and "split apart," Charlotte, helped bring clarity to my rambled thoughts, and was (as always) patient with my frequent mental departures from the here and now.

The publishing team at Davies-Black helped me think through critical components of my writing and offered creative marketing expertise. I'd like to especially thank my acquisitions editor, Melinda Adams Merino, who provided a high degree of encouragement during the course of this project, and who offered valuable suggestions relating to the organization and flow of my material. Melinda's commitment level was high enough to continue her support of this project even after she had made the decision to leave Davies-Black to relocate to London. I'd also like to thank Davies-Black's Director of Sales, Laura Simonds, whose business savvy has helped me formulate and execute an innovative marketing plan in support of this book.

When it comes to content contributions, the list is extensive. The folks at the Center for Creative Leadership in Greensboro, North Carolina, including Sara King, Valerie Sessa, and Craig Chappelow, provided substantial research related to the areas of executive selection, derailment, learning agility, and insight-focused executive education. Kay Lillig Cotter, Director of Consulting for Measurement Services at Wilson Learning, provided some sharp insights on the subject of executive assessment, both domestically and internationally. Thomas Saporito, Senior Vice President of RHR International, outlined some significant research that RHR had conducted related to the subject of CEO selection and assessment. George Klemp and Bernie Cullen, partners in Cambria Consulting, provided a very thought-provoking analysis of the field of executive selection and the important role culture "fit" plays in the selection process. Bruce Barge, IO psychologist with Anon Consulting, was willing to share his consulting experiences in integrating executive development with business strategy.

I'd also like to thank those individuals who helped me look ahead to see where the fields of executive search, competitive intelligence, and executive selection are headed in the future. Among these are Steve Balough, president of David Powell Associates; Joe McCool, editor of *Executive Recruiter News;* David Lord, president of Executive Search Information Services; Peter Felix, president of the Association of Executive Search Consultants; and Constance LaDouceur, principal of ExecuQuest, Inc. I'd also like to thank Thomas McCoy of Thomas McCoy Associates for sharing information on the subject of executive retention including the application of his company's LeaderShare™ executive incentive system. A special thanks goes to Geoffrey Smart and his father, Brad Smart, who were invaluable to me not only in being willing to share details of their selection interviewing process, but also for their assistance in networking me with other professionals in the field of executive selection and assessment.

One of the things I enjoyed most about this writing project was having the opportunity to explore cutting-edge methodologies related to executive assessment and development. Three members of the Strategic Management Group (SMG)—George Winnick, Managing Director; James Allen, Director of the Client Engagement Group; and Bridget Doyle, Best Practices Consultant—generously shared information regarding the application of business simulations to executive development. Kevin Thibodeau, vice president of the Caliber Learning Network, was kind enough to provide a detailed demonstration of how his company's sophisticated distributed learning system could be applied, while Alison Peirce, Program Director for Wharton Direct, was very helpful in outlining emerging trends in distributed learning. I'd also like to thank Joseph Sefcik Jr., president of Employment Technologies Corporation, who introduced me to the applications of video-based assessment technology, and Bob Schneiders, president of Educational Data Systems, who provided valuable information on the subject of computerized competency databases.

One of the most rewarding things about taking on a writing project like this is the opportunity it provides to learn from some of the leading scholars in the fields of business development and human resources. For this I'd like to thank David Butler, Associate Dean for Executive Education, School of Hotel Administration, Cornell University, for sharing his perspective on academic alliances, and Albert Vicere, professor of business administration and director of the Institute for the Study of Organizational Effectiveness, The Smeal College of Business Administration, Pennsylvania State University, for his insights into the field of executive development. A big thanks goes out to Professor Arnoud De Meyer, Associate Dean, Executive Education, INSEAD, in Cedex, France, and James Pulcrano, Dean of Executive Education, Institute for Management Development (IMD), Lausanne, Switzerland, for their advice on international executive development. Youssef Bissada, professor of entrepreneurship, INSEAD, and the owner of Bissada Management Simulations, provided a fascinating look at how distance learning can be integrated with the use of computerized business simulations. I received helpful advice on the area of CEO selection from David Sadtler, a Fellow with the Ashridge Strategic Management Center in London, while Michael Marquardt, management consultant and professor at George Washington University, shared his international expertise in the field of action learning.

Finally, I'd like to extend my appreciation to the many senior-level executives and corporate HR leaders who were willing to clear some time on their busy calendars to share with me their success stories in the field of executive resource management. Three individuals—Freddy Cabrera, Director of International Human Resources, PepsiCo; Chuck Bolton, VP of International HR, Boston Scientific; and my good friend and colleague Samir Gupte, at Choice Hotels International—all shared a wide range of expertise on the subject of international executive selection and development. Jim Dagnon, Senior Vice President of People, The Boeing Company, provided a very useful case outlining Boeing's use of succession planning to help integrate leadership within its postmerged organization. Michael McNeal, Director of Employment for Cisco Systems, introduced me to the intricacies of Cisco's Internet-based hiring system. Dan Stolle, Director of Human Resources for Tellabs, shared his company's experiences in the area of executive assessment. Another individual who deserves my thanks is Curt Mason, Vice President of Sales and Marketing for Henninger Media, for revealing how his company took a team approach to distributed learning. Tim Westall, Director of Management Development for Union National, provided a fascinating look into his company's approach to executive competency development and selection. Curt Clawson, president of the Chicago-based Beverage Cans Americas division, and Ed Lapekas, American National Can's chairman and CEO, deserve my thanks for sharing the story of how they applied the strategy of "topgrading" to achieve a strong performance turnaround in their company. Last of all, I'd like to thank Linda Krom, Director of Executive Development for GTE Services Corporation, for providing an excellent example of how business simulations, action learning, and the use of knowledge warehousing can be forged together to produce incredible learning results.

Robert Barner is Vice President of Organizational Development and Learning for Choice Hotels International, the second-largest hotel franchiser in the world, involving over four thousand properties in thirty-eight countries. In this position, Barner is responsible for overseeing his company's executive assessment and development, succession planning, employee development, electronic media development, and franchisee training functions. He has over twenty years of experience in the field of executive resource development.

Barner is the author of two other books, *Lifeboat Strategies* and *Crossing the Minefield,* and has contributed to several other volumes. He has also authored numerous articles on executive development, team building, and quality improvement. He can be reached at ibscribe@aol.com.

CHAPTER 1

PUTTING THE KEYSTONE IN PLACE

Place yourself in the following scenario: Some of your key executives have recently defected to your competitors. At the same time, recent performance problems have planted certain doubts in your mind about the capabilities of some of those senior managers who are still on board. These performance problems run the gauntlet—some of your biggest customers appear to be highly dissatisfied with the level of your field service; during the last two years your sales of new products have lagged way behind those of your competitors; and your company is falling behind in its plan to implement new manufacturing technology. The timing for these problems couldn't be worse since your company is planning to initiate a major marketing launch next year, one that threatens to fall apart unless you can quickly fill in the holes in your leadership bench. As a key member of your company's leadership team, you've been asked to help the vice president of human resources (HR) develop a game plan for rebuilding and strengthening your executive bench. What do you do?

Tough situation, isn't it? Yet in today's volatile and hypercompetitive market, this type of scenario is increasingly common. The fact is that we've entered an age in which human capital, as exemplified by the executive team, is becoming increasingly visible on the corporate balance sheet. Perhaps no organizational resource is more closely guarded or carefully acquired than the corporate executive team. It's not unusual for companies to spend several months and hundreds of thousands of dollars to attract and recruit executives who represent the right "mix" of organizational talent. Increasingly, the addition or loss of a key executive translates directly into a corresponding gain or loss in corporate stock value and in the overall assessment of a company's long-term viability. In a recent *Time* article entitled "Betting on a CEO," writer Daniel Kadlec noted that when the previous CEO of CBS, Michael H. Jordan, was replaced by Mel Karmazin, the company's stock rose 2⁵/8. Similarly, the stock value of Bank of America rose 3 points in two days when the company president, Hugh McColl, agreed to stay at this company until 2002.[1]

To closely dissect the effect that top-level executive changes have on corporate profits, witness the impact created by the unexpected resignation of James Dimon, one of Citigroup's top executives, in late 1998. Citigroup was created as a result of the merger of Citicorp Bank and Travelers Group Insurance, and Dimon was viewed by many insiders as a likely successor to Citicorp's Chairperson Sanford Weill. Dimon's resignation not only immediately impacted Citigroup's stock price (the stock fell almost 3 points in two days), but also resulted in a downgrading of the stock by analysts at two Wall Street investment firms. Thomas Hanley, a banking analyst for one of these firms, Warburg Dillion Read, offered his rationale for the downgrade by suggesting that the departure "could create a significant void at a time when the company needs stability."[2]

Hanley's comment is reflective of the incredible importance that analysts now place on the top-line value of executive leadership. The fact is that we've entered an era in which stock analysts watch the hiring and departures of high-level executives with the same level of anticipation with which a dedicated seismologist watches the jiggling needle of a seismograph. They recognize that even relatively small shifts in the organizational fault line can bring about significant changes in a company's operational performance. After emphasizing the importance of a good management team to a company's stock value, Daniel Kadlec warns that because today's executives are very mobile, "buying a stock for its management has become a bit like picking a restaurant for its chef. You need to check in once in a while to make sure old Pierre is still there and that he isn't suddenly trying to cook Chinese."[3]

Within certain fast-change industries such as network technology, effective talent is becoming such a scarce commodity that many companies have had to replace the traditional golden handcuffs used to ensure loyalty with more exorbitant platinum restraints. Now the offering may include expensive stock options, accommodating unusual relocation requests (one recent *Wall Street Journal* article mentioned that to capture a key executive the prospective employer agreed to move the candidate's horse!), and even offering job placement assistance for spouses. Another sign of the times is the "bounty" that a large number of high-tech firms are beginning to offer their employees for referrals that result in the capture of desired technical specialists and leaders. In many industries, the practice of conducting talent "raiding parties" on competitors has become so rampant that these platinum handcuffs have been fortified with harsher restraints, such as the use of strictly enforced noncompete agreements.

THE BIRTH OF THE KEYSTONE PHENOMENON

The effects just described are part of a larger change process now rippling through the corporate landscape. At the epicenter of this change process lies an entirely new way of thinking about the essential value of the executive leadership function and our ability to shape and mold this function. I've termed the new way of thinking "the keystone phenomenon" to reflect the pivotal, or keystone, position the senior team plays in securing the organizational infrastructure. The keystone phenomenon can be summed up in two principles:

1. Executive capability now holds the critical keystone position in the construction of any winning competitive strategy. More than any other factor—capital, technology, or resources—executive competence provides an organization with its most sustainable competitive advantage in the marketplace.

2. The secret to securing a solid keystone lies in building a comprehensive executive resource management system that effectively links an organization's business strategy to its executive talent base.

Several factors are fueling the growth of the keystone phenomenon and causing organizations to strengthen their ability to select, develop, and retain world-class executive talent.

- *Growth of the "Knowledge Workforce."* The rise of the knowledge organization means that much of a company's assets now reside in the technical and industry-specific expertise of its associates and executive team. One downside of this change is that any organization becomes much more vulnerable to competitive threat when its asset base can sprout legs and walk away. This is particularly true when we are dealing with executives who have developed entrenched relationships with key customer accounts or who have a keen and proprietary understanding of their company's core strategy, planned market entries, patent-directed research, or emerging technologies.

3

Recognizing that the loss of executive talent translates directly into the loss of competitive advantage, companies are responding more strongly than ever to what is viewed as the theft of leadership resources. In 1997, Microsoft Corporation was sued (the suit was settled a few months later) by software company Borland International for what Borland termed "predatory hiring practices."[4] The suit alleged that over a three-year period Borland had lost over thirty engineers, software architects, and marketers to Microsoft. Borland had accused Microsoft of recruiting Borland employees "for the specific purpose of damaging Borland's ability to compete with Microsoft in the [software] development tools market and to slow the company's financial success."[5]

As the executive talent base continues to contract, we can expect this type of talent tug-of-war to be reenacted within a variety of industries. Witness the recent lawsuit directed against the online bookseller Amazon.com by Wal-Mart for the alleged practice of luring away fifteen of Wal-Mart's information technology employees and consultants, including Wal-Mart's chief information officer. In this case, Wal-Mart had been particularly concerned about the loss of individuals who had access to proprietary information and trade secrets regarding the company's data warehousing and merchandise management systems.[6]

- *Wholesale Importing of Talent.* Recently the talent wars have escalated to a new level through the use of corporate acquisitions, aimed largely at importing intact work teams into the hiring organization. In some cases, the acquisition of innovative start-ups provides two related benefits: it clears the field of new competitors, and it can bring into the organization both cutting-edge technological skills and executives who have demonstrated entrepreneurial ability.

During 1994 to 1997, Cisco Systems, a major player in network systems, purchased nineteen new companies as a means of acquiring new-product development expertise.[7] According to Mike Volpi, director of Cisco's acquisition team, the average Cisco acquisition takes only six weeks—the kind of speed necessary in an industry where product life cycles can be as brief as eighteen months.[8] In explaining the importance of acquiring intellectual capital through acquisitions, Cisco's CEO John T. Chambers said, "Most people forget that in a high-tech acquisition, you are really acquiring only people. That's why so many of them fail. At what we pay, at $500,000 to $2 million an employee, we are not acquiring current market share. We are acquiring futures."[9]

Bethesda, Maryland–based AppNet Systems, Inc., a recent start-up that is attempting to create a one-stop-shopping concept in the field of electronic commerce, is another vibrant example of how fast a company can grow its executive talent base through the use of corporate acquisitions. Backed with over $100 million in venture capital, within a four-month period AppNet acquired six companies possessing a variety of e-commerce expertise, and has plans for acquiring several more. Chief executive Ken Bajaj's strategy calls for linking the right combination of technical expertise from many different areas to provide customers with a full array of e-commerce services.[10]

- *Executive Talent as Value Differentiator.* In an age when a company has the ability to mimic its competitors' resources and technologies, effective organizations recognize that one of the best ways of distinguishing themselves is by promoting the presence of high-performing executives. The presence of top-level talent is especially important to the large numbers of technical start-ups that have emerged in the past few years. Many of these companies have been able to attract large sums of venture capital, in spite of their new debuts within highly speculative markets, due largely to the high degree of faith that the stock market places in the competency and vision of the companies' owners and executives.

  Scient Inc., a recently formed San Francisco–based World Wide Web consultancy, was able to quickly raise $20 million in venture capital based in significant part on the strong reputations of Scient's executive team, which includes former executives from IBM, AT&T, and Gateway, Inc. In explaining what attracted her company to Scient, Kelly Scott, a senior vice president with First Union Corporation, one of Scient's corporate clients, explained that she "wanted a firm with senior-level people who are visionaries, but who also could be very tactical."[11]

- *Scarcity of Skilled Executives.* While it is true that the aging of the baby-boomer generation has produced a glut of midlevel managers, at the same time we are experiencing a dearth of good talent in the executive ranks. This is particularly true for such functions as information technology (IT) and HR, where increased demand is rapidly outstripping the availability of strong executive talent. Add to this the fact that we are now entering a vicious cycle in which the high demand for executive talent is beginning to create a logjam within many leading executive search firms, resulting in longer time-to-fill for executive placements. A recent McKinsey Company study on executive talent involving 77 large U.S. companies, 400 corporate officers, and 6,000 executives concluded that "companies are about to be engaged in a war for senior executive talent that will remain a defining characteristic of their competitive landscape for decades to come. Yet most are ill prepared and even the best are vulnerable."[12]

The scarcity of executive talent is particularly acute on the international front, where exemplary leaders have exposure to broader sections of employment opportunities. Those local managers and executives offering both leadership skills and an in-depth knowledge of local cultures, political systems, and distribution networks can command a high premium on the market. Describing the talent wars now under way in Warsaw and other Central European cities, a recent article in the *Wall Street Journal Europe* stated that, "In the region's talent-starved business world, almost anything goes in the competition to attract and retain the few experienced local managers who often bounce from job to job."[13] The same article goes on to explain the difficulties this regional talent war has created for employers: "That battle, in turn, has sent ripples through Central Europe's corporate ranks. Salaries are jumping by leaps and bounds, some top managers nearly doubling their salary between 1993 and 1995, a trend that continues apace in capital cities across the region."[14]

- *Environmental Complexity.* The value of the ship's navigator increases in proportion to the distance the ship ventures from known territory. It's one thing to be able to track your course when you have line-of-sight to a familiar shoreline, but quite another to know how to navigate by the stars, especially when your ship has been seriously blown off course. We live in a time in which many organizations have been blown off course by the consolidated impact of complex international market forces, the birth of entirely new technologies, and the emergence of competitors from unlikely fields (witness AT&T's emergence as a competitive threat to the banking industry). Faced with this unpredictable and highly fluid work environment, corporate boards and stockholders depend more on the abilities of executives who can assume the role of corporate navigator in charting a safe passageway through the market.

WHEN THE WELL DRIES UP

The cumulative result of these business factors is that companies that lack high-caliber executive leadership are finding both their performance and their corporate credibility seriously eroded. As Table 1 on page 8 illustrates, the shortage of executive talent eventually shows up in two types of corporate costs; those *opportunity costs* associated with not being able to aggressively pursue new opportunities, and those *operational costs* created by performance deficiencies that are directly associated with the lack of qualified leadership. Before reading further you may find it useful to identify from the list in Table 1 those cost factors that represent the most significant executive shortage costs for your company.

THE HR DIRECTOR AS TEAM ARCHITECT

The recognition that executive talent can provide a sustainable competitive advantage is also dramatically reshaping the functions and responsibilities of HR and training directors. This raises succession planning and executive assessment and placement to a much greater prominence within the organizational value chain. The increased value of these functions is reflected in part by the fact that directing boards incorporate executive talent review sessions into their strategic planning process, and by the escalating value of compensation packages being offered to HR executives. Professor Arnoud De Meyer, Associate Dean, Executive Education (1992–1999) for the prestigious business school INSEAD in France, notes that one of the trends he is seeing is "the higher level of quality in human resources professionals. Ten years ago HR was a bit of a parking lot for those 'good citizens' of the company who couldn't get to the top level of the company. Today, we find outstanding people, because CEOs see HR directors as a true asset to the organization."[15]

Together, these changes are forcing HR directors to transform themselves from their traditional roles of talent procurers and compensation administrators to the relatively new role of team architect. They are being asked to develop methods for securing these keystone leadership positions into the bedrock of the organizational infrastructure. At the ground level of executive decision making, they must be able to address such issues as the following:

- Determining how the current leadership pool will need to be reconfigured to support global expansion
- Anticipating areas of vulnerability, in which the loss of current players or the failure to gain new talent could pose a significant setback to a company's business plan

TABLE 1

COSTS ASSOCIATED WITH EXPERIENCING A SHORTAGE OF EXECUTIVE TALENT

Opportunity Costs

- Inability to enter new markets in a timely fashion

- Problems in managing mergers and acquisitions due to loss of corporate gatekeepers

- Difficulty in fending off intrusions by aggressive competitors

- Loss of credibility (and associated stock value) with market analysts, governing boards, and corporate stockholders

- Inability to pursue new technologies due to absence of technical leadership

- Difficulty in driving international expansion due to lack of executives having broad, multinational experience

Operational Costs

- Slowdown in time-to-market due to holes in executive bench

- Excessive costs in overhead and capital expenses due to lack of a disciplined financial gatekeeper

- Defection of key accounts due to inability to meet high service standards, or to absence of executives who know how to effectively manage large, sensitive accounts

- Gross operating inefficiencies due to lack of strong leadership

- Loss of technical expertise as your best high-potential technical performers leave due to lack of credible, motivational leadership

- Scheduling logjams due to lack of leaders who can play a strong role in arbitrating top-line priorities

- Selecting the most effective methods for obtaining an accurate "read" on the performance capabilities of the current senior management team

As I will discuss in later chapters, the ability to tackle such tough issues is quickly raising the bar regarding the competencies and business savvy expected of HR leaders, and is highlighting the importance of such innovative HR tools as computer-based executive training, Internet recruiting, and the use of sophisticated competency databases.

CLIMBING THE EVOLUTIONARY LADDER OF EXECUTIVE TEAMING

The ability to build and sustain a winning leadership team calls for innovative approaches to the task of executive resource planning. In coaching and consulting with a variety of organizations over the last twenty years, I have found that organizations vary widely in the effectiveness of their executive development and staffing functions. For the sake of simplicity, these variations can be described in terms of a three-stage evolutionary journey that begins with a minimal understanding of the true value of executive resource management and, in the best-case scenario, ends with the ability to fully leverage leadership capabilities to competitive advantage.

The Executive Resource Matrix shown in Table 2 on page 10 shows how companies vary by stage of development in terms of the approach taken in managing the five critical dimensions of executive resource planning. A good starting point for designing your own executive resource plan is to review this matrix with your senior team and jointly determine the stage at which you would place your company within each of the five dimensions.

For an organization that is operating at Stage 1 of executive resource planning, short-term work pressures typically push the issue of executive development and staffing far into the background. An organization frequently initiates the evolutionary climb through the remaining two stages only after it (1) is exposed to competitive benchmarks that point out the shortfalls of its executive staffing systems, and (2) becomes aware of the extent to which it can leverage corporate performance by upgrading its leadership talent pool. Stage 1 companies have only the barest inkling of where executive capability fits into the overall business strategy and are therefore willing to make only marginal investments in growing and retaining executive talent.

Moving up the evolutionary scale we encounter those Stage 2 companies that are somewhat invested in growing executive talent,

TABLE 2

EXECUTIVE RESOURCE MATRIX

Five Core Dimensions of Executive Resource Planning

Development Stage	Connections to Business Strategy	Corporate Investment in Executive Development	Degree of Executive Ownership	Integration of HR Systems	Real-World Anchoring
Stage 3	• Tight linkages • *Design* of business strategy is reexamined in light of changes in executive staffing	• Heavy time investment; senior executives design/deliver training, guide development assignments • Training is mandatory condition of job • Invest 3–5% of base salary in training	• Senior executives and HR codesign resource plan • High value placed on mentoring and coaching	• All phases of executive assessment and selection are integrated through a uniform competency model and database	• Heavy use of action learning and work projects • Job rotation used extensively with high-potential (HIPOS) candidates
Stage 2	• Marginal connections • *Implementation* of business strategy is impacted by changes in executive staffing	• Moderate time investment; seniors may kick off or wrap up training • Training optional, but will release people to attend training • Invest 1–3% of base salary in training	• Senior executives play an advisory and screening role; HR as designer • Moderate value placed on mentoring and coaching	• Rudimentary integration of some components of the executive resource system	• Heavy use of case simulations based on business problems
Stage 1	• No connectivity • Business strategy is not modified to reflect changes in executive staffing	• Senior executives are detached from training • Development placed at bottom of priorities • Invest <1% of base salary in training	• Executive resource plans viewed as HR paper process • No value placed on mentoring and coaching	• Executive development and selection is pursued as a series of isolated activities	• Heavy reliance on classroom-based executive education programs

but have not as yet learned how to formulate a comprehensive and disciplined executive development strategy. These are companies that are struggling to grow their executive talent bench, but do so in a jerky and disconnected fashion. Their focus tends to be on investing energy and money on correcting immediate deficiencies in the leadership bench rather than developing a long-term executive resource strategy that supports their overall business strategy.

As a company progresses to Stage 3, it becomes fully capable of building a strong executive team and discovers that it can take advantage of its superior leadership talent base to improve its competitive position. A Stage 3 company is characterized by an executive resource plan that is fully integrated. Human resource actions involving the recruiting, selection, assessment, and development of corporate executives are formed within the well-defined context of the company's business strategy. In short, these decisions are viewed by senior management as making good business sense by helping the company fulfill its long-term business objectives. To better understand the defining characteristics of the three stages, let's consider how these stages apply to the five dimensions of executive resource planning.

DIMENSION 1: CONNECTIONS TO BUSINESS STRATEGY

Stage 1: In Stage 1, companies tend to write off executive staffing and development programs as being simply more HR paperwork that has little bearing on the overall business plans. The top HR executive may not even be privy to business strategy reviews, and when he or she is involved, it is as a courtesy by the senior staff. Stage 1 organizations never sense the need to use information on the company's executive resource capabilities to shape business strategy.

Stage 2: By contrast, Stage 2 organizations are characterized by well-intentioned but disjointed attempts to connect executive staffing and development with business strategy. Although such organizations may create yearly executive talent reviews, a common mistake is the failure to develop databases that can help them incorporate this information into the overall readiness assessment for undertaking major projects, such as new market entries or acquisitions. Instead, this organization is likely to view its talent reviews as after-the-fact checklists to spot immediate holes in the leadership bench.

Stage 3: As Figure 1 on page 12 illustrates, a company's prerequisite for entering Stage 3 is that it must learn how to form linkages between its business strategy and its executive resource strategy. In this scenario, the yearly talent review process becomes an important method for evaluating the feasibility of alternative business strategies.

FIGURE 1 INTEGRATING EXECUTIVE RESOURCE MANAGEMENT
WITH BUSINESS STRATEGY

In the same way, when making decisions regarding competency identification, coaching, and development, Stage 3 executives can be
relied on to go beyond self-invested interests to focus on the long-
term needs of their companies. In examining the executive development programs created by four leading corporations (Motorola,
Xerox, General Foods, and Federated Department Stores), consultant
and previous Xerox HR director James Bolt noted that "the most
important emphasis of the four programs is on the executive's role in
implementing the corporation's strategies and achieving goals—
including bottom-line results."[16]

DIMENSION 2: CORPORATE INVESTMENT IN EXECUTIVE DEVELOPMENT

Stage 1: At this stage, an organization has little interest in investing time, attention, or money in development activities that can upgrade the performance of its executives. Instead, it is more likely to allow performance to degrade to the level where it can no longer be ignored, then attempt to solve the problem by replacing incumbents. Quite often, executives operating within a Stage 1 environment are unwilling to release their staff to attend training courses. In such organizations, executives and managers at all levels are given the not-so-subtle hint that, in comparison with attending development training courses, their time could be better spent in true "value-added" activities.

A related characteristic of Stage 1 is the belief that money spent on executive development activities is a wasteful overhead cost rather than a long-term investment in human capital. As a general rule of thumb, I have found that a company at this level tends to invest less than 1 percent of an executive's base salary, and the same percentage of that individual's work time, on executive education. Table 3 on page 14 shows sample investment levels of money and time for Stage 1, 2, and 3 organizations. Within Stage 1 organizations, when money is allocated for development, it is dispersed through a shotgun delivery method and spent on a variety of disconnected training programs.

Because Stage 1 senior executives view executive development as an HR function, they are not willing to commit their personal time and attention to the design or review of such programs. The end result, of course, is the creation of HR-built development programs that are viewed by senior managers as being academic and out of touch with the real world of business. Perhaps more important, because Stage 1 senior executives interpret *development activities* to mean *classroom training,* they do not view the development of associates as part of their day-to-day responsibilities and are therefore unwilling to invest their personal time in conducting development planning discussions or carefully structuring development assignments (see Chapters 8 and 9).

Stage 2: Over time, an organization begins to recognize that it can obtain big payoffs from investing in executive development. As shown in Table 3, Stage 2 companies translate this renewed interest into a willingness to invest additional time and money in development activities. Unfortunately, while Stage 2 executives are willing to allow their team members to attend management training courses, these courses are frequently not integrated into a cohesive training

TABLE 3			
CORPORATE INVESTMENT LEVELS FOR EXECUTIVE DEVELOPMENT			
Investment Areas	Stage 1	Stage 2	Stage 3
Money allocated for development	< $1,000	$1,000–$3,000	$3,000–$5,000
Time allocated for development	< 2 days	2–6 days	6–11 days
Allocation percentage	< 1%	1%–3%	> 3%–5%

Note: Analysis assumes an average base salary of $100,000 a year, with 225 work days available per year.

curriculum. Another characteristic of Stage 2 organizations is that senior managers are willing to make only minimal investments of their personal time and attention through such limited activities as kicking off or wrapping up executive development workshops, or development planning discussions with associates.

Stage 3: Organizations that have reached Stage 3 have committed to making a substantial investment in executive resource development. This investment makes itself apparent not only through the allocation of greater amounts of time and money to formal development programs but also in the personal attention and care that senior staff pay to designing and tracking such activities. In companies such as CitiBank, PepsiCo, and GE, senior executives spend a significant part of their time delivering training and auditing the results of development projects that have been assigned to trainees because they view such activities as unique opportunities to mentor and guide emerging executive talent. Another characteristic of Stage 3 organizations is that development activities are not offered on a hit-or-miss basis; instead, a core development curriculum is carefully designed for executives, with attendance in such training viewed as a mandatory and critical part of their job responsibilities.

DIMENSION 3: DEGREE OF EXECUTIVE OWNERSHIP

Stage 1: A clear symptom of Stage 1 management is when senior-level executives accept little or no ownership of the design and management of their executive staffing and development process, and instead pass off this responsibility to their corporate HR department. Inevitably, this abdication of responsibility has a nasty way of circling back by exposing companies to a variety of problems.

- The resulting HR-driven executive staffing decisions will be viewed with mistrust by the senior staff.

- The HR-generated executive development process inevitably will prove inadequate, as it fails to take into account the many business assumptions that drive the company's long-term strategy.

- Because the executive resource plan is not designed around their needs and concerns, executives are likely to quickly become disenchanted with this process and find creative ways to circumvent it, such as (1) working around HR directors to bring executive candidates in through the back door of the company; (2) disparaging any performance information that is obtained on job incumbents or candidates through such third-party vehicles as assessment centers or 360-degree feedback; and (3) ignoring the HR director's recommendations for the design and staffing of new functions in favor of their own "gut feeling" decisions.

Stage 2: At this stage, executive ownership is present but minimal and sporadic. The most common scenario is when an HR leader attempts to design in isolation components of the executive resource process, such as an executive competency study (see Chapter 4), and then after the fact selectively brings in senior managers to provide feedback and guidance on these components. While this degree of involvement represents a substantial improvement from that found in Stage 1, it still falls well short of an approach that reflects balanced ownership between the HR function and senior management.

Stage 3: As senior executives obtain a better sense of how they can benefit from a well-designed executive resource system, they begin to aggressively seek out additional opportunities to weigh in on, and take greater ownership for, the design of this process. Researcher James Bolt noted that a common feature of the executive development programs created by Motorola, Xerox, General Foods, and Federated Department Stores was the heavy involvement of the CEOs and senior executives in the design and delivery of these programs.[17] Observing that this involvement occurred at the early stages of the design process, Bolt notes that "at all four corporations, the staff responsible for the program design conducted extensive interviews with 12 to 80 of the company's most senior executives. Data from these interviews altered the objectives, scope, and content of each of the programs that were later put into place."[18]

This ownership includes such activities as working with the HR function to jointly determine how changes in corporate strategic goals will affect resource planning; offering suggestions for improving the initial design of projects such as competency identification, assessment designs, and development projects; and helping to craft specialized development programs for high-potential executive candidates. At this stage, senior executives are also more likely to seek out competitive benchmark data that can help them gauge the relative effectiveness of their executive resource process.

DIMENSION 4: INTEGRATION OF HR SYSTEMS

Stage 1: In Stage 1, executive resource management systems are typically created in a piecemeal fashion—without forethought regarding how these pieces should link together. The product of these disconnected efforts is similar to what you would find if a home builder had teams of plumbers, builders, and electricians perform their work in isolation without benefit of a general contractor, a project plan, or an integrating set of blueprints. When it comes to organizational design, the lack of integration shows up in many ways.

- Large amounts of time and money will be wasted on design components, such as 360-degree surveys or succession planning models, without first clearly identifying the objectives of these components.

- The HR system will contain discrepancies that send contradictory and confusing messages to senior executives and middle management. A typical example is when executives are exposed to one set of competencies in their performance appraisal forms, a second in their succession planning models, and a third in their 360-degree profiles. From a development perspective, such a situation leaves executives rightfully confused regarding the competencies that are most highly valued by their organization.

- From an HR planning perspective, this problem typically creates huge holes in the organization's database—a problem that is sometimes not uncovered until a company encounters an emergency situation, such as a sudden vacancy on the senior team.

Stage 2: By the time an organization evolves to Stage 2 it begins to recognize the importance of system integration and has started to align components of the executive teaming system. As I will point out in Chapter 4, a common starting point involves the creation of an executive competency assessment that serves as an orchestrating mechanism for helping the senior team make effective decisions regarding executive succession planning and placement.

Stage 3: In Stage 3 organizations, executive resource development takes the form of a totally integrated system: the senior staff and the HR department have a common understanding of the competencies needed to build a successful leadership team and have formally identified these competencies through a disciplined assessment process. The competency profile is then embedded into such documents as the company's performance appraisal form, its development planning guides, and its succession planning documentation. The glue that holds this system together is a competency database profiling the performance of all executive staff. In the best-case scenario, every element of the resource process, from initial recruiting to long-term development, is aligned with this executive competency assessment. A corporate recruiting strategy based on an integrated HR system will display the following features:

- External executive recruiters are given clear direction regarding the relative value the hiring organization places on different leadership and technical competencies.

- Recruitment advertising highlights the importance of these competencies.

- The selection interviewing process includes a behaviorally based interview model that allows interviewers to carefully screen prospective candidates in terms of desired competencies. (See Chapter 12.)

- Senior executives and HR leaders are aligned on the key criteria required for success for any new job position and the relative standing of candidates with respect to these criteria.

- Both external recruiters and senior managers use their executive competency database as a map for identifying those corporate "targets" that are most likely to yield executive candidates with the prerequisite competencies.

- This same database enables the organization to generate a comparative review of the competencies demonstrated by internal and external candidates. In other words, it provides an equitable field of play for both internal and external candidates.

DIMENSION 5: REAL-WORLD ANCHORING

Stage 1: At Stage 1, HR leaders tend to base executive staffing and development approaches on "pure" HR models that ignore the realities of the corporate workplace. Consider the area of executive assessment. Many assessment models portray the evaluation of executive talent as an analytical, totally objective, quantifiable process that is impermeable to personal bias. A more realistic approach, and one that is more prevalent within Stage 2 and 3 organizations, is to accept that human agendas and political realities are a fact of life. One can then take creative steps to manage, or at least mitigate, the more politicized aspects of the executive assessment process.

Another area in which the lack of real-world anchoring frequently shows up is executive development. Stage 1 organizations tend to take a limited view of executive development, treating it as an artificial experience that occurs outside of the world of work, within the boundaries of the classroom. Accordingly, senior managers are unwilling to take on instructional roles for executive development training, and instead pass off this responsibility to outside consultants or university professors. As I will discuss in Chapter 9, while I am a strong advocate of creative partnerships between corporate development programs and outside consulting firms and universities, innumerable problems are created when ownership of executive development is passed over to such outside partners.

Stage 2: At the second stage of evolution, senior leaders and HR directors begin to work together to ensure that all elements of the executive resource management process go beyond paperwork systems to reflect the true context of the organizational culture. This shift in focus is predicated on the assumption that HR-based, textbook-derived solutions to executive resource challenges must be modified to make them adaptable to a corporate work culture.

As an example, consider the design of a performance appraisal system. HR specialists love to create elaborate, lengthy, time-consuming appraisal forms under the theory that more is better. An executive who has a large number of direct reports will react to a cumbersome appraisal process by ignoring it or by taking a token check-the-box approach to it. Either option negates the underlying objective of the appraisal documentation, which is to provide a valid audit trail for the executive talent base. Recognizing this challenge, savvy HR leaders aggressively look for ways to streamline the appraisal process, knowing that the trade-off will be more thoughtful appraisal evaluations by their executives.

Concurrent with these changes, during Stage 2 development activities begin to shift away from pure classroom training to incorporate more real-world experiences. The device most commonly used to effect this transition is the use of business simulations designed to reflect the organization's work environment and primary business challenges.

Stage 3: Stage 3 organizations recognize that the most effective way to grow and strengthen executive teams is through the use of action-oriented learning approaches that test executive competencies against the mastery of day-to-day work challenges. A prime example of this concept is the "action learning" model used by such companies as GE and CitiBank (see Chapter 8). This model goes beyond the traditional case approach by requiring teams of executives to tackle business problems, to research and develop solutions to those problems, and to then report on their findings to their senior executives. A related real-world executive development technique employed by Stage 3 companies is rotating high-potential executives among assignments within different strategic business units or international divisions, as a means of exposing them to a variety of work challenges and team environments.

Stage 3 organizations are also characterized by a fluid approach to the design of their executive assessment, staffing, and development processes. That is, the human resource models used to direct these activities are continually modified to reflect the corporation's changing business landscape. One U.S.-based computer hardware company with which I consulted for several years exhibited this fluid approach to executive resource design when it made an aggressive move into the international market. To support the move, the company senior vice president of human resources asked me to work with her to update her company's executive competency model, with the goal of emphasizing certain leadership factors, such as cross-cultural sensitivity, interpersonal relations, and flexibility, that have been found to be associated with success on international assignments. Of equal importance, this company was willing to take the next logical step and make modifications to its selection, on-boarding, and executive development processes to ensure that the selection, development, and orientation of its international executives reflected these unique leadership competencies. Figure 2 on the following page outlines a few of the factors that might be considered in attempting to anchor a human resource system in the real-world context of a company's business environment.

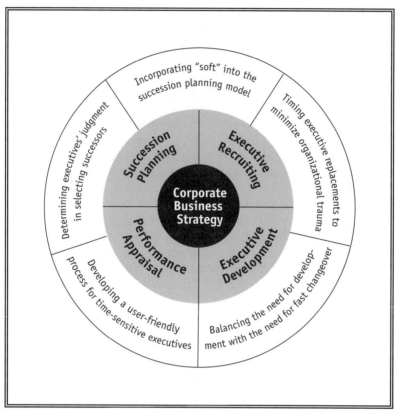

FIGURE 2 HOW TO ANCHOR HR SYSTEMS IN THE REAL WORLD

SETTING THE FOUNDATION
FOR SUPERIOR EXECUTIVE TEAMS

In reviewing the differences between Stage 1, 2, and 3 organizations, the question that naturally arises is, "How can I help my company develop the characteristics of a Stage 3 organization and in so doing improve our ability to build and develop a superior executive team?" The answer lies in developing an effective executive resource plan that makes use of the thirteen essential building blocks to executive teaming. Each of these building blocks will be covered in one of the remaining chapters.

Chapter 2: Developing an Executive Resource Strategy. Begin by developing an executive resource strategy that links your company's strategic business objectives to current and anticipated leadership needs.

Chapter 3: Uncovering Emerging Business Requirements. The first step in creating this executive resource strategy begins with understanding your company's long- and short-term business requirements.

Chapter 4: Identifying Executive Leadership Competencies. The next step involves identifying those leadership competencies that are essential for meeting your business requirements.

Chapter 5: Assessing Executive Capabilities. You then need to assess the performance and potential of individual executives against these identified competencies.

Chapter 6: Evaluating Your Leadership Bench. These individual assessments can then be rolled up to form an overall snapshot showing the performance capability of your executive bench.

Chapter 7: Managing Executive Transitions. A major challenge involves determining the most effective way to manage executive transitions, both to address the issues surrounding the movement of executives into, out of, or across your organization, and to minimize the disruption such changeovers can cause to your operation.

Chapter 8: Building Executive Competencies. Another challenge involves using the most innovative development methodologies to quickly enhance the overall leadership competencies of your team.

Chapter 9: Forging an Executive Development Strategy. Executive development must extend beyond activity-based programs to link competency development to corporate business strategy.

Chapter 10: Planning for Succession. An effective succession planning process can help you identify both immediate replacements for key leadership positions and long-term successors who can meet the changing needs of your organization.

Chapter 11: Uncovering Exceptional Talent. To grow your executive bench you need to be able to use competitive intelligence to uncover potential candidates, and to work with external search firms and your internal HR department to identify candidates who can truly add value to your organization.

Chapter 12: Selecting the Right Players. Once your search process has identified appropriate executive candidates, it is essential to have in place an effective method for selecting executives who represent the best "fit" with your company's business requirements and organizational culture.

Chapter 13: On-Boarding New Leaders. To ensure that incoming executives make a smooth transition to their new work environment, starting from the first day on the job, you need a solid on-boarding plan.

Chapter 14: Retaining Star Performers. Once you've acquired, assessed, and developed a strong leadership team, it is important to take action to prevent the defection of your strongest performers and to secure their commitment to your organization.

Together, these chapters constitute a viable approach to building exemplary executive teams. A good starting point for evaluating your company's executive resource needs is to identify, from the list shown in Table 4, those work challenges that are most pertinent to your own organization, and to then give special attention to those chapters that offer suggestions for addressing these challenges.

TABLE 4
IDENTIFYING YOUR COMPANY'S EXECUTIVE TEAMING CHALLENGES

How can we...	Related Chapter
1. Link our strategic plan to our executive staffing requirements? 2. Enlist the support of our senior executives for our executive resource plans? 3. Ensure that our executive staffing and development decisions support our primary business objectives?	Chapter 2 *Developing an Executive Resource Strategy*
4. Accurately anticipate future leadership needs? 5. Flag changing business conditions that may require significant changes in the way we recruit, select, and develop our leaders? 6. Anticipate emerging business requirements that signal the need for different types of executive leadership and technical skills?	Chapter 3 *Uncovering Emerging Business Requirements*
7. Identify those leadership competencies that are most important to organizational success? 8. Determine the appropriate blend of executive talent needed to sustain performance following a merger or acquisition? 9. "Depoliticize" the methods we use for selecting and promoting our leaders, by better aligning senior executives on executive selection criteria?	Chapter 4 *Identifying Executive Leadership Competencies*
10. Identify the unique development needs of individual executives? 11. Provide a balanced perspective when assessing leader performance? 12. Spot high-potential talent within our organization?	Chapter 5 *Assessing Executive Capabilities*

TABLE 4 (CONT'D)	
IDENTIFYING YOUR COMPANY'S EXECUTIVE TEAMING CHALLENGES	
How can we...	**Related Chapter**
13. Identify damaging "holes" in our leadership bench?	Chapter 6 *Evaluating Your Leadership Bench*
14. Implement an executive talent review process?	
15. Determine the types of executive competencies needed to grow new markets or product launches?	
16. Determine the most effective timing for executive transitions?	Chapter 7 *Managing Executive Transitions*
17. Accurately assess the business impact of changes to our executive bench?	
18. Ease the difficulties we might encounter as we undertake executive transitions?	
19. Advise our executives on the most effective methods for coaching/mentoring their staff?	Chapter 8 *Building Executive Competencies*
20. Construct development assignments that build long-term abilities?	
21. Anticipate the development requirements of high-potential executives, given the evolving nature of our industry?	
22. Link our development objectives to our business strategy?	Chapter 9 *Forging an Executive Development Strategy*
23. Go beyond development activities to create meaningful developmental learning systems?	
24. Match our development approaches to our organizational structure?	
25. Evaluate our ability to meet our company's long-term leadership requirements?	Chapter 10: *Planning for Succession*

How can we...	Related Chapter
26. Develop a succession planning process that prevents critical senior-level vacancies from going unfilled?	Chapter 10 *Planning for Succession*
27. Identify the most appropriate successors in post-merged organizations?	
28. Determine executive job requirements within our rapidly changing organization?	Chapter 11 *Uncovering Exceptional Talent*
29. Make the most effective use of executive search firms?	
30. Establish a recruiting process that attracts exceptional executive applicants?	
31. Identify executives who represent the right "fit" with our organizational culture?	Chapter 12 *Selecting the Right Players*
32. Determine the suitability of executives for international assignments?	
33. Uncover potential problem areas with executive candidates?	
34. Start new executives off on the right track?	Chapter 13 *On-Boarding New Leaders*
35. Eliminate the mistakes that are sometimes made during a new executive's start-up period?	
36. Quickly evaluate the adjustment level for newly hired executives?	
37. Find innovative ways to retain exceptional leaders and combat competitive "raids" on executives?	Chapter 14 *Retaining Star Performers*
38. Track down and address the underlying causes of voluntary turnover?	
39. Position our incentive plan as part of our overall competitive strategy?	

- A major influence on today's business environment is the "keystone phenomenon"—the growing recognition that senior executives hold the keystone position in securing the organizational infrastructure.

- The keystone phenomenon can be summed up in two principles: (1) an organization's executive capability now plays a dominant role in the construction of any winning competitive strategy, and (2) the secret to securing a solid keystone lies in building a comprehensive executive resource management system that effectively links an organization's business strategy to its executive talent base.

- As companies are coming to understand the critical role executive performance plays in obtaining competitive advantage, the war for executive talent is heating up.

- To compete successfully within this talent war, companies must know how to seek out, recruit, assess, select, develop, and retain high-performing executives.

- These changes are forcing HR directors to transform themselves from their traditional roles of talent procurers and compensation administrators to the relatively new role of team architect.

- Some of the factors fueling the war for executive talent are the growth of the knowledge workforce, the ability to undertake the wholesale importing of talent through mergers and acquisitions, the recognition that executive talent can be a true value differentiator, and the growing complexity and uncertainty of the business environment.

- The lack of a strong leadership bench can show up both in such opportunity costs as the inability to enter new markets or fend off aggressive competitors and in such operational costs as slowdowns in time-to-market and gross operational inefficiencies.

- Organizations can be characterized as being in one of three stages, depending on the relative effectiveness of their executive development and staffing functions.

- Stage 1 organizations are characterized by a lack of connectivity between executive resource plans and business strategy, senior executives who are detached from executive development, a low investment level in development, executive resourcing viewed as an HR paperwork process, the pursuit of executive development as a set of disconnected activities, and heavy reliance on classroom-based development activities.

- Stage 2 organizations are characterized by a marginal level of connectivity to business strategy, a moderate cost/resource investment in executive development, senior managers who play a tangential advisory/support role in executive resource planning, the integration of some elements of the executive resource strategy, and a learning process that incorporates case studies and business simulations.

- Stage 3 organizations are characterized by tight linkages between executive resource planning and business strategy, senior managers positioned as codesigners/deliverers of training, training as a mandatory and well-orchestrated process for all executives, a high value placed on mentoring and coaching, a thorough integration of all executive resource planning elements, and the heavy use of action learning and work projects to transfer development beyond the classroom.

CHAPTER 2

DEVELOPING AN EXECUTIVE RESOURCE STRATEGY

*S*trategy is generally defined as the ability to maneuver into a position that can secure a future competitive advantage. For an army this might mean determining where to position troops and artillery over a given terrain to increase the chances of securing a military objective. In the corporate world it means developing a business focus and supporting game plan that can help you achieve your long-term objectives.

Just as every company has an overall business strategy, an integral part of this business strategy needs to be the creation of an *executive resource strategy*. As I mentioned in Chapter 1, the recruiting, hiring, and developing of executive talent represents a heavy resource investment on the part of any organization, and exerts a decisive impact on a company's ability to compete successfully. An executive resource strategy serves as a coherent plan of action for focusing your investment efforts to obtain the best overall mix of leadership talent.

The fact is that all companies have an executive resource strategy. Consider whether your company is geared more toward pulling leadership talent up from within or importing executives from the outside. You probably know the answer. Or consider how quickly or slowly your company is moving to replace and build up your executive team. You probably know that answer, too.

That's because all organizations have an executive resource strategy. The problem is that quite frequently this "strategy" is developed incrementally and without foresight, as a knee-jerk response to whatever leadership challenges force their way to the top of the senior team's agenda. One month a key executive suddenly defects to a competitor, making the corporate leadership team aware that they have an executive retention problem on their hands. As they take action to correct the problem, the results of the annual talent review alert them to the existence of serious competency shortfalls in the senior team. A few weeks later, the results of the annual company opinion survey flag managers' concerns over the lack of internal promotional opportunities.

Over time, as an organization attempts to respond to such problems, it creates the framework for what becomes, by default, its corporate executive resource strategy. Such strategies are usually vaguely understood by senior teams, HR leaders, and corporate directing boards and are seldom explicitly outlined or placed against the backdrop of the company's strategic business plan. As a result, they typically contain a number of design flaws including staffing, development, and/or assessment components that are either not fully integrated into the overall design or completely missed from the HR "radar screen." In addition, the lack of a formal and detailed executive resource plan means that corporate stakeholders and decision makers never have the opportunity to bring into alignment their separate views regarding the major principles that should drive their corporate resource strategy.

The resulting lack of alignment and integration can punch a big hole in a company's ability to compete successfully. As HR researchers Karen Golden and Vasudevan Ramanujam have suggested, "The lack of integration between human resource management (HRM) and strategic business planning (SBP) processes is increasingly acknowledged as a major source of implementation failures. It is often alleged that companies develop strategic plans based on extensive marketing and financial data but neglect the human resource requirements necessary to successfully implement them."[1]

To counter these problems, HR leaders must work closely with their senior teams and directing boards to design and implement comprehensive executive resource strategies. A key function of leadership is to ensure the integration of an organization's operating values with its strategies, structures, and systems. As HR practitioners John Pickering and Robert Matson have contended, "Without this congruence between the purpose of the organization and its processes, system integrity is low. With low integrity, the system will enter a degenerative cycle."[2] Recognizing the pivotal role that strategy plays as a foundation piece for effective executive resource management, throughout this chapter we will consider how to systematically build the elements of your executive resource strategy, and address several of the critical design issues that need to be folded into the construction of this strategy.

To develop an effective resource strategy, the HR function must be willing to assume the role of strategic partner to the executive team. Unfortunately, in many organizations HR still has a long way to go in establishing itself as a strategic partner with top management. In the McKinsey study "The War for Talent," researchers found that although 78 percent of the 400 corporate officers that they interviewed (within 77 large U.S. companies) agreed that "HR should be a partner in efforts to build a stronger talent pool," only 27 percent of these respondents agreed that "HR currently plays this role at present."[3]

Employing the term *strategic partner* involves more than just a semantic shell game. As management consultant and University of Michigan professor Dave Ulrich proposes, "HR professionals become strategic partners when they participate in the process of defining business strategy, when they ask questions that move strategy into action, and when they design HR practices that align with business strategy."[4] The true test of an effective executive resource strategy is that it should enable you to accomplish the following objectives, all of which support exceptional business performance:

- Ensure that executive resource decisions are well aligned with strategic business objectives.

- Enable your company to obtain the most qualified leaders to secure a long-term competitive advantage.

- Effectively manage the timing, communication, and logistics of executive transitions to support the smooth continuity of business performance.

- Identify and leverage high-potential leadership talent across your organization.

- Flag leadership shortfalls that could pose serious roadblocks to business performance, and determine the best course of action for correcting these roadblocks.

- Use competitive intelligence to target and capture superior executive talent from the outside, while erecting barriers to competitive "theft" and the defection of high-potential performers.

- Establish plans for accelerating the development of core leadership competencies.

- Anticipate potential executive changeovers and develop succession plans to manage these changeovers.

PERFORMING A BASELINE REVIEW
OF YOUR STRATEGY

Before attempting to improve your executive resource strategy, it is useful to perform a baseline review, by examining your strategy in terms of the six success criteria shown in Table 5. Let's review these six criteria in detail and consider what they tell us about the characteristics of a successful executive resource strategy.

1. *Does your executive resource strategy provide logical linkages between your company's business objectives and important executive selection and development decisions?* An effective executive resource strategy should be able to tell you how anticipated changes in business conditions are likely to modify the required composition of your executive team. For example, the planned acquisition of a firm that lies outside of your company's historical market area might flag the need for entirely new technical or marketing skills. In the same way, if your company was trying to counter a strong downward trend in customer service satisfaction, it would highlight the need for executive competencies in the areas of customer support and market research.

A key characteristic of companies that have successful executive resource strategies is the ability to detect when changing business requirements signal the need for different types of executive competencies. Al Vicere, management consultant and coauthor of the book *Leadership by Design,* suggests that, "Most organizations make the mistake of implementing development activities that are removed from their business strategy and HR strategy. Those companies that are doing the most effective development work have a nicely defined business strategy, based on knowing the kinds of leadership skills they need to have, and the kinds of people they need to develop to build this strategy. Once a company has this together they next need to determine what initiatives they need to put in place to deliver on these development objectives, and finally, to consider how they resource them; internally or externally."[5] Knowing how to translate business objectives into executive resource plans is only half the challenge of linking business strategy to resource strategy. The other half of this challenge involves the ability to predict the success of proposed business objectives, given the limitations and constraints imposed by your current leadership base.

When business objectives are pursued without this type of preemptive screening, the results can be disastrous. This was the situation I encountered a few years ago while working as an HR

TABLE 5

**SIX SUCCESS CRITERIA FOR EVALUATING
AN EXECUTIVE RESOURCE STRATEGY**

1. Does your executive resource strategy *provide logical linkages* between your company's business objectives and important executive selection and development decisions?

2. Does your strategy *employ a data-driven competency assessment process* that enables your senior managers to make well-informed decisions on executive placement and development?

3. Does your strategy *reflect a tightly orchestrated HR system* that ties together your company's selection, recruitment, and development components?

4. Does your strategy *incorporate input from key organizational stakeholders,* including board members, senior managers, executives, and high-potential managers?

5. Does your strategy reflect a decision process that goes well beyond immediate concerns and short-term business pressures to *address the long-term needs of your organization?*

6. Does your strategy *allow you to focus your executive resource efforts* to obtain the most effective overall team?

---

executive for a previous employer. In this situation, a manager was promoted to head up a new marketing launch in the Middle East due largely to his successful track record in growing a mature domestic product line in the United States. That the manager failed was not a surprise to me, as the competencies required to lead a three-person market launch in the Middle East are far different from those needed to grow revenue within a mature market in the United States. In this case, our company should have realized that the ability to successfully lead a team that is largely isolated from its corporate support base, and to start up a new business operation within a totally new set of business conditions, regulatory constraints, and distribution channels, requires a unique set of executive competencies. An effective executive resource strategy guards against this type of failure by forcing senior teams to measure existing leadership competencies found in their executive talent pools against their leadership requirements for key initiatives.

2. *Does your strategy employ a data-driven competency assessment process that enables your senior managers to make well-informed decisions on executive placement and development?* The engine that powers an effective executive resource strategy is a well-constructed competency database. A comprehensive database provides everyone in the organization with a common language and assessment methodology for evaluating the comparative performance of executive incumbents and candidates. As Figure 3 illustrates, when designed properly, a competency database allows an organization to identify both the *depth* and the *breadth* of its leadership bench by highlighting patterns in executive competencies; for example, those strengths (in this case, the strength of team building) that permeate across management levels and work functions.

3. *Does your strategy reflect a tightly orchestrated HR system that ties together your company's selection, recruitment, and development components?* The test of this integration is that your executive resource management system should allow you to easily match and compare data that reside within different components of your HR system. In a valid system, executives are not expected to use one set of competencies when conducting performance appraisals, a second set of competencies when participating in selection interviewing, and still another one in their succession planning process. Instead, the same set of competencies and ratings scales should provide uniform performance metrics for calibrating HR actions across the organization.

One way to confirm that you have an integrated executive resource management system is to look for inconsistencies in the information that is generated on executives within different elements of this system. We are not talking about nuclear science here; these kinds of problems are easy to detect. If, for example, an executive or manager is identified as a high-potential candidate within your succession planning process, but the same individual is concurrently rated as weak or untested on several of the competencies expected of higher-level executives, you know that you have a problem. In the same way, if your company's executive search firms consistently offer up job candidates who fall far short of your expectations, you know that there is a disconnect in either *identifying* or *communicating* the essential competency requirements for these positions.

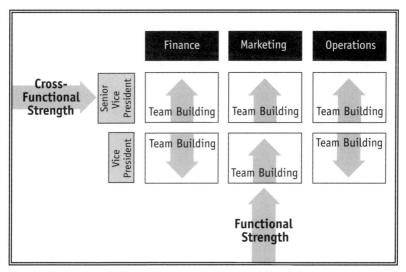

FIGURE 3 IDENTIFYING PATTERNS IN EXECUTIVE COMPETENCIES

4. *Does your strategy incorporate input from key organizational stakeholders, including board members, senior managers, executives, and high-potential managers?* Occasionally, HR leaders make the mistake of attempting to create their executive resource strategies on their own, without seeking input from other members of their executive team, in the hope of "wowing" their senior teams or governing boards with the elegant leadership staffing and development models they've developed. This type of insular model building usually fails to produce the desired results.

If your senior managers are not privy to the rationale that drives the design of your HR strategy, they are far less likely to support that strategy. In addition, without feedback from key stakeholders the HR department's final product will not take into account any changing business conditions that may significantly alter the requirements for executive success. Finally, if stakeholder feedback is not obtained early in the design process, the derived strategy will frequently overlook the requirements of certain specialized stakeholder groups. I know of a company that created an executive resource plan that included input from its corporate IT function but neglected to interview IT executives located in the field sites. The resulting resource strategy was rather lopsided, missing many of the key requirements for successful IT performance in field locations.

If, on the other hand, your organizational stakeholders buy into the design process for your executive resource strategy, they will be more likely to accept and support decisions regarding executive placement and development. Vicere suggests that "the most effective HR leaders have recruited in senior-level sponsorship, and have encouraged line executives to openly talk about their strategy. These HR leaders assume the roles of high-level OD consultants; they understand that part of their job involves getting senior executives to understand that executive resource management is the process by which they (the senior managers) leave their legacy with their organization, and create a new generation of executives who can fulfill that legacy."[6]

5. *Does your strategy reflect a decision process that goes well beyond immediate concerns and short-term business pressures to address the long-term needs of your organization?* Many organizations largely ignore their executive resource plans until faced with an emergency, such as the sudden departure of a key executive. These companies tend to consider only the most immediate, short-term executive resource issues. They view the executive resource plan as no more than a snapshot of the current performance capability of their organization.

A more effective approach is to use the executive resource strategy to perform an assessment of both your company's *short-term* and *long-term* leadership requirements. This approach can help you determine the degree to which your organization's current leadership talent pool poses a serious constraint on its ability to pursue critical long-term goals. Since establishing the right executive leadership is the first element to setting off in a new direction, it is important to create an early warning system that quickly detects changes in leadership requirements. Another consideration is that because the development path for an executive is often five to ten years, and represents a substantial time and money investment on the part of an employer, it is important to accurately predict the trajectory that this development path should follow to parallel the company's long-term business needs. One method for anticipating the long-term executive resource requirements of your company is the use of the scenario forecasting technique that will be introduced in Chapter 3. This technique can help you obtain useful feedback from your entire senior team regarding future business needs and associated leadership competency requirements.

6. *Does your strategy allow you to focus your executive resource efforts to obtain the most effective overall team?* The most dis-

tinguishing characteristic of a viable executive resource strategy is that it can *leverage talent and ability through a focused and sustainable game plan.* Since, by definition, having a strategy means valuing and selecting certain courses of action over plausible alternatives, it stands to reason that if you are attempting to be all things to all people, you don't have a strategy. Following this line of thinking, the creation of an executive resource strategy implies a willingness to make some tough decisions involving the most effective ways to leverage time, money, and talent to obtain a superior executive team. An effective executive resource strategy addresses a number of tough choices.

- To what degree should we balance our need for executive involvement and ownership with the time limitations faced by senior managers?

- To what degree should we focus on high-potential executive candidates as opposed to spreading our development investment across our entire population of executives?

- What tradeoffs do we face in taking a fast or slow changeover approach to replacing weak performers?

- To what extent should our executive resource strategy emphasize obtaining talent from the outside, at the cost of reducing promotional and developmental opportunities for our current executives and managers?

- How quickly or slowly should we move on the change-up process (the aggressiveness with which we are willing to place executives into "stretch" positions)?

- If we have only limited funds to spend on external consulting, within what area of our executive resource system will this investment provide the best payoffs?

- What type of leadership mentoring and coaching process will be most closely aligned with our organizational structure and culture?

- What emphasis will we place on the development of key leadership competencies?

DEVELOPING THE FRAMEWORK FOR AN EXECUTIVE RESOURCE STRATEGY

Of all the many executive resource decisions listed above, three decisions significantly affect organizational performance. I refer to these decisions as the *make-or-buy decision,* the *acquisition decision,* and the *transition decision.*

THE MAKE-OR-BUY DECISION

One of the most difficult decisions a company faces involves the degree to which it chooses to rely on internal or external placements to fill gaps in its executive leadership bench. While almost every organization employs both of these options, many companies encounter factors that predispose them to rely predominately on one of these options. Some of the factors that should be reviewed when weighing the relative pros and cons of make-or-buy decisions are presented in Table 6.

The way in which an organization formulates and executes its make-or-buy decision affects not only its ability to carry out its strategic plan but also the type of leadership culture it fosters. By this, I'm referring to such factors as the following:

- How the organization's employees view its commitment to internal development

- The types of performance standards the company sets for its executive leaders

- The value the company places on organizational experience as a prerequisite for managing executive functions

First let's consider the conditions that favor *internal placement*. The fact is, companies that live by the slogan "we promote from within" tend to be quite different from those whose motto is "we hire the best and the brightest." As Table 6 shows, there are several conditions under which a focus on internal development may be advantageous. One such factor is when your company is able to draw on a large talent pool of exceptional managerial performers. Note that we are really talking about two conditions here. The first condition involves the *size* of the pool. A general rule of thumb allows three to five potential internal replacements for every executive position within your company. The second condition involves the *quality* of your talent pool and whether those persons identified as potential replacements really are exceptional performers who are ready to move up. If your talent pool has been allowed to degrade over time, it is possible that selected replacement candidates will simply represent the best options within a mediocre reservoir of talent.

Another situation that favors internal placement is when you are operating within an organizational climate in which internal development (or the lack of it) is a volatile HR issue. This is often the case for companies that have experienced repeated downsizing, where job security is a strong concern among managers, or when there has been a strong precedent set over the years for promoting from within. In any of these situations, the decision to shift executive bench-building

TABLE 6	
FACTORS TO CONSIDER WHEN EVALUATING MAKE-OR-BUY DECISIONS o	
When to Rely on Internal Placement	**When to Rely on External Placement**
• You can draw on a *large* talent pool.	• You have a *limited* internal talent pool.
• *Internal development* is a key HR issue.	• *Performance capability* is a key HR issue.
• Business conditions are *stable*.	• Business conditions are *radically changing*.
• Building *cross-functional capability* is a strategic objective.	• There is a desire to *overcome thinking constraints* imposed by industry norms.
• Talent can be built *incrementally*.	• There is a sense of urgency for *quickly upgrading* the executive bench.

efforts to the external recruitment of executives will likely trigger concerns among executives and managers regarding the company's commitment to internal development.

Internal development tends to be a more viable option when a company is operating within a stable business environment. By this I mean that the company is operating within a mature market characterized by (1) established product lines, (2) a stable economic environment, (3) a moderate rate of technological growth, and (4) market boundaries that are fairly impermeable to intrusion from "wild card" competitors from outside the industry. These types of stable business conditions support internal development by favoring the archiving of industry and organizational knowledge. That is, a company will usually attach a premium to internal candidates who bring with them organizational and industry-related experience, in-house technical expertise, and knowledge of well-established work methods and processes.

Placement from within may also be preferred when companies are attempting to build cross-functional capability by moving talented high-potential managers and executives across development assignments and positions. The idea here is to build a pool of potential general managers who have a broad understanding of the workings of the organization. Still another advantage of focusing on internal development is that it helps attract high-potential talent by positioning an organization's work environment as being supportive of executive development, with ample opportunities for promotional advancement.

One last condition that favors internal placement is when a company has the luxury of building talent incrementally. This is usually the case when, as just mentioned, an organization is operating within a stable business environment and when a *baseline review* of the executive leadership bench (see Chapter 6) shows that at least 90 percent of the executive bench is staffed by solid performers. Given these two conditions, it is possible to make incremental adjustments to the leadership bench through external replacement, while relying on the gradual development of internal talent to meet the bulk of the company's bench-building requirements.

Now, let's review the conditions that favor *external placement*. As you were reading the conditions that favor internal placement, you probably thought to yourself something like, "Sounds good, but that's a description of an ideal work environment." The fact is, you're right. Quite often, as much as we would like to rely on internal development to meet our executive staffing needs, the reality is that we are often faced with expedient pressures that force us to turn to external recruiting to build our leadership bench.

The first condition for external placement is when you have a limited talent pool that yields a small average number (less than three) of qualified internal successors to executive positions. Having a limited talent pool can mean either that you have a relatively small base of potential executives from which to choose, or that the candidate pool you have, while large, is extremely weak. The discovery of a weak and spotty internal talent pool is a danger sign that indicates the need for importing talent from the outside. Unfortunately, the realization that there is a deficient internal talent pool is something that takes many organizations by surprise. A typical scenario is when a new CEO enters a company, performs a baseline review of the current executive team, and discovers that, as a result of historically low performance standards, the performance ratings for company executives have been grossly inflated.

A second factor that favors external recruiting is when performance capability supersedes internal development as a key HR issue.

Perhaps a company is facing short-term business pressures that require immediate turnaround actions and that cannot be successfully addressed with incumbent executives. In such a case, a company may not be able to afford the time delays involved in meeting these business challenges through internal development and promotion, and must instead rely on external recruiting. The time required to develop junior-level candidates is difficult to collapse. In a tight labor market, if a company is not willing to take the risk to promote candidates before they are deemed fully "ready," those same candidates may be snatched up by willing competitors, thus reducing the pool of qualified successors.

A third situation that favors external recruiting is when business conditions are radically changing. Simply put, if the business environment for the next five years is projected to be significantly different from that of the last five years, there is a strong argument for devaluing any premium historically placed on executives and managers who possess organization and industry knowledge. In this kind of scenario, the last words you want to hear from a senior management team are "but that's not how we've always done it around here." There is a wide spectrum of research suggesting that executives from outside the organization are frequently brought in specifically to support broad organizational change initiatives or company turnarounds.[7,8,9,10]

Still another factor to consider is the need to overcome the thinking constraints imposed by industry norms. This need is particularly strong when a company is attempting to "think outside the box" to challenge the dominant industry logic about how businesses within a given industry should operate, or when a company is attempting to expand into an entirely different field of endeavor.

There are, of course, several downsides to relying on an external recruiting strategy. The first is cost. In today's tight labor market, a company may have to go 20 percent over market value to attract exceptional job candidates, not to mention the additional costs required for search fees, relocation, and negotiated perks. In addition, there is a high risk in making midstride changeovers—that is, in bringing new executives on board and attempting to acclimate them to a new company when work projects are about to encounter critical milestones. A key variable here is the time available for effectively on-boarding new hires before they are able to gain the necessary corporate knowledge to weigh in on key business decisions. Finally, one has to consider the natural demoralization and confusion that often accompany the influx of outside executives into an organization.

THE ACQUISITION DECISION

This decision centers on whether an organization chooses to draw its talent from best-in-industry performers or go outside its industry to recruit world-class talent. The latter decision is usually fueled by one of the following two scenarios.

The Quarantine Scenario. The industry in question may have been historically sheltered from outside competitors, leading to a stable, well-defined, and fairly predictable competitive set. Companies operating within this scenario traditionally draw leadership talent from within their respective industry pools, with the long-term result of such "corporate inbreeding" being the development of executive leaders who are extremely knowledgeable about their industries, but who (because of a narrow range of industrial competition) may not represent world-class talent. As traditional market barriers dissolve, an organization finds that it must radically expand its definition of the term *competitor,* with the result that industry-specific expertise begins to erode in value. The banking industry illustrates the quarantine scenario—on the one hand attempting to expand into money market investment and on the other attempting to ward off intrusion by large giants (such as AT&T) that have decided to enter the credit card market.

The Outside-In Scenario. A company located at the other end of the change continuum also may have to go outside its industry in order to acquire executives who can provide fresh new perspectives on the challenges of increased competition, mutating technologies, and shifting customer requirements. An interesting example comes from Harrah's Entertainment Inc., a large gambling and resort company, which recently brought on board as its chairman and chief executive Philip Satre, a former corporate lawyer. Satre, in turn, pulled in Gary Loveman, a Harvard Business School professor and former Harrah's business consultant, as the company's new chief operating officer. Satre hired Loveman to tackle the problem of growing Harrah's despite a flat industry trend. One of Loveman's solutions has been to create a type of "frequent gamblers" program that provides incentives to Harrah's most loyal customers. The strategy seems to be working as these gamblers now make up as much as 18 percent of the company's revenues (up from 9 percent in 1995).[11]

If we view executive acquisition decisions as representing a balancing act between the need to attract world-class performers and the need to attract the best performers within a given industry, we arrive at the four acquisition options shown in Figure 4 and discussed below.

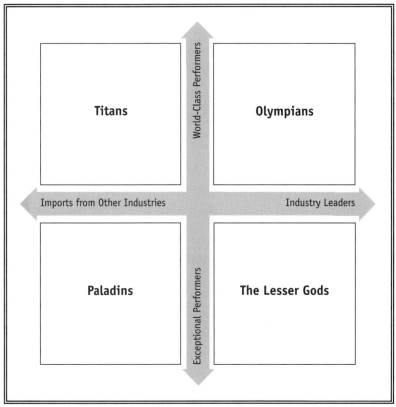

FIGURE 4 SELECTING AN ACQUISITION STRATEGY

Titans. These executives represent world-class performers that are imported from outside one's industry. Titans are key executives who have developed a reputation for being able to quickly master totally new fields. They are often brought in to free up companies from lock-step thinking and to redirect them along entirely new directions. AT&T's titan is Mike Armstrong, the former head of Hughes Electronics, who assumed the position of CEO in 1997. At the time of this writing, Armstrong is attempting to radically expand AT&T's traditional market boundaries, by considering alliances with major cable companies, such as TeleCommunications, Inc., and Time Warner, as well as Internet service providers such as America Online. The idea behind these moves is to enable AT&T to use cable networks to provide customers with television services, voice communications, and Internet access.[12]

The challenges posed by bringing a titan into a company are threefold:

- They tend to lack credibility with internally groomed executives who, having come up through the ranks, prize industry-related experience.
- They often find their new home a hostile environment, where they are subtly undermined by insiders who are politically "wired" to the senior team or the directing board.
- They must be able to operate within an extremely accelerated learning curve and quickly analyze the operational constraints of their new company and industry.

Despite these challenges, there are some indications that the ranks of titans are rapidly swelling. An article by John Helyar and Joann S. Lublin in the *Asian Wall Street Journal* cites two recent research studies that confirm this trend. The first study, conducted by Michigan State University, found that among 369 companies involved in the study, more than one-third were outsiders. The second study, conducted by the Harvard Business School, produced somewhat different results, suggesting that the number of "outsider CEOs" has doubled since 1980, comprising a current level of 17 percent of all CEOs.[13] Helyar and Lublin suggest several reasons for the growth of the outsider CEO, including the growing preference for superior general management expertise over industry knowledge; the increased authority of boards, which are attempting to seek out world-class talent; and the fact that titans often bring with them into their new corporate home a cadre of executive staffers from their previous organization.[14]

Additional evidence for the continuance of this trend comes from a 1998 study sponsored by the Association of Executive Search Consultants, involving interviews with three hundred CEOs, HR directors, and executives classified as being "up-and-coming CEOs." One of the study's conclusions is that the interviewees all agreed that, "it is not necessary for a CEO to be from within the industry to be effective. Rather the current thinking, held by over three-quarters of the corporate leaders we interviewed, is that *leadership ability* is far more important than *industry savvy*."[15]

Olympians. These executives represent world-class performers who are also best-in-industry performers. Olympians offer an organization the best of all possible worlds: a leader who understands the workings of the industry, who presents industry stock analysts with a known, risk-free leadership variable, and who also brings to the table world-class performance. An example of an Olympian is Steve Jobs, who agreed to come back as the chief executive for Apple Computer. Jobs's reemergence at Apple has given this company a healthy shot in the arm in terms of creative technological innovation, while at the same time rekindling the interest of the investment community. While the Olympian is certainly the most attractive candidate a company could opt for, such individuals are extremely scarce and are costly to import. Accordingly, the time-lag for locating and recruiting an Olympian can add several months to the standard three- to six-month executive search—an option that some companies can't afford to take.

The Lesser Gods. These are those best-in-industry executives who lag behind the comparative performance of their peers in other industries. An example would be a construction management firm acquiring a CIO who is widely regarded as a respected executive within the construction industry, though not necessarily someone who has gained distinction as being a world-class performer in the area of information technology. The advantage that the Lesser Gods bring to the table is that they require a shorter on-boarding ramp for learning the dynamics of their organizational homes and are often easier to acquire.

Paladins. These executives are neither world-class nor best-in-industry performers, but frequently represent solid and reliable talent that is readily accessible and affordable to an organization. Frequently, such individuals make up the primary candidate base for junior-level executive searches, and they are particularly attractive to an employer when they offer a means of achieving a significant talent upgrade over executive incumbents, without forcing a company to incur unusually high recruiting, relocation, and hiring costs.

THE TRANSITION DECISION

The third major decision that guides a company's executive resource strategy is the *transition decision*. This decision concerns the *speed* at which an organization takes action to strengthen its leadership bench. As Figure 5 on page 46 illustrates, we can view the transition decision as extending across two dimensions. The horizontal dimension relates to the rate of executive *changeover*—the aggressiveness with which a company imports external talent from the outside. The vertical dimension refers to the rate of *change-up*—the aggressiveness with which internal candidates are thrust into new executive challenges, through either promotions or lateral transfers. Together, these two dimensions produce four options for strengthening executive teams, each of which presents an organization with its own unique set of

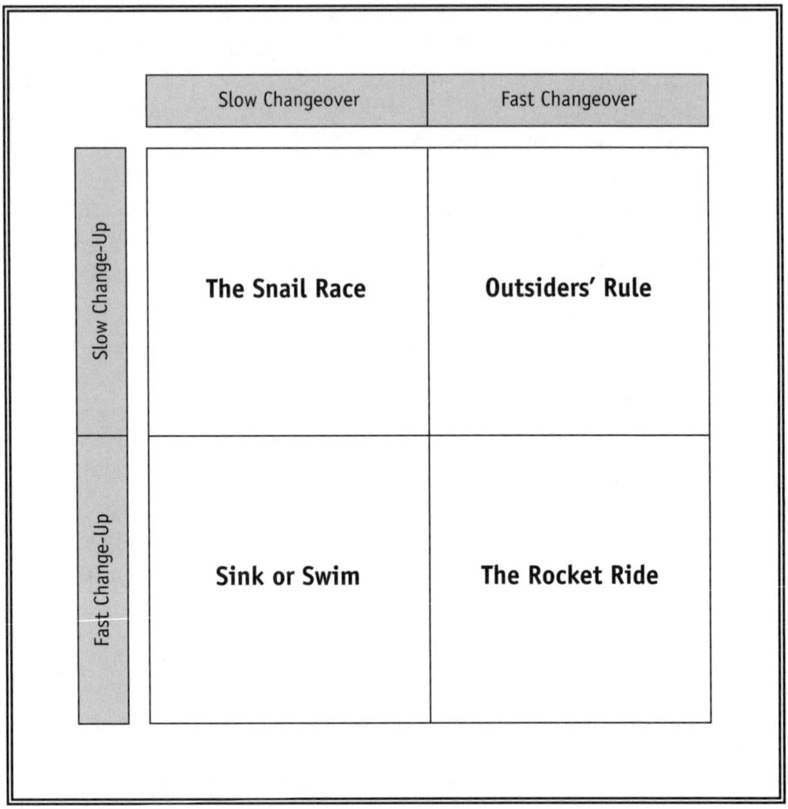

	Slow Changeover	Fast Changeover
Slow Change-Up	The Snail Race	Outsiders' Rule
Fast Change-Up	Sink or Swim	The Rocket Ride

FIGURE 5 FOUR TRANSITION OPTIONS

challenges and opportunities: (1) Outsiders' Rule, (2) the Rocket Ride, (3) Sink or Swim, or (4) the Snail Race.

The Outsiders' Rule Option. As its title suggests, this option is based on making a fast changeover in the replacement of executives from the outside, coupled with a slow, incremental growth of executive talent through internal promotions. The Outsiders' Rule option is frequently selected when organizational performance trends and accompanying competency audits show that a company has allowed its internal talent base to atrophy, producing a limited number of candidates for promotion.

The Outsiders' Rule option may also be warranted when a company has gradually created a large-scale mismatch of executives to their functions. This was the situation I encountered several years ago after coming on board with a company as its director of organizational development. I discovered that the organization had been experiencing tremendous difficulty in growing new sales sectors. Further investigation showed that part of this problem stemmed from the company's historical practice of combining its customer support and sales organizations, under the mistaken assumption that the same competencies were required to run these two different functions. In this situation, the senior team eventually recognized the need to separate those few internal leaders who comprised the true sales talent from the bulk of their sales/service leadership, whose strengths resided more in the area of building long-term customer relationships. This type of competency differentiation is sometimes referred to as the process of "separating out the hunters from the farmers."

The Outsiders' Rule option is often exercised when organizations need to quickly grow large chunks of the business through the wholesale importing of intact work teams and senior managers. Such is the case with Cisco Systems, Inc., which has used corporate acquisitions as a means of rapidly growing its talent base. A defining success feature of Cisco's acquisition strategy is that this company works hard to secure the loyalty and support of its acquired executives, both by assuring the acquired team that there is a valued, secure place for them within their new corporate home, and by quickly placing acquired CEOs and other senior managers into important leadership roles. This integration of talent is one of the reasons Cisco experiences only a 6 percent yearly turnover in acquired employees, far below the industry norm.[16]

While there is no arguing with the premise that the Outsiders' Rule option provides a method for quickly upgrading an executive talent base, at the same time it is fraught with difficulties that deserve serious attention. Chief among these is the fact that this option can lead to a self-fulfilling prophecy—the reliance on external recruiting to quickly plug talent gaps leads to the erosion of a company's internal development efforts, resulting in a further dependence on external candidates. Figure 6 on page 48 shows how this scenario often plays out with fast-growth companies, which frequently have extensive executive staffing needs during the first few years of existence. The challenge here is for a company to keep a dual focus and simultaneously import the best possible talent while vigorously working to strengthen its internal talent pool.

Another major problem faced by companies that adopt the Outsiders' Rule option is the loss of organizational expertise, history, and continuity as outsiders begin to displace internal performers. This problem can surface in a number of ways, including the weakening of long-term customer relationships ("Where did Jennifer go? Who is the new face here?") and the departure of key people who take with them an irreplaceable understanding of an organization's work

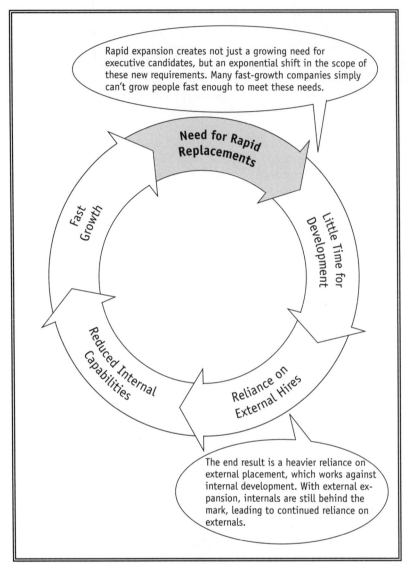

Rapid expansion creates not just a growing need for executive candidates, but an exponential shift in the scope of these new requirements. Many fast-growth companies simply can't grow people fast enough to meet these needs.

Need for Rapid Replacements

Fast Growth

Little Time for Development

Reduced Internal Capabilities

Reliance on External Hires

The end result is a heavier reliance on external placement, which works against internal development. With external expansion, internals are still behind the mark, leading to continued reliance on externals.

FIGURE 6 THE VICIOUS RESOURCE CYCLE CONFRONTING
MANY FAST-GROWTH COMPANIES

systems and processes. Still another problem created by this option is the demoralization of long-term employees, who may feel that they have been unjustly overlooked for key promotional openings. A related problem involves the difficulty of integrating many new leaders into the current executive team.

If you are committed to using the Outsiders' Rule option, there are a few steps you can take to mitigate these problems. The first is to clearly explain to your work associates the rationale for bringing in a large number of outside executives. Employees are likely to be more supportive of such a move if they can see how it has been grounded in the company's business needs. Second, if you have selected this option as an expedient, temporary solution for bridging critical staffing needs, send this message to your company. Let employees know that over the long term they can count on your company to maintain its emphasis on internal development and promotion. At the same time, take visible actions to support this position by conducting an audit of your internal development, job posting, and promotional processes and by initiating (if you have not as yet established one) the type of talent review process outlined in detail in Chapter 6. Finally, undertake a focused on-boarding and team-building process (Chapter 13) as a means of gaining alignment between new and established company executives.

The Rocket Ride Option. This is the most aggressive and ambitious of the four transition options and involves quickly pushing superior talent up through the ranks (often before they are completely ready to take the jump) while simultaneously importing a large number of outside candidates. The Rocket Ride is most likely to occur when two conditions exist: (1) a company is experiencing an organizational mutation in the form of rapid growth, an entry into a completely new market or product area, or a complete changeover in its product or service deployment strategy; and (2) the company's board of directors or CEO has a low level of confidence in the existing management structure.

True to its name, the Rocket Ride is an aggressive and fast-moving strategy for upgrading executive talent through the use of accelerated recruiting coupled with the rapid development and promotion of internal candidates. The Rocket Ride closely resembles what Bradford D. Smart and Geoffrey H. Smart refer to as "topgrading the organization," which they define as the practice of "not only finding, hiring, and promoting better people at all levels . . . but proactively hiring and promoting only the most talented people available, while sensitively but aggressively removing chronic underperformers."[17] (Additional information on the selection interview process the Smarts recommend to support topgrading can be found in Chapter 12.)

As it requires the rapid injection of new executive talent, the Rocket Ride always generates a certain amount of confusion and uncertainty in an organization. This situation is exacerbated by the replacement of underperforming members of the executive team. Under this scenario, you can anticipate encountering the following problems.

- Executives and managers who are loyal to the old guard are apt to resist the ideas and actions of the incoming executives. Steps will need to be taken to minimize this resistance and to provide a safe "incubation period" for newly imported talent (see Chapter 13).

- Discrepancies may occur in the criteria used in hiring decisions of internal versus external candidates. When you are moving fast to both hire and promote executive talent, first ensure that you have established a fair playing field for evaluating the comparative competencies of internal and external job candidates. Suggestions on how to do this can be found in Chapters 5 and 12.

- A high financial investment over a relatively short period of time is assumed. This includes the severance costs for terminated executives, recruiting and relocation costs for incoming executives, and relocation costs and bonus and salary adjustments for internal candidates. In addition, you must add to these direct costs the more hidden costs associated with high levels of executive transition, such as the attrition among angry and disgruntled employees, project disruptions that occur during the "changing of the guard," and ripple effects that are created as executives are promoted and leave open many lower-level executive positions.

- Organizational discontinuity occurs as new people flood into positions, often bringing with them entirely new performance expectations and operating assumptions regarding the best way to do business. At the same time, the rapid departure of existing talent may mean the concurrent exodus of company and industry knowledge that is essential to the smooth performance of the organization.

- Organizational uncertainty and trauma abound as employees mourn the loss of familiar co-workers and bosses, while simultaneously adjusting to the unknown expectations of new managers. In his classic article "Muscle-Build the Organization," Harvard Business School professor Andrall E. Pearson states that "only an aggressive approach can make a big difference, quickly. But it has its costs; at least initially, managers have to be willing to sacrifice continuity for a thorough shake-up."[18]

Despite these problems, sometimes there is no other viable way to effect the widescale changes required by the organization. The Rocket Ride is usually undertaken because a company's CEO or board has identified severe performance problems or a limited window of growth opportunity, which require an aggressive and rapid infusion of new leaders into the organization. Still, there are some precautions one can take to make this disruptive option more palatable to the organization.

- Make all required leadership changes over a short period of time. I am not referring to the time that should go into the leadership transition plan, which may be considerable, but rather the length of time needed to execute the plan. After all, as the old adage says, "when pulling a sore tooth, it is usually better to do it as fast as possible."

- Have an open discussion with your associates explaining the rationale for bringing in a large number of outside executives; and (if such is the case) explain the rationale for occasionally skipping promotional levels to pull up the most qualified candidates for open positions. This latter scenario usually occurs in technically driven functions such as IT or Operations, where there may be a dearth of talent in the next organizational level but a high degree of talent at lower levels.

- Encourage the use of on-boarding and team-building activities to gain alignment between new and established company executives. Detailed suggestions for how to create on-boarding plans can be found in Chapter 11.

- For those areas of the company in which the rapid replacement of executives will mean the loss of organizational history and systems knowledge, consider taking steps to retain critical portions of your technical knowledge base before certain executives are managed out. These steps might include creating an Intranet-based FAQ (frequently asked questions) file and electronic bulletin board for archiving project-related information, updating nondisclosure statements regarding the sharing of proprietary corporate information, installing transition leaders on key projects to ensure program continuity, and investing additional funds to keep selected executives on board (or retaining their services through temporary consulting contracts) while executive replacements are being moved into position.

The Sink or Swim Option. This option involves building the bulk of your executive bench strength through an aggressive internal promotional strategy, while relying far less on external recruiting to fill positions. The advantages of such a strategy are that it supports the organizational value of internal development and promotion, creates a motivational charge through the use of promotional opportunities, and ensures that organizational knowledge is passed on through internal promotion.

Concurrently, there are several drawbacks that are unique to this transition option. First, this option requires managers and executives to advance into new positions before they are fully ready. While such an option certainly provides a challenging stretch for performers, at the same time it necessitates a higher degree of risk taking. To make Sink or Swim a viable transition option, organizations must be willing to allow an increase in the failure rate for projects as relatively inexperienced executives struggle to adapt to their new positions.

A second concern is that for companies attempting to break into new territory, the Sink or Swim option may result in organizational inbreeding as senior-level managers attempt to clone junior managers in their own image. This problem can be partially offset through the use of organizationwide team reviews that force a check-and-balance system onto executive promotional decisions, and by emphasizing demonstrated performance and innovative thinking over seniority and experience in promotional decisions.

A third concern is that the Sink or Swim option is based on the assumption that there is sufficient internal leadership talent within the organization (although this may require multilayered searches for candidates) to fill all available executive positions. This talent will not be available if the company has not previously invested in executive development and coaching. In cases in which a sufficient talent pool is lacking, the organization will be forced to adapt a different transition option or to downgrade the quality of its executive team. To directly address this concern, I strongly recommend that before exercising this option you perform a complete competency assessment of your executive team (see Chapter 6). I also recommend that in evaluating the performance and potential of executives you go beyond their managers' personal evaluations to make use of supplemental, independent assessment vehicles such as 360-degree profiling and assessment center feedback (see Chapter 5).

The Snail Race Option. The Snail Race is the most conservative of the four transition options and is primarily used by organizations that are in a slow-growth, steady-state mode or that hope to minimize the risks associated with bringing on board new executives. The Snail Race offers a few obvious advantages, including a low degree of organizational resistance to change, ample time allotted for "shake-out flights" to assess the capabilities of newly placed executives, and a high level of continuity in transferring leadership and technical skills from outgoing to incoming leaders.

Unfortunately, these advantages are often outweighed by the disadvantages that accompany this transition option. An important disadvantage is that the Snail Race is demotivating for those high-potential (HIPO) executives and managers who see few promotional opportunities being made available to them, and who are disenchanted with the low caliber of top-level leadership in their organization. Companies that pursue this option therefore increase the probability of incurring heavy attrition among their HIPOs.

Another disadvantage of the Snail Race is that it tends to reinforce complacency among executives, by encouraging them to regard their positions as tenured and completely secure. While I in no way endorse the idea that fear and intimidation are the ways to build a good executive team, it is equally true that leaders who see little or no movement in the executive ranks are likely to begin to nestle comfortably within their comfort zones and to adopt an insular and retracted view of their business environment.

The Snail Race can produce a "hardening of the arteries" with respect to a leadership team that, through the lack of new leadership blood, becomes increasingly introspective and prone to lock-step thinking. A final drawback with this option is that an extremely slow transition of a company's leadership team can prove to be a major obstacle when attempting to break into new markets or exploit new growth opportunities.

As a general guideline, if your company is committed to employing this option, it is important to look for creative ways to breathe new life into your executive team. Some steps you might take are

- Make an extensive investment in development options (see Chapters 8 and 9) that can help your team continue to build its skill strengths.

- Develop a succession planning model (see Chapter 10) that points out to team members gaps that cannot currently be filled through internal backups and that may require the selective use of external recruiting.

- To create a "burning platform" for change, consider conducting benchmarking studies for work functions that are regarded by your company as its core competencies. (Core competencies are discussed in detail in Chapter 4.)

- Consider making use of rotational job assignments to develop a broader cross-functional skill base and to shake selected executives out of their comfort zones by encouraging them to take on new responsibilities.

IS THERE A "BEST STRATEGY"?

As you might deduce from the examples provided throughout this chapter, an effective executive resource strategy should embody a flexible game plan for action, rather than a rigid methodology that imposes an immutable HR staffing and development logic on an organization without regard to changing business conditions. Indeed, changes in the business picture or organizational structure often denote the need for modifications to a company's executive resource strategy. Thus, a new CEO who uses the Outsiders' Rule option to quickly replace a low-performing executive team with strong outside talent might shift to the Sink or Swim option once poor performers have been pruned from the company and several outside leaders have been installed. In the same way, a company facing a severe performance decline might launch into the Rocket Ride to effect a quick turnaround, then downshift to a slower transition strategy once the company is again on stable ground. The point is that the selection of an executive resource strategy is not a paint-by-numbers process; it requires a high level of intuition and business savvy on the part of its primary architects—the corporate CEO and the vice president of HR.

CASE IN POINT: AMERICAN NATIONAL CAN COMPANY
Curt Clawson, President

A dynamic example of the steps a company can take to link its business strategy with its executive resource strategy can be found in American National Can Company. Curt Clawson, president of the Chicago-based Beverage Cans Americas division, provides the following description of how his company has applied the concept of "topgrading" (refer back to the Outsiders' Rule transition strategy; also see Chapter 12 for more information on topgrading) to strengthen its leadership bench.

> Our company was formed ten years ago from a merger of two older companies. We've been around a long time, with our average employee having over twenty years of work experience. As has been typical of other American companies, for a long time there was a trend within our company to downsize—every year shedding more of the fat that typified our bureaucracy—with very little outside hiring. As a result, when I took over the Beverage Cans Americas division I encountered a company that had a good history and some awesome technical strengths and customer relationships, but that had stagnated because it had become too internally focused and was not bringing in new people. As a result, over the last five years, we had become less competitive and were losing market share to more nimble competitors. Ed Lapekas, chairman and CEO of American National Can, realized that given these circumstances, a heavy dose of change was vital to restore the company's health. Accordingly, he hired me to

be the initial change agent targeting the Beverage Cans Americas division. Moreover, he has provided the senior support necessary for any real change process.

This was the situation when I walked in the door. A recent *Fortune* article said that most CEOs fail because of poor execution. I believe this. We felt that in the short term we needed to out-execute our competitors, and that the way to do this was to have a simple strategy that everyone could buy into. The vision statement we subsequently drafted was "to be the leading can company in the world." We said that we would do this through three actions: having the best customer service, the lowest costs, and the best people. I'm a firm believer in the fact that you need to continually reiterate your business strategy to your organization, so we framed everything we did in terms of "customer," "cost," and "people."

Given the business context we inherited, we felt that in order to get the best people in the industry we needed a heavy dose of topgrading in our company. In different circumstances I probably would have taken another approach, but in this case I felt we lacked the internal skill set necessary to be competitive, and that it was important to attract the best people to our company. We went about doing that in a very systematic way, starting at the top and working down the organization. We kicked off the process by having everyone read Bradford Smart's book *Topgrading*. Later, Brad and Geoff Smart were brought in to lead a series of topgrading seminars, which were outstanding. This gave us the conceptual foundation that our people needed to understand and later implement our upgrading plans.

From the start we prepared our company for these changes by being very honest in our communications and explaining the rationale behind topgrading, and why we were doing what we were doing. We explained that we would need to bring in new managers to pull in the skills needed to catch up to our competition. I personally got in front of everyone and told them about our three themes: customers, costs, and people. I also used a weekly voice-mail to tell them how we were doing on our three themes.

We have over 2,000 hourly associates at our company and a salaried workforce of 700 people. Through our topgrading process we brought in about 100 managers and threw them into the mix. As a starting point we ranked our managers as "A," "B," and "C" players, using the topgrading competencies. I found that when I brought in "A" players that reported to me, they in turn brought in topgraders to report to them.

We used the same competencies to evaluate everyone in the company on both performance and potential. This generated a matrix that included high potentials, solid contributors, and low performers. Once we brought in "A" players, the "C" box began to get more crowded. Using our formal review process, I personally worked with our HR people to evaluate such positions as senior engineers and production managers. I got on a plane and spent a day at each of our twenty-two plants to verify what I was told. As we worked through this process we had all managers rank their people. On our first attempt we weren't well calibrated, but with input from our newcomers we've become better calibrated to the talent levels of benchmarked companies.

When going outside for the kinds of managers and executives we needed, we looked for certain competencies. In manufacturing we wanted people who were experienced in leading "lean" manufacturing efforts, while in purchasing we brought in people with supply-chain skills because we wanted this to be a value differentiator. Regarding leadership skills, we generally reviewed everyone in terms of the leadership competencies outlined in *Topgrading*. Along with new skills, we also wanted people who could handle pressure, and so we tried to draft people from companies that represented the types of work culture we wanted to create—companies such as Emerson Electric, General Electric, and so on.

In looking at the lessons learned from this experience, I'd have to say that if I had it to do all over again I would probably start by topgrading our HR function first, rather than the manufacturing function, because having HR people experienced in topgrading is a great benefit during times of great change. I usually did the assessment without much HR involvement because I wasn't sure of their calibration. The point here is that you need good, experienced HR people from the start.

We've accomplished a lot through our efforts. Originally I had wanted to accomplish everything in a two-year time period, but we've found that we've been able to move much faster than that. Because of our topgrading and our other actions, in the first year we were able to improve our operating income by 60 percent. This year looks even better.

- The starting point for building an effective leadership team is crafting an executive resource strategy that links a company's business objectives to its executive staffing and development needs.

- The three decisions that provide the context for an effective resource strategy are the *make-or-buy decision,* the a*cquisition decision,* and the *transition decision.*

- The make-or-buy decision relates to the extent to which your strategy is based on importing fresh talent from outside an organization or on developing from within.

- The acquisition decision concerns whether your leadership acquisition efforts are focused on hiring world-class performers or exceptional executives who are not regarded as being world-class, and whether your search is directed within or outside of your industry.

- The transition decision involves the speed at which you are attempting to make changes in your executive bench—whether these transitions will occur quickly or incrementally.

- Together these decisions articulate how a company intends to upgrade its talent base, the risks and investment commitment that will be associated with this improvement, and the speed with which a CEO or board intends to implement this upgrading.

- An effective executive resource strategy should be a flexible game plan for action, not a rigid HR methodology. Therefore, it is important to try to anticipate changing business conditions that may require a reassessment of your current strategy.

CHAPTER 3

UNCOVERING EMERGING BUSINESS REQUIREMENTS

Whenever I ask one of my colleagues in HR or training to walk me through the first steps they take when designing an executive resource plan, they typically start off by describing how they design their leadership competency models, or how they build the components of their executive staffing or development systems. While these elements are certainly important, such answers miss an important point, which is that we cannot begin to talk about executive staffing requirements until we have first clearly articulated our organization's business requirements. In other words, it makes little sense to attempt to identify essential leadership capabilities unless we've first determined the business context in which those leaders will be expected to excel.

If my company is planning to shift 30 percent of its market base overseas during the next five years and I don't really understand the problems we are likely to encounter in managing this expansion, how can I possibly anticipate the types of international leadership skills that will be needed to support this effort? In the same way, if as an HR executive within a public service agency I do not understand the types of customer complaints that are driving the overhaul of our service delivery process, how can I possibly determine whether we have in place the leadership skills needed to tackle these challenges?

Al Vicere, management consultant and coauthor of *Leadership by Design,* explains it this way: "A lot of companies are basing their leadership development up front on the design of their competency models, but the problem is that they've designed these models strictly in terms of behavioral models which are disconnected from their business strategies. It shouldn't be the competency model that is the driver—it should be the business strategy that's the driver. This means answering questions such as, 'Where are we going? Where is our technology and IT strategy going? What skills sets do we need to grow now to prepare for the future?'"[1]

In a similar line of thought, Dave Ulrich suggests that HR planning approaches can be arrayed across a continuum. At one end of this continuum lie those "add-on" HR plans that are, as Ulrich suggests, created as an afterthought to business planning and are "no more than a postscript to the business planning process."[2] At the other end of this continuum lies the "isolated" approach, in which HR attempts to carry out HR strategy with little or no input from line management. Ulrich argues that the most effective HR strategies are located midpoint on this continuum and have as their intended outcome "an architecture or framework for incorporating HR practices into business decisions to ensure results."[3] As an example, Ulrich points to the HR team at Frontier Communications, which forced its company to review such critical HR issues as, "Will the acquired firm's talent add value to Frontier?" and "Will the acquired firm's management style and culture be consistent with Frontier's?" before acting on a business acquisition.[4]

In short, the first step in articulating an executive resource strategy is to step back and take a big-picture view of those long- and short-term business requirements that determine the need for certain types of leadership competencies. A clear understanding of your company's business requirements serves as the linchpin that connects business strategy to organizational capabilities. The underlying operating principle here is that HR leaders need to move in front of corporate business initiatives to help senior managers anticipate the potential implications of executive resource issues.

This type of front-end alignment between HR considerations and business objectives is a hallmark of an effective HR function. This chapter introduces three techniques for obtaining this alignment by clearly identifying your company's business requirements. Two of these techniques, *strategic planning reviews* and *scenario forecasting,* can be used for analyzing the long-term business needs of your overall organization. As such, these are techniques that are best performed as group exercises by your entire senior leadership team. A third technique, *business analysis,* can help you identify the short-term business requirements of individual work functions and operating units. This tool can be independently completed by different executives, with the composite results rolled up to provide an overall organizational profile. Together, these three predictive tools can help you answer the question, "What types of leadership competencies can help us successfully meet anticipated business challenges?"

THE STRATEGIC PLANNING REVIEW

If you manage your organization's HR function, a good starting point for executive resource planning is to conduct an off-site review of your strategic plan with your senior management team. If you are a member of your senior team, you can help initiate this process by proposing such a session to your company's senior HR executive. The strategic planning review is not intended to serve as a detailed tactical discussion of your business plan. Instead, it can help your leadership team reexamine the long-term organizational and leadership requirements of their business. A strategic planning review should enable your senior team to address three questions that can help them obtain a clearer picture of your company's future direction.

The first question is *"What changing business conditions do we anticipate encountering over the next few years?"* These changing conditions might include new market entries, changes in your customer base, the appearance of new competitors, emerging technologies, evolving relationships with key customers or vendors, changes in your approach to service delivery, planned mergers or acquisitions, or a shift in your company's competitive posture (for example, shifting from a niche position to a direct assault on your competitor).

The second question you need to pose to your senior team is, *"What adaptations will these changes require of our technology or organizational structure?"* This question requires your senior team to look inward to consider how organizational processes, technology, and structure will need to be modified to accommodate new market and business conditions. The idea here is to form a clear picture of how changes in your external operating environment are expected to shape the design of your organization. Three representative organizational adaptations are as follows:

- *Corporate Merger.* Two formerly separate organizations are faced with the challenge of creating a uniform and transparent operating system that can meld together previously different work systems, such as their financial databases and reporting software. This change may extend far beyond system changes, to include a massive technical training effort and a careful review of how these changes will affect the new company's financial reporting process.

- *New Service Offerings.* A banking chain decides to extensively diversify the array of financial services it provides to its customers, with the goal of positioning itself as a one-stop shop for customers' investment needs. The bank recognizes that this move will require a totally new marketing and sales strategy and extensive changes to its backroom support systems. This shift will also require the bank's Financial Service Advisers and executives to quickly master new skills in commercial marketing.

- *Customer Partnerships.* A small supplier discovers that to retain the business of one of its key customers, a Fortune 50 corporation, it must participate in a "supplier-customer quality partnership" program designed by the customer. The contractual requirements associated with this process include becoming certified as an ISO 9000 supplier, the creation of a detailed quality reporting structure, the formation of an interorganizational quality team, and the creation of sophisticated product tracking and inventory systems.

In each of. these examples, organizations find that they must quickly adapt to changes in external business conditions by modifying their information systems, transforming their organizational structures, and/or designing totally new work processes.

The third question is, *"How will these adaptive responses change the expectations we have of our corporate leaders?"* The strategic planning review session offers an excellent opportunity for your senior team to engage in solid dialogue on this subject, and to seek alignment on the types of technical and leadership skills that will take on critical importance over the next few years. At the same time, since this question can only be completely answered through a more detailed evaluation of each department's unique leadership requirements, it will therefore be explored in much greater detail later on in this chapter during the topic of how to perform a business analysis.

THE SCENARIO FORECAST

The scenario forecast is an excellent technique for encouraging senior teams to think "out of the box." The scenario forecast goes beyond a simple straight-line extrapolation of a company's projected financial performance to paint a clear, detailed picture depicting an organization's probable future performance within alternative operating environments.

The benefits of scenario forecasting go well beyond executive resource planning. When performed correctly, this technique serves the same function that robust design does for product engineering;

that is, it forces management teams to develop business plans that can accommodate a variety of interacting change factors. It also provides a valuable tool for building alignment among senior executives on future opportunities and threats. Still another derived benefit of scenario forecasting is that it helps members of executive teams better understand how their disagreements on key issues *are often based on very different assumptions about how the future will unfold.* Finally, if your senior team has not recently reviewed its strategic plans, performing a scenario forecast in advance of this discussion will help team members create a more thorough and well-developed plan.

I strongly recommend that scenario forecasting be performed as a team activity by your entire senior management group. In addition, during the first three action steps of this process, it is important to obtain input from individuals who can expose your top leadership team to different assumptions and inputs. These individuals might include technical leaders who have a reputation for accurately tracking industry trends, industry leaders, and even key customers and vendors. This is an area in which a trained outside consultant can provide value both in helping test those assumptions and in providing needed facilitation support for your team discussion.

Table 7 on pages 64 and 65 outlines the basic steps that constitute a scenario forecast. Prior to experimenting with this technique you should first carefully review the recommended readings noted at the end of this chapter.[5,6,7]

One of the most potent applications of scenario forecasting is to look far down the road to anticipate emerging requirements in the area of executive competencies. This forecasting process is particularly important in situations in which the resulting forecast suggests that a there is a good probability that a company will soon enter a new market area, or product or service segment—changes that could require a major injection of new technical and leadership skills and the creation of entirely new organizational career paths. Table 9 on page 66 provides four examples of how business changes could translate into evolving executive leadership competency requirements.

THE BUSINESS ANALYSIS

Just as a strategic planning review or scenario forecast can help your senior executives jointly identify the long-term leadership requirements of your organization, a business analysis can help each senior team member evaluate those short-term leadership requirements that are unique to his or her respective work function or operating unit. The term *business analysis* has a variety of connotations, depending on the business context in which it is applied. In this book it refers to

---

TABLE 7

HOW TO COMPLETE A SCENARIO FORECAST

1. *Identify influencing factors.* With your team, brainstorm a list of external factors that are likely to strongly shape the business environment in which your company operates. For a U.S.-based petrochemical company this might include such factors as changes in environmental regulations pertaining to petrochemical removal, disposal, and transport; gasoline consumption levels in the U.S.; or petrochemical production levels in other countries, including OPEC.

2. *Rate influencing factors.* Rate each factor on a 1-to-10 (low to high) scale on both *degree of impact* and *scope of change. Degree of impact* refers to the degree to which changes in this factor may affect the performance of your company. A score of 10 means that this is a factor that could have an intense impact on your business performance. *Scope of change* refers to the degree to which this factor is likely to change over the next two years. A rating of 10 means that you believe that a factor will undergo extreme change over the next two years.

3. *Identify key influencing factors.* Now multiply the ratings received for each factor on degree of impact by those for scope of change. You should now have a scoring range that extends from 1 (1 x 1 = 1) to 100 (10 x 10 = 100). Select from your list the two factors with the highest overall scores. These become your *key influencing factors.*

4. *Create alternative scenarios.* For each factor, describe two alternative possible scenarios. In the petrochemical example, a key influencing factor was "gas consumption levels in the U.S." One future scenario might therefore be "increased business and leisure travel create a 15 percent increase in gasoline consumption over the next two years," while an alternative might be "domestic economic pressures cause a reduction in business and leisure travel of 20 percent over the next two years." Create both optimistic and pessimistic scenarios while avoiding highly improbable scenarios.

5. *Combine scenarios.* Fold your scenarios into a *combined scenario matrix,* as shown in Table 8. Next, create a title that best describes the combined scenario, represented by each cell of the matrix. In the

example presented in Table 8, the label "The Golden Window" is used to indicate the window of opportunity that is created for increased gasoline sales, given both a strong increase in domestic gasoline consumption and a decrease in worldwide production.

6. *Describe each combined scenario.* Generate a one- to two-page summary describing the details on each of the four combined scenarios you have identified, including the sequence of actions that would likely lead to the combined scenario.

7. *Assess probability.* Use any and all available information to assess the relative probability for the future occurrence of each of these combined scenarios. In the example shown in Table 8, there is an estimated probability of 16 percent that the Golden Window scenario will occur during the next two years.

8. *Assess the implications.* Have team members jointly identify the probable implications of the four combined scenarios for your business strategy.

TABLE 8

THE SCENARIO MATRIX

Scenarios Related to Worldwide Production	Scenarios Related to Domestic Consumption	
	15% *increase* in gas consumption	20% *decrease* in gas consumption
20% *increase* in petrochemical production	Everyone Wins (24%)	The Sharp Fall (36%)
10% *decrease* in petrochemical production	The Golden Window (16%)	Export Express (24%)

TABLE 9	
IMPLICATIONS OF SCENARIO FORECASTS FOR EXECUTIVE COMPETENCY	
Scenario Forecasts	**Implications for Competency Requirements**
We will make a major shift into the commercial market from the defense market, with 70 percent of revenues coming from commercial sales in five years compared to 30 percent today.	• Less emphasis on importing executives who possess a military background and have experience in marketing to the military • Need to import or develop marketing executives who have strong skills in customer focus and commercial marketing and sales
Within the next five- to ten-year period, over 50 percent of our revenues will come from new product developments.	• Need for executives having ability to manage fast product development and design for manufacturing • Need executives who can effectively bridge marketing, production, and legal to shrink development times
We anticipate streamlining our direct overhead expenses, with our entire field support and audit functions being outsourced to external providers.	• Require leadership competencies in negotiating and managing large outsourced work functions • Need organizational development executives who can help us plan a smooth transition from in-house to outsourced work functions
We will open our first e-commerce site on the Internet next year, with the objective of having 15 percent of all sales coming through the Internet within the next four years.	• Need IT executives who are able to identify appropriate e-commerce target markets and manage web site design, including integration of inventory, tracking, credit, and billing

the process of having each executive generate a brief (one- to two-page) assessment of the business challenges his or her work function expects to encounter during the coming year, and the types of leadership competencies that will be needed to successfully meet these challenges. When these individual assessments are consolidated into a single report, the *composite organizational business analysis* can help your senior team determine those leadership competencies that will take on particular significance over the coming year. The five steps that make up the business analysis are discussed below. They are

- Step 1: Summarize business objectives and accountabilities
- Step 2: Identify anticipated challenges
- Step 3: Specify assumptions
- Step 4: Determine implications
- Step 5: Troubleshoot your analysis

STEP 1: SUMMARIZE BUSINESS OBJECTIVES AND ACCOUNTABILITIES

Summarize your major business objectives and accountabilities for the coming year, paying particular attention to those that represent significant changes in the scope of your current work responsibilities and that represent entirely new responsibilities. It is also important to highlight objectives that may exert a substantial impact on the overall performance of your company.

STEP 2: IDENTIFY ANTICIPATED CHALLENGES

Identify the major challenges you anticipate encountering as you set out to meet your objectives. These could involve changes in organizational structures or reporting responsibilities that will require your team to take on very different leadership roles. Other challenges could include identifiable shortfalls in technical or leadership skills, the need to create new and untested work systems or processes, and the need to accomplish more with limited resources. These anticipated challenges establish the *demand features* for your company's leadership positions. They provide a clearer context for understanding the difficulties your work functions and their leaders will face in attempting to meet new objectives.

STEP 3: SPECIFY ASSUMPTIONS

The next step involves specifying any assumptions on which your business analysis is based. In so doing, try to remain sensitive to uncertainties that can shape your assessment of both the feasibility of your business objectives and the degree of difficulty embedded in the challenges you have identified. A good method for checking assumptions is the use of a technique I call "Running the Gauntlet." It involves having executives individually test their readiness for pursuing different business objectives, given alternative performance scenarios. To better understand this technique, consider an individual preparing for an extended camping trip. Someone planning within a narrow set of contingencies may take only a few bare essentials: sleeping bag, tent, flashlight, and matches. However, the person creating a more robust plan will prepare for a wider range of environmental conditions by including foul-weather gear, a cookstove, water purification tablets, and a first-aid kit.

Running the Gauntlet means testing the robustness of your business objectives against three or four short-term business scenarios. While this technique is similar to that of scenario forecasting, it differs by focusing exclusively on the evaluation of business objectives that are slated for the coming year. Table 10 shows how this application could be used with the four scenarios shown earlier for our petrochemical example. The executive who has completed this analysis has discovered that in undertaking this first objective her team is well prepared to handle any of the four future business scenarios. On the other hand, Objective 3 is not very robust since the executive has rated her readiness to execute against this as "low" for three of the four scenarios.

Looking at this example from another perspective, we can see that, overall, the scenario for which this executive is least prepared is that of the Export Express, while she is most prepared to deal with The Golden Window.

How accurate is this type of comparative assessment? If it is performed entirely by the same executive who has written the objectives, then it will probably be flawed and biased. To obtain a more balanced assessment, the executive could invite her team and peers to perform the Running the Gauntlet exercise as a team activity. In this approach, the entire group would jointly discuss the probable impact that each of the four scenarios would likely have on the first objective. Participants would then be asked to independently evaluate the team's readiness level for addressing identified challenges, with the team discussing ratings that are highly discrepant. The team would then follow this same approach to obtain readiness ratings for the second and third objectives.

The usefulness of Running the Gauntlet is that quite often executives incorporate into their planning a set of implicit assumptions much like a strong bet—a "Plan A" that is based on the assumption

TABLE 10				
TESTING READINESS FOR PURSUING DIFFERENT OBJECTIVES				
Alternative Scenarios	Everyone Wins	The Golden Window	The Sharp Fall	Export Express
Objective 1	High	High	High	Moderate
Objective 2	Moderate	Moderate	Low	Low
Objective 3	Low	Moderate	Low	Low

that a given scenario will come to pass—while ignoring the need to plan for other contingencies. Running the Gauntlet forces leaders to explicitly examine their operating assumptions and evaluate the overall robustness of their plans. For the purpose of executive resource planning, the most important point to note here is that *a critical part of this readiness assessment lies in determining whether we have in place the types of executive leadership we need to successfully execute against key objectives.*

STEP 4: DETERMINE IMPLICATIONS

This step in the business assessment involves determining the implications of your business analysis for executive resource planning, and determining your company's readiness for executing against key business initiatives. To better understand this point, consider how the New York Stock Exchange conducts its annual "HR Review." Frank Z. Ashen, senior vice president of HR at the New York Stock Exchange, explains, "We ask our business line managers to review the upcoming year's priorities and initiatives and look at their current organizational structure. We ask what skills are necessary to meet their business goals and fill any gaps that may exist; then we ask them to identify key positions, backups, and replacement candidates for those positions."[8]

A business analysis forces your executive team to address the question, "Given the objectives, responsibilities, and challenges that I am facing, what kind of executive leadership do I need to have in place?" While you will not be able to completely answer this question until after you have performed a competency assessment (Chapter 6), at this point you can begin to sketch out at least a rough outline of your executive resource needs. Some of the considerations that should be incorporated into your thinking are

- Are there shifts in responsibilities? Will the leaders of certain work groups be expected to take over work functions that are now performed by other departments?

- Are we increasing the span of control of selected work units?

- Are we planning to take on any new responsibilities or objectives that will require the application of completely new technical skills?

- Are we making any changes to our work structure that will make selected work functions more complicated or difficult?

- Are there objectives or accountabilities for which the performance bar will be raised significantly over the coming year?

- Within this array of objectives and accountabilities are there any responsibilities that could significantly affect the overall performance of my company?

- Will certain executives be required to assume greater responsibilities for the management of external stakeholders such as key accounts, customers, board members, vendors?

STEP 5: TROUBLESHOOT YOUR ANALYSIS

This step involves reviewing your business analysis with your manager or a peer—someone who can provide an impartial critique and who can point out the weak spots in your analysis. The troubleshooter's role is to encourage you to critically examine the assumptions you have built into your business analysis and to provide alternative ways of interpreting your analysis. Figure 7 shows what a business analysis of the future might look like for the vice president of HR with a midsize manufacturing company. Note that the analysis provides a firm linkage between current and anticipated business changes, and explains how these changes will affect the need for related HR staffing and management activities. This type of analysis clearly sets the stage for reviewing a company's leadership needs.

During 2000 our organization took the first steps in making the transition from a domestic sales organization to an international one, by bringing on board plant sites in Canada (Toronto and Ontario) and Mexico City. Our 2001 sales plan calls for continued expansion with launch teams into Costa Rica and the Caribbean. This expansion will involve a total of five separate sales teams, each of which will be led by a Senior Director of International Sales. To meet this objective, the HR department will need to finalize our international compensation guidelines by the first quarter of 2000. In addition, to ensure that our sales department will meet its objective of having these teams fully staffed by April 1, 2001, we will need to shift from the part-time use of our domestic HR Recruiting Director to obtaining a full-time placement for a Director of International Recruiting.

In support of our international team, we will also need to bring on board local HR managers in Toronto and Mexico City who can manage HR policies and (in Canada) collective-bargaining activities. These are areas that are currently being only sporadically managed through the assistance of an external HR consulting service, resulting in a very poor level of service support for these areas and a high level of turnover in our Toronto plant. The absence of a full-time HR manager at these locations also significantly increases our risk exposure to regulatory violations in these areas.

Another major change that will severely impact the HR function is the planned extension of our IT platform across all sites next year, concurrent with the integration of our field and headquarters IT groups and supported by the newly created position of CIO. A recent benchmark study has suggested that our IT executives and managers are currently being compensated well below market value for comparative industries. Exit interviews with IT professionals who left our company this year suggest that if this problem isn't quickly addressed, the recent exodus we've experienced among our IT ranks (turnover of 18 percent for 2000) could worsen, with key defections going to our competitors. Should this occur, it would severely hamper the achievement of our 2000 IT objectives. Accordingly, the HR department has set as a major objective for 2001 the creation of an IT retention plan that calls for the identification of "at risk" IT executives and managers within key positions, appropriate salary adjustments, and a complete review of our IT objective bonus plan for 2001.

The third major business objective affecting our HR function involves plans for the piloting of high-performance work teams at three of our production sites (Chicago, Cincinnati, and Atlanta) over the next two years. This will represent a completely new organizational design effort for these plants. While the initial design of the team structure has been achieved through the use of external consulting support, the Team Readiness Study that was completed in March of this year strongly recommends that we provide substantial training support for both the members of these teams and their supervisors, who will be required to make the transition into the new role of team adviser. The delivery of this training, along with the need for supplemental coaching for these teams and supervisors,

FIGURE 7 BUSINESS ANALYSIS: HR DEPARTMENT

- The first step in designing an executive resource strategy involves identifying the business challenges that currently shape, and will come to shape, the types of executive leadership required of your company.

- While you can't be expected to be a crystal-ball gazer, there are three techniques you can use to identify the competencies that your organization will need to build or import over the next few years to sustain a competitive advantage. They are *strategic planning review, scenario forecasting,* and *business analysis.*

- The strategic planning review links strategic planning to leadership capability by addressing three questions: (1) "What changing business conditions do we anticipate encountering over the next few years?" (2) "What adaptations will these changes require of our technology or organizational structure?" and (3) "How will these adaptive responses change the expectations we have of our corporate leaders?"

- A scenario forecast is a technique for articulating alternative scenarios about how business conditions will unfold, and your company's readiness for effectively performing within each scenario.

- A business analysis provides a one-year breakout of key business initiatives, along with a gap assessment that enables a company to determine whether it has the leadership and technical capability in place to successfully execute against these initiatives.

CHAPTER 4

IDENTIFYING EXECUTIVE LEADERSHIP COMPETENCIES

One of the defining characteristics of an effective resource strategy is its ability to clearly delineate the leadership competencies that are essential to an organization's success. A company that is unable to isolate these essential requirements inevitably encounters serious obstructions as it travels downstream in the execution of both its business objectives and its executive resource plans. For one thing, it will be very difficult to establish the criteria for successful performance at different executive levels. These success criteria become a moving target as senior managers and board members discover that they have no common language with which to align their separate views regarding expected leadership performance. The confusion about what the organization is looking for in executive candidates will also show up in longer time-to-fill for positions and in a higher "miss" rate for executive candidates—all because the hiring company has not clearly communicated to its executive recruiters the essential job requirements for executive positions. Companies that are unable to identify and articulate their essential leadership requirements also encounter an important trust issue with subordinate managers, who are likely to believe that their organization arbitrarily reshuffles promotional standards and lacks a set of equitable and reasonable criteria for making selection and promotion decisions.

On the other hand, companies that take the time to accurately identify prerequisite leadership competencies and assess their leaders against these competencies generate several competitive advantages. First and foremost, when managed correctly a well-designed competency model can help senior teams reach agreement on such issues as the key leadership and technical competencies required for organizational success and the types of developmental experiences that will exert the strongest impact on executive growth. Moreover, by accepting ownership for both the *design process* and the *intended outcomes* of the competency model, the corporate leadership team sends to the rest of the organization a clear message regarding their common support of any sensitive personnel decisions that may later be based on this model, such as the placement, development, and even termination of key executives.

An executive leadership competency model also helps employers distinguish superior performers from other members of the pack, and in many cases to isolate and clone the "best practices" used by superior leaders. This same common language provides a unified framework for orchestrating all related personnel actions, such as performance appraisal, executive recruiting, and executive assessment. It also creates an even playing field for fairly and equitably assessing internal and external candidates using the same selection criteria.

From a development viewpoint, an executive leadership competency model puts into the hands of line managers tools that allow them to take greater ownership of the development process and to become less dependent on the HR department as an intermediary for directing their professional development. Instead these executives are better able to self-identify these competencies, self-assess their readiness for promotion, and self-initiate development plans for strengthening key competencies.

An executive leadership competency model is especially important during times of rapid organizational change, since periodic updates of this model will indicate when rungs of the promotional ladder are missing or have been changed. This situation frequently develops when a downsizing or restructuring greatly modifies or totally eliminates selected executive jobs, resulting in a widening competency gap between certain positions and those positions that lie higher on the promotional ladder.

This kind of periodic review is also critical for recalibrating organizational success measures; simply speaking, an updating of the competency model can point out whether downtrends in organizational performance are the result of an influx of less competent executive performers or whether the "competency measuring stick" has subtlety shifted over the last few years.

LEADERSHIP COMPETENCIES
AND CORE COMPETENCIES

Given all of these reasons, you would think that every organization would be working diligently to develop a comprehensive executive leadership competency model. Unfortunately, many people just do not know where to begin. In their study "The War for Talent," the researchers for McKinsey Corporation found that only 16 percent of responding companies even knew who their high performers were, and only 3 percent felt that their company was effective at developing people or moving low performers out quickly.[1]

Very little has been written on how to systematically design an executive competency model. In attempting to lead you through the basics of this process, we first need to make the distinction between an organization's *leadership competencies* and its *core competencies.* If you have read any Dilbert™ cartoons you probably know that the term "core competencies" is one of the most maligned and misused management concepts in vogue today. A large part of the problem is that many professionals have an incomplete understanding of what a core competency actually is and how this concept can be successfully applied to improve business performance.

Core competencies are unique technical skills that a company exhibits consistently and exceptionally better than others in its field, and that give the company a sustainable advantage over its competitors. Core competencies are always tied to a company's strategic position; that is, they define what the company does that adds unique value to its customers. Core competencies represent a "performance road map"—an overview of those special abilities that not only are currently required but will take on even greater significance for an organization in the future.

Wal-Mart provides one of the most well-known examples of a company that has managed to leverage the core competencies of logistics and distribution to a competitive advantage. It is one of the most effective companies on the planet when it comes to knowing how to pull sales data back through its system on a real-time basis, and to instantly feed that information back through its distribution and supplier channels. As a result, Wal-Mart is able to move products through its stores in an incredibly timely and cost-efficient manner, and to quickly respond to changes in customer buying patterns.

Over the years I have encountered many companies that consider a half-day executive workshop to be sufficient for their senior teams to identify their core competencies. This kind of cursory review usually only leads to dead-end discussions, and worse, can result in superficial and meaningless competency breakouts that, if acted upon, can actually damage an organization's performance capability. Core competencies function as a kind of lighthouse beacon for guiding an organization's long-range planning efforts. A superficial analysis that results in the misidentification of core competencies is a beacon that guides its ships onto the rocks.

One of the reasons it is very difficult for an organization to identify its core competencies is that, by definition, core competencies are not simply those performance areas in which a company *wants* to excel, but those in which a company can actually *demonstrate* that it holds a *sustainable, unique,* competitive advantage. Note those three key words:

- *Demonstrate* means that the company is able to track the leveraging role that selected competencies play in its success formula. Most organizations have never developed the performance metrics necessary to do this.

- *Sustainable* means performance abilities in which the company can maintain a continued advantage over time.

- *Unique* means that the core competency is not easily duplicated or cloned.

To uncover competencies that share these three criteria requires substantial time, financial analysis, and often the assistance of external consultants—an investment many companies are simply unwilling to make.

Not all well-performing companies owe their success to their core competencies. It is entirely possible for a company to become successful because it knows how to ride a market wave of demand, because it is a solid performer within a relatively noncompetitive arena, or because it is more effective on a number of fronts, such as logistics, customer sales, and frontline service.

Let's proceed to outlining the difference between core competencies and leadership competencies. First, remember that an organization's core competencies reflect not only the knowledge and abilities of its employees, but also its work systems and processes. Wal-Mart's core competencies weave through its organization, involving the creation of sophisticated data warehousing and logistical systems. In other words, when a company decides to execute against its core competencies, the result is not as simple as bringing on board executives and professionals who know how to do things differently. This execution also requires a careful analysis of an organization's infrastructure. Individual competencies are only one part of the equation.

Next, recall that core competencies represent those *technical* competencies that provide an organization with a demonstrated, unique, sustainable advantage over its competitors. As such, core competencies are *vertically distributed* across different levels within selective organizational functions. They encompass the competencies and experience of not only key executives, but also managers and professionals. At the same time, an organization may discover that the leadership competencies it requires for success do not represent organizational core competencies, but actually include certain generic leadership competencies that are common to the success of other companies.

In conducting a variety of executive competencies studies over the last fifteen years, I have found that there is a large degree of overlap in the leadership competencies identified by different companies. This personal observation has been largely confirmed by a study jointly performed by the Corporate Leadership Council and Cambria Consulting. The study identified ten central leadership competencies that were frequently referenced in the fifty corporate competency models reviewed by the researchers.[2] The top four of these competencies were "drive for results" (cited by 84 percent of respondents), "people development" (cited by 71 percent), "conceptual grasp/big-picture awareness" (cited by 64 percent), and "team player" (cited by 62 percent).[3]

The fact that many companies have identified the same leadership competencies as critical to success does not lessen their importance, as each organization holds a different set of expectations regarding how its executives are expected to successfully apply these competencies. To better understand this idea, let's take the leadership competency of "team player." Although this competency appeared in 62 percent of the companies included in the Corporate Leadership Council study, each company probably has its own unique view regarding how this competency should be demonstrated in its work environment. Depending on the company, this might mean

- Creating effective teams with key vendors to resolve difficult quality and pricing issues
- Leading cross-functional project teams
- Building alliances between different corporate subsidiaries
- Successfully managing corporate culture and system alignment during mergers or acquisitions
- Functioning as the corporate good-will ambassador to key customers
- Bridging cross-cultural barriers when leading international teams

The point is that, while at the highest level of abstraction different companies may value the same leadership competency, at the ground level this generic competency could easily translate into very different sets of performance expectations. A good competency analysis will ferret out these differences and build them into the model.

HOW DO YOU PLAN TO APPLY YOUR MODEL?

Before embarking on the creation of a competency model, it is important to have the members of your senior team agree on how they would ideally like to be able to apply such a model to their business decisions. Common areas of application include the following:

- Succession planning
- Performance appraisal
- Decisions regarding internal promotions and external selections
- Development planning
- Individual coaching and mentoring
- Accelerated tracking and development for high-potential performers
- Competency mapping (mapping the principal strengths and weaknesses exhibited by the leadership bench)

The point of undertaking this front-end discussion is not just to obtain clear alignment on the goals and priorities of the executive resource program, but also to ensure that the program you design will be sufficiently broad and vigorous to meet desired applications.[4] As an example, if one of the intended purposes of your competency model is to enable your company to evaluate its unique competency requirements for international and domestic offices, your competency database will need to be able to provide separate competency breakdowns for these different organizational units. If a second desired outcome of your program is to ensure that you select and hire the best possible external candidates, your competency database will need to be translated into an interview format that can be applied to executive selection interviews.

Obtaining up-front agreement on how your competency model will be applied will also prove helpful in shaping the structure and implementation of your competency research process. Some of the areas on which you need to seek agreement are

> *Data Categories.* Which job levels and functions will be included in the study, and how will these data be broken down for analysis? Will you require a breakdown by job level, work site, or job

function? How about a correlation of data by years in position or years of service? What about performing an analysis by age, gender, or race of respondents to ensure that the competency study is not biased toward selected groups of performers?

Unique Technical and Functional Competencies. Will your executive competency study be restricted to an analysis of generic leadership competencies (strategic thinking, team building, communications)? Will you also attempt to isolate those technical and functional competencies that are unique to successful performance within individual work functions (such as knowledge of international compensation for an HR executive, or knowledge of data warehousing for a finance executive)?

Competencies Required for Current Versus Future Success. Will you focus solely on those executive competencies required for current success, or will you extend your analysis to include those emerging competencies that are viewed as critical to the future success of the organization?

Format for Data Collection. How will your senior team and board prefer your competency data to be formatted and formally communicated to your organization? A thorough competency study can generate a large amount of data. One method for keeping from being overwhelmed by these data is for the members of your senior team to decide early in the design process what type of information they will need and in what format.

How and with Whom Information Will Be Shared. Who within your organization will see the results of your competency study? Most employers divide their communications strategies into three components.

- All employees learn of the executive leadership competencies that are identified as being essential to successful performance. This can be accomplished either through small-group discussions that are cascaded down through the organization or through more formal mechanisms such as printing executive development directories or publishing these directories on the company's intranet system.

- Training and HR departments, as well as the executive team, learn of the summary of the executive team's overall strengths and development needs. This information is used to plan executive development curricula (see Chapters 5 and 6).

- The assessed executive, his or her manager, and the head of the HR department learn of individual competency assessment data that are derived from performance appraisals, 360-degree feedback, or talent assessment reviews.

Where the Competency Database Will Reside. Who will be the primary process owner responsible for archiving and analyzing information on executive leadership competencies and for periodically updating this information? For large organizations that have both divisional and corporate HR departments, the primary process owners are usually the corporate HR leaders, with the heads of OD, Compensation, or Executive Development having the accountability for competency data gathering.

How to Develop a Competency Model

Once you have identified your long- and short-term business requirements, you need to identify the executive competencies that address these requirements and from these data design an executive leadership competency model that will serve as the centerpoint for your executive resource strategy. The six steps to developing a competency model are summarized in Figure 8 and are discussed below.

Step 1: Review Templates

The creation of an executive resource strategy is a major undertaking, yet most HR leaders and senior managers are extremely time limited. It is therefore often useful to begin with a generic template of the leadership competencies that have been previously identified by HR consultants as critical to the success of executives. Using a template not only helps you jump-start an otherwise time-consuming process, but also provides a solid research base for justifying your final recommendations regarding competency identification and assessment.[5] There are many commercially available competency models on the market, each of which can help identify the performance requirements of executives and professionals and can be used as self-directed tools for supporting development planning. In this chapter, I will reference only the former application and will hold off on discussing development planning applications until Chapter 6.

One of the best tools available is the Leadership Architect® package developed by Lominger Limited. This tool involves a card deck with descriptions of sixty-seven essential competencies and nineteen career stallers and stoppers (such as lack of ethics and values and lack of composure) that have been found to derail the career success of professionals.[6] Mike Lombardo and Robert Eichinger, at the Center for Creative Leadership, compiled these competencies and career

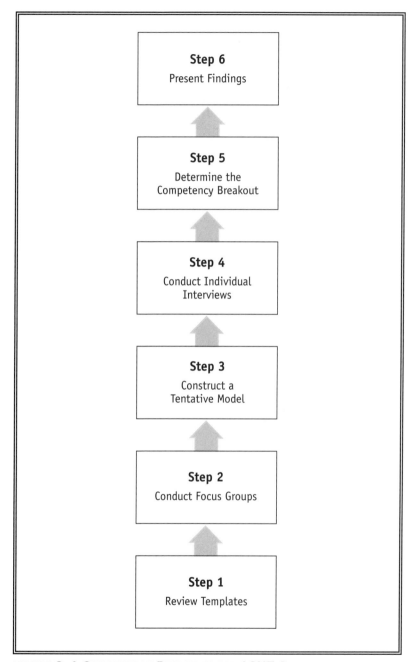

FIGURE 8 A COMPETENCY BREAKOUT FOR ACME CORPORATION

stallers from years of long-term studies with such companies as AT&T and Sears.[7] Using the deck, participants can sort the cards according to different categories, such as prioritizing the cards/ competencies from "essential" or "mission critical" to "not impor-tant." Lominger Limited also sells a related software program called The Career Architect® Expert System: Electronic Version 8.1, which includes two important tools: a self-directed development and coach-ing tool and a computerized card-sorting tool.

Another useful tool for initiating the development of a compe-tency model is the package called *Competency Model Handbooks, Volumes 1–4*, published by Linkage, Inc. Each volume provides a set of competency models gathered from different organizations. For example, Volume 2 includes competency models for the functional areas of Finance, Sales and Marketing, Information Systems/ Technology, and HR. It also includes ten different models for Leadership, including the positions of senior manager, executive, branch manager, business unit head, team leader, and plant manager.

STEP 2: CONDUCT FOCUS GROUPS

The initial breakout of competencies contained in your template can be reduced to a more manageable list through a series of focus groups. The selection of focus group participants is extremely impor-tant to ensure a complete and in-depth analysis. I recommend adher-ing to the following guidelines for managing the selection, communi-cation, and delivery of these sessions.

Selection and Format

- Limit focus groups to no more than twenty participants to encourage full participation. These participants should be excep-tional performers who have been nominated for participation in this study by their managers.

- Form focus groups along executive levels. One group might be composed entirely of executive board officers, while a second might include all remaining vice presidents, and a third might be restricted to senior directors and directors. Typically you will require assistance from your corporate HR leader and senior team to determine the most appropriate methods for categoriz-ing executive levels within your company.

- Pull participants from a variety of site locations to provide a bal-anced view of competency requirements.

- Divide focus group activity, and the subsequent roll-up of com-petency data, according to division. If you are operating within a large corporation, a grand roll-up and comparison of competency data can then be performed to identify those competencies that are unique to certain divisions versus those that permeate the entire organization.

Communication

- Explain the purpose of the sessions. Point out the importance of participants' input to helping your organization gain a better understanding of the development needs of your leadership bench.

- Explain that this is *not* an assessment of participants' performance, but rather the creation of a competency map based on their joint feedback.

- Tell participants how and when you will feed results back to them (via published report, posting on intranet, informal meetings, and so on).

Delivery

- Allocate three to four hours of time for each focus group.

- Use only skilled facilitators to direct focus group sessions.

- Ask participants to jointly rate the relative importance of each competency to the successful performance of executives in their organizational level. If you are using the competency cards contained in *Leadership Architect*® or some similar tool, participants can sort competency cards into different preestablished rating categories. If you are not using a card-sort tool, it is essential that you provide an unambiguous definition for each competency. Otherwise, you will find that terms such as *teamwork* and *strategic thinking* convey very different meanings to different focus group participants.

- As an alternate competency-rating method, assign a point-rating scale for each importance category, then use tally marks to record the number of votes gained for each category. A total score can then be obtained by multiplying category points by votes. In the example shown in Table 11, a ten-person focus group voted on the relative importance of four executive competencies. Their voting results, from the most to least important competency, were project management, strategic thinking, team player, and—last—people development.

This rating process can be augmented or supplemented by having executives rate the competencies required of their direct reports. The information can then be combined with subordinates' self-assessment ratings to form a composite competency model. Two

TABLE 11

USING A VOTING PROCESS TO IDENTIFY CRITICAL COMPETENCIES

Competency	Essential (4 points)	Very Important (3 points)	Somewhat Important (2 points)	Unimportant (1 point)	Total Score
Strategic Thinking	✓✓✓	✓✓✓✓✓	✓	✓	30
Team Player	✓✓	✓✓✓	✓✓✓✓	✓	26
Project Management	✓✓✓✓	✓✓✓✓	✓✓		32
People Development	✓✓	✓✓✓	✓✓	✓✓✓	24

conditions require managers to directly evaluate their reports' competency requirements: (1) When a company's CEO and chief HR executive lack confidence in the performance capability of a certain organizational level or functional unit, and question whether executives within this group are able to accurately self-assess the key leadership competencies required for their own success. (2) When the performance requirements for a given organizational level have abruptly changed (through a reorganization, merger, or entry into an entirely new market) and incumbents lack the perspective needed to determine the competencies required for success under the new set of business conditions. Under either of these scenarios, it is essential to have competency assessments generated by both executive incumbents and their managers.

Still another version of this technique is to ask participants to rate executive competencies according to their anticipated importance to future performance. If your senior team has previously generated a scenario forecast and assessed the implications of this forecast to future competency requirements (Chapter 3), this document can be used to jump-start the thinking of focus group participants. Once you have identified the top-rated competencies for a given executive level, it is helpful to ask for recommendations regarding the types of performance that can demonstrate proficiency within each competency. For example, when discussing the competency of "project management," the question you should direct to your focus group is, "What does someone who is skilled in the area of project management do that sets him or her apart from other performers?" Another version of this question is, "Think of someone whom you consider to be skilled in the area of project management. What does this person do that sets him or her apart from others who perform poorly in this competency?"

STEP 3: CONSTRUCT A TENTATIVE MODEL

Once you have gathered a wide array of data from your focus groups, the next step is to consolidate it into a coherent competency model. In constructing your model, one of the most difficult judgment calls you will need to make is where to draw the line for selecting competencies. Try to avoid the common trap of creating a model of monolithic proportions. It is not uncommon to find companies that have identified twenty or more "essential" executive competencies. Keep in mind that a good model should keep your organization focused around a few pivotal performance areas. As a general rule of thumb, if you are working with more than twelve competencies, your model will be too diffuse and cumbersome to be of much use in identifying or assessing executive talent. One way to work around this problem is to limit your competency model to the five to ten top-rated competencies on your list. You can then eliminate any competencies that are redundant in relation to those on your top-rated list.

Next, use the focus group and interview data you have gathered to identify, for each top-rated competency, four or five behavioral statements that best demonstrate proficiency within that competency. Table 12 shows how a final competency model might appear. Note that this example provides sample behaviors for only three executive competencies, whereas your completed competency model might include six to twelve competencies.

In completing the process of creating a model, keep the following cautionary thoughts in mind. First, supporting behaviors should be described in concrete, action-oriented terms. Avoid statements that describe *intentions* rather than *actions,* such as, "displays a positive attitude with peers" or "exhibits a strong self-concept." Also, to provide a balanced competency framework, use the same number (I recommend four or five) of behavioral statements for each competency. Finally, avoid statements that reference two or more behaviors, as this feature will make it difficult for you to apply your competency model to executive assessment and development. As an example, if an individual is told that he or she is not performing effectively on the behavior of "Makes decisions in a timely manner with input from key stakeholders," is the problem a lack of speed, the lack of stakeholder feedback, or both? To avoid this problem, each statement should describe only a single behavior.

One way to test the validity of your model is through the use of the following card-sort technique known as the affinity diagram:

1. Write each behavioral statement and competency on a separate notecard.

2. Spread the competency cards out on a table. These will become your "title" cards for arranging the card sort.

3. Shuffle the stack of behavior cards.

4. Have small, five- to eight-person groups of representative managers and executives conduct the card sort. Before beginning, explain to them that the objective is to get their input on identifying key behaviors that demonstrate performance within a given competency.

5. Ask the group to take the first behavior card from the deck and determine in which of the competency piles the card best belongs. Each card can be matched to only one competency. Have the group repeat this process for each of the behavior cards.

TABLE 12
EXECUTIVE COMPETENCIES AND SUPPORTING BEHAVIORS FOR ZYX CORPORATION

Decision Making

The ability to make effective, timely, and well-determined decisions based on available information.

1. Makes decisions in a timely manner; knows how far to go in data gathering before reaching a decision; doesn't become frozen through "analysis paralysis."

2. Exhibits a high success rate in the quality of business decisions.

3. Makes decisions based, in part, on input from key organizational stakeholders.

4. Is able to deal with ambiguity and complexity; can sort out critical pieces of information and synthesize a variety of data into a well-constructed decision.

5. Is able to deconstruct complex problems to assess underlying causes and determine appropriate courses of action.

Strategic Thinking

The ability to analyze information to determine the most appropriate courses of action for long-term gain.

1. Considers the long view when making tactical decisions.

2. Analyzes potential actions from the perspective of external stakeholders, such as board members, stockholders, or customers.

3. Is able to determine those actions that will most effectively sustain our company's competitive position.

4. Accurately anticipates future trends and the most probable consequences of actions; doesn't get taken by surprise.

5. Is able to translate strategic thinking into a compelling plan of action.

TABLE 12 (CONT'D)

EXECUTIVE COMPETENCIES AND SUPPORTING BEHAVIORS FOR ZYX CORPORATION

Organizational Impact

The ability to exert positive and affirmative leadership within our organization.

1. Builds effective team partnerships with external players such as key vendors and customers.

2. Is able to identify "influence peddlers" within the organization and enlist their support; understands how things get accomplished within our company.

3. Seeks common ground for developing win-win solutions to problems involving others; effectively manages conflict.

4. Establishes rapport and exerts a leadership role with a wide cross-section of the organization, regardless of position.

5. Creates strong teamwork across functional boundaries; is perceived as a team player by internal customers.

---

6. Perform this exercise for a representative sample of your executive population, identifying those behavior cards for which there is at least 90 percent agreement among participants. These are the behaviors that truly discriminate between performance on different competencies.

STEP 4: CONDUCT INDIVIDUAL INTERVIEWS

Having used your focus groups to rate the relative importance of different executive competencies, you are now ready to delve into your competency analysis. The best way is to conduct a series of ninety-minute individual interviews with the members of your senior team and with any exemplary lower-level performers who have been identified by the senior team.

Before beginning your competency interviews it is essential that you clearly spell out for participants the purpose of these interviews and the payoffs that they are likely to gain through their involvement in this study. You may find it helpful to emphasize the following points in your introductory letter:

- These are not assessment interviews intended to evaluate the performance or capability of the interviewees. These are data-gathering interviews intended to capture information that can help your company target only the most critical requirements for key executive positions.

- Participants have been selected for the interviews based on their knowledge of your company's business environment and performance needs.

- If business conditions have significantly changed during the last two or three years, the competencies needed to drive successful performance will also have changed. A competency study can help you identify these changes.

- A competency-modeling process will encourage greater alignment among your team members on key executive selection and promotion decisions.

I recommend that you use individual interviews to explore the following five subject areas. Table 13 on pages 90 and 91 gives sample questions that can be used to obtain the information you seek.

- Examples of *demonstrated performance* through a comparative review of how superior performers differ from other performers in their application and mastery of key competencies.

- Examples of current and emerging *technical skills* that are deemed essential to successful performance within a given executive function.

- Examples of workplace *demand conditions* that test an individual's proficiency within a given competency area. For the competency of executive decision making, two demand conditions might be (1) making decisions under conditions of extreme ambiguity, such as analyzing competitive intelligence to forecast the moves of corporate opponents, and (2) identifying who, within and outside one's company, needs to be brought in as stakeholders to provide input on a sensitive decision, such as the most effective way to manage the restructuring of an operating unit.[8]

- Examples of career derailers—leadership behaviors that the interviewee feels are extremely detrimental to job performance, and that limit an individual's ability to perform at higher levels in the organization.

- Examples of on-the-job *development assignments* that have been found to build strength within identified competency areas.

TABLE 13

QUESTIONS FOR THE COMPETENCY INTERVIEW

Part A: Competency Application

- "Let's start with the competency of strategic thinking. Think about someone on your team who you feel exhibits a high degree of proficiency in this competency. Now think of someone on your team who does poorly in this area. What are some of the differences you've noted in the performance of these two people?"

- "What are some of the things you look for to determine whether someone is performing extremely well on this competency?"

- "What are some common performance problems you've encountered with people who would be rated poorly on this competency?"

(Continue this line of questioning for each top-rated competency you have identified.)

Part B: Emerging Technical Skills

- "What technical competencies do you feel are essential for executives who perform within your work function?"

- "During the next three to five years, what technical competencies are going to be much more important than they've been in the past (for example, because of changes in work processes)?"

- "What technical skills will become less essential for job success?"

- "What is the biggest technical competency gap for your work team as a whole?"

Part C: Demand Conditions

- "Every organization presents its associates with a unique set of demands that test their abilities. Within our company, what are some of the demand conditions that test an executive's ability in the competency area of strategic thinking?"

- "What are some of the things you look for that let you know whether an individual is highly proficient in this competency area? How would you expect the results of this demonstrated competency to translate into work results?"

(Continue this line of questioning for each top-rated competency you have identified.)

Part D: Career Derailers

- "Within every organization there are a few significant, problematic behaviors that could severely limit an individual's effectiveness or prevent him or her from moving upward in the company. What are some of the behaviors that you consider to be key 'career derailers' within this position?"

Part E: Development Activities

- "What are some key assignments that you've given your reports to build their strengths in the competency of strategic thinking?"

- "What external programs support the development of this competency?"

(Continue this line of questioning for each top-rated competency you have identified.)

TABLE 14

**HOW TO PROBE FOR ADDITIONAL DETAIL
DURING THE INTERVIEW**

Interviewer: What are some of the technical competencies that are essential to the successful performance of those executives who perform within your work function?

Interviewee: They need to understand the unique nature of our customer base.

Interviewer: Can you be a little more specific? How is your customer base unique?

Interviewee: Our customers, which comprise the big three auto manufacturers as well as second- and third-tier suppliers to these companies, have unique quality requirements that someone in our business has to understand.

Interviewer: Can you give me an example of what you mean by "unique requirements"?

Interviewee: One example involves the ability to determine the risk exposure we incur if we fail to meet contract requirements. Those customers that have just-in-time inventory systems often put into their supplier contracts rigid nonperformance clauses. By this I mean that they severely penalize any supplier that fails to ship parts on time, or that ships substandard parts, and in so doing creates a production shutdown.

Interviewer: So when negotiating customer contracts, executives in your function have to exert good decision-making skills in being able to weigh out the financial risks and compensating benefits laid out in a contract.

Interviewee: Exactly!

If interviewees provide vague or incomplete answers, use the technique of *successive probing* to encourage them to elaborate on their responses. Table 14 shows how this technique could be applied to a competency assessment for a finance department.

STEP 5: DETERMINE THE COMPETENCY BREAKOUT

So far you have worked to create an overall competency model, one that identifies the compctencies associated with your overall leadership bench. If you stop at this point, however, you do yourself a great disservice, as you lack information on how performance requirements vary by executive level and function, such as departmental functions, corporate divisions, and domestic and international operations.

One way to gain this information is to have representative executives rate the relative importance of each of your selected competencies. (Note: When determining the size of your rating group, I recommend that you obtain feedback from all executives located within the two highest levels of your company and at least 20 percent of all remaining company executives.) To encourage participants to make fine-line distinctions between the relative importance of different competencies, try giving them 100 rating points and then asking them to allocate these points according to the relative importance of each competency. This means that every point "spent" on a given competency is one less rating point that can be spent on another. Thus, if you have previously identified ten top-rated competencies and all of them were equally valued by respondents, each would receive ten points. The relative importance of competencies can then be determined by averaging rating scores, generating a comparative ranking among competencies. Finally, you can add to your competency profile those technical competencies that were identified as being unique to selected functional groups.

Figure 9 shows what a competency profile might look like for our hypothetical organization, ZYX Corporation. From this organizational chart we can discern a number of implications regarding ZYX's executives.

1. The competency rated as most important to the overall executive group is strategic thinking, followed by team building, problem solving, and customer focus.

2. Divisional units display some differences with regard to the value each places on the four competencies, with the greatest differences showing up in the competency of customer focus, valued more highly by Division A than by Division B or C.

3. A competency breakout has been provided for Division B by executive level. The breakout shows that two of the competencies listed, customer focus and strategic thinking, are in the top four rankings for all three executive levels. In addition, within the top four competency rankings there is greater alignment between vice presidents and directors when the ratings for either

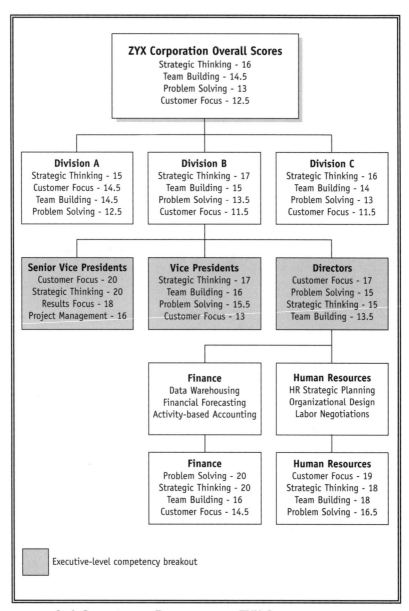

FIGURE 9 A COMPETENCY BREAKOUT FOR ZYX CORPORATION

of these groups are compared with those of senior vice presidents. Note that the senior vice presidents have placed in the top four rankings two competencies—results focus and project management—that were not top-ranked by the lower two executive levels.

4. The example also shows the comparative ratings for leadership skills by two functions, finance and HR, and also identifies the executive technical competencies unique to these departments.

5. The interview data gathered from these respective subgroups would be used to determine the underlying causes of scoring differences by division, level, and function. The following alternate explanations would need to be reviewed:

• The score differences may be attributed to the fact that each subgroup interprets the competency terms in different ways. Using the divisional difference as an example, Divisions B and C may have interpreted the term *customer focus* to mean both internal and external customers, while Divisions B and C may focus only on external customers.

• The score differences may reflect underlying differences in organizational values. Division A may actively emphasize customer focus in its external selection, reward, and appraisal programs. The high rating given to the competencies of results focus and project management by Division B's SVPs may be due to the fact that these competencies are regarded as residing more at the senior level in this division.

• Rating differences between subgroups can also reflect the fact that we are dealing with different population compositions. If several of Division B's SVPs were external hires, they may bring with them a different set of business priorities and associated corporate rules from those of Division B's VPs and directors.

STEP 6: PRESENT FINDINGS

The last step in developing your competency model is to present your findings to your CEO and senior team, and, if requested, to your governing board. This presentation should present a high-level overview of the following components of your study:

1. Your rationale for undertaking the study (the need to assess the company's readiness to move forward on new business initiatives, the challenge of breaking out leadership competencies for newly integrated corporate teams following a merger or

acquisition, the need to update a competency database that is several years old).

2. The study's objectives.

3. The methodology used (the use of focus groups and interviews, criteria for selecting focus group and interview participants, the use of a research-based template).

4. Your findings (competencies identified for your overall organization, competency breakouts for subunits, unique and emerging technical skills).

5. Implications. Some of the more significant implications you should consider in your final report are:

   • To what degree are the members of your senior team aligned regarding the competencies needed to drive business performance?

   • Where is alignment lacking, and what are significant causes for this lack of alignment; in other words, where are the fault lines visible along the organizational interface? (Whether, for example, newly imported executives and experienced incumbents differ in the importance they attach to certain competencies.)

   • What surprises did you encounter? What unique technical or leadership competencies were identified that were not previously considered by your executive team? To what degree are executives and their reports in agreement regarding the relative importance of selected competencies?

   • What's coming up on the horizon? Based on the interview data you have obtained, what emerging technical or leadership skills must your executive team begin to build to prepare them for anticipated business challenges?

6. Recommended next steps. These would include any actions you plan to take over the next year to refine or strengthen your model (such as extending it down to lower-level executives or managers, or incorporating interview data from others in your organization), and a restatement of your plans for integrating the competency model into your company's HR system.

INTERNATIONAL EXECUTIVES: A WHOLE NEW SET OF CHALLENGES

So far we've approached the subject of executive competency identification from the point of view of executives who are based in U.S. corporations. When we shift to the global scene, we have to recognize that international leadership assignments carry with them their own particular set of challenges and demands. These requirements show up in a number of ways, not the least of which is a high failure rate, particularly for U.S. expatriates. One expert places the failure rate for international assignments between 20 and 50 percent, with each failure costing an employer an estimated $200,000 (1991 figures).[9] Another study showed that "up to 25 percent of United States expats 'black out' in their assignments and have to be recalled or let go. Between 30 percent and 50 percent of the remainder are considered 'brown outs'; they stay in their posts but underperform."[10] Still another study suggests that the failure rate for U.S. expatriate managers is three times that of European and Japanese managers (30 percent versus 10 percent).[11]

There are five factors to which this failure rate can be attributed:

1. *The Challenges of Managing a Virtual Team.* International executives operate in a distributed environment, frequently separated by thousands of miles from both their home offices and team members. Even with the assistance of modern technology, skewed travel schedules and different time zones make it difficult to establish regular communication channels. As Kay Lillig Cotter, Director of Consulting for Measurement Services for Wilson Learning Corporation, points out, "Working on an international basis, you may need to manage virtual teams. In a global organization, managers/executives may have people reporting to them that they never see. So questions arise about how you manage from a distance, especially when you don't have a common cultural viewpoint."[12]

2. *Conflicting Agendas.* International executives are often placed in the middle, attempting to balance the expectations of the home office with the day-to-day expectations of their partners and co-workers in their host country. A few years ago, I was involved in a consulting project for a shipping transport company that involved an extended stay in the Virgin Islands. During my visit, I found that local executives were continually frustrated by the unwillingness of their U.S.-based senior managers to listen to their input on how to formulate their shipping schedules. The head of the VI office, a U.S. expat, found that one of the formidable tasks he faced involved resolving skirmishes between these two warring groups.

3. *Stringent Adaptive Demands.* International executives often have to deal with simultaneous adaptations to new jobs, different teams, unanticipated relocation problems, and different national laws, customs, and cultural norms.

4. *Family Adjustment Problems.* At the same time, expats also face the challenge of ensuring that their families adjust to their international moves. Management consultant and George Washington University professor Michael Marquardt cites a survey involving eighty U.S. companies on expatriate assignments that indicated that the number one reason cited for failure was "inability of the manager's spouse to adjust to a different physical or cultural environment," with "other family problems" also mentioned as an important adjustment factor.[13] Researchers Jean Woodall and Dianna Winstanley claim that a large part of this adjustment problem is due to the fact that many companies are operating from an antiquated notion of "family." As Woodall and Winstanley see it, "At the center of this is the problem of the 'trailing spouse.' The notion of the expatriate assignment is grounded in a social reality that has been out of date for twenty years: male managers with a dependent spouse who did not have a career of her own."[14]

5. *Lack of Training.* Expats are frequently simply not provided with any training designed to help them take on their new international roles. In the study cited earlier, showing the comparative failure rates for U.S., European, and Japanese executives, researchers found that 68 percent of U.S. companies that are involved in international business provided no training to prepare their expatriates.[15] For many U.S.-based firms, this lack of formal training is largely associated with the misguided belief that high-potential executives come equipped with all of the requisite competencies needed to made a ready adjustment to a new culture.

IDENTIFYING LEADERSHIP COMPETENCIES FOR INTERNATIONAL EXECUTIVES

We can see that it is essential to determine the unique competencies associated with success on international executive assignments, given the high failure rate encountered for expatriate executives and managers. Studies on the performance of international executives suggest that the following competencies are important to success:

- Management and career consultant Beverly Geber claims that "flexibility, interpersonal skills, adaptability, knowledge of business are key success factors for international managers."[16]

- Samir Gupte, Senior Director of Human Resources for Choice Hotels International, suggests that another important competency is the ability "to adopt the best problem-solving solution, without any nationalist or ethnocentric barriers that might cause the expatriate to overlook the ways that people solve problems in other cultures." Gupte adds that this factor is related to that of being able to adapt communication styles to different cultures. As an example, Gupte notes the cultural norms of Brazil and the Middle East, in which "a leader would not have an 'all staff' meeting, but would instead rely on his or her leaders to disseminate information."[17]

- Extensive research conducted by Marshall School of Business professor Morgan McCall suggests that "three things are particularly important in an international business context: commitment to making a difference, insightfulness, and the courage to take risks."[18]

- Two additional research studies cited language skills, adaptability, cross-cultural sensitivity, openness, behavioral flexibility, and knowledge of the host culture to be important variables for international success.[19, 20]

- Michael Marquardt has extracted from several studies the following ten factors necessary for success on international assignments: "Cultural self-awareness, language proficiency, global perspective and mind-set, respect for the values and practices of other cultures, patience and tolerance with ambiguity, sense of humor, communication skills, creativity, emotional resilience and adjustment skills, and self-management of learning."[21]

When you boil down these findings to their areas of commonality, three competencies appear to emerge as essential to the success of international executives.

1. *Adaptability/Flexibility.* The ability to readily adapt to new cultures and work environments and to demonstrate flexibility in continually adjusting one's behavior to new situations.

2. *Cross-Cultural Sensitivity.* Respect for, and a willingness and ability to understand and respect, the new culture and people in which one is immersed.

3. *Interpersonal Skills.* The ability to remain sensitive to the needs and concerns of others, and to communicate in a way that builds rapport.

CASE IN POINT: BOSTON SCIENTIFIC
Chuck Bolton, Vice President, International HR

One company that has met this challenge head-on is Boston Scientific Corporation, a worldwide leader in noninvasive medical treatments based in Natick, Massachusetts. From 1994 to 1998, Boston Scientific grew from 2,500 to 14,000 employees. During this same period, international sales exploded, moving from 18 percent to 47 percent of revenues. Chuck Bolton, Boston's Vice President of International HR, explains, "A big challenge caused by our expansion has been hiring people for specific positions and then ensuring that they weren't surpassed by the scope of the job as the job expanded. Another major challenge involved maintaining a high-performance company."[22]

According to Bolton, an analysis of the company's leadership competency model, which centered around nine major competencies, suggested that three of these competencies—leadership style, broad management perspective, and people developer—were found to be strongly tied to successful international performance. In highlighting the reason for the importance of these competencies, Bolton explains that: "Leadership style is important because on international assignments we need leaders who can stimulate creative ideas from others and coaches who can use all possible business experiences, such as budget reviews, as learning opportunities for teaching subordinates. People development is critical to allow us to quickly grow our business. 'Broad management perspective' is important to understand that on an extended international assignment you are not a 'lone soldier'; you need to know that you have the backing of the company, and you need to understand how to leverage resources for support. Finally, it is critical that people placed on international assignments be able to understand the long-term view of the company and match their actions against this view."[23]

The competency model developed by Boston Scientific is used in a number of applications, including selection for international assignments and executive development.

SOME FINAL CAVEATS

In developing your executive competency model, it is important to keep in mind a few caveats:

1. Invest whatever level of time and energy is needed to build stakeholder support for your project. No matter what kind of research template you start with, or the thoroughness and

integrity of your design, your senior team will not support your model if they do not feel that they have been heavily involved in its design. Build into your project plans several opportunities for team reviews. In addition, look for an influential senior manager who can provide a strong troubleshooting and sponsorship role for your project.

2. Recognize that at times you have to compromise a "pure HR design" for the sake of political reality. A classic example is when a key senior executive (such as your CEO!) wants to include in your study an additional competency, although this competency was not highlighted by any of your focus group or interview participants. A purist approach would be to resist efforts to include this competency since it does not match the data you have generated. A more realistic approach would be to see if the requested competency addition is at least marginally synonymous with an existing competency (so that you can blend the two through some creative wordsmithing), or whether you can subsume the competency under another related competency by presenting it as one of four or five behavioral anchors that support and substantiate that competency.

3. Since you will want your results to reflect a current review of your organization, and you want to maintain support for your project, it is important that you move quickly in completing your competency analysis. As a general rule of thumb, once approved you should be able to complete a competency project within three to six months. If it takes more than nine months, either you do not have the right level of executive support for your project or you are working with a poorly constructed design.

4. Once developed, it is important that your competency model be updated every two to three years, to reflect your organization's changing business requirements. This is particularly true if you work in a fast-changing industry.

5. Keep it simple. If your initial focus group efforts produce more than twelve competencies, consider consolidating competencies into a final field of twelve. If others appear confused by your competency descriptions, look for ways to simplify your language.

6. Do not become defensive if you meet some initial resistance early in the implementation of your competency project. It is common for managers and executives to have misgivings about such studies, fearing that their participation will be meaningless and merely result in a white paper that is lost on someone's shelf.

A stronger concern may be that your study is masking some kind of clandestine assessment of the participants themselves. The best way to prevent such miscommunication is through the use of clear and frequent communication earlier in your initial design regarding the intended purpose and objectives of your study. This might entail departmental presentations, e-mail general notices, and simple brochures that provide examples of the types of information you hope to gain from participants.

7. Communication is also a critical feature at the close of your study. If you have done your homework, you should have obtained a high level of involvement from managers and executives through your focus groups and interviews. After presenting your findings to your senior team you have an obligation to

- Send a follow-up letter to these participants, thanking them for their assistance and presenting a brief overview of your findings.

- Send a secondary communication to your general executive population, presenting the final breakout of competencies that will now be applied to each executive level in your company. For development purposes, your executives should also have access to information on those important technical competencies required of each function, as well as on emerging leadership and technical competencies that are likely to become more important over the next few years.

SUMMARY OF KEY POINTS

- An organization must be able to identify the *leadership competencies* that are essential for its success.

- An organization's *core competencies* are those unique technical skills that a company does consistently and exceptionally better than others in its field, and that provide the company with a sustainable advantage over its competitors.

- By contrast, *executive competencies* are those competencies required for successful leadership within an organization.

- Before launching a competency assessment project, gain up-front alignment from your senior team regarding (1) the job levels/functions to be included in your model, (2) unique technical/functional skills to be included, (3) whether your model will include both current and future competencies,

(4) the desired format for data collection, (5) how data will be shared, and (6) where the competency base will reside.

- The steps for building a competency model include (1) reviewing a competency template, (2) conducting focus groups, (3) constructing a tentative model, (4) conducting individual interviews, (5) determining the most appropriate competency breakout, and (6) presenting your findings.

- Some cautionary guidelines to follow when implementing an executive competency assessment are (1) build solid stakeholder support for your project, (2) recognize that at times you have to compromise a "pure HR design" for the sake of political reality, (3) try to complete your competency project within three to six months to ensure relevancy, (4) update your model every one or two years to reflect your organization's changing business requirements, (5) keep it simple, and (6) don't become defensive if you meet some initial resistance early in the implementation of your project.

CHAPTER 5

ASSESSING EXECUTIVE CAPABILITIES

Before moving on, take a moment and see where we are in the process. In the first four chapters I explained how designing an effective executive resource strategy can help you make effective leadership staffing and development decisions. You have also taken a look at some of the elements that go into a good strategy and learned how to identify the emerging business requirements and the leadership competencies needed to meet these requirements. In this chapter you will be introduced to several assessment tools you can use to evaluate executives against these leadership competencies and determine both their current performance and long-term potential. In Chapter 6 we will take this assessment process one step further by introducing you to a four-step method for consolidating these individual assessments into an evaluation of your overall executive bench.

THE IMPORTANCE OF ASSESSMENT

As a starting point, let's consider what an executive assessment is designed to do. The question of how a given executive is likely to perform in the future, whether in his or her current position or in a completely different leadership role, is high-stakes poker. That is, there is usually so much riding on this question that we cannot afford a cursory guess about a given leader's performance capability. We have to know, as accurately as possible, how a leader can be expected to perform when put to the test, in a number of different work situations.

An essential part of this decision process involves identifying the 5 to 10 percent of the executive talent pool who represent your organization's high-potential managers and executives. These high-potential leaders (HIPOs) offer the strongest contribution potential to your company and represent a significant investment opportunity for its future. To identify and develop them you must have in place a reliable executive assessment process.

Unfortunately, we often find ourselves unexpectedly confronted with difficult executive management decisions. An executive abruptly terminates, a merger is suddenly announced, or the corporate office makes the decision to implement a companywide reorganization. These are but some of the situations in which we are expected to make quick decisions regarding the relative capabilities of our executive leaders. In these types of fast-change scenarios, it is absolutely essential that we have taken the time, well in advance of the change curve, to map out the comparative strengths and weaknesses of our leaders.

Still another factor that complicates the picture is the trend toward importing leaders from outside a company or industry. In such a situation, it is imperative that we be able to create an even field of play for assessing the comparative performance of internal and external candidates who are competing for the same positions. Forming such an evaluation is extremely difficult without having in place the right assessment methodology.

Finally, if you are an HR or OD specialist, you will often be called upon to assume a performance-coaching and advising role to your executive team. A good assessment process can help you work around time and budgeting constraints to identify both the development needs of your overall leadership team and the leadership requirements of specific work functions. It can also enable you to target development plans to the unique needs of individual executives. At the same time, a reliable assessment process can help you diagnose the underlying causes of performance problems and spot challenging leadership behaviors before they contribute to the derailment of executives.

WHAT DOES AN EFFECTIVE ASSESSMENT METHOD LOOK LIKE?

Five criteria characterize an effective assessment process. First, an assessment method should *be valid*; that is, it should evaluate performance areas that have been shown to be related to job success. Second, as closely as possible, the assessment process should *replicate the job conditions under which selected competencies are used*. If one of the demand features of an executive's job is considered to be the ability to negotiate with aggressive and hostile vendors, an assessment simulation that attempts to evaluate these negotiation skills should include role-plays involving difficult vendor situations.

Third, an assessment method should be *as free as possible from subjective biases*. Obviously, given the complexities of the real world and the many subtleties that make up an executive's position, this criterion is very hard to achieve. However, as I will explain later in this chapter, there are a few assessment guidelines we can follow that will at least partially mitigate this type of bias.

Fourth, the purpose of the chosen assessment method should be *clearly understood* by participants and their managers. It is important to distinguish assessment methods that are specifically targeted to evaluating current performance from those that predict an executive's chances of success under yet-unmet work conditions—for example, assessing the leaders of a company's functional groups on their readiness to advance into the role of general manager.

Fifth, an assessment method should be *easy to administer and interpret, and relatively cost-effective*. This is an area in which assessment methods vary widely. Some methodologies, such as assessment centers, are extremely expensive to operate, require specialized training on the part of the assessment center administrator and raters, and can be implemented with only a small number of participants at any one time. While expense and time factors are usually not insurmountable obstacles when the assessment is aimed at a few carefully chosen executives, these factors can easily make the difference in being able to manage large-scale assessment projects involving broad groups of executives.

In this chapter we will compare four methods for assessing leadership performance, illustrated in Figure 10 on page 108. I call these methods the "fabulous four" because they constitute the central core of almost any executive assessment process. They are: (1) single-rater evaluations, (2) multirater evaluations, (3) assessment simulations, and (4) assessment interviews.

SINGLE-RATER EVALUATIONS

The first assessment method involves evaluating an executive's overall performance through a single rater. This type of assessment forms the crux of most talent review and performance appraisal processes. Senior executives usually defend this assessment method on the grounds that it is administratively simple and quick, and that it is based on feedback from the most reliable information source: the executive's manager. There are, however, several drawbacks with this assessment process that make it only marginally useful. The first is the problem of rater bias. Individuals vary widely in their ability to

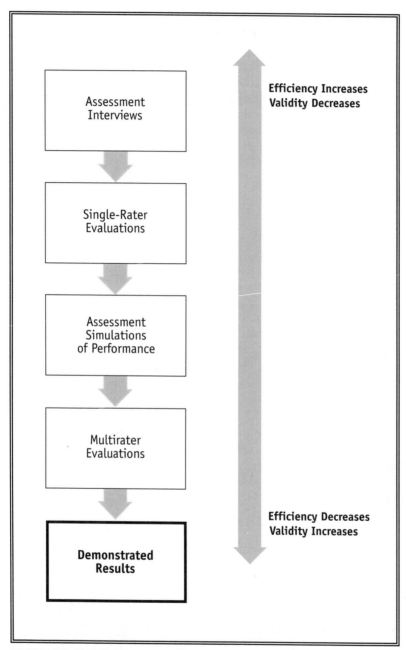

FIGURE 10 THE COMPARATIVE VALIDITY OF ASSESSMENT OPTIONS

accurately assess the performance of other people. Personal biases also tend to enter the picture. Another problem involves the phenomenon of "cloning"—the tendency of executives to evaluate (and select) individuals on the basis of how closely they resemble their raters. Other problems involve the inaccuracies that occur with memory distortions (reflecting on performance that has occurred over a twelve-month rating period) and the invalid assessments that we are likely to obtain from substandard managers.

There are, of course, several steps we can take to counter these drawbacks. These include the use of rigorous competency models, such as those described in the previous chapter, and providing executives with in-depth training in how to make objective selection and promotional decisions. In addition, we can partially compensate for the skewed ratings obtained by poorly performing executives by having senior managers weigh in on the performance ratings of direct and second-level reports.

MULTIRATER EVALUATIONS (360-DEGREE FEEDBACK)

Many of the drawbacks that are associated with single-rater evaluations can be overcome through 360-degree profile systems. As Figure 11 on page 110 illustrates, a 360-degree assessment process draws feedback from a professional's complete circle of influence, including that person's manager, peers (internal customers), and work team. Usually three to five raters are selected to provide team feedback, and an equal number are selected for peer feedback. Larger group sizes can be used, although this adds to the costs and administrative burden of the process. Executives having fewer than three direct reports should not solicit feedback from these individuals, as respondents will not have adequate anonymity.

The most productive feature of a multirating process is its ability to provide a diverse array of feedback. Research has shown that leaders often reveal different aspects of themselves to these different rating groups. An example would be the executive who is extremely accommodating with her manager, but overly controlling with her work team and excessively demanding with peer-level managers. This broad, inclusive data-gathering approach serves the same function as does a three-sided mirror in a clothing store. While those new clothes may look pretty good from the front, the side mirrors catch perspectives that normally are not within our field of view. By comparing their self-assessments against the feedback provided by others, participants are able to identify blind spots. Accordingly, when compared against single-rater evaluations, 360-degree evaluations offer a

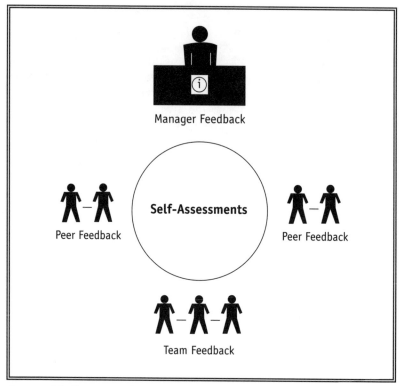

Manager Feedback

Peer Feedback

Self-Assessments

Peer Feedback

Team Feedback

FIGURE 11 FEEDBACK SOURCES FOR 360-DEGREE PROFILES

more balanced and in-depth competency assessment approach.[1] In addition, the use of input from a variety of anonymous raters reduces the perceived risks that many people associate with giving critical feedback, particularly when that feedback is directed to their supervisors or other senior-level managers in the organization.[2]

The use of multiraters also provides a way to compensate for the faulty assessment evaluations that are sometimes obtained by inexperienced or poorly performing executives. Figure 12 shows how this situation might be enacted. In this case Jack Smith, VP-Accounting, has previously given a negative evaluation to one of his reports (Michael Howard) on the company's yearly talent review. Since Smith's own performance record has not been very good, his boss, Jane Darnell, SVP-Finance, has decided to solicit alternative feedback on Howard, in the form of a 360-degree evaluation. The results of the evaluation, shown in Table 15 on pages 112 and 113, indicate that on almost every measure, Howard's peers and team accord him much higher ratings than his manager does. While no final conclusions

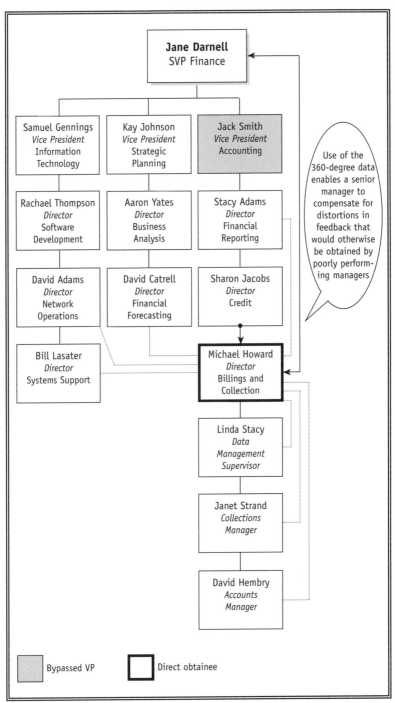

FIGURE 12 APPLYING 360-DEGREE DATA AS A CHECK AND BALANCE

TABLE 15					
360-DEGREE PROFILE OF MICHAEL HOWARD					

Competency Area

Decision Making The ability to make effective, timely, and well-determined decisions based on available information.	Team	Manager	Peers	Total	Self
1. Makes decisions in a timely manner—knows how far to go in data gathering before reaching a decision; doesn't become frozen through "analysis paralysis."	4.6	2.0	4.0	4.9	4.0
2. Exhibits a high success rate in the quality of business decisions.	4.2	2.0	3.8	3.81	4.0
3. Makes decisions based, in part, on input from key organizational stakeholders.	3.0	2.0	3.0	2.90	5.0
4. Able to deal with ambiguity and complexity; can sort out critical pieces of information and synthesize a variety of data into a well-constructed decision.	4.1	1.0	4.5	4.13	4.0
5. Able to deconstruct complex problems to assess underlying causes and determine appropriate courses of action.	4.5	2.0	4.6	4.31	3.0
Total	4.08	1.8	3.98	3.82	4.0

Competency Area					
Strategic Thinking The ability to analyze information to determine the most appropriate courses of action for long-term gain.	Team	Manager	Peers	Total	Self
1. Considers the long view when making tactical decisions.	4.7	3.0	3.0	3.77	5.0
2. Analyzes potential actions from the perspective of external stakeholders such as board members, stockholders, and customers.	4.7	2.0	3.0	3.68	5.0
3. Able to determine those actions that will most effectively sustain our company's competitive position.	3.1	2.0	4.0	3.18	4.0
4. Accurately anticipates future trends and the most probable consequences of actions; does not get taken by surprise.	4.0	1.0	4.0	4.0	4.0
5. Able to translate strategic thinking into a compelling plan of action.	2.8	2.0	4.0	3.23	3.0
Total	**3.86**	**2.0**	**3.6**	**3.57**	**4.2**

could necessarily be drawn from these data, the SVP now has additional data to warrant a closer look into the situation.

A 360-degree evaluation ideally should rate an individual's performance on each of the behavioral anchors that have been previously identified through the competency identification process (see Chapter 4). Ratings are usually made in terms of a five- to seven-point rating scale. In addition, some organizations include in their surveys one or two open-ended questions, such as the following.

- "How would you describe this individual's strongest competency?"
- "What is the most important leadership development area for this individual?"
- "What one competency could this person improve that would generate the greatest improvement in his or her performance?"

While some companies include external customers as a discrete part of their reporting group, there are several reasons why it may be advisable to exclude your customers from this rating process. First, keep in mind that external customers can become somewhat confused regarding the purpose of a 360-degree evaluation and may find it difficult to separate their ratings of individual executives from their customer satisfaction ratings for your organization as a whole. In addition, external customers seldom have the option of attending orientation sessions that can provide useful background and context on executive assessment. A third caveat is that external customers lack opportunities to observe the full spectrum of an executive's performance, such as how he or she directs and manages work teams. A better option for obtaining customer feedback is the use of customer satisfaction surveys that are completely separate from the 360-degree profile.

CREATING A 360-DEGREE PROFILE

To begin, obtain alignment among the senior staff and chief HR leader regarding the purpose and objectives of the 360-degree review. Specifically, is the program restricted to development or will it also be applied to appraisal and promotional decisions? Senior managers should also be aligned on the basic guidelines for program implementation, such as who within the company will have access to the 360-degree scores, whether scoring profiles will be archived by the HR department, and who in the company (the individual's manager, a designated HR specialist, or an outside consultant) has the responsibility for providing coaching support to those executives who request this service.

Next, establish a design team to determine the specifications for the system. This should include determining how far down the organization the 360-degree assessment will extend, the minimum and maximum numbers of raters that will be included in each assessment, how the 360-degree implementation will roll out across the organization, and the communication, orientation, and training plans that will be put into place.

Identify the leadership competencies and supporting behaviors that will be evaluated as part of the 360-degree process. If you have already completed the competency identification process that was outlined in the previous chapter, you will be able to skip this step and move on to a senior-level review. Conducting a senior-level review affords your senior managers an opportunity to provide input and revision of the design process and recommended assessment form.

The next step is to provide a formal orientation session for your entire respondent group to explain important program features. An orientation session is especially important for organizations in which there is a strong trust issue between executives and their work teams, and where participants are expected to have a number of concerns and questions about how their 360-degree results will be communicated and used. Some of the topics that need to be covered in your orientation include the following:

- Purpose of the 360-degree profile

- Payoffs obtained through the use of the 360-degree process

- Benchmark data on other companies that have successfully applied 360-degree methodology

- Examples of the evaluation form that will be used and an explanation of how it has been designed or selected

- Time frames for orientation, distribution of the forms, completion of the forms by raters, data inputting and analysis, and follow-up training

- How the completed profiles will be used and who will have access to them

- Explanations regarding the competency dimensions and behaviors being assessed

- How to avoid common rating problems such as the "halo effect"—when one positive behavior influences the ratings on other behaviors; or using the rating form as an overall evaluation of performance instead of an assessment of relative skill strengths and weaknesses; or how to rate behaviors that have not been directly observed, though most 360-degree profiles provide the option of leaving these statements blank

- How to select raters and how to achieve self- and manager alignment on selection

- Addressing participants' concerns regarding the rating process

Now, conduct a pilot rollout of the 360-degree process prior to full-scale implementation. A pilot can help you uncover unanticipated problems, such as software glitches (for internal designs), misinterpretations of rating instructions, and employees' concerns regarding the planned use and application of the profile assessments. Only then, after the pilot has been reviewed and any changes made, conduct the full implementation of the 360-degree process, including form administration, data inputting, and collation of results.

At the point that you are ready to distribute the 360-degree profiles to respondents, a second orientation session should be held to explain

- How to interpret completed scores (making use of representative rating forms)

- How to form development plans based on typical scoring profiles

- How to look for blind spots in performance feedback—discrepancies between self-scores and feedback scores provided by others

- Options that will be made available to participants who would like individual coaching on ways to apply 360-degree evaluations to development planning

Finally, use the 360-degree results you have obtained to create targeted group competency profiles for each executive level and function. I will discuss the details of this last step in the next chapter.

ISSUES IN THE DESIGN OF 360-DEGREE ASSESSMENTS

An important design issue is determining whether the 360-degree process will be *internally* or *externally* designed. There are advantages to both options: with internal design you achieve better control over form administration and management of the software database, and you decrease the chances that disconnects will occur between executive participants, respondents, your senior team, and your HR department. Internal design should not be attempted, however, unless your HR department has on board individuals who are experienced in the design and interpretation of multirater instruments.

On the other hand, external design allows you to move faster without getting bogged down in a potentially heavy administrative burden. External administration usually raises the comfort level of respondents regarding the confidentiality and anonymity of their responses. By mailing their responses directly to an outside consulting firm, respondents know that their scores will not be intercepted and reviewed by the HR department or their managers. But these advantages come at a price. The costs for purchase, administration, and feedback can easily run $400 to $1,000 per participant, and the cost of the custom design itself may run an additional $20,000 to $50,000.

Another design issue is whether the 360-degree process will be administered via hard copy or software. Hard copy is preferable when you are dealing with a limited number of respondents, have limited funds for design, and are faced with a tight turnaround schedule. Hard copy is also a better choice when the evaluation process is not likely to be extended or replicated, or if your respondents are not computer literate. Some respondents feel more comfortable with a paper copy they can mail directly to an outside consulting firm.

Computer-based assessments provide much faster response and collation time, decrease the administrative burden, and make it easy to create reports for selected executive subgroups. These advantages can become very significant when processing a large number of respondents, or when you anticipate that the use of 360-degree assessments will continue as an ongoing program.[3] One final advantage is that computer-based approaches provide greater document management control than do hard-copy alternatives, eliminating the problem of stray evaluation forms surfacing around the office.

Before jumping into a computer-based system, there are three things to keep in mind. First, all respondents must have ready access to a computer. Second, plan on spending some money. Most software vendors typically will charge a one-time fee per site license, ranging from $5,000 to $20,000. Multiple-site licenses can usually be obtained at discounted rates. Finally, while the use of a computer-based system inevitably saves a lot of downstream administrative time, it requires much more time to design, retrofit (for externally purchased systems), and debug than do hard-copy evaluation methods. It should be noted that there are currently a few consulting firms, such as the Center for Creative Leadership, that are experimenting with the use of Internet-based delivery of 360-degree tools.

If you are seriously considering purchasing 360-degree evaluation software, or obtaining design or administration assistance from an external vendor, you may want to start with the following vendors, all of which have had years of experience in this field. (See the Resources section at the back of the book for contact information.)

Personnel Decisions, Inc.

The Center for Creative Leadership (ask about their Benchmarks® and SkillScope® tools)

TEAMS, Inc.

Lominger, Limited (ask about their Voices® tool)

Another critical issue for review is the decision regarding *who selects raters* for participating executives. There will always be attempts by executives to generate a favorable assessment for themselves by prior screening of the raters. One way of minimizing this problem is to have ratees select a large pool of prospective candidates, and then have the ratee's manager make the final selection from this list. This approach supports the concept of employee empowerment, while ensuring that managers have input into this process.

Still another important design issue involves *the scope of the evaluation effort.* I offer the same advice here as I did regarding competency identification—namely, keep it simple. One of the most common mistakes made by designers of 360-degree evaluations is that they use such extensive and elaborate competency models that respondents get lost in the data. David Bracken, Director of Organizational Assessments and Research Services for Personnel Decisions, recommends including no more than sixty behaviors in your 360-degree profile and cautions that employees will spend no more than ten to fifteen minutes filling out a multirater assessment form.[4] Remember that because participants will be receiving feedback from multiple sources during a full-scale 360-degree review, it is common for respondents to be asked to provide feedback for several of their peers—a task that can require several hours.

A final issue concerns the proper application of 360-degree evaluations. Applications fall into two categories: *development* and *assessment.* Development is by far the more innocuous application. In this scenario, 360-degree evaluation data are returned directly to participants, who exert a high degree of control over their use. When 360-degree evaluations are extended to use for performance assessment, the process becomes more anxiety provoking for participants. Excessive concerns regarding the intended use of these data can skew rating scores in a positive (or if the participant is strongly disliked, a negative) direction.[5] I have found that when the 360-degree process is directed toward evaluation, respondents make a cognitive shift from attempting to discriminate between the participant's strongest and weakest competencies, to focusing on an overall assessment of the participant's performance.

My recommendation is that the application of 360-degree profiles should be limited to executive development in the first year. Then wait until this methodology has been successfully debugged and accepted as a part of your corporate culture before attempting to use it for performance evaluation. If you do decide to use the 360-degree for performance evaluation, it will be critical, from a liability protection standpoint, that you provide respondents with adequate communication and training regarding the suggested use of this evaluation method. Always be very candid and honest in letting participants know in advance the intended uses of the 360-degree evaluation process.

The intended use of the 360-degree profiles will affect the optimal timing of this process. No matter how much you claim that this feedback process is only intended to be used for development purposes, if the forms are mailed out a month before your annual performance reviews your organization will automatically view the 360-degree process as a covert part of the annual appraisal review.

Before closing this discussion of 360-degree assessments, it is important to caution that before attempting their design it is critical to have on board, or available through consulting assistance, a professional who has experience in psychometric testing and assessment. An excellent reference in this regard is the book *Choosing 360°: A Guide to Evaluating Multi-Rater Feedback Instruments for Management Development* by Ellen Van Velsor, Jean Brittian Leslie, and John W. Fleenor. The authors advise that a well-designed 360-degree instrument should meet the following criteria:

- The test should show a correlation coefficient for inter-rater reliability (agreement on rating scores within same rating groups of peers or direct reports) of at least 0.4.

- The characteristics of the sample group on which you are testing your 360-degree assessment should closely resemble those of the population group on which you intend to conduct the test.

- The test should be shown to be valid (that it measures what it claims to measure) through evidence of at least a moderate (0.3 or more) correlation between the test scores and job performance (managerial ratings of effectiveness), or positive correlations with another testing instrument that has already been shown to be valid.[6]

A useful feature of this text is that it contains an "Instrument Evaluation Checklist" for comparing the relative utility of different 360-degree instruments.

ASSESSMENT SIMULATIONS

Assessment centers are very structured learning laboratories where participants participate in a battery of work-related simulations typically spanning one to three days. Assessment centers have different target audiences: those targeting managers and executives make use of assessment exercises that help to evaluate an individual's performance on generic leadership competencies; those targeting professional employees tend to evaluate interpersonal competencies. Still others are custom designed to evaluate specific functional competencies, such as sales competencies. Assessment center simulations have been shown to be a valid and useful tool both when applied to executive development and when used as a supportive methodology for executive selection and promotion decisions.[7]

WHAT A CENTER LOOKS LIKE

Although simulations can involve a variety of content, they tend to follow the same format. Participants are given background data related to a work situation and asked to assume the role of a leader in a hypothetical scenario. They are then involved in a sixty- to ninety-minute exercise in which they are asked to make a decision, solve a problem, or intervene in an interpersonal situation. Most leadership simulations fall into one of three categories: in-basket exercises, case scenarios, and role plays.

In-basket Exercises. Participants assume the role of a new manager who is taking over a work function. They are given an "in-basket" that contains memos, handwritten notes alluding to work problems or success stories, work schedules, angry letters from customers—in short, all of the puzzle pieces that form a typical work situation. After spending a brief time organizing the data, participants are asked to draw conclusions from them and recommend a course of action, as well as to determine the order in which they would go about attacking each of the work problems (the ability to assess priorities).

Case Scenarios. Participants are presented with a detailed business case detailing a challenge faced by a hypothetical company or work function. A variety of background information is offered, including key financial reports, marketing research, or performance data on hypothetical team members. Participants are asked to analyze the data and, depending on the nature of the simulation, must either develop a solution to a problem or recommend a strategy for advancing a business objective.

Role-Plays. Participants are given background information on a difficult leadership challenge that requires the use of interpersonal competencies. Examples include arbitrating a conflict between two coworkers, resolving a problem with a key customer account, pitching a sale, or managing a grievance issue. Participants then confront the challenge directly through a role-play exercise, which is conducted face-to-face or over the phone. The role-plays are conducted by "actors," who have been trained to disclose certain data when prompted though the use of insightful questions, and to respond in certain ways to participants' actions. The attempt here is to provide the same relative demand feature to all participants so that the only variable under observation is the degree of competency exhibited by each participant.

Generally, each work simulation is designed to evaluate no more than two or three different competencies. Attempts to evaluate more than three competencies at once will produce diluted evaluation data, since the raters who are observing and documenting each simulation find it difficult to simultaneously track multiple evaluation areas. Figure 13 on pages 122 and 123 shows a representative schedule for a two-day assessment center program, while the Competency/Simulation Matrix shown in Table 16 on page 123 illustrates how the competencies being assessed within this program might be paired with simulations.

During the assessment process, trained observers evaluate competencies using structured rating sheets. They also document examples of competencies and competency shortfalls (for example, someone who is so domineering that he or she misses opportunities to listen and gather information). This completed documentation goes into a final assessment report. Unlike 360-degree scoring profiles, the final report does not usually contain quantitative ratings of participants, but rather a narrative description of each participant's competency strengths and shortfalls. It is important to note that this assessment summary is not normative; that is, participants are not compared against each other in the use of competencies. Instead, each participant is ranked against a series of general guidelines that describe the types of behavior the participant should be expected to demonstrate in a given competency. The final assessment report is usually shared with participants within two weeks following completion of the assessment activities. Most assessment centers offer report debriefings and associated development coaching sessions as supplemental services that can be offered to client companies. Figure 14 on page 124 illustrates part of an assessment report for one of the participants in our hypothetical assessment center.

THE EVOLUTION OF ASSESSMENT SIMULATIONS

As with every other form of assessment technology, assessment centers have gone through some interesting evolutionary changes since some of the first pioneering studies were carried out some forty years ago by AT&T.

Day One

8:00–8:30 a.m. Participants arrive at center and are given an overview of what they can anticipate encountering over the next two days, as well as general guidelines for completing the program (e.g., "Don't 'play-act.' Just be yourself.")

8:30–Noon *Participants divide into two teams and rotate between the following exercises:*

Exercise 1 Participants are given sixty minutes to review an in-basket package describing a marketing problem. Next, each participant takes twenty minutes to deliver his or her findings to "management."

Exercise 2 Participants take sixty minutes to review a background case describing a declining performance trend for a high-performing employee. Each participant then takes twenty minutes to conduct a performance improvement coaching session with the employee.

Noon–1:00 p.m. Participants meet for lunch.

1:00–4:00 p.m. *Participants conduct the following exercise as a single team:*
Exercise 3 Participants are given sixty minutes to individually review a case regarding a hypothetical quality improvement problem. They then have ninety minutes to reach consensus regarding the most effective approach for solving the problem and restoring the confidence of their customers.

4:00–4:30 p.m. *Participants debrief and have the opportunity to share questions and concerns.*

Day Two

8:30–Noon *Participants divide into two teams and rotate between the following exercises:*

Exercise 4 Participants are given forty-five minutes to analyze financial and business data related to a performance decline in a hypothetical business unit. They are then individually given twenty minutes to interview two "company managers" and probe further into the causes of the business problem. Finally, they have an additional ten minutes to provide a debriefing of their conclusions to their "manager."

Exercise 5 Participants are given forty-five minutes to review case information pertaining to a business objective that requires the support of a peer manager, who (according to

---

FIGURE 13 TYPICAL ASSESSMENT CENTER AGENDA

the background data) tends to be inflexible in his think-ing. Participants then spend twenty minutes in a role-play exercise to see if they can capture the support of the peer manager.

Noon–1:00 p.m. Participants meet for lunch.

1:00–4:00 p.m. *Participants conduct the following exercise as a single team:*

Exercise 6 Participants are given sixty minutes to individually review a case regarding a resource allocation problem among competing departments. Each participant is assigned a role as a different department head. They then have an additional sixty minutes to use their influencing skills to persuade each other to support their respective depart-mental agendas. At the end of the session, participants take thirty minutes to jointly vote on how they choose to allocate funds.

4:00–4:30 p.m. *Participants attend a final debriefing and are given infor-mation regarding how and when their assessment reports will be shared with them.*

FIGURE 13 TYPICAL ASSESSMENT CENTER AGENDA (CONT'D)

TABLE 16						
COMPETENCY/SIMULATION MATRIX						
	Simulation Exercise					
Assessed Competency	1	2	3	4	5	6
Problem Solving	✓	✓		✓		
Decision Making			✓			✓
Team Leadership			✓			✓
Organizational Influence	✓				✓	
Sensitivity/ Relationship Building		✓			✓	
Strategic Thinking			✓	✓		

Organizational Influence

Part A: Assessment Simulations

This competency is assessed through two simulations. In the first exercise, participants are given twenty minutes to use their influencing skills to present a business case for a marketing decision to their managers. In the second situation, participants are given twenty minutes to gather support from a hostile peer-level manager for an important business objective.

Part B: Observations and Conclusions

Mr. Veck scored very high on the behavioral dimension of "building team partnerships." In presenting his findings to his manager, he identified the key stakeholders who had already weighed in on the marketing problem and attempted to anticipate the concerns they might have with this issue. This behavior was also evidenced during his meeting with his peer, when he set the stage for discussion by telling his angry partner, "It's important for me to know that you feel comfortable supporting this decision."

Mr. Veck also scored high on the behavioral dimension of "seeking common ground for win-win decisions." In both exercises he carefully took notes on the respective concerns voiced by his manager and peer. When meeting with his manager, he took the time to look for the hidden concerns behind objections. For example:

Manager: I just don't feel comfortable making that adjustment to our brand position.

Veck: Tell me a little more about that. What's the source of your discomfort?

An important area for improvement is in "exerts an influencing role in the decision process." In the marketing exercise, Mr. Veck showed a willingness to immediately relinquish his position and adopt his manager's suggestions, even when options were available within the guidelines of the case for melding these respective views. In a similar way, when the discussion with a peer began to move to the point of confrontation, Mr. Veck allowed himself to be persuaded to accept his partner's position, despite background material indicating that other organizational stakeholders were strongly opposed to this position.

Summary: Mr. Veck displays the competencies needed for building rapport and stage setting with organizational stakeholders, and in listening effectively to opposing views. He needs to strengthen his competency in the area of exerting influence in team decision making.

FIGURE 14 ASSESSMENT REPORT FOR JOHN VECK

Portability. The first assessment centers were conducted at fixed sites. Participants went to the center and camped out for two to five days. Increasingly, consultants are providing clients with portable assessment centers that they can set up near a corporate office—an arrangement that reduces travel time and costs.

Versatility. Assessment centers have become much more diverse in recent years, with many centers focusing on discrete management levels or targeted work functions. Over the last twenty years, I have been involved in setting up assessment centers to

- Evaluate the readiness of hourly workers to assume the transition to first-level supervision
- Assess the suitability of managers for extended international assignments in Saudi Arabia
- Provide an assessment of team leadership capabilities as part of a diversity training process for executives at combined sites in the United States and the Virgin Islands
- Evaluate customer delivery skills for managers and professionals within a customer service department

Computer-Based Assessment. The newest movement in the field involves the migration from traditional live assessments to interactive, computer-based simulations. In discussing the evolution of the assessment process, Kay Lillig Cotter, Director of Consulting for Measurement Services for Wilson Learning, suggests that in the future, computer simulations will allow us to create more realistic simulations of executive job demands that, "take on the form of a virtual job, a seamless simulation, that gives an accurate feel of the job." She adds that

> We are going to see more and more simulations that make use of computers, with e-mail and voice-mail built in as part of the simulation. I don't believe the assessment will necessarily be computer based at the CEO level, but do feel that the assessment can be more computer-driven at the director and vice president level. Computerization provides more standardization and also allows us to move away from the kinds of time-limited tests that are often part of executive assessments. Timed tests are not especially appropriate to assess the senior managers for several reasons. Most of these tests do not involve providing context, and yet most executive decisions rely on understanding the context. These individuals often feel the pressures of their jobs, but normally have a reasonably high degree of control over the time they take to make

decisions. Computer-generated assessments allow executives the latitude (which they have in their real jobs) to make judgments on where, when, and how they choose to use their time to explore issues, which ones to deal with, and what they need to explore before they make decisions and set directions.[8]

One company that has taken a lead in automated assessment is Employment Technologies Corporation (ETC). ETC's president, Joe Sefcik, describes the focus of his company as providing performance-based assessments and exploring ways to use technology to automate the selection process. ETC focuses primarily on entry-level and mid-level managers. The typical ETC simulation involves a video that depicts a realistic job preview with multiple scenarios showing work teams, customers, or managerial situations. At designated points, the video freezes and participants are given multiple-choice questions and asked to select from among four alternative options. Each option is scaled from the best to worst choice. Participants' answers are entered into a computer, and their responses are automatically scored and processed. The average simulation takes about an hour.

Sefcik provides the following examples of simulations offered by ETC.

> Our Success Skills 2000™ program depicts four managers: a department manager in a data processing department in a number of interactions with clients and staff, an engineer managing a project, an accountant working with clients and dealing with internal issues in an accounting firm, and a sales and marketing representative working with a client. The simulation evaluates three primary competencies and seven subcompetencies, which are "Applied Problem Solving" (subcompetencies: problem solving and critical thinking), "Interpersonal Effectiveness" (subcompetencies: influence, building rapport, and teamwork), and "Accountability" (subcompetencies: self-management and initiative). This simulation has been used by Prudential, GTE, several banks for selection decisions involving branch manager positions, and Saturn, which is using the program to select some of their management teams for their dealerships. ETC also provides simulations in the areas of financial sales assessment and customer skills assessment.[9]

Sefcik believes ETC's automated assessments offer several advantages over live assessments.

- *Reduced Cost and Time.* A standard two-day live assessment can cost up to $100,000 for design, with a delivery cost of $1,500 to $5,000 per person, which limits how far down in the organization you can take the assessment. Time is a factor as well. Our average assessment can be performed within an hour. While such an assessment process may require us to invest $300,000 in design costs, the cost for our customers is only $20 to $40 per participant.

- *Flexibility.* One of the reasons we've placed our simulations on video is that they can be administered to individuals or groups. We've had as many as 250 people complete an assessment at one time. In addition, these assessments are portable and can be brought to the client's site.

- *Immediate Feedback.* One of the trends we are seeing in assessment design is linking assessment results to development as soon as possible, so that someone can be assessed and then immediately go into a coaching dialogue to improve performance. Our automated assessment design provides participants with diagnostic feedback immediately following the assessment.[10]

While ETC targets most of its assessments at the midmanagement level or lower, Sefcik claims that you can apply this assessment technology "to assess any work activity at any level . . . [the only caveat is that] the higher the level of the job, the more complex the simulation needs to be."[11]

COMPARATIVE ADVANTAGES AND DISADVANTAGES

Assessment centers offer a number of advantages over alternative assessment methodologies.

- Centers can provide a fair field of play for comparing the competencies of external and internal job candidates.

- Simulations can be used to test competencies that have not as yet been put to the test by candidates, making them a great method for assessing readiness for promotion.

- Assessment centers can collapse a variety of job challenges into a short time frame, providing a concentrated developmental experience for attendees.

- Unlike single- or multi-feedback methods, the raters who conduct assessment center simulations are not work associates who carry with them residual "relational baggage" that can distort the assessment process. By being completely impartial, they help to depoliticize the assessment process. This conclusion is supported by independent research data that indicate that, when compared against other assessment approaches, assessment centers are viewed by participants as more fair and equitable.[12]

- Research studies show that assessment centers have a high rate of predictive validity. When compared with other assessment approaches they are better at predicting the future performance of individuals.[13]

- By having competencies assessed through multiple simulations, you can build a picture of how they are displayed within different work contexts. Thus, an executive may discover that he or she has excellent persuasion skills in one-on-one situations but has difficulty getting his or her point across in a group forum. This detailed contextual review makes the assessment process an excellent development tool for executives and executive candidates.

Overall, assessment centers offer a reliable and thorough method of assessing executive performance and potential. Their successful implementation, however, depends on our ability to overcome the following implementation obstacles:

- Because of the complexity of the observation process and the fact that many simulations require time-intensive, one-on-one role-plays, assessment centers usually limit attendance to a small number of participants (five to ten) at a single time. This factor and the incredible time investment required to analyze and prepare reports on assessment data make assessment centers a costly proposition. Count on spending $1,500 to $5,000 for each center participant.

- The small number of people who can participate in a single assessment center session make the center a narrow funnel for processing job candidates. Thus, it tends to be reserved for critical development or selection decisions, or is used as the final stage in a selection or promotional competition.

- In order to be valid, the assessment center's simulations and competency assessment system need to reflect the leadership competencies that are critical within your own organization. My strong recommendation here is to not consider using an assessment center until your organization has first completed the type of competency identification process outlined in the previous chapter.

ISSUES IN THE DESIGN OF ASSESSMENT CENTERS

A major design issue involves managing clear communications about the purpose and objectives of this assessment method. Attending an assessment center can be a very anxiety-provoking and draining experience for an executive. Thus it is important when communicating the rationale for using a center that you highlight the in-depth development feedback that this method can furnish. In addition, consider designing into your program an informal and nonintimidating introduction piece that puts participants at ease with the process.

The success of an assessment center is directly tied to the job-relatedness of the simulations used by the center. A sales simulation that evaluates cold calls by phone is not valid if most of your cold calling occurs face-to-face. Before making use of off-the-shelf assessment simulations, conduct a walk-through of all in-basket and case materials to evaluate their relevance to your own organization.

As I have already warned, cost will be an important issue. If you plan to use an assessment center to evaluate a large group of candidates over a long period of time, you can use a "funnel" procedure to substantially reduce costs. If the assessment center offers six exercises conducted over three days, for example, consider running an initial batch of candidates through the full three-day program, then conduct a study correlating performance on each assessment simulation with follow-up performance on the job. Statistical analysis of this type is very tedious, but it will often show that only one or two assessment center exercises are highly correlated with on-the-job performance. The next step involves designing a streamlined version of your assessment center, based solely on the use of the most performance-discriminating exercises.

Another important variable involves the "face validity" that an assessment center has with your executive team. In other words, does the process look and feel like a valid assessment method to the senior executives who will be depending on the results of this process? In my experience, some executives are intimidated by the idea of relying on an assessment center to evaluate performance, for fear of losing control over the selection and promotional process. Here are some suggestions for countering these concerns:

- Engage your senior team in a review of alternative centers. Ask each consultant who is bidding for your business to give your senior team an outline of their assessment process, their history and expertise in assessment methodology, and a list of corporate clients.

- Ask vendors to discuss the types of training programs their raters attend as well as the "actors" who take part in role-play exercises.

- When you have narrowed the final selection, invite a few members of your executive team to accompany you on a site visit to see a representative center in action.

- Alternatively, ask competing vendors to allow one of your executives to attend their assessment center at no cost to your company.

ADAPTING ASSESSMENT CENTERS
TO THE NEEDS OF EXECUTIVES

Assessment centers have been applied to managerial groups ranging from candidates for first-line supervisory positions to senior executives. It is thus important to stop and consider how such centers must adapt to meet the unique needs and expectations of senior-level managers. Kay Lillig Cotter offers several suggestions for making assessment services more palatable to executives.

- I have very rarely seen senior managers go through a group assessment center, but instead find that they tend to favor individual assessments. An individual assessment allows the executive to go through the process at his or her convenience and without the scrutiny or challenge of performing with colleagues.

- It is important to prepare the executive. I've found that lower-level managers are more compliant and used to taking direction. Executives are used to being in control and don't like to do things that they don't understand.

- I think it's important to have material they can read beforehand. They should know with whom they are going to be working, what the process will involve, and how the information is going to be used by their company. At the start of the process they should meet the person who will be the primary assessor—in other words, the person most responsible for interpreting the results and providing them to the client company.

- As for preparation, they should be encouraged to get a good night's sleep and come in ready for a day of interesting work. They might want to think about their career interests, since they will likely be discussing their career in the interview.

- If the assessment is a positive experience for the executives, they will promote it, even if the experience provides critical feedback. However, if the executives feel that they are not being treated with respect or, in other words, feel jerked around by the process, no matter how accurate or helpful the results are, they are likely to respond negatively and won't support the use of the assessment process for others.

- It's important to provide executives with information in advance and preferably in writing as well as orally. Any written material provided to executives should be carefully proofed, presented professionally, and written succinctly. Most of them do not have a high tolerance for sloppy work.[14]

ASSESSMENT INTERVIEWS

The last assessment technique to review is the use of the targeted behavioral interview. The premise behind this interview technique is that one of the best ways to predict future performance is to ask a series of structured questions that trigger previous mastery of selected competencies. The design of the targeted behavioral interview process generally follows four steps: (1) identify key leadership competencies, (2) develop associated questions, (3) provide a scoring key for "levels of response," and (4) conduct interview training.

IDENTIFY KEY LEADERSHIP COMPETENCIES

As with the creation of the 360-degree profile or the assessment center simulation, the design of the assessment interview starts with the identification of key leadership competencies and the behavioral anchors that delineate each of these competencies.

DEVELOP ASSOCIATED QUESTIONS

The second step is to develop interview questions that can help you extract demonstrated performance within each competency. Frequently, interview questions are developed through in-depth *design interviews* with incumbent executives who demonstrate exemplary competencies. The design interview seeks to determine which job demands test the performance of a given competency and how outstanding performers differ from average performers in their approach to these job demands.

To better understand this, let's consider the competency "organizational influence"—the ability to capture the support of others in the pursuit of business objectives. An example of the type of question that might be used during the design interview is: "In what types of work situations is it absolutely essential for an executive in your function to be able to obtain the support of peers, senior managers, and team members?" A typical answer might be, "When the leader needs to introduce a new business initiative that requires the use of scarce resources, such as IT network support." From this line of questioning, the interviewer could develop the following targeted behavioral interview question: "Tell me about a time in which you had to introduce a new business initiative, one that required the use of scarce resources. Take me through the first series of steps you went through in driving this initiative."

PROVIDE A SCORING KEY FOR
"LEVELS OF RESPONSE"

It does no good to identify a set of interview questions without knowing how to analyze the responses you obtain from interviewees. Once again, information collected during the design interview can help you develop a range of responses, from "very effective" to "minimally effective." In the "organizational influence" example above, you could ask as a follow-up question in the design interview: "Can you think of an executive who performs extremely well in this situation—someone who always seems to be able to get approval for new business initiatives? What is it that this person does that sets him or her apart from people who don't perform well in this area?" The idea behind this question is that leadership competencies need to be applied differently, depending on the organizational context and culture. What constitutes a successful leadership approach in one company might be very different from what works in a totally different corporate cultural setting. Assume that in this case the interviewee's response is, "I know of two people who excel in this area. They are both great at sizing up key stakeholders, determining, for example, who needs to be brought into critical decision-making meetings, who needs to be copied on e-mail, and who needs to 'test run' ideas before they are brought up to the senior staff for review." Based on the design interview, the interviewer might put together the scoring key for this question shown in Figure 15. The intent of the scoring key is not to grade interviewees on their ability to parrot the representative responses shown in the key, but rather to provide a framework to help the interviewer interpret the effectiveness of different types of interview responses.

CONDUCT INTERVIEW TRAINING

The final design step involves training interviewees to effectively apply the interview questions and answer guides for each leadership competency. Interview training is essential, since for many applications of the targeted behavioral interview process, such as promotion and selection decisions, interview scores can be dramatically skewed by rater bias if such training has not been provided.

Question: "Tell me about a time in which you had to introduce a new business initiative, one that required the use of scarce resources. Take me through the first series of steps you went through in driving this initiative."

Response Level	Sample Response
Very Effective Response 5 Points	• The respondent demonstrated a detailed understanding of the role played by key stakeholders and influencers and formulated a very successful approach to gaining their support, demonstrating good planning and the most effective sequencing of actions. • Demonstrated a high level of insight in reflecting how previous actions could now be modified to be more successful. • Typical response: "Because we had just undergone a budget and personnel freeze, I knew that my request was going to be an uphill climb. The first thing I did was confer with the VP of Marketing, someone I regard as a senior mentor to me, and identify all of the senior managers who would be likely to weigh in on this decision. I also put together comparable options for reaching my objective, including outsourcing and vendor support, as a means of weighing out costs. I then approached each of the three key members of our senior management group and outlined my case, tying it to their own objectives and priorities. I also asked them to play devil's advocate to help me test out my plan. This approach took longer than I would have liked, but my request was accepted during a time in which no other staff increase was permitted."
Effective Response 3 Points	• The respondent understood the role of key stakeholders and influencers, but formulated only a moderately successful approach to gaining their support and influence. • Little insight in terms of how previous actions could have been changed to have been made more effective. • Typical response: "I knew before I ever approached our senior team for review that because my staff had a direct bearing on the success of our customer support function, I'd have to get the backing of the Senior VP of this function. I spent three different meetings laying out my requirements to this individual, and eventually she gave her support."

FIGURE 15 RESPONSE KEY FOR COMPETENCY:
ORGANIZATIONAL INFLUENCE

Response Level	Sample Response
Minimal Response 1 Point	• The respondent perceived success due only to own actions, and displayed only marginal awareness of the role that others played as change advocates and supporters in the change initiative. • Little understanding of key stakeholders necessary for project success. May rely heavily on manipulation or coercion to achieve goals. • Typical response: "At first I encountered a lot of resistance to the idea that I needed additional staff, but I just kept hammering on the issues until I got my way."

FIGURE 15 RESPONSE KEY FOR COMPETENCY: ORGANIZATIONAL INFLUENCE (CONT'D)

I recommend a training format in which interviewers are first introduced to the concept of behavioral interviewing, then become acquainted with the interview questions and scoring keys they will use. The final stage of training should involve interviewers evaluating videotapes of "interviewees," who are actors reading responses to preselected questions from prepared scripts. Interviewers can use this training approach as an opportunity to compare their assessment scores, and to examine the variability among their scores for selected questions. Having repeated access to interviews via videotape is a powerful method for gaining alignment on scoring profiles.

CASE IN POINT: TELLABS
Dan Stolle, Human Resources Director

To obtain a more in-depth evaluation of their executive talent and to gain senior staff alignment on candidates, Tellabs, a Chicago-based designer and manufacturer of telecommunications equipment, has made use of assessments provided by impartial, third-party consulting firms. Dan Stolle, Tellabs' Director of Human Resources, provides the following overview of his company's approach to executive assessment.

Because of the volatility of our market and the amount of rapid growth our company has encountered, it doesn't make sense for us to try to predict the "boxes" into which executives will be placed over the next few years. As an example, rapid growth could cause a single
..

job to grow into two or three different jobs, each having its own requirements. Instead, we try to determine the leadership role each person can play. We ask ourselves:

- Is this a person who could handle product responsibility, which would include both R&D and market planning?

- Is this someone we want to have in new-business development, focusing on the long-term strategic side of our business?

- Is this someone we could see leading one of our major organizational functions?

We use 360-degree feedback, psychological tests, and IQ/aptitude tests. Based on this assessment profile, an Individual Development Plan is created jointly by the executive, the executive's boss, and the industrial psychologist. A roundtable succession review is conducted, with each level of executives reviewing the level below them. During our succession review, the industrial psychologists give their assessment first, explaining how they view each executive's strengths and weaknesses. Then the individual's boss presents the individual's development plan and his or her own point of view. Participants in the roundtable also provide input and ideas based on their experience with the individual. The combination of 360-degree feedback, involvement by the executive in reviewing and processing the assessment, and the objective third-party view provided by an independent consultant who has nothing to gain or lose by the outcome provides a high level of integrity and credibility.

The competencies in the 360-degree assessment are determined by the CEO and the presidents of the company. The focus of the assessment and roundtable review session is on development of the executives and on gaining broader understanding of the individual's capabilities and determining the most beneficial assignments and positions for the person and the company. After the roundtable review session, the individual executive is provided feedback from the session by his or her boss, and may revise his or her development plan accordingly. Human resources maintains a copy of the development plans and works with the executives to assist in meeting their development needs. A summary of the roundtable session is also kept by the roundtable participants, for reference as they make decisions regarding staffing and assignments.[15]

SUMMARY OF KEY POINTS

- A well-designed executive assessment process can help you identify high-potential (HIPO) talent, assess your readiness to tackle new business initiatives, compare the relative abilities of internal versus external candidates, evaluate the overall capabilities of your leadership team, and provide diagnostic data for executive coaching.

- An effective assessment process should be valid; should replicate as closely as possible the job conditions under which selected competencies are used; should be as free as possible from subjective biases; should enable you to assess performance within current and anticipated work conditions; should be easy to administer and interpret; and finally, should be relatively cost-effective.

- The four types of assessment methods reviewed in the chapter are single-rater evaluations, multirater evaluations, assessment simulations, and assessment interviews.

- Single-rater evaluations are the most common evaluation method, and while easy to administer, suffer from rater bias and provide incomplete and limited information on ratees.

- Multirater (360-degree) evaluations provide a more equitable and comprehensive evaluation process, as well as enabling assessors to see how different stakeholder groups (peers, subordinates, managers, customers) view assessments.

- Assessment centers reveal how individuals might perform when confronted with the job demands emulated in a series of in-depth business simulations. While imposing a high cost and administrative burden on a company, assessment centers can provide targeted diagnostic information showing how internal and external candidates are likely to perform when faced with certain job challenges.

- New advances in assessment center technology have resulted in assessments that are more portable (can be brought on site), more versatile (can be customized to reflect unique work demands), and computer based to allow more complex simulations in a relatively short time period.

- To be adapted to the needs of senior-level executives, assessment simulations must be given on an individual basis, and must start with a thorough briefing including well-developed and polished materials.

- Assessment interviews consist of behaviorally based questions that capture how individuals have performed in the past against a variety of leadership competencies. Such interviews take time to develop but can provide a wealth of information regarding candidates' overall leadership abilities.

- The design of the targeted behavioral interview process generally follows four steps: (1) identify key leadership competencies, (2) develop associated questions, (3) provide a scoring key for "levels of response," and (4) conduct interview training.

CHAPTER 6

EVALUATING YOUR LEADERSHIP BENCH

I n the previous chapter you were introduced to several techniques for assessing the performance of individual executives. In this chapter you will learn how to compile individual assessments to perform an executive team evaluation (ETE). As Table 17 on the next page suggests, the ETE enables you to determine whether you have in place the leadership talent needed to meet current and emerging business requirements.

Without a coherent process for evaluating the strength of your leadership team, it is almost impossible to determine whether your organization is ready and able to move forward on critical business initiatives. In fact, some would argue that the assessment of leadership capability is a key factor in the survival of any senior manager, including the CEO. In a recent *Fortune* article, consultants Ram Charam and Geoffrey Colvin targeted this factor as representing an essential competency that differentiated the performance of successful and unsuccessful CEOs. As Charam and Colvin summarize it, "So how do CEOs blow it? More than any other way, by failing to put the right people in the right jobs—and the related failure to fix people problems in time. Specifically, failed CEOs are often unable to deal with a few key subordinates whose sustained poor performance deeply harms the company."[1] One way to avoid this tripping point is to systematically evaluate the performance of your overall leadership team, and to study the implications of such an evaluation on your ability to successfully carry out your objectives.

TABLE 17
EXECUTIVE TEAM EVALUATION MATCHES BUSINESS REQUIREMENTS TO EXECUTIVE CAPABILITIES

Business Requirements	Executive Capabilities
• Web-based development	• IT development
• Union avoidance	• HR competencies
• Global development	• International marketing
• Acquisition planning	• Strategic thinking
• Creation of customer-supplier partnerships	• Team leadership

If your company has never conducted an ETE, your senior managers might initially resist the idea of having other executives provide input on personnel actions that affect their direct reports. To overcome this resistance and obtain the stakeholder support you need to successfully launch the ETE, you will first need to assure your executive team that this process is objective and equitable, and generally provides more valid and complete data than can normally be obtained solely by an executive's manager.

A number of actions can help build stakeholder support for implementing an ETE. The first is to share with your team those research studies that confirm the prevalent use of the ETE as a best practice by such leading corporations as PepsiCo, GE, and IBM. To better understand emerging trends in the use of 360-degree profiling for executive development and assessment, you may find it helpful as a starting point to review two studies published by the Corporate Leadership Council, a Washington, D.C.-based for-profit organization providing best-practice research in the area of executive education in human resources:

360° Feedback—Lessons Learned (January 1998)

The Role of 360° Feedback in the Performance Appraisal Process (June 1995)

The second action you can take is to clearly communicate the advantages that can be obtained through the ETE, including

- Creating a uniform assessment process for evaluating the entire executive team

- Learning how direct reports are perceived by senior-level managers who work with them on a cross-functional basis

- Providing a check and balance on the different performance measures and standards used by different executives

- Identifying, from your executive talent pool, those individuals who constitute the best of the best, the high-potential executives (HIPOs)

- Ensuring that HIPOs are not hidden away in an isolated area of the company, but have broad exposure to the entire leadership team

- Creating a competency map of the overall leadership bench, and identifying problematic holes in that bench

- Developing a common language and assessment process that enables you to track the performance of leaders as they move across your company

- Surfacing the most important development needs for the entire executive team and for selected subgroups within this team

Apart from these applications, it is important to let your senior team know that the ETE can help determine whether you have in place the leadership needed to meet current and anticipated business challenges. Among the issues an effective ETE can resolve are the following:

- *Competitive Advantage.* How does our leadership compare with that of our competitors? In what areas of leadership are we leading the pack? Where are we falling behind?

- *Competency Gaps.* What critical gaps are emerging between current leadership capabilities and our changing business requirements? Are there any widespread deficiencies within our leadership team? What does our ETE say about our ability to meet our strategic objectives? In what areas do we lack the necessary leadership muscle to aggressively move forward?

- *Depth and Scope.* Do we have a sufficient level of *redundancy* in our leadership skill base? Is our talent pool broad enough to ensure an adequate depth and breadth in required leadership competencies?

- *Risk Exposure.* What critical technical skills or leadership experiences are limited to a few executives? To what degree are these individuals considered to be at risk? If they were to leave our organization, how big of a hole would they leave in our bench?

- *Trend Performance.* Based upon comparative reviews with 360-degree profiles previously conducted for our organization, what is the emerging trend for our leadership competency base? In what areas do we appear to be gaining or losing strength over time? How does this trend line match up against the dominant logic for our industry; for example, within our industry what technical and leadership competencies are taking on greater importance?

A third step for garnering stakeholder support is to involve representative executives from across your company in a team that collectively selects and designs the ETE methodology. There are two commonly used approaches to conducting the ETE: (1) *consolidating data from 360-degree reports* (incorporating performance feedback from peers, work teams, and managers) on your entire executive population to create a composite snapshot of executives' competency strengths and development needs, and (2) the *executive team review* (ETR), in which each executive is evaluated by his or her own manager, and then the evaluations are reviewed (and in some cases modified) by the entire executive team. Each of these approaches is discussed below.

The primary use of 360-degree feedback is in individual development planning, not executive assessment or the selection of high-potential talent—although some companies (at individual managers' discretion) have used 360-degree feedback as one of the data sources that feed into performance appraisals.[2] The ETR is used not only to identify team development needs, but also to compare the relative performance potential of different executives and for reaching agreement on recommended personnel actions (promotion, transfer, termination) for selected executives.

APPROACH 1:
CREATING AN ETE FROM
360-DEGREE PROFILES

The 360-degree profile is the first of two ETE approaches that you will be introduced to in this chapter. In Chapter 5 you saw how 360-degree profiles can be used to pinpoint the strengths and development

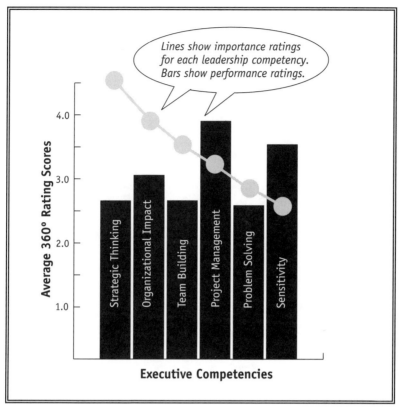

Lines show importance ratings for each leadership competency. Bars show performance ratings.

FIGURE 16   EXECUTIVE COMPETENCY PROFILE FOR
ALL CORPORATE DIRECTORS

needs of individual executives. When rolled up into a composite report, this information can also be used to generate a snapshot of your overall leadership team. Figure 16 shows a representative scoring profile for director-level executives in a hypothetical company. Note that the vertical scale of this figure shows the *weighted value* for each competency—that is, the relative *importance ratings* this organization has assigned to each leadership competency. The bars show executives' average *performance ratings* for their perceived ability on each competency. It is important to identify competencies for which there are significant gaps between these two measures. In Figure 16 we can see that one such gap occurs for the competency of strategic thinking, a skill area that is highly valued by directors and their managers (5.0), but on which directors scored relatively low (2.7) on

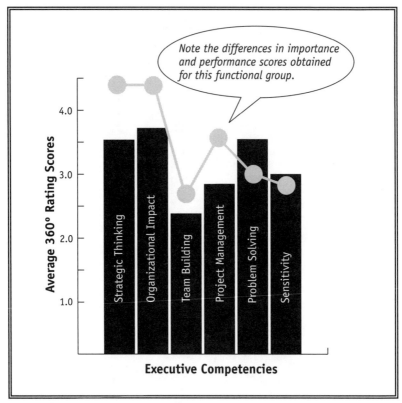

FIGURE 17 EXECUTIVE COMPETENCY PROFILE FOR
MARKETING DIRECTORS

ability. Figure 17 provides a separate scoring breakout for the company's marketing directors. Note that when compared with all corporate directors in Figure 16, marketing directors show a very different scoring profile, a finding that highlights this leadership group's
unique strengths and development needs.

From this type of 360-degree data analysis, it is possible to put
together an *executive competency summary* that highlights the
respective strengths and weaknesses for each executive subgroup. A
portion of a representative executive competency summary is presented in Figure 18 on pages 145 through 147. It summarizes the
executive team's strengths and weaknesses as well as the implications
of these scores for the company's ability to meet its strategic business
objectives. (Note: The figure's average rating scores are the combined
ratings received from each executive's peers, manager, and work
team; self-report scores are not included.)

Part A: Design Overview

Early this year, a 360-degree feedback survey was completed for 239 of 254 director-level personnel within our company. The survey encompassed 85 directors located at our corporate office, 128 directors at our six field offices, and 26 directors in our European offices in London and Madrid. Fifteen directors were unavailable at the time the survey was generated.

The 360-degree evaluation was based on having participants rated on fifty key leadership behaviors associated with performance on ten leadership competencies. Participants were rated by their managers, co-workers (internal customers and support groups) and team members on a five-point scale (5 = completely agree, 1 = completely disagree). Participants' self-report scores were gathered for the purpose of supporting individual development plans but were not included in this study. The reliability of this reporting data was increased by having all participants and respondents attend a half-day orientation session, which explained scoring protocol, guidelines for scoring, and how to avoid common scoring bias errors. All reporting scores were averaged to provide one set of averaged scores for each participant. Participants' average scores were then averaged together to provide reports for each of the nine locations, as well as an overall scoring profile for the entire director group.

Part B: Overall Results

Company directors display moderate strengths in the competencies of project management (4.0) and sensitivity (3.8), with a minor deficiency in the area of organizational impact (3.2). Significant weaknesses were found in the competencies of strategic thinking (2.7), team building (2.7), and problem solving (2.6).

Given the fact that as a company we pride ourselves on our customer service skills and our construction engineering expertise, it should come as no surprise that our directors display moderate strengths in the areas of project management and customer support. While these rating scores are not as high as we might hope, they are not low enough to warrant a high level of development investment activity.

Of greater importance is the relatively low group score for the competency of organizational impact. Weak performance in this area could hamper our ability to grow strong cross-functional leadership in our organization, an important factor given our aggressive growth plans for next year and the increased organizational complexity we face as we continue our corporate-wide reorganization.

The most important finding that can be taken away from this study is the relatively low scores shown for all directors in the competencies of strategic thinking, team building, and problem solving. Of these areas, problem

FIGURE 18 EXECUTIVE COMPETENCY SUMMARY: COMPANY DIRECTORS

solving can be most easily isolated and addressed through targeted training and development assignments. Given the relatively low priority score assigned to this competency, we can position this development need as significant but not critical. By contrast, strategic thinking and team building show wide gaps between their high organizational value and executive performance. The low scores found for team building are aligned with those found for organizational impact, as the behaviors required of these two sets of competencies are strongly associated. The impact of this skill deficiency is likely to show up in several performance areas, including our ability to aggressively grow our cross-functional process improvement network and to create sustainable customer-supplier partnerships.

The most detrimental deficiency found for our directors is within the area of strategic thinking. The low rating scores found for this area suggest that our company directors may find it difficult to step up to the expanded job roles being cast for them under the current reorganization plan. Two other points need to be made here.

1. This deficiency is most strongly noted by directors' managers (senior directors and vice presidents), who report an average rating score of only 2.2 for their director-level reports. This finding is critical, given that our senior directors and vice presidents constitute a relatively large percentage (30 percent) of external replacements, many of whom were chosen specifically for their strategic thinking capabilities.

2. Research has shown that the competency of strategic thinking is one of the most difficult to develop and often involves a protracted development period. The challenge our organization faces is being able to quickly build our bench strength in this area to meet our aggressive marketing and product development goals for the next three years. This will require a significant development effort (recommendations are outlined in Appendix A of this Summary Report), and places us on alert to the fact that over the next twelve months we may need to "seed" the director level with additional external placements who have demonstrated strengths in the area of strategic thinking.

Part C: Scoring Profiles by Subgroup

Some of the scoring patterns that appear to be unique to our nine separate locations are as follows:

- Our two international offices both assign a much higher value to the competencies of team building (Madrid: 4.5, London: 4.2) and sensitivity (Madrid: 4.0, London: 4.5). Interview follow-ups suggest that directors and their managers view these competencies not only as critical to success within our international market, but also as important "career derailers" for those executives who exhibit serious deficiencies in these areas. Accordingly, scoring profiles for our two field offices show almost a full

FIGURE 18 EXECUTIVE COMPETENCY SUMMARY: COMPANY DIRECTORS (CONT'D)

---

point increase for each of these competencies when compared with directors overall. This is an important point to keep in mind when selecting candidates for international assignments.

- It is interesting to note that scores for organizational impact vary directly as a function of location, with the highest scores received for those directors located in our corporate office, and much lower scores received for directors in our field and international locations. Follow-up interviews conducted at these locations suggest that these score variations are indicative of the degree of influence directors are viewed as having in companywide decisions, and their participation and leadership level on key work projects. The data suggest that development of this competency will require specific training geared to this competency and also exploring ways to increase the participation level for field and international directors on key decision-making activities.

FIGURE 18 EXECUTIVE COMPETENCY SUMMARY: COMPANY DIRECTORS (CONT'D)

APPROACH 2: THE EXECUTIVE TALENT REVIEW

The second approach for accomplishing the ETE is the executive talent review (ETR), an annual evaluation of executive-level talent by the senior team. Because the ETR is often confused with the annual performance appraisal review, it is important to take a few moments to highlight the significant features that differentiate these two assessment tools.

One of the most important distinctions is that a performance appraisal is a *standards-based assessment*. Whether directed toward an executive, a manager, or a nonmanagerial professional, an appraisal should be based on clearly defined performance standards. If the appraisal includes the review of written objectives, the manager also has a responsibility to specify the success criteria by which those objectives will be evaluated. If we are truly comparing performance against set standards, there is no resulting "quota" for a given performance category. Thus, one executive might have a high number of team members who "exceed standards," while another might have a disproportionately high number of people who fall into the "below set standards" category. A good appraisal system will not arbitrarily "rack and stack" performers, regardless of their actual performance against standards. Such an appraisal system will not label a certain executive as "underperforming" simply because "someone has to fall into that category." A good appraisal system does not force-fit performers into a bell curve when the evidence suggests otherwise.

While the appraisal ratings for a single team of five to ten executive reports might fail to follow the ideal symmetry of a bell curve, the much larger numbers of participants included in a companywide ETR often mean that the performance rollups for all company executives are more likely to approximate such a curve. As Figure 19 illustrates, the ETR normally takes the form of a *two-tailed review*—that is, a review of those executives who fall in the upper and lower "tails" of the bell curve. This means both those high-performing executives who are ready for promotion or who have the potential to quickly advance and those poorly performing executives who need to be managed out of the company.

If a review of the resulting ETR evaluations suggests that this curve is radically skewed to one side, the answer is to consider the need for an adjustment of executive performance standards, while simultaneously determining whether the performance standards that are currently in place have been explicitly communicated to all executives. An organization that is attempting to upgrade its leadership capabilities by aggressively replacing its poorest leaders should achieve this goal by raising the performance bar in a way that supports the tougher, more competitive business conditions the company is encountering. The organization then has a responsibility to give its executives an opportunity to meet this tougher standard.

The alternative scenario—and one, unfortunately, I have too often witnessed—is for an impatient CEO to assume that performance standards have been traditionally set too low, and then arbitrarily select a specified number of executives (supposedly the poorest performers) for the chopping block.

While the bottom tail of the ETR needs to be standards based, the identification of the upper tail of this curve is both standards based and normative based. By this I mean that, given the limited number of slots normally available for executive promotions and the amount of time and cost that long-term assignments for high-potential talent entail, once we have compared people against standards, we then need to be able to compare people against people, as a means of selecting the best of the best. At the same time, many companies find it useful to conduct periodic industry benchmark reviews to determine where their "best" would rate against industrywide standards. The resulting information can help you determine how much you can reasonably rely on ETR data to formulate make-or-buy decisions regarding the promotion or hiring of executive talent.

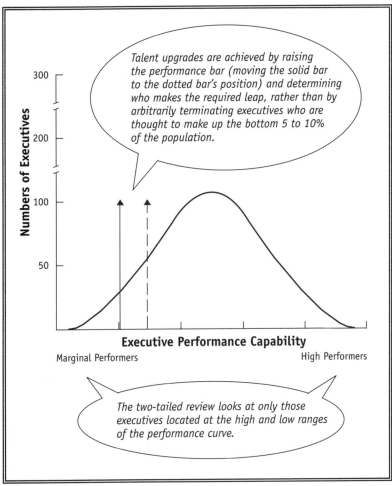

FIGURE 19 MANAGING THE TWO-TAILED ETR

ETRs focus on the executive's *performance capability* and *performance potential,* while appraisals are more results focused. Accordingly, the ETR may include discussions of recurring performance problems or noted career derailers (see Chapter 5) over the last several years that present serious obstacles to further career advancement. The ETR may also include developmental and work activities that, although not a central part of the individual's current job responsibilities, shed significant light on his or her performance potential.

The final difference between the ETR and the appraisal is one of ownership. Because performance appraisals evaluate performance on manager-assigned tasks, accountabilities, and objectives, these are largely controlled by an executive's manager. In contrast, ETRs are companywide assessments of executive talent that are designed to track the organization's overall leadership talent. For this reason, although ETRs are initially prepared by each executive's manager, they are "owned" by the entire organization and it is completely expected that during the ETR process other senior managers will provide performance feedback on reviewed executives.

In summary, when compared with the appraisal, the ETR is a much more comprehensive and far-reaching assessment tool, with recommendations that shape a company's overall leadership bench.

GETTING ALIGNMENT ON PURPOSE AND OUTCOMES

Before undertaking the ETR, senior managers and HR leaders must agree on its purpose, its intended outcomes, and guidelines for its implementation. Getting this alignment will go far in ensuring that participating senior managers gather the right kinds of background information on executives who will be included in the review. Clear alignment also helps avoid communication breakdowns regarding the role senior managers are being asked to play in team decision making and how the results of the ETR will be communicated to the company's top-level management and board of directors. Capturing alignment from senior stakeholders also encourages individual senior managers to endorse the team recommendations emanating from the ETR.

Getting the senior team and the HR department aligned on the implementation process for the executive team review means resolving the following three questions.

What is the scope of the review? In other words, how inclusive will it be? If the purpose is to reach alignment on identifying executives who are either high-potential or marginal performers, the senior team will generally be reviewing only the top and bottom 5 percent of the executive talent pool, or twenty executives out of population of two hundred. If we assume that this review is performed by the top two executive levels of the company, and that approximately thirty minutes is invested in each executive under review, then each review team can count on investing a full day in the review session. If the intended purpose of the review is to jointly evaluate all two hundred executives in the organization, then the time requirements will mushroom tenfold, and the resulting executive evaluations will tend to be shallow and cursory. At the other extreme, we could restrict the review to evaluating only those executives for whom some personnel action (promotion, transfer, termination, position upgrade) is planned over the next year, with the result that each executive level would be evaluating only a few executives.

Often the top-level management group of the company also participates in a secondary review of *all* executives and managers who have been identified as being high performers. Thus, a group of senior vice presidents who report directly to the president and the CEO might be responsible for evaluating their organization's vice presidents, while staging a secondary review of all HIPO executive candidates nominated at lower levels in the organization.

How often will the review be conducted? Generally, ETRs are annual events, but midyear, interim reviews may also be required when: (1) you want to gauge the performance of any new executives who have recently entered your company, or (2) your organization needs to quickly recalibrate executive capability in preparation for an impending organizational change, such as a merger or restructuring.

What is the optimal timing for the review? In other words when, during the calendar year, should the review be conducted with respect to other HR initiatives, such as a rollout of 360-degree profiles or the yearly performance reviews? My recommendation here is to coordinate the review to follow the annual appraisal process by thirty to sixty days. This accomplishes three things. First, it reduces the amount of administrative and logistical work required of your executives, since the commentary provided for the appraisal forms can (with some changes) be summarized for use in the ETR. It also forces congruence between the ratings generated on appraisals and ETRs, and enables the appraisal process to screen critical personnel recommendations proposed through the ETR. Finally, having your executive staff work through the appraisal process in advance of the ETR will usually increase the thoroughness of the analysis that goes into their ETR ratings.

IMPLEMENTING THE ETR

The ETR usually consists of four steps. First, each senior manager independently reviews the performance and potential of his or her direct reports. Executives who are lacking a manager (the manager has left the company and a replacement has not yet been hired) are usually jointly rated by the company's chief HR executive and the CEO. The CEO also rates the performance of his or her direct reports, including the head of the HR department. If the company's board of directors requires a rating of the CEO, the board itself may initiate this rating, or create it in dialogue with the company's chief HR executive.

Second, the reviews are audited for completeness and validity by the HR department.

Third, the senior management team conducts a joint review of its executive bench. Assessments that appear to be unsupported by demonstrated performance can be challenged during this review, and senior managers can make suggestions regarding proposed personnel actions for those executives under review.

And fourth, the head of HR incorporates the evaluations and the associated recommendations developed through the ETR into a summary report, which is personally reviewed with the company's top-level senior management team. A separate report, containing selected evaluations (usually of the company's top management level along with director-level HIPOs), is presented to the company's board of directors.

Figure 20 shows a representative rating form for use in the ETR that contains most of the elements that would normally be required for a review—including HR-related background data, ratings for individual leadership competencies, and the executive's overall rating for performance and potential (the Performance/Potential Matrix). Rating definitions for "performance" and "potential" differ greatly by organization. Definitions for these two categories are presented in Table 18 on page 154.

EVALUATING EXECUTIVE PERFORMANCE

Defining Performance. The "performance" category refers to *demonstrated* performance. A senior manager rating an executive who has been in the company for only two months will be hard-pressed to accurately rate this leader's performance or potential. The manager should skip the current review for that executive and seek an interim review after at least six months on the job.

An increasingly common tweak on this problem is the junior-level executive who eventually follows his or her boss into a new organization. In this situation, senior managers might argue that given their previous work relationship with the new hire, they have no difficulty in rating the individual's performance and potential. Nonetheless, the senior manager will be unable to substantiate the new hire's ability to master perhaps a totally different set of work demands. Of equal importance, other senior managers will have had no opportunity to weigh in on this assessment. As a result, the junior-level executive should be excluded from the current review and included in an interim review.

To be completed by HR department

Hire Date: _____   Department: _____

Time in Current Position: _____   Dept. Code: _____

Current Salary: _____   Languages: _____

College Degrees: _____

Please complete

Name: _____   Reviewer: _____

Title: _____   Date: _____

Leadership Competency Ratings

Competencies	Low	Medium	High
Strategic Thinking			
Customer Focus			
Problem Solving			
Team Building			
Organizational Impact			

Performance/Potential Matrix

Leadership Potential

Performance	Low	Medium	High
High			
Medium			
Low			

1. Describe demonstrated performance and related activities that support
   your ratings: [Provide ample room for response]

2. Describe this individual's readiness for promotion and alternative positions
   to which this individual could be promoted: [Provide ample room for response]

FIGURE 20 SAMPLE EXECUTIVE TALENT REVIEW

	Performance	Potential
TABLE 18		
DEFINITIONS FOR LEADERSHIP PERFORMANCE/POTENTIAL		
High	• Consistently exceeds standards	• Capable of advancing two to three levels in the next five years
	• Over-delivers on performance targets	• Extremely learning agile
	• Requires little or no direction	• Possesses broadest range of technical and leadership competencies
Medium	• Consistently exceeds or meets standards	• Capable of advancing one level within the next five years
	• Occasionally meets performance targets	• Moderate learning agility
	• Requires a moderate level of direction	• Possesses sufficient range of technical and leadership competencies
Low	• Consistently fails to meet standards	• Little liklihood of advancing
	• Seldom meets performance targets	• Low level of learning agility
	• Requires a high degree of direction	• Possesses narrow range of technical and leadership competencies

Defining High Potential. When compared with leadership performance, the factor of "leadership potential" is much more difficult to evaluate. There are several reasons for this. First, consider that, by definition, the category of "potential" requires us to project forward in time and predict an individual's untested capability to successfully tackle job challenges never before encountered, as he or she advances to increasingly complex leadership positions. Therefore, the evaluation of potential must be more than just as a straight-line extrapolation of current performance. It represents our best guess about how a person is likely to perform when faced with new and unknown tests of his or her leadership ability.

Another factor that impedes our ability to assess potential is something I refer to as the paradox of trying to "look over our own heads." Whenever we make high-potential determinations, we are attempting to identify people who are capable of advancing two or three levels—one or two levels higher than where we are now. This means that a senior director might be asked to identify, from a pool of director candidates, a few executives who are capable of advancing to the level of senior vice president. That is a tall order, even for the most astute individual. One way to offset this deficiency is to have second- and third-level managers provide input into the final identifications of high-performing executives.

THREE FACTORS FOR EVALUATING HIGH POTENTIAL

To counter these problems we have to have a well-defined methodology for evaluating executive potential. As Table 18 illustrated, there are three factors that we can use to evaluate executive potential.

Factor One: Learning Agility. The first of these factors is the degree of *learning agility* displayed by the candidate. A recent study by Michael Lombardo and Robert Eichinger, cofounders of Lominger Limited and former researchers with the Center for Creative Leadership, suggests that the ability to learn from experience plays an underlying role in an executive's ability to master new challenges and serves as a strong predictor of executive potential.[3] Simply put, people who are learning agile are able to more quickly and adeptly adjust to new work challenges. Lombardo and Eichinger suggest that learning agility can be divided into four components:

> *People agile:* Possessing self-knowledge, calmness under pressure, and the ability to seek and respond to feedback

> *Results agile:* Performing well and encouraging others to perform well under tough conditions

> *Mental agile:* Coping with complexity and ambiguity, and taking a creative approach to problems

> *Change agile:* Seeking new learning experiences, enjoying experimentation and trying new things.[4]

The concept of learning agility is supported by a rather extensive study performed by University of Southern California professor

Morgan McCall, involving 838 managers within six international corporations. McCall found that several of the eleven characteristics that distinguished high potentials from other performers—such as "seeks new opportunities to learn," "learns from mistakes," and "seeks and uses feedback"—were directly related to the concept of learning agility.[5]

So how do you go about measuring learning agility? Two useful tools are

- *Learning Agility*™: *The Learning II Architect*™ *Questionnaire.* A 67-item self-assessment and feedback survey developed by Lominger Limited, Inc., that evaluates learning agility on the five factors of mental agility, personal agility, source agility, change agility, and communication agility.

- *Learning Tactics Inventory.* A 32-item self-assessment inventory developed by the Center for Creative Leadership that looks at four discrete clusters of behaviors that denote learning preferences: action (learning by direct experience), thinking (learning through personal reflection), feeling (recognizing when one is anxious or uncertain about new challenges), and accessing others (looking to others for information and direction).

Factor Two: Scope of Competencies. While an evaluation of learning agility tells us a lot about an individual's general ability to grow and advance, it does not tell us whether that individual has the potential needed to advance within a particular career track. When assessing potential, the question we need be asking ourselves is, "Potential for what? Potential to eventually take over what types of responsibilities?" Are we suggesting that a high-potential candidate is some sort of protean superstar who is capable of advancing two or three levels up within *any* major company function, or do we have in mind a clearly defined position against which this potential will eventually be tested? To complicate the picture even further, keep in mind that our target is continually shifting. When we identify people as being "high potential" and capable of rapid advancement, we are making determinations about their ability to perform against nonexistent job challenges and in a future business environment that may well be radically different from what it is today.

A second test point for determining whether an individual is a "high potential" is whether he or she possesses a sufficient *scope of prerequisite leadership and technical competencies* to advance within a given function.

Factor Three: Time Required to Advance. It could be argued that given sufficient hand-holding and preparatory time, a large number of executives could eventually advance in grade. The problem is that in most cases we do not have infinite time for development. The question, therefore, becomes, "Given a moderate degree of developmental support, who will most likely be able to advance two or more levels within the next five years?"

As a case in point, I have over twenty years of experience with organization development, training, consulting, recruiting, and process improvement, and I currently hold the position of Vice President of Organizational Development and Learning. I have, however, little background and experience in the areas of compensation, safety, employee relations, employment law, and labor relations—all of which are critical prerequisite skills for managing an overall HR function. As the eventual successor to the role of senior vice president I would have to rate myself as "low potential." This is not a reflection on my performance ability (high) or degree of learning agility (high), but is instead an honest assessment that it would simply take me too long to absorb these prerequisite skills.

OPEN-ENDED QUESTIONS ON THE ETR

Referring back to the ETR rating form in Figure 20, the first of two open-ended questions asks senior managers to substantiate their ratings with performance documentation. This might include performance on key job responsibilities or annual objectives, or anecdotal information that substantiates the use of important leadership competencies. The second question on the rating form asks the executive's manager to comment on the ratee's readiness for promotion and the promotional challenges that the ratee is prepared to tackle. The reason for including this question is that a rating for "potential" is meaningless unless it is directly applied to a stated promotional challenge. Explicitly stating these challenges helps to ensure that ratings for potential are effectively translated into "readiness for promotion."

COACHING ASSISTANCE ON THE ETR

As senior managers complete the talent reviews for their direct reports, they usually require some degree of coaching assistance from the company's HR department. This is an important function that should be handled by senior-level HR staff with extensive experience in conducting the ETR process. The coaching process inevitably deals with the following kinds of issues:

- Confronting a senior executive who recommends immediate personnel action for a report, without providing adequate justification and documentation

- Advising a senior executive who is having difficulty making final decisions as to the ETR rating for a direct report

- Functioning as devil's advocate for a senior manager whose written ratings for a report contradict anecdotal feedback by other senior managers

- Advising a senior manager to postpone a review on a team member who is new to the company

- Helping a senior manager plan the timing and implementation strategy for recommended personnel actions

- Advising a senior manager about the "wordsmithing" of ETR rating forms

PLANNING AND CONDUCTING THE ETR MEETING

Once the coaching/advising process has been undertaken and all executive evaluation forms have been completed, it is time to set up the actual ETR meeting. The meeting should be restricted to the senior managers who will be performing the reviews, the head of the company's HR function, and (optional) a meeting facilitator—such as the company's director or vice president of organizational development—who ensures that team members adhere to the meeting guidelines. Meeting participants should free up the morning following the meeting in case the planned agenda flows over into the next day.

At the start of the meeting each participant should receive a binder containing ETR rating forms for all participants who will be reviewed. Typically the senior HR manager will compile a copy of this binder for the CEO. Each binder should be numbered and assigned to a specific senior manager, so that the ETR documentation can be carefully tracked. All copies of the rating forms should be returned to the senior HR manager.

Figure 21 shows a typical agenda for a one-day session. The ETR meeting usually begins by stating the purpose and objectives of the ETR and the desired outcomes for the meeting. After the introduction, the team reviews the meeting agenda and facilitation guidelines. Some of the most important guidelines to set for this meeting are as follows:

- The meeting is critical to the success of our organization. Give it your full involvement.

- Make a commitment to clear your agenda for the meeting. Avoid interruptions if at all possible. If a participant has to excuse him- or herself from the meeting, it is better to call for a five-minute minibreak and delay the discussion than to have a key member

8:30–9:00	Introduction by SVP, HR, and CEO
9:00–9:30	Review of Agenda and Session Guidelines
9:30–4:30	Departmental Reviews
9:30–10:15	Marketing and Sales
10:15–10:30	*Break*
10:30–11:30	Operations
11:30–12:00	International
12:00–1:00	Lunch
1:00–2:00	IT
2:00–2:30	Finance
2:30–3:00	Legal
3:00–3:15	*Break*
3:15–4:00	Customer Support
4:00–4:30	Human Resources
4:30–5:00	Evaluation Summary and Close (SVP, HR)

FIGURE 21 ETR MEETING AGENDA

of the team out of the discussion while recommendations or personnel actions are being discussed.

- Stay with the agenda. Unfortunately, the HR department is often the greatest violator of this guideline. Like a greedy senator who tries to attach all sorts of unrelated addenda to a pending bill, some HR directors try to bring unrelated HR issues into the discussion, such as the need to beef up executive recruiting. If you want the session to achieve its stated objectives, your facilitator may need to put a hold on such "kitchen sinking."

- Stick to an agreed-upon time limit. Prior to the meeting, presenters will be allocated a certain time period to complete their presentation based on the number of executives they will be reviewing. Participants should make every effort to stick to this agenda. One of the facilitator's jobs is to track meeting time and determine, by early afternoon, whether the meeting will need to flow over into a second day.

- Follow the agreed-upon presentation format. A consistent format makes it easier for participants to compare the performance of different executives and provides a much easier review piece for the organization's governing board.

- Let all presenters have their say. Departmental presenters should be allowed to complete their review of their entire team before questions and challenges are offered.

The next section of the meeting consists of having each senior manager make presentations on those executives within his or her respective function. Before jumping into this review, it is helpful to have each presenter give participants a brief summary of the emerging business requirements (see Chapter 3) and work challenges in his or her area. This provides useful context for understanding the organizational impact of proposed executive replacements, additions, and/or promotions. Next, the presenter should provide a summary of each executive being reviewed. The easiest way to do this is to have all ratings summaries loaded onto a laptop and LCD viewer for concurrent viewing by all participants. Another advantage of this technique is that any recommended changes to ratings, or added documentation, can be made directly in the computer, for real-time review by the team. Presenters should limit their discussion of each reviewed executive to the following:

- A brief overview of the executive's current work responsibilities

- The performance/potential ratings assigned to the executive

- A brief rationale regarding the justification for these ratings, referencing the two most important competency strengths and weaknesses noted for the executive on the rating form

- Any proposed personnel actions for the executive

- A summary of the executive's development plan

Following each presentation, questions and suggestions are solicited from the participants. This interaction constitutes the most sensitive part of the meeting facilitation, as different senior managers may well have very different views regarding the competency and potential of certain junior-level executives. In cases in which different team members become deadlocked in discussion, the facilitator can use one of four techniques to move the discussion back on track.

- Call a break and try to resolve the issue with the conflicting team members, or privately ask for their suggestions for resolving the dispute.

- Volunteer to take the discussion off-line with these members, with the head of HR or the CEO on call as final arbitrator.

- Invite other participants to weigh in with their input.

- Suggest that proposed rating evaluations or personnel actions be postponed for a few weeks while additional information is gathered by the HR department, and/or by those senior managers who may be involved in a sponsorship or mentoring role with the executive.

The HR department presenter is last on the agenda for two reasons. First, being the departmental archivist for the ETR information, and the occasional arbitrator of intrateam disputes, it is a professional courtesy for the chief HR manager to allow other team members to precede him or her. Second, the team facilitator is likely to be a member of the HR department and one of the individuals being reviewed. Placing the HR department last on the agenda allows that individual to be excused so that the team can evaluate selected HR executives in confidence.

In the last part of the meeting, the head of HR performs an evaluation summary and then closes the meeting. The purpose of the evaluation summary is fourfold.

1. It steers senior managers away from focusing only on their own department, and toward the big picture of how the team's recommended changes might affect the leadership bench. An example would be to point out probable disruptions to project schedules or new business initiatives as the result of planned large-scale replacements of executives.

2. It highlights any holes in the leadership bench and allows participants to determine its overall strengths and weaknesses. These findings can be matched against the companywide profile—such as the one shown earlier in this chapter (see page 143) for aggregated 360-degree data—compiled from the senior managers' potential/performance ratings.

3. It offers suggestions for any additional follow-up meetings or actions that might be required to close unresolved issues, or (should time run out) to complete any outstanding reviews.

4. Finally, it also constitutes a "check-in" process with the senior team to ensure that all participants are fully supportive of their joint recommendations.

INTERPRETING DATA FROM THE ETR

Figure 22 on the next page shows a performance/potential matrix that is frequently used to collate executive ratings from the ETR. The figure is an elaboration of the performance/potential matrices found

Executive Potential

High Potential
- Capable of advancing two to three levels
- Extremely learning agile
- Possesses broadest range of technical/leadership competencies

Moderate Potential
- Capable of advancing one level
- Moderate learning agility
- Possesses sufficient range of technical/leadership competencies

Low Potential
- Little likelihood of advancing
- Low level of learning agility
- Possesses narrow range of technical/leadership competencies

	Low Performance	Moderate Performance	High Performance
High Potential	Develop Competencies Overcome Derailers		Advanced Place on HIPO Track
Moderate Potential	Closely Monitor Performance Implement Turnaround Plan	Bedrock	
Low Potential	Manage Out		Maintain Momentum Reposition

Executive Performance

Low Performance
- Consistently fails to meet standards
- Seldom meets performance targets
- Requires a high degree of direction

Moderate Performance
- Consistently exceeds or meets standards
- Occasionally meets performance targets
- Requires moderate level of direction

High Performance
- Consistently exceeds standards
- Overdelivers on performance targets
- Requires little or no direction

FIGURE 22 EXECUTIVE PERFORMANCE/POTENTIAL MATRIX

162

in the ETR rating form. All executives who are placed within this matrix can be grouped into the following six categories.

Low Potential/Low Performance. These executives fall far short of the company's performance standards for leaders and have low potential for advancement. One would normally expect 5 to 10 percent of the executive population to fall into this category. These individuals need to be aggressively managed out of the organization.

High Potential/High Performance. These are the superstars of the executive bench. Again, only 5 to 10 percent of the executive population falls into this top-performing category. These leaders not only outperform their counterparts, but they have demonstrated leadership potential indicating that they could eventually advance successfully two or three levels within the company. Their managers need to outline options for their immediate advancement or development plans for extending their contribution potential to the company. In addition, it is also important to flag those HIPOs who are viewed as being "at risk" of defecting to a competitor (see Chapter 12 for suggestions on steps you can take to retain "at risk" executives).

Low Potential/High Performance. Executives in this category have usually reached a career plateau. They are performing very well, but they are deemed unable to advance further for one of the following reasons:

- They have great difficulty implementing the requisite competencies for advancement.
- They exhibit a career derailer that, while troublesome at the current level, would pose a great impediment to further advancement.
- They seem unable to keep up with the rapidly changing requirements of their job (organizational obsolescence).

The challenge here is to build into the job structure exciting and challenging work that will continue to engage the efforts of the individual.

High Potential/Low Performance. This rating usually accompanies one of two scenarios. It may be that the executive in question is new to the job and believed to have excellent long-term potential despite initial adjustment problems. Such a situation might justify the use of an interim review for confirmation. Or, the executive displays exceptional talent in many areas but is struggling with a career derailer or competency deficiency that is affecting performance. In this case, the executive's senior manager should include a development plan for addressing these problems along with the rating evaluation.

Moderate Potential/Low Performance. These executives are normally deemed to have serious performance problems, but also sufficient potential to be worthy of salvage. Ask their senior managers about the plans they have put in place to help such individuals turn around their performance. Concurrently, these executives need to be closely monitored over the next few months for any signs of continued performance degradation. Consider them to be good candidates for an interim review.

Moderate Potential/Moderate Performance. These individuals serve as the bedrock of the leadership team. Unfortunately, all too often the ETR meeting is so focused on the review of high-potential executives, or of those who need to be managed out, that this group is largely ignored. Keep in mind that frequently up to 80 percent of your entire executive team will fall into this category, and these individuals constitute a source of dependable, reliable performance. They may be individuals who, with some additional coaching or development assistance, could significantly raise their leadership contribution potential. Ask their managers about the development plans they have put in place to encourage the development of these executives.

The way in which an organization's executives are arrayed on the performance/potential matrix can tell us a lot about the degree of the leadership team's strengths and vulnerabilities. There are four princial areas of leadership vulnerability that I like to track.

1. The degree to which specific work functions are "underpowered" by the presence of poor performers. One way of assessing this area is to compare the Business Analysis prepared earlier by each department (Chapter 3) with its ETR and thereby identify business objectives and initiatives that are unlikely to be successful given the current leadership.

2. Holes or gaps in the company's succession plans, such as areas in which only two or fewer qualified successors are in place. By "qualified successors" I mean executives who could immediately step in, if required, to take over a function.

3. Competency gaps—that is, areas in which the entire leadership team is deficient in certain competencies that are deemed necessary to grow the business according to the strategic plan. An example would be a company that plans to reorganize to provide stronger, more targeted customer support, yet finds through the ETR that many executives are evaluated as deficient in the leadership competency of "customer focus." Another example is when critical technical competencies appear to be restricted to a few "irreplaceable" executives—leaders whose sudden departure would create large holes in the leadership bench.

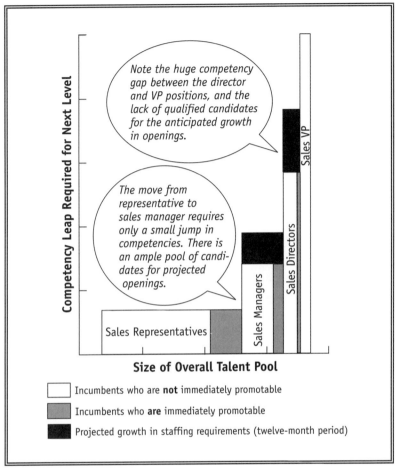

FIGURE 23 EVALUATING THE STRENGTH OF YOUR TALENT POOL

4. Stretch gaps, or large gaps that occur between the competencies found for a given leadership level and those required for success at the next promotional level. Stretch gaps sometimes occur when senior managers recognize that a given executive level has been underpowered, partially as the result of low entry requirements for the position. Raising the entry requirements for this position will often dramatically reduce the competency gap between that level and succeeding leadership levels. Stretch gaps can also occur when corporate restructurings eliminate management or executive levels that have historically served as bridge points—that is, positions that provide for the testing, training, and screening of junior-level executives who are in transition to senior management. Figure 23 illustrates some stretch gaps that

exist for three different leadership levels in a hypothetical sales department. For each level we can see the type of competency leap required to move to the next level, as well as the projected supply of and demand for executives who are qualified for advancement.

MANAGING CONTROL OF
ETR DOCUMENTATION

Given the sensitive nature of the evaluations and recommendations emanating from the ETR, the ETR data collection and collation for it are usually handled by a small, senior-level HR team. A "fire wall" is often created to separate these data from other information that is stored in the company's human resource information system (HRIS) database. Because the handling of ETR documentation involves a high level of confidentiality, all hard-copy materials should be maintained in a secured desk and office. Due to the sensitivity of these and associated personnel evaluations, the permanent hard copies and computer disks containing the ETR results are usually held exclusively by the head of the HR department and the CEO. The chief HR manager is also responsible for incorporating the ETR evaluations and the associated recommended personnel actions into a summary report that is personally reviewed with the company's top-level senior management team. The HR leader will also typically prepare a separate report for the company's board of directors that deals with evaluations of the company's top management levels (usually vice presidents and higher).

CASE IN POINT: FIRST UNION
Tom Westhall, President of Westhall & Associates

At First Union Company, the ability to identify and develop leadership talent is a key element of their long-term success. To address this critical need, Automation and Operations, the company's support group (which includes Information Technology, Branch Operations, General Services, and the Service Center Division), has developed an integrated process called "Building Human Capacity." Its goal is to ensure the availability of leadership talent to accomplish current business objectives, and to develop the leadership bench strength needed for key roles throughout the organization. Tom Westall, president of Westall & Associates, who helped develop the process while at First Union, explains that starting with a clear picture of the leadership competencies required, based on the organization's strategy, was a key to the design of this process.

Our first step was the development of the Leadership Competency Model, which defines the critical success factors and supporting behaviors of exemplary leadership. This established the foundation of our process.

To develop the competency leadership model, we started with a series of focus groups made up of our senior leadership team, key customers, line managers, and HR representatives. Each focus group was asked to identify the key challenges and opportunities the organization will face over the next three to five years. Based on this information, we asked our executives to identify what they see as the critical leadership competencies required to be successful in that environment. These lists were compiled, and when the groups met a second time they were given the composite list and asked to rank the items in proper order. Then the groups were asked to nominate individuals who were exemplary performers in these competencies. After this list was compiled, each group completed a one- to two-hour behavioral event interview. The data were recorded and transcribed and returned for analysis (over 1,800 pages of data). This information was then coded and painstakingly analyzed to identify the success factors and supporting behaviors of exemplary leaders. This profile then became the Leadership Competency Model.

The competency model establishes the foundation of the Building Human Capacity process. It includes three primary steps: (1) an inventory of leadership talent, (2) a readiness assessment of potential and promotability, and (3) development planning/coaching. The first step comprises two elements: the employee background information summary and the 360-degree leadership assessment. The summary updates each individual's experience, accomplishments and results, and career goals. The assessment provides feedback to participants based on the leadership competency model.

The first year the 360-degree results were used only for developmental purposes. The second year this feedback served as input for succession planning, the second step in the Building Human Capacity process. Each division's inventory of leadership talent (Step 1) was reviewed using the 360-degree results, key developmental experiences, significant accomplishments, performance, and other leadership factors.

Then the division heads met as a leadership team to review the individuals designated as "high readiness" (Step 2) and match them against the competency requirements of key organizational roles. We defined *high readiness* in terms of being part of the leadership pool, rather than being designated for a specific position. Consensus was reached and a development strategy was created for each key individual.

The third step, development planning/coaching, involves feedback sessions for all participants based on their leadership inventory results. In these sessions we provided tools to analyze the data, relate them to their business results, create development strategies, and involve their managers in development coaching sessions.

This overall process for Building Human Capacity is completed annually by the organization's senior leadership team. Once the annual process is completed, the senior leadership team conducts quarterly progress reviews. These monitor the key results measures targeted: number of candidates designated as "high readiness," progress on development plans, turnover of "high-readiness" candidates, number of internal promotions to key positions, and improvement of individual and cumulative results on the 360-degree assessment.

Senior leadership commitment and sponsorship for this process is the key, Westall explains. "Leaders who understand that human capital is the organization's chief competitive advantage and are committed to leveraging that advantage will be the winners long-term."[6]

SUMMARY OF KEY POINTS

- An executive team evaluation (ETE) is a methodology for determining whether an organization has in place the leadership needed to meet current and emerging business challenges.

- An ETE includes a uniform assessment process for evaluating the entire executive team, a check and balance on the different performance measures and standards used by different executives, a method for identifying high-potential candidates for succession planning, a competency map of the overall leadership bench, and a means of identifying problematic holes in that bench.

- An effective ETE helps you determine where your company has or lacks competitive advantage, any critical gaps between current leadership capabilities and changing business requirements, the depth and scope of your leadership team, your company's risk exposure to the loss of key executives, and significant trends related to the performance of your executive bench.

- One way of conducting an ETE involves consolidating data from 360-degree reports to create a composite snapshot of executives' competency strengths and development needs.

- A second approach, the executive team review (ETR), involves having each executive evaluated by his or her own manager, and then having all or some of these evaluations reviewed by the entire executive team.

- An ETR normally takes the form of a two-tailed review—that is, a review of those executives who fall in the upper and lower "tails" of a bell curve. This includes both high-performing executives who are ready for promotion or who have the potential to quickly advance and poorly performing executives who need to be managed out of the company.

- It is important to gain senior team alignment on three aspects of ETR implementation: the scope of the review (or the degree to which it will encompass different organizational levels), how frequently the review will be conducted, and the optimal timing for the review.

- The ETR usually consists of four steps: (1) Senior managers independently review the performance/potential of their direct reports. (2) The reviews are audited for completeness and validity by the HR department. (3) The senior management team conducts a joint review of its executive bench. (4) A summary report summarizing the strengths and development needs of the entire leadership bench is prepared and reviewed with the company's top-level senior management team.

- The evaluation of an individual's "potential" is more than just a straight-line extrapolation of current performance; it represents our best guess about how a person is likely to perform when faced with new, unknown tests of his or her leadership ability.

- Attendance at an ETR meeting should be restricted to the senior managers whose direct reports or lower-level high potentials will be included in the review, the head of the company's HR function, and (optional) a meeting facilitator, such as the company's director or vice president of organization development, who ensures that team members adhere to the meeting guidelines.

- A performance/potential matrix is a graphic method for representing the performance of each executive along the separate dimensions of performance and potential.

- It is important to track four factors related to leadership vulnerability: (1) the degree to which specific work functions are "underpowered" by the presence of poor performers, (2) any holes or gaps in the company's succession plans, (3) any competency gaps found for the entire leadership team, and (4) any "stretch gaps," or large gaps that occur between the competencies found for a given leadership level and those required for success at the next promotional level.

CHAPTER 7

MANAGING EXECUTIVE TRANSITIONS

I n the previous two chapters we learned how to assess the performance of individual executives and to consolidate these assessments into an evaluation of your overall executive team. It would be easy to assume that the conclusions generated by this evaluation process are self-activating and somehow effortlessly transform themselves into action.

The visual image that comes to mind is that of a fairy tale: The company's guiding leadership team members meet together for the annual talent review to outline their individual recommendations for changes in the executive bench. These recommendations are so detailed and carefully constructed that they quickly result in a smoothly implemented and angst-free changeover in executive personnel. The closing words in our imagined scenario might as well be "they lived happily ever after." In the real-life version of this tale, as I am sure you know, executive transitions are much more likely to be incompletely designed, poorly communicated, and sloppily executed.

WHO NEEDS A PLAN?

Senior managers and HR leaders alike tend to assume that if they devote sufficient attention to executive assessment and selection, then the execution of executive transition—the process by which executives are moved up, down, in, and out of the organization—will virtually take care of itself. In truth, there are several factors that make executive transition a fairly convoluted and messy experience, one that cries out for judicious planning and execution.

Keep in mind that executive transitions usually carry with them a host of subtle complexities. This is especially true for wholesale changeovers in an organization's executive teams. Such variables as delays in filling open positions and maintaining the continuity of workflow during changeovers need to be considered during the transition planning process. A thorough executive transition plan enables a senior team to manage these factors by orchestrating the many logistical details that make up the executive transition process, and forces the team to apply the same discipline to this process that it would to any other major business project.

What compounds this complexity is that executive changeovers are seldom self-contained but instead exert a strong ripple effect across the entire organization. Changes in a company's IT department, for example, can have a widespread impact on other departments that are heavily dependent on IT's day-to-day hardware support and help-desk functions. In a well-constructed transition plan, the senior team and the HR department form a composite picture of how anticipated personnel actions fit together. Good planning minimizes transitional disruptions by giving senior managers advance notice regarding the executive movements that are being planned for other departments, and how these changes may impact their own work functions.

The executive transition plan also allows the senior team more input on planned staffing changes. After listening to other team members, a company CIO who had planned to immediately replace a poorly performing director of network development may recognize that her company would be better served by postponing this move for another six months, until a current networking project has been completed. Or, the SVP of marketing may discover that other senior team members favor making substantive process improvements instead of replacing a current marketing service executive. In short, by developing a common game plan for change, organizational leaders are better able to pool their collective thinking and develop a change strategy that works in the best interests of their entire company.

When transition plans involve multiple changes to the executive bench, it is usually due to a major reorganization. In such a scenario, transition planning becomes far more than the planned movement of chess pieces on the corporate game board. It includes changes to work process flows, reporting levels, grade structures, and key functional accountabilities. Completing the process can be compared to the challenge of replacing some of the pilots and executive support staff for an airline while most of the planes are in midflight and your engineering (in this case "reengineering") team is simultaneously attempting to modify features of the planes' hull or equipment design.

The point of this analogy is that it is impossible to stop the clock and take a company off-line during times of executive changeovers. Because of this, managing the *timing, pacing,* and *political aftermath* of executive moves requires a high degree of sensitivity to a company's underlying needs. While an executive transition plan cannot guarantee this insight, it can build in the necessary checks and balances to ensure that executive moves are implemented with the big picture in mind.

MANAGING THE PEOPLE SIDE OF TRANSITIONS

So far we have discussed some of the more task-focused elements of the transition process, but the fact is that executive transitions also hold a high symbolic value for the members of an organization. Associates watch executive changeovers with the same wary attention a Kansas farmer gives to a wind funnel forming overhead in the sky. They tend to read into even the smallest of staffing changes strange portents and symbols of impending doom.

Given the high level of apprehension and anxiety that often accompanies movement in the executive ranks, it is important to carefully think through the communication and timing of such moves. A good transition plan does more than help us analyze the logistics of organizational transitions; it encourages us to think about the underlying meaning such changes are bound to convey to others in our organization, and how we can go about shaping the context and subtext of these messages.

At the deepest personal level there is the matter of the affected executives themselves. Executives who are being managed out need particular care and handling. Apart from the obvious liability issues that stem from the improper handling of employee terminations, the risk of damaging an individual's self-esteem during a clumsily handled termination is high. An inevitable by-product of such treatment is that once the word gets out that an employee was treated callously in the termination process, trust and respect among the ranks for the leaders in charge quickly evaporate. While this is problematic for any poorly handled employee termination, it can be especially devastating when dealing with terminated executives, given the high degree of visibility they have both inside and outside the organization.

There is an irony at work here, that while we become sensitized to the concerns of employees who are about to be managed out, we fail to attend to the anxieties and concerns of those executive "survivors" who are also deeply affected by executive changes. These include both newly promoted leaders who are trying to adapt to previously untested job demands and "outsiders" who are valiantly trying to grab the reins of ongoing projects and establish leadership within new (and occasionally hostile) work teams.

Still another leadership group we need to consider are those executives and managers who may be bitter and apprehensive about having been passed over during the transition process. It does not make good business sense to invest a significant amount of time and energy in bringing exceptional performers on board if, at the same time, a poorly managed transition process causes equally good performers to disappear out the back door. Accordingly, a transition plan should include actions that will be taken over the next twelve months to retain the commitment of high-performing at-risk executives.

PREPARING THE EXECUTIVE TRANSITION PLAN AND TIMELINE

While no executive transition plan can ever be detailed enough to address the concerns of all affected parties, a good plan can help us anticipate and address the primary concerns of those individuals and work groups who are most likely to experience a high degree of anxiety, anger, or disorientation as the result of planned transitions. Let's step back now and look at how to prepare an executive transition plan. We will then look at the elements that make up a good transition plan. Finally, we will review some useful guidelines and caveats for managing the implementation of these plans.

STEP 1: PREPARE THE INITIAL DRAFT

The initial draft of the executive transition plan is usually prepared by a chief HR executive. It is based on information obtained from the company's annual executive evaluation and refined through feedback obtained from the senior team during, and subsequent to, the corporation's annual talent review. A common scenario is for the author of the transition plan to pass the rough draft on to other members of the senior team for their individual feedback. As was true for the written executive assessments and the executive performance/potential matrix that were introduced in the last two chapters, the transition plan should be regarded as a highly proprietary document and should be treated accordingly.

STEP 2: TROUBLESHOOT THE PLAN

Once the chief HR executive has obtained the senior team's feedback, he or she must assume the role of troubleshooter and devil's advocate and review with individual senior managers any elements of the plan that require improvement—such as discrepant or inaccurate information, poorly constructed milestone schedules, or significant plan components that are either missing or underdeveloped. The "talking boxes" shown in Figure 24 on page 176 show the types of feedback the chief HR executive might share with members of the senior team. The transition plan at this point will probably contain all relevant information, except for any planned changes involving personnel actions pertaining to senior team members themselves. The final version of the transition plan that contains this information is usually prepared in tandem by the company's chief HR executive and CEO, then retained for board review and for use as a planning document.

STEP 3: CONDUCT A TEAM REVIEW

Following the consolidation of feedback from senior executives, the chief HR executive will ask the senior team to evaluate the feasibility of the refined plan and make any final revisions to it. As part of the review process, the senior team will discuss the business implications of the transition plan, such as identifying projects that will have to be delayed or reassigned pending the hiring of new leaders, or making sufficient allocations in the next budget cycle to support the planned hiring and termination of executives (search costs, relocation costs, stock option allowances, sign-on bonuses).

ELEMENTS OF THE TRANSITION PLAN

While each transition plan is somewhat unique, these will generally include the following four components: transition timetable, areas of impact, related HR initiatives and activities, and overview of the new structure.

TRANSITION TIMETABLE

The timetable is the heart of the transition plan, as it provides an orchestrating function for all major actions that will be taken as part of the executive transition process. Figure 24 provides a representative timetable that is divided into three components. The first component addresses the timing of planned changes to the executive team, the second shows changes to organizational structure, and the third indicates related HR initiatives. The "talking boxes" show some of the concerns that might be raised regarding this plan, including questions relating to the timing and recommended execution of selected activities. The advantage of using a graphic timetable is that

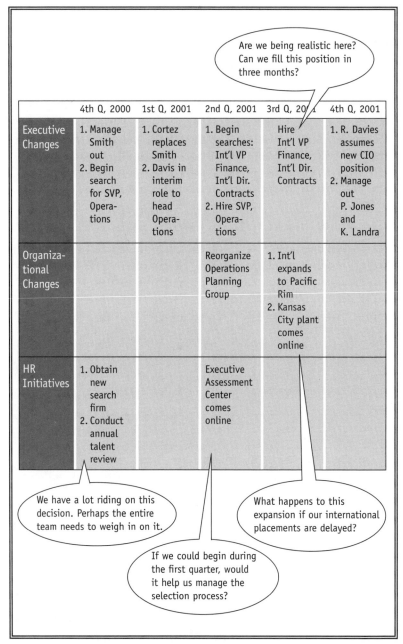

FIGURE 24 EXECUTIVE TRANSITION TIMETABLE 2001 (FIRST DRAFT)

as executive positions change against the backdrop of HR activities and organizational changes, the senior team can better understand the possible interactions between these variables.

AREAS OF IMPACT

This section provides an overview of those business areas that are likely to be affected during the executive transition process, as well as the actions that are being taken to minimize potential disruptions to business operations. The idea here is to ensure that changeovers occur as quickly as possible, with the goal of minimizing the time that teams spend stranded in the "dead zone" between the departure of one executive and the hiring of a replacement. A related task is to evaluate the probable impact of executive movements on key projects. For example, the senior team can appoint temporary "project stewards" to play an interim guiding role on key projects until incoming or newly promoted executives are fully integrated into their new positions.

Another impact area involves maintaining the quality of internal and external customer service during times of transition. In the transition timetable shown in Figure 24, one of the anticipated changes in executive leadership calls for the company's IT function to be pulled out of the finance department and established as a separate function reporting to a newly created CIO. If not correctly managed, the changeover in IT leadership could cause service disruptions such as delays in software development or hardware installation. In this situation, the chief HR executive or CEO might add to the transition plan a description of steps that will be taken to mitigate such problems.

One last component that is often included in this section is the plan for managing second- and third-tier position vacancies that will result from internal promotions to the top level of the executive team. Thus, the anticipated timing for filling a top-level executive position will determine the timetables and options for successive layers in a company.

RELATED HR INITIATIVES AND ACTIVITIES

This element of the transition plan calls for a summary of any significant HR initiatives and activities that will be occurring during the transition period that could influence the successful completion of executive changeovers. In Figure 24 you can see that the HR department is considering changing executive search firms during a period in which key searches will be well under way. The executive team may want to provide recommendations regarding the timing of this change and the selection criteria for choosing a new firm. The executive team may also want to discuss the feasibility of bringing the new assessment center online during the first quarter instead of the second, as a means of assisting in the selection process for new candidates.

Another way to look at this element is to ask ourselves whether we require any additional types of HR activities that are not currently encompassed in the transition plan. From Figure 24 we can see that this company intends to open a new plant during the third quarter, yet the plan shows no activities related to executive hiring for this facility, nor for the on-boarding and orientation of the plant's new leadership team.

OVERVIEW OF THE NEW STRUCTURE

This element normally involves the preparation of a pretransition and a posttransition organizational chart. The charts should be formatted to provide a clear delineation between new positions and replacements. In cases where executive changeovers occur as part of a larger restructuring effort, an entire work function may be isolated for review. Figure 25 shows a representative posttransition organization chart for a hypothetical finance department. In this example, the transition plan might include the following information:

- A short paragraph summarizing the rationale for the creation of the International Finance section
- An estimated timeline for filling the open VP of Accounting position
- A brief summary highlighting the background and qualifications of the new VP of Information Technology and Director of Software Development

HOW TO EASE THE TRANSITION PROCESS

Even the best-laid transition plan can go awry if it is not properly executed. Here are suggestions for increasing the success of the executive transition process.

GAUGE ORGANIZATIONAL TRAUMA

Every change creates some degree of discomfort. As the old saying goes, "the only one who likes change is a wet baby." It is important to attempt to gauge the degree of organizational trauma that will result from the planned changes to the executive bench—from the top

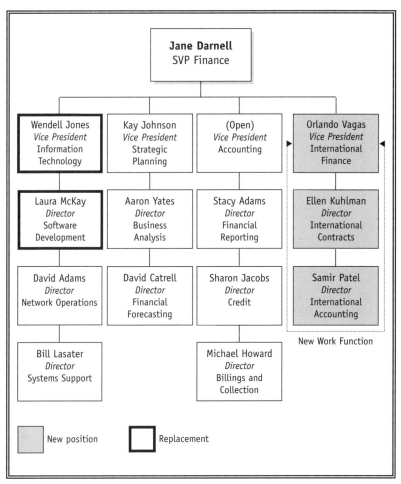

**FIGURE 25 POSTTRANSITION ORGANIZATION CHART
FOR FINANCE DEPARTMENT**

level to successive subordinate levels—and concurrent changes to key work processes and organizational structure. Each senior manager should evaluate planned executive transitions in the larger context of the organizational changes his or her function is likely to encounter over the next year and what impact these changes will have on major business initiatives.

The idea of gauging organizational trauma is based on the assumption that every organization has a certain "saturation point" for change, beyond which its adaptive capacity begins to erode. As

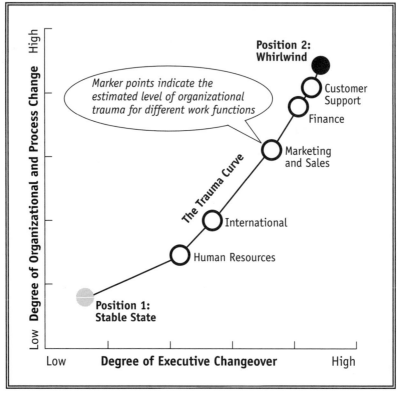

FIGURE 26 ESTIMATING THE DEGREE OF ANTICIPATED
ORGANIZATIONAL TRAUMA

Figure 26 illustrates, every work function can be placed somewhere on a curve with respect to the degree of organizational trauma it anticipates over the next year. Functions may range from operating within a "stable state" to those that are caught up in the high-change "whirlwind." By gauging this change threshold and knowing when your work functions are about to exceed their change capacity and go into overload, you can take steps to minimize this trauma. These adaptive steps might include the following:

- Conducting open forums with groups of employees to explain the rationale for proposed organizational changes

- Initiating a task force composed of associates within your work function, your company's organization development manager, and internal customers to develop recommendations for better managing planned organizational changes

- Looking for ways to alter the timing or sequencing of planned changes to ease the stress level of your work group
- Scaling back ambitious business objectives to take into consideration likely work disruptions or the orientation period for new executives
- Developing a thorough on-boarding process to ease the transition for incoming executives (described below)

Tom Saporito, senior VP with RHR International, a Chicago-based management consulting firm, emphasizes the importance of timing executive moves so that the organization is prepared for change.

> The movement of senior managers must sometimes be supported with organizational redesign. Inevitably it will require some tinkering and aligning, so that the evolution of business strategy, organizational strategy, and succession plan come together. It's not just about taking the right person, it's also about building the right team, so that when the person is selected the team has continuity and functions effectively.

> An example involves a client we are now working with, in which the CEO has agreed to leave one year from now. The company wants to name its successor in October and have the new CEO installed in February of next year. To make this work, there are several key questions that need to be addressed. Will any internal people be ready by February, and will this time frame be sufficient for the organization to prepare for the degree of change involved? Also, because the incumbent CEO has a fairly dominant leadership style, and because of what has been an involved strategy into new lines of business in other parts of the world, the top team is not near to being a solid team. So the risk of handing the ball over to a new CEO without a team ready for continuity of support, combined with the dominating leadership style that the team's been used to, could create major problems. It's not about picking Charlie or Joe, it's about orchestrating the entire organization to be ready so that when a senior-level move occurs there can be a smooth transition.[1]

CONTAIN POLITICAL FALLOUT

As we have reviewed, the executive transition process is more than just a series of analytical chess moves. The successful execution of this process is largely dependent on accurately determining the extent of political fallout that you will inevitably encounter as you undertake changes to the executive team, and then planning accordingly. To better understand this point, ask yourself the following questions:

- Are your senior team and CEO fully aware of, aligned with, and supportive of planned changes to the executive team? Have they all had opportunities to weigh in on the details of your transition plan?

- Are you planning to manage out key executives who have close ties to your organization or governing board? If so, have you given some thought as to how and when you intend to communicate the rationale for these changes to these respective stakeholder groups?

- Are there any executive moves—terminations, promotions, or transfers—that are likely to be viewed by organizational associates as unfair or arbitrary? Have you considered the steps you will need to take to address these concerns?

- Have you developed a communication plan for alerting key customers to planned changes that could affect their operations?

- What message are you sending about your organizational culture by the way you are handling your executive moves? If these changes are handled with at least a minimal amount of sensitivity and compassion, you are sending the message that your company tries to do the right thing by its employees, even in the case of terminating poor performers. If terminated executives are treated in a callous manner, or incoming leaders are thrown into their new work functions with little preparation or guidance, you send a very different message about how employees are valued by your organization.

- If you are planning to move leaders into or out of your organization who have a high level of visibility by the outside investment community, have you given careful consideration as to how you are going to position these moves to the press?

These are only a few of the questions that address the political fallout that can ensue from changes to your executive bench. To undertake a more dedicated review of such issues I recommend that you spend part of your executive transition planning session identifying and addressing these types of questions, using the above rough list as an initial primer.

EXPLORE "WHAT IF" CHANGE SCENARIOS

One of the functions of an executive transition plan is to uncover and critically challenge the assumptions on which you have developed your planning. In doing so, your goal should be to test alternative implementation options and to keep your transition plan as flexible as possible.

One common assumption involves the expected turnaround time for selecting and hiring new executives. For each leadership position that needs to be filled, you should be challenging your team with the following questions:

- What is your "Plan B" if we are not able to bring on board an acceptable candidate in the time frame indicated?

- If this position is not filled within the expected time frame, how flexible would you be regarding changing the hiring criteria? How about adapting the search parameters by taking such actions as making creative use of the Internet, or accelerating the interview process through the use of team interviews?

- What is your plan for maintaining project continuity if the search runs over by three to six additional months? Who within your company could assume an interim role?

- What is the worst-case scenario in terms of how such a delay could adversely affect the work performance of your function?

Pose a series of "what if" questions to your senior team concerning possible changes to the transition plan. Assume, for example, that your current transition plan calls for managing out and replacing six members of your executive team over the next eighteen months. You could ask yourself what adjustments would be required should your board ask for this transition to be accelerated and completed during the next calendar year. Given this situation,

- How much money would you need to budget for severance, hiring, and relocation?

- What changes would you need to make in your selection and hiring strategy to accomplish this goal?

- How would you shorten the on-boarding and orientation process for new executives?

- What would be the impact on the organizational trauma level for your associates?

MANAGING THE CHANGING OF THE GUARD

Occasionally a company may ask an exiting executive to stay on board for a period of time while a new leader is brought into position. Redundancy of this type is called for whenever the leadership move is due to changing business needs rather than performance problems on the part of the incumbent executive, and when the job to be mastered is extremely complex and demanding, requiring at least some initial guidance by the exiting executive.

Managing the changing of the guard is also an important component of facilitating executive transitions between groups of incoming and outgoing executives, such as during an organizational reengineering effort or merger. In directing these group transitions, exiting executives are sometimes promised a "stay bonus," which is made conditional upon their willingness to delay their departure and complete a minimum period of employment. A recent study conducted by Right Management Consultants showed that 44 percent of 829 surveyed companies used stay bonuses, with a 98 percent retention rate for executives who were willing to stay for the agreed-upon period of time.[2]

When an overlap period between the departure of incumbent executives and the on-boarding of new executives is expected, the senior managers of the affected group need to work closely with the company's HR department to create a well-articulated breakdown of responsibilities between the outgoing and incoming executives, specifically:

- The role each will play in providing input on upcoming performance appraisals, talent reviews, the setting of yearly business objectives, and the annual budget planning process
- Who the single point of contact will be for managing sensitive customer accounts during the transition period
- The time frame for rolling over responsibilities to the new executive
- Projects that will be completed or brought to closure by the outgoing executive
- Details of the shared reporting relationships both executives will assume with their common work team

- There are several factors that make transition planning—the process by which companies determine how to move executives in, out, and across their organizations—a difficult process that requires careful planning.

- These factors include the complexity of transitions, the fact that they exert a ripple effect across an organization, the impact that open positions have on the accomplishment of key objectives, and the challenge of maintaining a continuity of workflow during times of executive changeover.

- Effective transition planning provides senior executives with opportunities to weigh in on the feasibility of proposed staffing changes.

- Given the high level of apprehension and anxiety that often accompanies movement in the executive ranks, it is important to carefully think through the communication and timing of such moves. A transition encourages us to think about the messages such changes convey to others in our organization, and how we can shape the context and subtext of these messages.

- Creating a transition plan involves preparing the initial plan, troubleshooting the plan, and conducting a team review to assess the feasibility of the plan.

- Three steps you can take to ease the transition process are (1) gauge the degree of organizational trauma that is likely to be created as a result of planned changes to the executive team and look for ways to minimize this trauma, (2) contain the political fallout that may be associated with executive transitions, and (3) manage the "changing of the guard" as replacements move in to supplant incumbent executives.

CHAPTER 8

BUILDING EXECUTIVE COMPETENCIES

I have never yet walked into an organization where the top leadership is dead set against the idea of developing their executives and managers. Unfortunately, there are a number of reasons why these good intentions often fail to translate into substantive development efforts.

- *No Time.* It should make sense as we ascend the corporate ladder for organizations to invest more in the human assets they've taken such pains to acquire. The paradox, of course, is that because the executive team plays such a critical role, it is difficult to free up these individuals to attend the standard multiday classroom training programs.

- *Virtual Team Structure.* Time by itself is not the only obstacle. In many international companies the sheer dispersion of leaders around the globe limits the types of formal development opportunities in which they can participate.

- *Lack of Context.* Traditional executive development programs frequently take place within an academic "box" that is completely outside the context and setting of the executive's work environment. Increasingly, today's leaders are looking for learning options that integrate competency development with their actual job demands.

- *Resource Constraints.* Many companies are attempting to draw deeper into their organizations for future leadership talent, and to extend rich development opportunities down to lower-level

<table>
<tr><td colspan="2" align="center">TABLE 19</td></tr>
<tr><td colspan="2" align="center">BEST PRACTICES IN BUILDING EXECUTIVE COMPETENCIES</td></tr>
</table>

TABLE 19

BEST PRACTICES IN BUILDING EXECUTIVE COMPETENCIES

1. Use *action learning* to link developmental activities to real-life work challenges.

2. Use *job simulations* to accelerate learning.

3. Use *formal mentoring programs* to provide needed support and coaching.

4. Use *corporate and academic consortia* to leverage developmental resources.

5. Use *distributed learning and cybertools* to extend developmental opportunities.

managers. The result is that HR leaders and executive develop-ment experts are finding themselves under pressure to uncover creative ways to stretch development dollars over a much larger leadership pool.

To address these challenges, today's leaders are looking for train-ing options that offer flexibility in the learning process, as well as a seamless transfer of skills and knowledge from the learning setting to their work environments. In this chapter I introduce five learning methods and technologies that can help meet these needs. They are generally considered to be best practices in the area of executive development, and a variety of organizations have applied them to enhancing the effectiveness of their executive development efforts. These practices are summarized in Table 19.

BEST PRACTICE #1: ACTION LEARNING

One of the most effective vehicles for linking developmental assign-ments to work experience is *action learning*. In its simplest form, action learning can be viewed as the combined use of classroom and field activities. It extends learning beyond the formal training process by assigning projects to cross-functional work teams. Projects might require participants to research business problems and issues proposed by their CEO or senior-level managers, develop solutions, actually implement those solutions, and review their results with their senior management. Action learning teams have been created in a number of companies ranging from GE and Honeywell to Citibank and Anderson Consulting. Uses for action learning have ranged from improving delivery performance for customers (National Semiconductor), to analyzing market dynamics and opportunities and supporting sales strategies (Bristol-Myers Squibb), to helping a U.N. volunteer develop strategies for increasing public health awareness for residents of Atiu in the Cook Islands.[1]

According to Michael Marquardt, there are six essential components to the action learning process.

1. *The Chosen Problem for the Action Learning Process.* This should be a problem that is important to the organization and connected to the system of the organization. There are two kinds of action learning: *single-problem* and *multiproblem.* Single-problem action learning presents one problem for all participants to work on. The more traditional multiproblem action learning presents participants with multiple problems, and each person has time to discuss his or her particular problem. We make a distinction in action learning between a "puzzle," in which the answer is known but just isn't discovered yet, and a "problem," in which the solution is completely unknown. True action learning teams deal with problems, not puzzles.

2. *The Composition of the Group.* Action learning teams should consist of four to eight members. They should also be diverse, representing different parts of the organization and possibly vendors or customers. The important thing is to not just include "experts," but rather to encourage people to have fresh perspectives. It is possible to have people reporting to others on the team, if the leader is someone with whom others feel comfortable.

3. *The Process Itself.* In typical problem-solving groups, the focus is on quickly generating solutions to a problem. In action learning we encourage reflective inquiry—spending time up front asking questions about what you are trying to accomplish, and then reflecting on options. If the focus is on solving the problem, the organization will tend to crunch the time cycle; whereas, if it is on development, it will spread out the process so that executives can integrate learning with work.

4. *Commitment to Action.* Action learning groups must have power to take action. This distinguishes an action learning model from a task force or committee. It puts more energy on the team,

since team members know the organization will be taking action on their solutions. The "work out" process used by GE is a form of action learning, since [in GE's program] 99 percent of the time the manager immediately commits to implementing the solution or action proposed by the group.

5. *Commitment to Learning.* This means asking, "What have we learned? Why did this problem exist to begin with? What are our individual learning styles? What kinds of learners are we? How can what we've learned here be applied to other parts of the organization?" This is where you get a tremendous amount of team and individual development.

6. *The Need for the Group to Be Facilitated or Advised.* The facilitator may be external to the group or organization, or the role may be rotated among group members. The group may meet once for three hours or in two-hour segments over a period of weeks or months. The facilitator's primary focus is on learning. This is the person who will be asking questions to help people determine *what* they've learned, *how* they've learned, and how they can *apply these learnings* to other areas of their work lives.[2]

Marquardt concludes that some of the most common potholes that people encounter in using action learning include

- Attempting to put more emphasis on *action* than on *learning*

- Not having a facilitator who enables the action learning team to focus on the learning

- Our natural tendency to jump into solutions, as opposed to sitting back and asking questions and reflecting

- Being unwilling to trust that the group process will work, and that the solution the group will come up with is better than that which will be developed by any single person[3]

BEST PRACTICE #2: JOB SIMULATIONS

One of the most exciting trends in executive development has been the creation of realistic business simulations that effectively mimic the demands of an executive job. Simulations come in all forms and sizes, ranging from simple exercises that can be completed within an hour to detailed simulations that span several days of effort by an entire team.

For some people the term *business simulation* is synonymous with *business case,* although the two are very different. Perhaps the biggest difference is that a case is passive. It requires a learner to review, analyze, and develop recommendations for action based on a written summary of an actual or hypothetical company or business unit. A simulation is interactive. It requires the learner to make decisions based on a business issue or problem; then, regardless of whether the simulation is live or computerized, it provides the learner with consequences based on the results of those decisions. If the wrong cost evaluation is made, profits can go down. Failure to detect market trends can result in the loss of key customers. A decision to invest in production capital may temporarily reduce profits but expand sales revenues in the long run.

A second major distinction between business cases and simulations is that a business case is usually *a singular learning event,* while a simulation is an *iterative learning event.* No matter how complicated and detailed a business case may be, once the learner has reached the review cycle, the learning is essentially over. The exciting thing about a business simulation is that learners get feedback on their performance. Based on this feedback, they can reflect on those aspects of their performance that may be contributing to success or failure, and alter their leadership approach and business decisions accordingly. The iterative design is a very powerful learning experience for organizational leaders.

A third difference between business cases and simulations involves systems design. A business case allows only limited interaction among its elements, while a business simulation—particularly one with a computerized database—allows unlimited interaction among the various components. The decisions the learner makes with regard to market strategy, production costs, selection of service options or distribution channels, and cost are all interactive. A business simulation provides the learner with a realistic modeling of how the business and organizational elements of a company interact to produce sometimes unexpected effects. Thus, in a computerized simulation the decisions to expand into several new market areas and to implement a severe cost-cutting program may cancel each other out.

There are six significant advantages to the use of business simulations as an executive development tool.

1. *Provide Low-Risk Learning.* Business simulations lower the risk level that is normally associated with real-life trial and error. Roger Schank, director of Northwestern University's Institute for the Learning Systems and a pioneer researcher in the field of business simulations, suggests that a key ingredient for learning is the creation of an "expectation failure"—a situation that forces learners to reevaluate their assumptions when the results

of their efforts do not match up to their expectation and they experience a failure in their work situation.[4] The problem, as Schank defines it, is that in the real world *failure* is associated with loss, shame, and fear. The great thing about computer simulations is that "they enable users to fail in private."[5] Schank goes on to say that "failure should be a private experience in which a learner has the opportunity to reflect and think about other options not chosen."[6]

2. *Uncover Potential Failure Points.* Business simulations accelerate learning by intentionally directing learners to the most common failure points in a given business activity. Feedback by experienced executives that is built into the simulation design captures many of the toughest potholes that leaders are likely to encounter. These may be failure points not normally encountered until one has spent months or years on the job.

3. *Provide Anticipatory Training.* Business simulations allow participants to temporarily step into senior-level leadership roles that they have not yet mastered or to stretch financial, global management, and marketing skills that they have only marginally acquired. Simulations can help leaders plan adaptive strategies for unanticipated large-scale events, such as a sudden downturn in the economy or the aggressive intrusion of an unforeseen competitor.

4. *Support Team-Based Learning.* Simulations serve as an effective vehicle for team-based learning, by requiring team members to work together to overcome difficult challenges and providing opportunities for members to jointly reflect on the outcomes of their team decisions.

5. *Compress Decision Making.* The use of simulations saves time by allowing participants to compress the impact of business decisions that would usually unfold over the course of years and to see the long-range impact of business decisions. In a real-life scenario, the impact of a disastrous business decision might not be fully recognized for two or three years, long after the responsible individual has moved on to another company. Business simulations not only enable learners to obtain immediate feedback about the efficacy of long-term business decisions, but help them make the connections between cause and effect.

6. *Mimic Real-Life Complexities.* Computerized simulations permit the crunching of large amounts of financial and market data, with the option of getting real-time feedback that increases the complexity of simulations and lends a real-life texture.

One company that is taking a leading role in the design and delivery of computer-based business simulations is the Philadelphia-based Strategic Management Group (SMG). George Winnick, SMG's managing director, James Allen, director of SMG's Client Engagement Group, and Bridget Doyle, SMG's Best Practices consultant, provided the following overview of their company's approach to business simulations.

In describing how SMG designs its programs, Winnick explains that SMG "builds an abstraction of reality" by systematically determining

- The organization with which SMG is working
- The company's business environment
- Key levers that drive the business
- The role and impact (positive or negative) of each member of the senior team
- The relationship between key drivers and key leadership. Winnick cites as an example, "If an organization wants to drive cost out of the business, the key driver may be to standardize the business. However, if the sales organization is out meeting with customers and saying, 'We can customize the widgets,' and the organization isn't equipped to handle that—there is a major misalignment among the components of strategy."[7]

Doyle and Allen add that there are several factors that weigh into the design of a simulation, including the following:

- *Defining the problem* the organization wants to solve as well as the desired solution
- *Determining the context* in which the business problem or challenge takes place
- *Establishing the time frame* for the simulation
- *Establishing clear objectives* by identifying the key things the company is trying to achieve in its simulations
- *Identifying the variables* on which the client measures performance
- *Describing the roles* that participants need to assume within their simulation. Doyle explains that this can be "either a current organizational role or a role to which you aspire. An example might be that if the role is customer service, the simulation might place the individual in a junior sales position."[8]

A typical SMG simulation involves the following components.

1. Participants are given a preworkshop assignment in the form of a hard-copy review of a business case. This assignment provides context for the introduction of the business simulation.

2. The whole group participates in lecture and discussion for related training in areas such as strategic planning and customer focus, and receives an explanation of how the simulation will operate.

3. Participants are divided into teams. During the first breakout session, each team takes thirty minutes to develop its plans and build strategies. During the remaining two to two-and-a-half hours, the team reviews quantitative information on a hypothetical company and makes business decisions in the form of sales levels, sales prices, cost controls, growth objectives, manufacturing, and quality investment decisions.

4. Participants reconvene. Each team's decisions are transferred to a disk and analyzed on computer by the course's data administrator. Each team is given a detailed report showing the impact of its decisions. At the same time, team members may be given general information that indirectly alludes to the strategies and decisions that are being formulated by other teams.

5. This process of team review, team decision making, analysis, and feedback on results is continued over three to four sessions.

6. The teams jointly analyze their final business performance and engage in a debriefing session to identify the lessons learned that they can export to their organizations.

Minimum and maximum class size for an SMG simulation are ten and fifty, respectively. An important factor in determining the ratio of facilitators to students is that some simulations require extensive real-time data processing, necessitating the presence of both a facilitator and a data administrator in the class. The facilitator leads the class while the data administrator processes the simulation data, developing reports for participants. Other simulations are self-processing, in which students evaluate and interpret their own decisions. In such cases only one facilitator is required.

SMG offers three types of simulations: *enterprise* simulations, *best-practice* simulations, and *hybrid* simulations. In explaining the differences between these three models, Allen says, "Our best-practice simulations require participants to choose between a series of options, in the form of multiple-choice responses or ranking their preferences with a series of decisions, such as moving a slider on their PC to indicate the degree of time or staff they wish to invest on a problem. The results are comparative, in that you compare your results to those of other teams, but the teams don't interact among themselves." An example of a best-practice simulation is SMG's "The Complete Project Manager," in which participants assume the role of a project manager and direct a project from inception to completion. Doyle explains that "throughout this process you are managing your team, stakeholders, and clients and balancing the competing interests of all parties with regard to their impact on your project."[9]

Doyle also says that, "In an enterprise simulation participants are actually required to load numeric inputs into their decisions, so they are constructing the data rather than selecting from a choice of options. The numbers are crunched and you can see the impact of your decisions in the marketplace. In these simulations teams are competitive, with participants making financial decisions that will affect their company's performance in a simulated marketplace."[10]

An example of an enterprise simulation is SMG's "Olympus," which Winnick describes as "a simulation that is designed to teach participants how to implement a strategy and align others around a strategy, while managing in a changing environment. In the Olympus simulation, the model company is in a high-tech industry and operates in a cross-functional environment involving hardware, software, and system support. The simulation helps team members evaluate the factors of trust and teamwork in work success because any decision made by a team affects other teams. Another trust issue is that if, after committing to following a given decision path, a team decides to change its business approach, the performance of the entire company can be adversely affected."[11]

Winnick explains that SMG's hybrid simulations combine features from both enterprise and best-practice simulations, through the fusion of both "hard" and "soft" leadership skills. Such simulations "give participants opportunities to assume a role in their organization, but to actually see the systemic impact of their decisions from a quantitative and financial point of view. The objective is to allow the participants to see the impact of their leadership behavior on the financial results of their company."[12] One of SMG's hybrid simulations is the "Essentials for Business Leadership" program, which teaches beginning managers the impact of their leadership behaviors on financial and organizational results.

Winnick, Allen, and Doyle suggest that companies should adhere to the following caveats when designing business simulations:

- *Take a Systems View.* Allen suggests that, "We use systems dynamics in our simulations to underscore the impact of leadership behavior on the entire system. Rather than thinking of things in terms of a simple, linear, cause-and-effect model, it is important to determine the multiple impacts of a given leadership behavior on a company."

- *Build in the Right Level of Realism.* Winnick explains that, "You don't want to strive for the simulation to be real. You want to 'simulate' not 'emulate.' You want the simulation to be real enough to involve the model while not exactly replicating the organization. You need to preserve a learning space for participants by helping them step back from their organization, so we typically create an imaginary simulation. If a client is an airline, we might take them into a different transportation company, such as a railroad company." To this Doyle adds, "You don't want people to play the simulations and say 'that's not the way things work.' Instead you have to find a way to capture their version of reality. You want to capture something that models their best practices and speaks their languages. You want to get into their world."

- *Understand Your Time and Financial Investment.* Allen cautions that some clients "think that they can just turn over a simulation to a consultant. Clients need to be aware of committing time and involvement in the design stage, which requires a lot of dialogue between them and the simulation designers."

- *Watch out for Cookie-Cutter Programs.* Doyle adds this final caveat, "Don't assume there is a fixed formula to designing or selecting a simulation. It is a function of whether you have internal expertise and how far you want to go in the simulations. This, in turn, depends on the length and complexity of a simulation, such as whether it involves an elaborate model or a straightforward decision tree, and whether the client has already developed case-related managers."[13]

Another company that specializes in the design and delivery of computer-based business simulations is Executive Perspectives (EP) a Brookline, Massachusetts-based education company. EP's roster of corporate clients includes such notables as IBM, Microsoft, Chemical Bank, United Technologies, AT&T, Kodak, and Texaco. In its simulations, EP provides participants with hard-copy case materials outlining the problems and issues facing hypothetical teams or companies. Participants make a series of business decisions affecting the outcome of their "company," with each iteration of review and decision making constituting a "year" of operation. After each iteration, participants receive feedback on their performance to enable them to make midcourse corrections to their strategy and implementation plan. At the conclusion of the program, participants take part in a debriefing session to identify the lessons learned from their exercise and to discuss the applications of their learning to their work situations. Some of the business simulations available through EP include

"Leading Cross Functionally," in which participants are tasked to work across functional boundaries to tackle enterprisewide business problems; "Achieving Service Advantage," which helps participants determine how they can differentiate their company by creating a unique service advantage; and "Global Perspectives," a simulation developed through EP's experience as an education provider to Unilever PLC, which simulates the issues inherent in managing a global business.

BEST PRACTICE #3:
FORMAL MENTORING PROGRAMS

The use of senior-level mentors is gaining wide acceptance across organizations as an effective vehicle for developing executives and managers. While the term *mentor* is frequently thrown around, mentoring in its truest sense is a method for providing employees with structured opportunities to develop competencies and address career roadblocks, through personal guidance by exemplary performers in an organization. The key words used in this definition suggest that mentoring is clearly not impromptu discussions without clear, well-articulated agendas; one-shot training programs; or mentoring by the expendable.

A number of payoffs are associated with mentoring programs. Among the most important are the following:

- Help to bridge developmental gaps by enabling learners to obtain advisement from individuals who reside in other parts of the organization.

- Accelerate learning by learning from the best.

- Provide guidance in the subtle side of leadership—those competencies that are normally difficult to pick up through a text or a training course.

- Create for the mentee a balanced mirror for self-reflection by providing feedback from someone other than one's manager.

- Can often provide women and minority executives with access to mentors through formal mentorship programs. Research suggests that in a work environment that supports only informal mentoring relationships, women and African Americans usually develop fewer mentoring relationships than do white males.[14]

Organizations tend to adopt the following ground rules in developing formal mentoring programs:

- To encourage participants to establish open and candid relationships with their mentors, mentors are usually chosen from outside the chain of command. They are frequently senior-level managers who either are located two to three levels higher in the organization or come from other companies that participate in mentoring consortia arrangements.

- Mentoring relationships are never forced on mentees, who must formally request participation in the program on a voluntary basis.

- Written guidelines should detail such issues as minimum expectations for participation (preliminary screening, minimum amount of contact time, willingness to participate in a follow-up interview) and the procedures that will be used in selecting and matching mentors and mentees.

- Many programs attempt to avoid mentor burnout by ensuring that no mentor is matched with more than two or three mentees within a twelve-month period.

- The company's HR department usually serves as the matchmaker and monitor for mentoring relationships. This means performing a preliminary screening of mentees to determine career goals and the appropriateness of a mentor relationship for meeting those goals, ensuring that mentees are matched with individuals who possess the experience and competencies that mentees are attempting to develop, providing program guidelines, and conducting follow-up interviews with mentees and mentors.

- Some of the legitimate roles assumed by mentors are those of senior-level advisers, career guides, and advisers to help mentees think through their approaches to difficult work projects or issues. Mentors are not expected to run interference for mentees with their bosses, manage or direct the mentees' jobs, or evaluate mentees' work performance.

Before deciding to proceed with a formal mentoring program, I advise that you adhere to the following cautions:

- Make certain that your organization is willing to ante up the investment required to orient, train, manage, and monitor the program.

- Set clear expectations regarding participation in the program for all potential mentors and mentees. Make certain that participants realize that participation in a mentoring program requires adherence to established guidelines.

- Emphasize that program participation does not guarantee job advancement. Mentors should be carefully screened in terms of three criteria: (1) their willingness to participate in the program and to freely share their time with mentees, (2) their reputation as developers of leadership talent, and (3) their mastery of at least some of the leadership competencies that you hope to transfer to mentees.

- Before launching into a full-scale program, start off small with a test pilot involving two or three mentee-mentor pairs. The book *The Center for Creative Leadership Handbook of Leadership Development* provides a series of questions that, when addressed, can help match learners to the types of developmental relationships from which they can most benefit.

BEST PRACTICE #4:
CORPORATE AND ACADEMIC CONSORTIA

A strong emerging trend in the field of executive development is the use of consortia arrangements with either multiple universities or other noncompeting corporations. Two companies that are making use of consortia arrangements are Whirlpool and Dow Chemical. Whirlpool's executive development program combines the use of traditional academic coursework and applied business projects, and was created through a consortium of schools, including INSEAD in Fountainbleu, France, the University of Michigan, and Indiana University.[15] Dow Chemical cooperates with a consortium of noncompeting companies to send their respective leaders off to study business best practices at universities.[16] Still another example is the Center for Advanced Human Resource Studies (CAHRS) at the School of Labor Relations, Cornell University. CAHRS boasts more than forty corporate members, representing senior-level HR positions in such companies as IBM, PepsiCo, and AlliedSignal. Together with Cornell faculty, CAHRS members conduct research related to HR within subfields such as organization development, education, and communications.[17]

Arnoud De Meyer, Associate Dean, Executive Education (1992–1999), for the prestigious French business school INSEAD, noted that there are several trends that are driving the growth of learning consortia. They include broader scope, accelerated pace, globalization, and strategic partnerships.

BROADER SCOPE

The first trend is the recognition that a single academic provider may not be able to provide all of the business experience and expertise required for a given program. Over the last ten years there has been a corporate shift from offering executive education "on an 'as exception' basis by a few leading companies, available to only a few of their leading people," to a position in which "virtually all managers feel that their company will, and should, invest in their development, and the individual expects this investment as part of the 'package' he or she gets from his or her company."[18] De Meyer adds that as many large companies attempt to stretch their resources to provide comprehensive education for this larger body of leaders, they are "putting more pressure on their external educational partners to be more effective and cost efficient."[19] One way of responding to this challenge is for universities and companies to develop consortia agreements, which can sometimes significantly reduce the costs for executive training, by having several companies and/or universities share the costs required for design and delivery.

ACCELERATED PACE

Corporate merge mania is forcing organizations to bring training on-line more quickly. As an example, De Meyer points to Daimler-Chrysler. "Daimler-Chrysler is looking for enormous training programs to help them create a common culture and practices within their newly merged organization. A few years ago this would have been a request for a four-year project. Now they are asking for it in six months."[20]

GLOBALIZATION

Companies are attempting to find executive educational solutions that can be adapted to a multicultural, and multinational, business environment. De Meyer suggests that, "Many business schools will have to grow beyond their current size to meet the growing global need. A major distribution company, Carrefour—the Wal-Mart of France—which has gone strongly international, has come to us looking for a program to meet their needs in France, but at the same time is asking for this program to be held partially in China, their big growth market. We can respond to this, but many business schools would only be able to handle this through a partnership."[21]

STRATEGIC PARTNERSHIPS

The fourth trend is the corporate movement toward seeking out a few universities and consulting firms that can serve as long-term, close-quarter partners in their executive development process. According to De Meyer, "Companies are looking for partnerships with a limited number of providers (not necessarily business schools). On the one hand, companies are trying to outsource their development activities, while at the same time their purchasing departments are telling them to raise their quality by reducing their number of suppliers and by developing long-term relationships with suppliers. This partnership may mean recruiting M.B.A. students, having privileged access to newer education on executive education, having access to faculty, or having faculty who know them well enough to help their companies conduct tailor-made programs."[22]

This trend toward a limited number of fully integrated partnerships is substantiated by David Butler, Associate Dean for Executive Education at the School of Hotel Administration, Cornell University. Butler suggests that the executive development industry is making the transition "from a highly decentralized system of not-for-profit and for-profit providers, to a system that will be dominated by a few powerful alliances. The dominant alliances will typically combine leading universities with for-profit companies specializing in technologically intensive forms of delivery and marketing. The alliances will distribute learning globally, and will offer highly competitive combinations of cost, convenience, and quality. We are still in the early stages of the transition from today's decentralized system to this heavily consolidated one, but the shift is accelerating rapidly. It will be largely accomplished within a decade."[23]

In assessing the implications of these strategic academic alliances for corporate development, Butler contends that, "Externally, they will need to be astute indeed in picking the probable winners in the coming shakeout among providers. Those who build early relationships with the winners will themselves enjoy a competitive edge. Internally, they will have to be skilled in accomplishing the massive changes in systems and in attitudes that effective use of these new alliances will demand."[24]

De Meyer provides the following advice for corporations attempting to establish a strategic partnership with a university:

- Be relatively clear, but not too detailed, about what your specifications are. Know what you want to achieve through your executive educational goals, but don't make your needs too limited, because the business school faculty can provide a host of creative ideas.

- Understand that the objectives of university faculty are different from the objectives of the consultant. Most of us have chosen this job because we like the creative freedom we have, and because we quickly become bored with doing the same thing many times. The point here is to keep your program intellectually stimulating for participating faculty.

- Many consultants can provide a good education, but you go to a business school to obtain new ideas. So look for the research base of the business school you are considering, and ask what kind of exciting new ideas these faculty members have.

- You go to a business school because it has depth of faculty. Look carefully at the team the school is providing you—at both its depth of talent and how well the faculty plans to integrate the program it offers you—versus presenting a smorgasbord of disconnected educational activities.

- Some business schools view executive education only as a means of making money. At these schools, executive education tends to be viewed in a negative way by the younger faculty members. At other schools, executive education is considered essential to what the school does. Look for the latter type of school for a partner.[25]

BEST PRACTICE #5:
DISTRIBUTED LEARNING AND CYBERTOOLS

A number of excellent executive development programs are available from some top-rated universities. The roadblock many executives face in using these programs is the difficulty involved in setting aside one or two weeks to attend them. In addition, if large numbers of executive students are to be included, then training costs can become a serious impediment. To get around these problems, colleges and corporations are looking at innovative alternatives involving the use of distance learning techniques and self-paced learning through CD-ROM.

One university that is taking a strong lead in distance learning is the Wharton Business School, which has implemented a series of management and executive development courses through its Wharton Direct program. To provide this delivery mechanism, Wharton has teamed up with Caliber Learning Network, Inc., which is itself the result of a combined effort between MCI Communications and Sylvan Learning Systems. Caliber uses a combination of satellite broadcasting, video conferencing, and networked training to link a series of forty class sites across the United States and Canada. Each class site houses three classrooms, and each classroom supports an average of twenty-five students.

Walk into a Caliber classroom and you enter rows of desks with embedded computer monitors and recessed keyboards at strategic points. Overhead microphones and large-format viewing screens (two per room) give exceptionally clear sound and video. The keyboard provides a number of features that encourage student interaction. At selected points during the lecture the presenters pose questions for discussion. Students formulate joint responses to these questions, and student representatives send their teams' responses to the instructor through the use of "connect" buttons. A videoconferencing system allows students to respond to instructors' questions "live" on-screen. Or, students can elect to hit the "whisper" button to contact a live subject matter expert for a more detailed explanation or to send a question to other students. As the instructor moves through the lecture, key learning points appear on the students' computer screens. The "review" icon enables a student to move ahead to scan learning points, or go back to points that might have been missed. Instructors can also provide students with backup hard-copy materials, which can be scanned and printed out by clicking on the "resources" icon on the screen. Another nice feature is that the system allows instructors to immediately poll students about how they feel about certain issues, or quickly determine the background that students have in a certain subject area through the use of preloaded multiple-choice questions that appear on students' computer monitors.

Wharton Direct is using distance learning to deliver a number of programs, ranging from "Building a Business Case" (how to make a case for a new business or product) to "Using Financial Statements." The typical program lasts six weeks and consists of six three-hour evening sessions. Tuition averages about $2,500. To make the courses integrated, they are frequently team-taught by several instructors. Because the programs reach such an extended audience, Wharton can afford to put its very best on-screen. Instructors include such notables as Dr. John Percival and Jeremy Siegel, author of *Stocks for the Long Run*. Another advantage of the distance learning option is that having multiple sites means that students may be able to continue with their courses when traveling on business.

Alison Peirce, Program Director for Wharton Direct, makes a sharp distinction between the terms *distance learning* and *distributed learning*. As Peirce explains it, "Distance learning is one-dimensional; it's just information dissemination, it doesn't assume integration and two-way interaction between the instructor and the student. In distributed learning, distance is not a factor."[26] Peirce sites the following advantages in the use of Wharton's program:

- *Increased Productivity.* One of the advantages of distributed learning is that it makes learning more productive and enables you to integrate multiple functions of the university in one place. If you are an engineer, instead of saying "tomorrow you can work at that in the lab" or "tomorrow you can look it up in the library," you can obtain information when and how you need it.

- *Academic Leadership.* One of our goals for Wharton Direct is that this program will reinforce Wharton's reputation as a leader in executive development.

- *Learning Transfer.* Another advantage is that whatever "course-ware" [the information that students can access via the web between classes] we develop for Wharton Direct can be used for other programs. For example, the courseware we use in "Building a Business Case" will be applied to the prework for our M.B.A. program. In addition, the program allows us to create new revenue sources.

- *Ease of Use.* There are occasions in which total immersion is essential, but there are many cases where a person cannot get away for a week. Our programs run late afternoon (for someone on the West Coast it would be 4 P.M. to 7 P.M.) to evening (7 P.M. to 9 P.M. for people on the East Coast).[27]

Peirce is quick to explain that the Wharton Direct program applies to a very targeted audience. "Twenty percent of our students already have an M.B.A. Over 40 percent of the students in our 'Building a Business Case' make over $100,000, and 50 percent of these students have over ten years of job experience. We are going after professionals who have an immediate learning need. Our format gives students an opportunity to apply learning between classes. In addition, the whole notion of having access to a national group of fellow students provides an exceptional learning experience."[28]

In looking ahead to where we may eventually go with such distributed executive programs as Wharton Direct, one improvement that comes to mind is for program sponsors to create greater opportunities to build learning nets comprised of present and past students. In the case of Wharton Direct, the "whisper" command button enables students to interact with subject matter experts at Wharton and with other students, but only for the program's duration. In the Wharton Direct course that I attended ("Building a Business Case"), a contact list of students was distributed but their titles, phone numbers, and e-mail addresses weren't included, so networking opportunities were rather limited. By providing this information for students across the network site, Wharton (or any other sponsor of distributed learning) could greatly extend its impact by expediting the creation of learning networks of professionals who could continue to exchange learning experiences long after the conclusion of a course.

Extending this idea even further, I envision a time when distance learning will be enhanced by collecting the lessons learned from a distributed network into a central knowledge archive, enabling each new class to continually build on the experiences of its predecessors.

Such a marriage of distributed technology and knowledge databases would provide executives with a powerful, integrated learning experience.

Another trend that may quickly emerge from the growing application of distance learning is the extension of executive development programs on a truly global basis. Wharton Direct currently covers both the United States and Canada. Another example is the Global M.B.A. program offered by San Diego–based National University, a private university at which enrollees include executives from Banco National de Mexico (Banamex), one of the largest banks in Mexico.[29] The University of Western Ontario runs a video conference–based M.B.A. program to reach the more remote parts of Canada, while Henley Management College in the U.K. is now partnering with the Certified General Accounts of Ontario (CGA) to conduct an international M.B.A. program in Canada.[30]

APPLYING HYBRID TECHNOLOGY TO INTERNATIONAL DEVELOPMENT

When you couple the use of computerized simulations with distance learning, you arrive at a very powerful and creative hybrid learning methodology. One of the experts in the use of this type of distributed learning approach is Youssef Bissada, who is both a professor of entrepreneurship for the international French business school INSEAD and the owner of Bissada Management Simulations, a company that designs computerized management simulations that are used for professional and executive education. According to Bissada, most of the simulations his company provides are geared toward, and involve competitions among, different teams. These simulations are iterative, involving a series of business decisions that successively build upon one another, becoming more complex over time. All simulations are fully computerized. Participants receive an in-house-designed software product that enables them to test different sets of assumptions on their desktops. The results are often sent back to a central site via the web for processing.

Bissada explains that he has worked with computerized simulations via distance learning for the last seventeen years. "Back in 1982 we wanted to be location independent, so we provided learners with portable computers and diskettes. Now we run the simulations both by disk and by the Internet." The business simulations used by Bissada begin "when participants receive a manual or rule book explaining the guidelines for the simulation, which are often downloaded by participants through the Net. In the manual there is a quiz to ensure that learners understand the basic rules. They then attend a plenary seminar together, and from this point are split up into their separate groups."[31]

Heineken is one international corporation that is actively using the technique of computerized business simulations via distance learning to strengthen the skills of its corporate leaders. Bissada provides the following description of this simulation:

An international competition involves about fifty teams, including teams in Indonesia, Europe, and the United States. The fifty teams are organized into seven separate markets, with seven or eight teams competing within each market. A winning team is selected in each market, and the seven winning teams are invited by Heineken to compete in Amsterdam as finalists in the competition. The teams work through seven weeks of activity. Each week they are required to make one key business decision, which sets the stage for the next week's activity. The business challenges become more complex as the simulation progresses. One week they are working on importing and marketing products, the next in manufacturing, and then on exporting products. They are primarily working with wholesalers, but can also opt to work with retailers. The types of decisions that must be addressed in this simulation involve sales management. We left it up to each team to decide how they wanted to organize themselves. Some teams communicated primarily through the phone, while others used the Net or video conferences.[32]

Bissada points to three key payoffs that can be generated through the use of distributed computerized business simulations.

These simulations provide one of the best ways to create good teamwork and networking among people. They also emphasize the importance of operating in a truly global environment, and how the decisions that they make in one area directly impact other people. In other words, they come to understand the relationship between different business decisions. Another benefit is that participants learn to implement strategy in a fast-changing environment, and how to link business strategy with operational decisions.

Regarding some of the constraints that have to be considered when conducting distributed simulations, Bissada points to the difficulties encountered in working through corporate fire walls on the Internet, and having limited access to the Internet from some global locations (when working in Indonesia he had only one hour of access a day). Finally, he suggests that another difficulty is "motivating people who are not doing very well. There is a need to explain that this is not a test, but a learning experience."33

SOURCES FOR CYBERTRAINING

As a starting point for exploring distance (distributed) learning options for your own organization, take a stroll through the web sites shown in Table 20 on pages 208 and 209. Executives who like to take a self-paced approach to learning may find it helpful to review the sampling of executive training programs available through CD-ROM shown in Table 21 on page 210. (Note: at the time of writing, prices for these products averaged $295.) One caution is that the large majority of CD-ROM training programs that I have reviewed are generally geared to the lower- and middle-management levels rather than to executive leaders. They do, however, provide a means of offering an introduction to management techniques that may be out-of-field for an executive. For example, the "Why Finance Matters" course would serve as a good introduction to someone who was not familiar with financial statements.

One company moving aggressively into the area of CD-ROM and web-based training is Arthur Anderson, which recently launched the Arthur Anderson Virtual Learning Network (VLN). Anderson has contracts with more than a dozen content providers and offers more than 400 courses delivered via the web or CD-ROM. All web-based courses are offered through a single user interface. One of the advantages of using VLN as a program provider is that every course is broken down into a series of topics or lessons, each of which can be completed in about twenty minutes. Participants can choose any topic that interests them without having to take the entire course.

For a more detailed look at how some companies, such as Anderson Consulting, are taking CD-ROM training one step further in the design of customized in-depth business simulations, I strongly recommend reading *Virtual Learning: A Revolutionary Approach to Building a Highly Skilled Workforce* by Roger Schank, professor at Northwestern University (McGraw-Hill, 1997).

TABLE 20	
HOT WEB SITES FOR CYBERTRAINING	
Web Site Address	**Services Provided**
Asymetrix Corporation www.asymetrix.com	Bellevue, Washington–based provider of multimedia tools for use over the Internet
Arthur Anderson Virtual Learning Network www.aavln.com	Web-based and CD-ROM training programs for corporations
Caliber Learning Network www.caliberlearning.com	Baltimore-based North American network of forty distance learning centers making use of PC and videoconference technology
California Virtual University www.california.edu	Clearinghouse service listing ninety-five online courses available through California colleges
Colorado State University's M.B.A. www.biz.colostate.edu/homer	M.B.A. program making use of Internet discussion groups and videotaped lectures
Databeam Corporation www.databeam.com	Lexington, Kentucky–based provider of "live" distance learning and communication software
Horizon Live Distance Learning www.horizonlive.com	New York–based provider of training live via the Internet
Macromedia Inc. www.macromedia.com	San Francisco–based provider of training and communication tools for the Internet
Ohio University's M.B.A. http://mbawb.cob.ohiou.edu	M.B.A. program that combines distance learning and on-site residence (three weekends plus three full weeks)

Web Site Address	Services Provided
Rochester Institute of Technology www.distancelearning.rit.edu	Distance learning program leading to an M.S. in information tech-nology
Stanford Online www.standford-online.standford.edu	Offers an online program leading to a master's degree in electrical engineering
Strategic Management Group www.smginc.com	Philadelphia-based consulting firm that designs generic and customized computer-based and CD-ROM training, and also designs and delivers computer-based, team-based business simulations
University of Phoenix www.uophx.edu/online	Offers online degrees in business and other areas
U.S. Distance Learning Association www.usdla.org	San Ramon, California–based association that supports the development of distance learning for training and education
Wharton Direct http://direct.wharton.upenn.edu	Provider of executive learning through the Wharton Business School via distance learning (partnered with Caliber Learning Network)

TABLE 21

A SAMPLING OF EXECUTIVE DEVELOPMENT PROGRAMS AVAILABLE ON CD-ROM

Title and Publisher	Developmental Focus
Business Strategy: Fast Track Management Development GeoLearning 800-970-9903	Situation analysis, industry analysis, portfolio analysis, and strategic decision making. Includes two business cases.
Pacific Dunlop China (A): Beijing Harvard Business School 800-587-8573	Operations management and improvement, set within an interesting cultural context: a sock manufacturing plant in Beijing. (Recommend that you also purchase the hard-copy instructor's guide, $20.)
Service Success Harvard Business School 800-587-8573	Understanding the service profit chain. Applying steps to build service capability.
Time Management American Management Association 800-262-9699	Priority setting, delegation, and time management techniques. Includes a simple simulation.
Understanding Project Management Strategic Management Group, Inc. 215-387-4000 www.smginc.com	Project management skills. Includes an introductory project simulation for applying project tools.
Why Finance Matters Strategic Management Group, Inc. 215-387-4000 www.smginc.com	Understanding financial statements, EVA, shareholder value, budgeting, and cost of capital.
Yes! The Interactive Negotiator Harvard Business School 800-587-8573	How to prepare for a negotiation, negotiating with different types of individuals, use of negotiating tools and techniques. (Based on the work of Dr. Roger Fisher.)

CASE IN POINT: HENNINGER MEDIA SERVICES

Curt Mason, Vice President of Sales and Marketing

One company that has reported significant gains from its involvement in Wharton Direct's program is Henninger Media Services, an Arlington, Virginia–based company that provides production and postproduction tools and services for film, video, and interactive media clients. Curt Mason, Henninger's Vice President of Sales and Marketing, explained that his senior managers participated in the "Building a Business Case" course as a common team, with involvement by Henninger's CEO, CIO, COO, and Director of Marketing.

According to Mason, "I went into the program skeptical because I used to teach college, and thought, 'Here we go, another academic program.' Instead, I found that during the program we worked on projects that were applied to our company. For my project, I worked with our COO in developing a business case for a new business involving a major capital and labor investment. We made the decision to buy hardware and software and to hire people—decisions we wouldn't have made had we not gone through this program. We learned how to create a reverse investment statement to look ahead and assess the opportunity costs of determining where else we could invest, and whether this particular investment represented our best investment opportunity. We determined the profit we needed to make, the sales we needed to generate to obtain this profit, and then worked backward to build our business model. We also built in other financials to test our assumption that the market was viable for us. On the basis of this we went forward."[34]

Mason lists several payoffs from attending the Wharton Direct program: "It gave us a common language and methodology to step back and address our own bias on how to build a business case. It also provided a very safe venue for learning. Finally, it placed us outside the organization, in a learning environment in which we understood we all were equal and went in with no title. The instructors were application oriented, not theory oriented. One of the greatest payoffs from our involvement with this program was that it provided us with a common language and a model that we all understood, so that any new product entry or service will be tested against this model."[35]

- Some of the reasons companies fail to take action in developing their executives include lack of time, the difficulty of developing the members of a virtual team, organizational frustration with traditional classroom training that is disconnected from work, and the growing pressure of resource constraints.

- Best practices in building executive competencies include the use of action learning, job simulations, formal mentoring programs, corporate and academic consortia, and distributed learning and "cybertools."

- Action learning attempts to link developmental activities to real-life work challenges by assigning cross-functional teams to research business problems and issues proposed by their CEO or senior-level managers, develop solutions to these problems, implement those solutions, and review results with their senior management.

- Job simulations require learners to make decisions based on a business issue or problem, then issue consequences based on the results of those decisions. In contrast to business cases, simulations are iterative learning events that permit learners to continually modify their performance based on feedback regarding previous decisions and actions.

- Formal mentoring programs provide employees with structured opportunities to develop competencies and address career roadblocks, through personal guidance by exemplary performers within the organization.

- Corporate and academic consortia help companies leverage developmental resources and meet global executive development needs through the use of creative partnerships among universities and/or noncompeting corporations.

- Distributed learning and cybertools involve the use of web-based training, video conferencing, and CD-ROM training to extend developmental opportunities to executives in remote locations, to stretch resource dollars, to provide broader access to top-rated business experts, to support self-directed learning, to increase the efficiency of learning, and to build geographically distributed teams.

CHAPTER 9

FORGING AN EXECUTIVE DEVELOPMENT STRATEGY

W henever the subject of executive development comes up, the classic executive development program comes to mind, in which either leading consultants and academics are flown in to teach at a corporate site or executives are sent off to a self-contained training program at some Ivy League university. Indeed, one of the drawbacks with the five development tools that I introduced in Chapter 8 is their seductiveness. Executive development experts tend to confuse development tools with development strategies, and in the process they try to force-fit their tools of choice to organizational settings for which they might be maladapted.

Fortunately, senior managers and HR leaders are beginning to move away from this rigid and limited one-size-fits-all model of development. Instead, a variety of innovative techniques provide executives with learning experiences that are far more substantive and more closely tied to the business requirements of their organizations. In this chapter I will outline nine elements that make up a true executive development strategy, and that separate such efforts from program- and activity-based executive development efforts. These elements are outlined in Table 22.

Meanwhile, I offer up the following sources for those who are interested in evaluating traditional M.B.A. and executive development programs.

> **TABLE 22**
>
> **ELEMENTS OF A COMPREHENSIVE EXECUTIVE RESOURCE DEVELOPMENT STRATEGY**
>
> 1. Link development objectives to business strategy.
>
> 2. Match development approach to organizational structure.
>
> 3. Match development plans to levels of learning agility.
>
> 4. Create developmental learning systems.
>
> 5. Evaluate leaders' commitment to leadership development.
>
> 6. Focus development on preventing failure.
>
> 7. Understand that performance improvement stems from self-awareness.
>
> 8. Develop for the future.
>
> 9. Keep a global focus.

- "The Best B Schools," *Business Week* (published annually)
- *Peterson's Guide to M.B.A. Programs and University-Based Executive Development Programs* (Peterson's Guides: 800-338-3282)
- *Bricker's International Directory: Executive Development Programs Guide* (Albert & Company: 561-697-3430)

ELEMENT 1: LINK DEVELOPMENT OBJECTIVES TO BUSINESS STRATEGY

This concept is an extension of the position I articulated in Chapter 2, that in order to be successful executive resource plans must be linked to business strategy. For the creation of an executive development program, this guiding principle translates into two subordinate practices.

First, start from a clear identification of one's executive target audiences. This means not only delineating how training is expected to vary by organizational level and functional group, but also defining target subgroups as women, people of color, high-potential performers, potential and current expatriates, and executive new hires.

Next, clearly define how executive development efforts are expected to support and enhance business objectives. A research study performed by the International Consortium for Executive Development Research concluded that, "Executive and [leadership] development must be focused strategically on both the target population and the issues that enable companies to create and sustain superior organizational capabilities. The cultivation of those capabilities is the strongest contribution that executive development professionals can make to improve firm performance and competitiveness."[1] Table 23 on page 216 provides three examples from my own experience showing how different organizations have adapted development efforts to support strategic business objectives.

For most companies, this focus on strategy translates into a reduced dependence on off-the-shelf external development programs and a greater investment in creating their own. A second conclusion by the Consortium's study is that, "In order to leverage their investment in learning, organizations are using fewer external development opportunities and are focusing instead on development activities specific to their organization and more tightly linked to their workplace."[2]

Bruce Barge, an industrial organizational psychologist and SVP of Chicago-based human resources consulting firm Aon Consulting, works with a number of companies that are attempting to link their executive development programs to their business strategies. As an example, he cites a municipal utility company that was attempting to perform within a deregulated environment and move into new markets, such as seeking new customers or bundling electricity with consulting services to help customers find ways to reduce their overall electric costs. According to Barge, "The company recognized that it needed skill sets in terms of the ability to develop vision and mobilize people around a new direction, as well as leaders who were more market savvy and who were able to sell the company's services in terms of customer-based solutions rather than product-based solutions. While the CEO was very oriented this way, he was challenged to get people one and two levels below to build these skill sets. An associated problem was the cultural inertia the CEO needed to overcome, given that his company had a history of promoting based on seniority."[3]

Barge explains that the training program created by the company used a variety of learning methods, all with the intention of getting the company's executives to take a fresh look at an old business.

	TABLE 23	
HOW TO LINK BUSINESS STRATEGY TO EXECUTIVE DEVELOPMENT EFFORTS		
Strategic Business Objective	Developmental Learning Objective	Related Development Effort
Quickly grow the business globally.	Provide domestic-focused leaders with a global perspective on business problems and break down walls between the international group and corporate support staff.	Mix international and corporate executives in teams within a business simulation, with the goal of determining how to counter the intrusion of a hypothetical global competitor.
Recapture market share through a renewed emphasis on customer focus.	Develop competencies in customer focus: enable leaders to make decisions that balance customer focus with financial profitability.	Create a series of action learning teams that are challenged to identify and address performance factors related to recent customer defections.
Develop reapplication of existing technologies that, with required organizational restructuring, will ensure successful entry into a new market area.	Help leaders understand their roles as change catalysts by anticipating broad-scale business changes and beginning to plan for those changes. Provide a safe environment in which to explore the business impact of alternative risk taking and innovation scenarios.	Engage teams of executives in a three-day retreat that requires them to develop and test scenarios of future business performance, and evaluate their current leadership capability in terms of these models.

The first phase of the training included having the CEO accompany different teams of managers and executives on a series of off-site retreats, ranging from outdoor experiential programs to soup conditions, with the goal of getting company leaders to experience what it was like to function in a totally foreign environment.

The CEO used action learning, in which teams of managers were chartered to study an important organizational issue, such as suggesting entirely new ways to treat wastewater, or how to modify the utility's brand in the marketplace. This phase of training was designed to get people to engage in out-of-the-box thinking, while simultaneously solving an important organizational problem. The company then put together a mentoring program that made use of both company mentors and senior-level managers who were external to the organization. All these things taken together have been well received by the utility. Based on these experiences, some people recognized that they lacked the skill sets needed to adapt and opted for early retirement, but they left with a better taste in their mouths. For most people it was a motivational experience.[4]

Barge explains that as a result of changes developed from this program, the utility has "rolled out seven new services in one year, versus the norm of one per year. They also have a better ability to attract and retain high-caliber people, and have every expectation that they will increase their revenue base."[5]

ELEMENT 2: MATCH DEVELOPMENT APPROACH TO ORGANIZATIONAL STRUCTURE

While focusing on business strategy enables an organization to formulate executive development objectives in terms of business strategy, the next step is to create an executive development model that meshes well with your organization's structural constraints. To better understand this concept, consider the relative size of your company. As outlined in Table 24 on page 218, in attempting to develop their leaders large and small companies bring to the table very different strengths and challenges.

Small companies are able to focus a high level of attention on the development of their executives. Large companies, because of the numbers of executives involved, are limited to applying a uniform, noncustomized format to executive development programs. Without careful attention as to how development efforts need to be adjusted to accommodate different executive levels, functions, and population groups (high-potential executives versus mainstream executives, special programs to advance the development of women and minorities), executive development programs can easily end up looking like

	TABLE 24	
	WEIGHING THE COMPARATIVE EXECUTIVE DEVELOPMENT CHALLENGE	
Challenge	**Small Companies** (Executive Pool < 100) and Start-Ups	**Large Companies** (Executive Pool > 500)
Ability to Provide Individual Focus	*High*—Can provide personal attention to the few candidates in the pool	*Low*—Greater pressure to develop according to formulas
Range of Development Options	*Low*—Few divisions or strategic business units in which to rotate high performers	*High*—Variety of job niches means a much larger array of development options
Maintenance Requirements	*Low*—Often performed informally	*High*—Large volume of candidates and options requires tight database management
Investment Capability	*Low*—Biggest hurdles include initial set-up costs and replacement costs	*High*—Economies of scale lead to greater investment ability
Calibration Process	*Low*—If external benchmarking is not performed, result may be "organizational incest"	*High*—Have access to a broader base of executives among different significant business units, resulting in more effective internal benchmarks
Talent Pool	*Narrow*—Few candidates within pool limits the range of candidates for succession planning	*Broad*—Large talent pool means greater redundancy in succession design
Cross-Functional Development	*Narrow*—Exception is fast-growth companies forced to take risks through out-of-field reassignments	*Broad*—Ability to provide leaders with exposure to a wide range of work challenges

broad-stroke sessions that are only marginally linked to individual development needs.

On the other hand, large companies have available a number of options for formal development. If the development goal for a given executive involves working with a new product start-up or gaining international exposure, there is a greater chance that such development opportunities will present themselves within large companies. Smaller companies offer less breadth of diversity in developmental experiences, but they can compensate for this by requiring executives to take on broad job assignments that encompass a number of leadership roles. As a result, larger companies can rely more on job rotation as a development assignment, whereas smaller companies tend to broaden the current existing structure.

Still another difference between large and small companies involves their respective maintenance costs for implementing development programs. Smaller organizations can afford to construct programs more loosely, with less need to formally track the development of candidates. Within larger companies it is all too easy for high-potential leaders to become lost within the system, and for companies to be unaware of development concerns until high-potential performers leave to join their competitors.

Another challenge that smaller companies face is in the initial investment costs required to underwrite formal development programs. It becomes very difficult to recoup training design costs for an in-depth executive development program that may only be conducted twice a year for a handful of leaders. As the executive population base increases, these costs become easier to recover.

Still another factor involves the ability of an organization to achieve what I term *performance calibration*. In a company of only twenty executives, four of whom are listed as high potential, it is very hard to establish leadership performance measurements. Given a candidate pool with only three potential successors to the position of vice president of finance, how do you determine whether the best of these performers is actually performing to world-class standards? It is important for smaller firms to use *external benchmarks* of leadership and technical competencies. In planning assessment strategies such as 360-degree profiling, smaller companies may want to consider using outside providers, such as the Center for Creative Leadership, which can make 360-degree scores to large, normative databases. By contrast, because larger companies have access to a broader range of executive candidates from different business units, these find it easier to establish *internal benchmarks* that allow them to determine the floor and ceiling for leadership performance within the organization.

A second issue faced by smaller companies is that of establishing an adequate talent pool for succession planning—a particularly acute problem for fast-growth companies. Larger companies, on the other hand, usually have a greater safety net in their ability to gather a greater number of succession candidates for positions. They also have the ability to provide individuals with exposure to a wide range of work challenges.

ELEMENT 3: MATCH DEVELOPMENT PLANS TO LEVELS OF LEARNING AGILITY

Earlier I proposed that high-potential executive candidates could be assessed partly in terms of their level of learning agility, which is composed of their adaptability to new work situations and their ability and willingness to learn new things. It is also possible to match development plans to these levels of learning agility (see Table 25). The basic premise behind this model is that people who have different levels of learning ability will approach development opportunities in very different ways.

Executives and managers who have been assessed as having low levels of learning agility are probably people who have not availed themselves of development opportunities over the last several years, and who have convinced themselves that they do not need to change. ("This leadership approach has always worked before; why do I need to change now?") This unwillingness or inability to learn can become particularly problematic if an organization encounters a volatile business climate that requires high levels of flexibility and adaptability.

To get past this roadblock, executives with low levels of learning agility need a greater degree of structure, support by mentors and managers, and peer modeling to encourage them to extend their learning and to link their learning to their business objectives. Such people might also benefit greatly from insight-oriented programs, such as the Center for Creative Leadership's Leadership Development Program, that encourage participants to take a fresh look at their interpersonal and leadership styles. A final consideration is how learning agility links to performance. In the case of an executive who has both a low level of learning agility and a poor performance record, the best course of action may be to either redesign that individual's job to compensate for the weakest performance areas or to help that individual seek employment outside the company.

Midrange leaders are those who have a moderate degree of learning agility. These are individuals who, although they may not aggressively seek out new learning opportunities or may have difficulty translating developmental learnings into changes in

	TABLE 25	
MATCHING EXECUTIVE DEVELOPMENT PLANS TO LEARNING AGILITY		
Target Group	Characteristics	Recommended Development Options
"A" Performers	*HIPOs*—Assessed as having a high level of learning agility	Look for stretch assignments and promotional options that provide high challenge and ensure retention. Explore cross-functional projects. Consider the option of international assignments. Provide access to options such as distance learning and Internet forums that leverage self-directed learning.
"B" Performers	*Midrange Learners*—Assessed as having a moderate level of learning agility	Develop within position; look for development experiences that broaden the individual's competency base. Consider experiences that provide structured feedback. Use team-based learning to model the use of aggressive inquiry and cross-functional perspectives.
"C" Performers	*Plateaued Learners*—Assessed as having a low level of learning agility	Provide options such as structured coaching to accurately assess the limits of learning agility and to create targets and limited goals for improvement. Consider insight-based programs to build the case for change. If poor performance continues, consider job redesign or managing out.

performance, are able with some guidance to fully profit from developmental experiences. They are leaders who have ample room to develop within their current positions. With these individuals one can look for development experiences that broaden their competency base. Another option is to use team-based learning, such as the simulations discussed later in this chapter, to model the use of aggressive inquiry. By this I mean having the opportunity to watch how their teammates aggressively deconstruct problems, probe for missing information, and attack problems from totally new and cross-functional perspectives.

Leaders who have a high level of learning agility aggressively seek out new learning opportunities. These are the individuals who are the first to sign up for benchmark studies, who continuously track new market trends and technologies, and who seem to track the lessons learned for any new learning experience. Such individuals can benefit greatly from self-directed learning opportunities, such as books, videos, and CD-ROM and distance learning programs. These are also the individuals who demonstrate the greatest degree of adaptability when faced with an entirely new learning environment, such as an international assignment or a stretch promotional assignment. Given the high level of motivation such individuals have for learning, the greatest challenge they pose is the need to continue to expose them to engaging and involving work experiences.

ELEMENT 4: CREATE DEVELOPMENTAL LEARNING SYSTEMS

Executive development programs can be visualized as stretching across a continuum. At one end of the continuum are what I call "sheep-dip" programs—one-shot courses that constitute a misplaced attempt to immerse executives into several days or weeks of concentrated study. While single-shot development courses vary in content and format, they are based on the same faulty learning assumptions:

- Executive development training is best approached through a single, consolidated program of study that is removed from day-to-day challenges on the job.

- Formal development programs provide leadership theory, which is tempered with on-the-job application.

- The best learning is provided by outside consultants or academics who are isolated from the organizational culture.

- All leaders enter training at the same baseline of learning readiness. No advanced preparation is necessary.

- Learning is self-contained. Program participants can easily translate the "take-aways" from the course to their work experience.

Fortunately, this antiquated view of learning is rapidly dying out as organizations begin to understand that the bulk of executive learning occurs on the job, through experiences that test and challenge leadership abilities.[6] This is not to say that formal development courses serve no function, but rather that they provide true value only when they are integrated into a complete developmental learning system. Arnoud De Meyer proposes that there are five basic components to executive and management development: (1) formal education, (2) on-the-job training, (3) special projects with a learning goal, (4) mentoring, and (5) job assessment. He adds that, "Today we are getting more and more questions from companies regarding how these components can be integrated. They say, 'We want to create a tailor-made program, which should have some special assignments with application to participants' jobs.' "[7]

We now know enough about the dynamics of the development process to know that there are certain factors that can increase the value obtained from developmental experiences. The first factor concerns the *timing of developmental experiences*. The idea here is to offer a difficult assignment at the point where an individual has sufficient context to take away something of value from the experience, but still allow room for stretch. Accordingly, it would make no sense to send new hires on a series of customer or supplier site visits until they have first been provided context on the types of partnerships their company is attempting to forge with customers and suppliers, a basic understanding of the differentiating value of the company's products and services, and an idea of where these particular customers and suppliers fit into the company's overall business picture.

Second, it is more valuable to interconnect training and work activities over an extended period of time than to segment learning activities as an isolated event. Michael Marquardt, professor with George Washington University's Global HR Development and the author of *Action Learning in Action* (Davies-Black, 1999), suggests that "instead of sending people off to an executive development program for a month, executives may go off to training for a week, obtain practice and feedback, and learn how to carry out what they've learned on the job site, then go back into training. Still another trend is the push to get information to people before or after training—through 360-degree feedback or some other form—to give executives some sources of information they can use to change their behavior."[8]

Third, managers need to prepare executives for developmental experiences by emphasizing what they hope learners will be able to take away from those experiences. This not only serves to ensure that executives target the right components of the learning experience, but also converts what might otherwise be perceived as a threatening or anxiety-provoking experience into a motivational experience. In addition, managers need to reach agreement up front with their reports regarding how these learners will self-assess the learning they take away from their experience and establish a process for follow-up review. This same principle also holds true for off-site seminars and leadership courses. Before sending an executive off to a seminar or training program, a manager needs to meet with his or her reports to establish learning objectives and a follow-up review process.

Fourth, research suggests that the most effective learning experiences fall into five categories: (1) *making job transitions* that require the use of new roles and competencies; (2) *creating change,* or functioning as a change agent for helping a company set out in a new direction, such as a business start-up or shut-down; (3) dealing with a *high level of responsibility* involving a dramatic increase in job scope, complexity, and pressure; (4) forming *nonauthority relationships,* such as a shift from line to staff or the management of a cross-functional project team where the leader must depend on influence skills to accomplish objectives; and (5) *handling external job pressures,* such as collective bargaining agencies or federal regulatory agencies.[9]

Last, organizations can interview current and former job incumbents to audit job functions in order to determine which assignments engender which developmental experiences and to better match individuals to assignments.[10] This type of audit can also be broken down by business unit or function. As researcher Morgan McCall suggests, "A corporate profile can be essential for determining which parts of the organization develop the skills needed for the future, what kinds of developmental opportunities are missing relative to the business strategy, which cross-boundary moves can be justified by strategic need, and where developmental interventions might be most useful."[11]

For additional tools you can use for determining which skills you can extract from different kinds of developmental assignments, I recommend the following:

- *Handbook of Leadership Development* by the Center for Creative Leadership

- *The Lessons of Experience: How Successful Executives Develop on the Job* by Morgan McCall, Mike Lombardo, and A. M. Morrison

- *Eighty-Eight Assignments for Developing in Place: Enhancing the Development Challenge of Existing Jobs* by Mike Lombardo and R. Eichinger, Center for Creative Leadership

ELEMENT 5: EVALUATE LEADERS' COMMITMENT TO LEADERSHIP DEVELOPMENT

One of the major conclusions presented in *The McKinsey Quarterly's* "The War for Talent" is that most companies simply do not make substantial investments in developing their executives. Only 10 percent of the study's respondents indicated that their companies made effective use of development assignments. As the study concludes, "Forty-two percent have never made cross-functional moves, 40 percent have never worked in an unfamiliar business unit, 34 percent have never held a position with P&L responsibility, and 66 percent say they have never had a leadership role in starting a new business."[12]

The question arises as to why corporations are willing to invest so much effort and time in formal executive training programs that seem to perform so poorly. The answer, I believe, lies in the concept of ownership. In too many organizations, people development is not viewed as a critical executive responsibility. Even for companies that do give lip service to executive development, seldom is people development included in their managerial selection or appraisal decisions. Again, the McKinsey research suggests that, "Although 78 percent of corporate officers questioned in our survey agree that companies should hold their line managers accountable for the quality of their people, only 7 percent believe that their companies actually do so."[13]

What can organizations do to encourage their leaders to place greater emphasis on leadership development? Here are some suggestions:

- Set clear executive development objectives for managers, as you would for any other area of business responsibility. As an example, at Hoeschst Celanese Corporation, diversity goals constitute 25 percent of senior managers' bonus goals.[14]

- Tie performance in executive development to executive compensation. The authors of "The War for Talent" state that, "At Monsanto, half a senior executive's bonus is based on his or her people management skills. At First USA, the ability to recruit talented new people is understood to be a criterion for promotion."[15]

- Make people development a key criterion for the identification of high-performing executives. Include as part of your formal succession review process questions that uncover the developmental ability of executives. Examples might include: "What is the voluntary turnover rate for exceptional performers within this executive's function?" "What executive development projects—job rotation programs, mentorships, cross-functional team development projects—has this executive established for his or her team?" "What percentage of direct reports to this individual have formal development plans for improving their performance? What percentage of these plans were actually implemented during this reporting period?" "Is this an individual who appears to be able to attract, develop, and retain superior performers? Are you impressed with the caliber of team this individual has built?"

- Make use of methods such as action learning, which break down walls between "development" and "work." Another way to spread ownership over line functions is to include senior executives on design reviews when creating mentor programs.

- Make use of team feedback instruments, such as 360-degree profiles, to help you target executives who are performing poorly in the area of people development. When you come down to it, the best source of information on an executive's developmental capabilities is his or her team.

ELEMENT 6: FOCUS DEVELOPMENT ON PREVENTING FAILURE

Executive development efforts tend to focus almost exclusively on building or enhancing the types of executive competencies that have been shown to correlate highly with successful leadership performance. There is nothing wrong with this; certainly competency development should occupy center stage in this arena. But in focusing exclusively on competency development, we sometimes overlook the fact that the factors that cause leaders to succeed are not necessarily the same factors that cause them to fail. Over the last fifteen years there has been substantial research conducted on the subject of executive derailment—that is, the reasons for failure in individuals who have been viewed as high-performing leaders. Some of the most important derailment factors appear to be the following:

- *Inability to adapt to changes*—changes that occur in transitions, such as a new boss's leadership style, a new job's leadership skills requirements, or a new corporate culture. An offshoot of this is the inability to make the transition to strategic thinking and planning.

- *Insensitivity to others*—becoming intimidating, abrasive, or unwilling to listen to the views held by others.

- *Arrogance*—the belief that one can't make mistakes, or a critical view of the contributions others have made to one's success. (I call this the "hubris factor," a reference to the concept of prideful arrogance that in Grecian tragedies often leads to the downfall of the central character.)

- *Failure to meet business objectives*—often associated with the syndrome of self-promotion and overpromising, and then failure to meet expectations with solid business results.

- *Difficulty developing and leading a team*—difficulty shifting from an aggressive to a participative leadership style.[16]

- *Lack of a broad business focus*—lacking sufficient breadth to manage the next level of performance, according to recent research by Ellen Van Velsor and Jean Brittian Leslie of the Center for Creative Leadership (CCL).[17]

Morgan McCall, a CCL researcher who has worked on the problem of executive derailment for more than fifteen years, suggests that there are three scenarios in which the process of executive derailment appears to unfold. The first is a situation in which an executive, in part blinded by past successes, becomes arrogant and desensitized to the importance of continuing to learn from experience. A second common scenario is when a leader attempts to rely on the same skills and leadership style that have proven valuable in the past, when confronted with a completely new and unrelated work challenge. In this situation, past successes, coupled with the inability to adapt to changing conditions, lead to failure. A third scenario is when an executive has serious flaws that are either ignored early in his or her career due to the executive's ability to produce outstanding results, or only partially visible to others. As the executive continues to rise in the organization and encounter new work situations, these flaws become more and more apparent and eventually lead to the executive's downfall.[18]

Viewed in this context, derailment behavior can be regarded as the mirror opposite of learning agility, the central ingredient necessary for high-potential performance. McCall draws the following conclusion: "Three of these [behaviors]—early strength becoming weakness, preexisting flaws becoming important under changing conditions, and success leading to arrogance—can be seen as learning disorders. All reflect a failure to learn and develop as the surrounding context changes."[19] Craig Chappelow, a product manager for CCL, stresses the importance of both willingness and intent in the learning process, suggesting that, "You have to talk about both an individual's *ability* to learn from experience and his or her willingness to learn from experience. The concept of derailment takes into account one's *willingness* to take and learn from feedback."[20]

The challenge of applying the concept of derailment to executive development is that all too often derailment studies provide after-the-fact analyses of executive performance. To detect problem performance in advance of derailment, Chappelow suggests that to stay ahead of this problem, managers should watch for the following warning signs in their associates: "(1) A sense of arrogance and an insensitivity to other people—the arrogance being 'I've had some early success; what I do works great; I don't need to develop other skills.' (2) Overly ambiguous—not minding the shop while you work your career. (3) Betraying a trust—not doing what you told others you were going to do; in other words, not fulfilling your promises."[21]

To better gauge executives' potential for derailment, you may want to consider using the Benchmarks® multirater profile, distributed by CCL. Section Two of Benchmarks deals with several behaviors that have been shown to be related to executive derailment. In addition, Craig Chappelow is currently developing a stand-alone, approximately twenty-question inventory that will be used for self-assessment only, to raise an individual's awareness of derailment and encourage him or her to consider participating in a more detailed 360-degree process such as Benchmarks.[22] Finally, I strongly recommend the book *Preventing Derailment: What to Do Before It's Too Late,* by Michael M. Lombardo and Robert W. Eichinger (Center for Creative Leadership, 1991).

The question naturally arises as to whether the derailment factors that I've outlined in the preceding paragraphs are a uniquely American phenomenon, or whether they've been shown to contribute to the demise of managers in other countries. Research on international derailment has been performed by Ellen Van Velsor and Jean Brittian Leslie of the Center for Creative Leadership, through a study involving sixty-two executives from the United States, the United Kingdom, Belgium, Germany, France, Italy, and Spain. In the study, participants were asked to describe both a successful executive (who had risen to the top of his or her organization) and one who had derailed (who, although initially viewed as a high-potential performer, had either failed or plateaued in his or her job). Some of their conclusions were as follows:

- European managers placed greater emphasis on attributing executive derailment to having an authoritarian (dictatorial, intimidating) leadership style and problems with interpersonal relationships.[23] "Problems with interpersonal relationships were mentioned in two-thirds of the cases in Europe, as compared to one-third of the cases among derailed American managers."[24]

- Failure to meet business objectives, difficulties in building and leading a team, and inability to adapt to change were factors noted as important by both European and U.S. managers (noted in two-thirds of examples cited by both groups), although a particular derailment problem faced by European managers involved "difficulties in adjusting to other countries' cultures."[25]

Once again the factors of adaptability, cultural sensitivity, and interpersonal relationships are key factors, as are the ability to meet business objectives and, for leaders, the ability to build and lead an effective team. Building on available research on the success factors associated with international performance, three University of Southern California professors, Gretchen Spreitzer, Morgan McCall, and Joan Mahoney, have developed a measurement tool, *Prospector*, that can be used for evaluating the potential of international executives (available through the Center for Creative Leadership). The tool evaluates participants on eleven dimensions that have been shown to be important to the ability to learn from experience.[26] These four dimensions are divided into four primary clusters.

- The ability to get organizational attention and investment
- The ability to take or make additional learning opportunities
- The ability to create an effective context for learning
- The ability to change (to make use of feedback and learn) as the result of experience[27]

ELEMENT 7: UNDERSTAND THAT PERFORMANCE IMPROVEMENT STEMS FROM SELF-AWARENESS

The very factors that cause executives to advance rapidly early in their careers frequently become the reasons for their eventual downfall. A classic example is the executive whose self-confidence eventually develops into a self-defeating arrogance—a personal belief that he or she is impervious to failure. A related situation is when leaders advance so quickly and with such success that they become unwilling to adapt their previously successful leadership style to meet changing work conditions. As Morgan McCall suggests, because they are talented, exceptional performers find themselves frequently moving into new positions, entailing different roles, responsibilities, bosses, and job demands. Together, these adaptive requirements "call into question the continued success of a person's particular pattern of strengths and weaknesses. Finding themselves in situations that no longer play to their strengths, they are left with only their weaknesses to draw upon."[28]

This type of perceptual blindness is a common focal point for executive derailment, representing as it does the mirror opposite of the concept of learning agility. The irony is that the same senior-level executive who rigorously places every aspect of his or her business under a microscope for analysis—who adheres to such disciplines as activity-based accounting and process analysis—will very often exempt his or her own behavior from examination. Such executives simply do not stop to consider the major influence their personal leadership style exerts on their company's culture and performance.

The fact is that, regardless of how advanced and sophisticated the development tools we have at our disposal, if executives are not willing and able to periodically subject their own behavior to objective review—to ask how they fit into the leadership equation—the development process is doomed to fail. The special challenge that HR leaders face is that at the executive level, attempts to break through this kind of "perceptual armor" can be very difficult. One study drew conclusions that I believe many HR leaders can confirm from their own experience: that the power exercised by CEOs and other senior-level managers, along with their tendency to exert a dominating communication style and their unwillingness to take in critical feedback, all work against executives' ability to gain insight into behaviors that could prove detrimental to their long-term success.[29]

So the roadblock we face in attempting to develop executives is that while it is difficult, if not impossible, for people to change unless they first accept the need for change, many high-performing executives remain somewhat isolated from the types of day-to-day feedback that could alert them to the need to modify ineffective leadership behaviors. As a result of this dilemma, it is absolutely critical for executive development programs to provide a safe environment in which leaders can obtain performance feedback from others and to provide opportunities for self-reflection based on this feedback.

Sara King, Program Director for the Center for Creative Leadership, provides the following explanation of CCL's approach to executive development: "Our growth as an organization and our reputation center around individual assessment for development, a process whereby an individual receives a lot of information about his or her strengths and development needs through such activities as self-report instruments, 360-degree instruments, and simulation-based feedback. Our largest and most well-known program is our

Leadership Development Program®, which utilizes a variety of methods for assisting executives in personal development. These include: psychometric instruments, 360-degree instruments, videotaped exercises, business cases, studies, outdoor activities, one-on-one conversations, and peer consultant groups. Participants receive feedback on how their behaviors impact other individuals, teams or group settings, and organizational environments."[30]

King explains that one of the advantages of the assessment-for-development approach is that it enables executives to separate those aspects of their leadership behavior that are situation-specific from those that represent consistent leadership patterns across a variety of work situations. "The program helps individuals to discover whether they perform in the same way in different environments, for example, in both individual settings and team settings. If, for example, an individual has confirmed that he or she has a high need for control, you can see whether this control-seeking is played out in different situations and begin to form a composite view of their behavior. We establish a kind of 'theme building' in which we tell clients, 'You know that in one-on-one situations you are getting this kind of data, and in family situations you are getting this information, and in group exercises you are getting the following kinds of information—what does all of this mean to you?'"[31]

ELEMENT 8:
DEVELOP FOR THE FUTURE

Executive development efforts are often myopic in their perspective. There is a tendency to formulate executive development strategies solely in terms of *current* organizational needs, when in fact we need to simultaneously *scan forward* by three to five years to prepare executives and high-potential executive candidates to successfully anticipate and address future challenges. After all, isn't this the time frame we usually plan for when setting our succession plans?

In fact, there is widespread understanding among top-level executives that competency requirements for future CEOs and executives are likely to change significantly over the next few years. In a 1998 survey conducted by the London Business School for the Association of Executive Search Consultants (AESC), involving two hundred CEO and COO survey respondents representing fifteen countries, "managing change," "vision," and "adaptability to new situations" were cited as being the top three competencies required of today's European CEOs.[32] Respondents also agreed that their successors needed to outperform them in five key areas that are likely to take on greater importance in the next few years:

- Adaptability in new situations
- International strategic awareness
- Ability to motivate cross-border teams
- Sensitivity to different cultures
- International experience[33]

While you can't safely predict the future, you can take the following five steps to ensure that your organization's development programs take into consideration the ever-changing business environment:

1. Before launching an executive development program, spend some time helping your top-level leadership team get aligned regarding how they believe the business picture for their company will unfold over the next few years. The three "future forecasting" techniques introduced in Chapter 3 are a useful methodology.

2. Make "scenario forecasting" and "decision making under conditions of uncertainty" two overriding focal points for your company's development efforts. I regard both of these leadership competencies as metacompetencies that help individuals "learn how to learn" in an uncertain world.

3. Review studies, such as the ASEC study just cited, that can help your organization formulate a clearer picture of how other executives view future challenges and competency requirements. In particular, seek out future studies conducted by experts in your own industry regarding anticipated market trends.

4. Identify both the current and future leadership competencies required of your executives. (If you are not sure how to do this, review the suggestions provided in Chapter 4.)

5. Set up an executive development advisory council composed of current exemplary executives, high-potential executive candidates, and HR specialists. Provide an oversight function for your development program; this council can also help you troubleshoot your program proposal to ensure that you have addressed both the current requirements and the future needs of your organization.

ELEMENT 9: KEEP A GLOBAL FOCUS

Over the last several years, as I've networked with HR leaders in a variety of organizations, I've noted that even though most senior managers realize that their international markets are likely to fuel the lion's share of their market over the next few years, they typically still focus 90 percent of their development resources in support of their domestic executives. This is true even for companies that pride themselves on being global.

Following are six steps you can take to counter this kind of domestic myopia.

1. Fold anticipated changes (identified in your assessment of international business requirements in Chapter 3) into your executive resource plans. This planning process will help keep your senior team focused on the broader, international picture.

2. Include in your executive competency model (Chapter 4) a separate breakout for the competencies required for international success in your industry. This type of competency breakout can help you identify any competency gaps that could adversely affect your company's ability to successfully execute against your international business initiatives. To ensure that these issues receive sufficient review, consider creating an executive council composed of HR leaders across your divisions—both domestically and internationally. Such a diversified sponsorship team can provide a more balanced perspective to decisions that impact your annual talent review and succession planning processes, and your executive development programs.

3. Consider partnering with organizations such as the Institute for Management Development (IMD) in Lausanne, Switzerland, which has fifty-three years of experience in the area of international executive development, or such international schools as INSEAD, in Cesex, France, which can provide invaluable perspectives on international development.

4. Consider benchmarking companies such as Unilever, PepsiCo, and British Petroleum, which have built strong track records as international players.

5. Commit to an adequate level of resource support to do the job right. James Pulcrano, Dean of Executive Education for IMD, says, "Development efforts on the international scale should be given the same serious thought and analysis as the strategy that takes a company onto the international stage. The same applies to the people involved; use your best talent (if they have the people skills and curiosity previously mentioned). Do not leave it till the end, or as an afterthought. One could even argue that international development efforts should precede international operations."[34]

6. Be ready to adapt your learning approach to the needs of your international audience. Arnoud De Meyer suggests that when

attempting to build an international executive development effort it is important to adhere to the following principles:

- People from different cultures have different value systems and different priorities.
- The people in your classroom each have a very different model of how the world works. If you don't understand this, you can teach and actually get a totally different output than what you intended.
- Behavior is very different by culture and this will affect your teaching approach.
- You should realize that as soon as you get into international education you are working with people who are filtering through their second, third, or fourth language versus the language of instruction. The more you can do in terms of teaching through examples that they can understand, the better off you are. While the general principles of a subject may be applicable from one place to another, the examples, stories, and analogies you use need to be adapted to the local environment.
- As a teacher you should be very sensitive to values issues. You can upset your participants if you don't understand their values. In the United States you tend to have a very realistic view of its value system, you tend to tell the world what is good and bad, and to try to impose what you feel is ethically correct on other areas of the world. If you don't respect the values of other people, they tend to become defensive, and defensive people don't learn.[35]

THE KEYS TO DEVELOPMENT

The field of executive development is rapidly advancing, including such new technologies as computerized simulations, action learning, distance learning, and the use of self-paced CD-ROM and web-based instruction. Perhaps the most interesting advancement, however, comes not from these new tools and techniques, but from an entirely new way of looking at the concept of executive development. Executive development is no longer viewed as a series of self-contained activities performed within the cloistered confines of the corporate training department, but as learning systems that must be fully integrated with a company's business strategy and organizational structure.

These changes are reflected in a shift in ownership, from the HR department to senior management, and an understanding that development is an interactive process that occurs between the individual executive and the organization. CCL spokesperson Sara King says that one of the more interesting trends in the field of executive development is the increased understanding by companies of the need for organizational support for insight-based learning. As King explains, "If Joe completes one of our leadership programs and goes back to his worksite, we want to be able to work with his organization to determine how to support this change process within that organization. For example, recently an organization that sent twenty people to one of our programs asked us to lead a focus group and ask, 'What are the factors in this organization that really helped you create and maintain positive change? What factors impeded your development efforts?'"[36] As this example suggests, over the next few years we can anticipate that companies will begin to discard the view of executive development as a set of prescribed activities that lie apart from the day-to-day experience of work, to ask about the types of organizational adaptations that are required to fully support and nurture leadership change.

CASE IN POINT: GTE
Linda Krom, Director of Executive Development

One company that has done an excellent job of integrating business strategy with the design of its executive development program is GTE. GTE's learning approach integrates the use of business simulations and action learning (reviewed in Chapter 8) with an internal knowledge base that allows individuals to extend learning well beyond the classroom. GTE's program design and implementation involved support from two external providers: the Center for Executive Development (CED) and Executive Perspectives (EP). Linda Krom, Director of Executive Development for GTE Services Corporation, provides the following overview of GTE's executive development program.

> The design of our program involved a year of planning, with the simulations built from scratch. To guide our design we created the "Leadership Development Advisory Board," consisting of representatives from GTE, the Center for Executive Development, and Executive Perspectives. These individuals served as customers for both the design and evaluation of the simulations. In our case our own internal program designers, along with representatives from EP and CED, met with our senior team in advance to include all of GTE's goals (revenue, and so on) in the simulation, along with real challenges they were facing.

GTE's simulations involve four iterations of simulations, which together are equivalent to four "years" of work. GTE's program consists of four courses, called Leadership Development 1–4, with each course directed to a different level of management. We refer to our simulations as "learning labs" to emphasize that these workshops provide participants opportunities to make decisions about GTE. The purpose of the learning labs is to give participants an enterprisewide view of the challenges facing GTE, the decisions they face in meeting these challenges, and the tools necessary to make those decisions. This helps them understand what other people in our company are facing and to develop a sense of ownership in understanding that it is every manager's job to help our business succeed.

The simulation is introduced with preclass readings three weeks before class. Then at the beginning of the simulation we communicate GTE's strategy as a setup for the first year in which the participants run the company. During the simulation the instructors mix teams cross-functionally, with each team reflecting actual team and functional structures. There is no competition among teams; the teams must work together to meet enterprisewide goals. All teams work together to meet market leadership, critical thinking, leadership, and continuous improvement. The simulations provide opportunities for people to apply leadership skills to real-life work situations.

As part of the process, we ask each participant to pursue an action plan that he or she brought to class and refine it during the class. Each team rolls out its action plan for improvement, and on the last day they review their plans with their senior executives. After the class, they work individually or in teams to implement their plans and we work with them over a period of three months.

Following the completion of the action plans, we conduct "After-Action Reviews" in which we have participants ask:

• What did we set out to do?

• What were the results we expected?

• What really happened?

• What were the successes we realized?

• What could we have done differently to enhance our outcomes?

Each participant is then asked to write a success story, which we post on our "Center for Lessons Learned" site found on our intranet. You can pull data on the intranet by subject matter, region, business unit, or products and services to apply to different projects. As an example, if I were given the project of introducing paging service into a rural area, I could go into our database and type in the words "pager service" and "rural areas" and pull up success stories related to these topics, as well as the names of the individuals who produced them.

Now we are enhancing this process. We don't want it to be just a repository of information, but an action tool. Periodically we sit down with the heads of our business units and give them a "report card" on how their units are performing. As part of this process, we review with them the success stories we've obtained for their unit since the last review. The unit president then writes each individual a personal recognition letter. This gets the president involved and shows him or her what is going on in the organization. The approach we are taking is that you can learn a lot more from learning about your successes than you can from learning about your weaknesses.[37]

SUMMARY OF KEY POINTS

- Executive development experts tend to confuse development tools with development strategies. In the process, they try to force-fit their tools of choice to organizational settings, for which these tools are maladapted.

- A substantive executive resource strategy is based on nine basic elements.

- The first element is to link development objectives to business strategies by starting from a clear identification of one's executive target audiences (levels, functions, special needs of women executives, high-potential candidates, and so on), and by defining how executive development efforts are expected to support and enhance business objectives.

- The second element is to match your development approach to your organizational structure. While smaller companies can focus closer attention on the development of each executive, larger companies have other countervailing advantages, such as greater resources and a larger pool of executive candidates.

- The third element involves matching development plans to levels of learning agility. While low-potential learners may benefit from such options as structured coaching and job redesign, mid-range executives (those assessed as having a moderate level of learning agility) should be encouraged to broaden their range of competencies. When dealing with high-potential executives, the emphasis should be on providing development options that provide high challenges and ensure retention.

- The fourth element is to create developmental learning systems, not single-shot courses, by carefully considering the timing of developmental experiences, by interconnecting training and work activities, and by clearly defining what you hope executives will gain from developmental assignments.

- The fifth element is to evaluate leaders in terms of their commitment to leadership development time through such actions as setting clear development goals for managers, tying performance in executive development to executive compensation, and making people development a key criteria for the identification of high-performing executives.

- The sixth element is to focus development on preventing failure as well as on ensuring success. This means working with executives to overcome such potential derailment factors as lack of flexibility, insensitivity to others, the inability to build supportive relationships, and arrogance.

- The seventh element involves understanding that the starting point for change is self-awareness. The challenge here is to use such techniques as insight-focused training and 360-degree feedback (see Chapter 5) to encourage executives to realize that behaviors that may have worked for them in the past may need to be adapted to support new business challenges or different work settings.

- The eighth element is to develop for the future, by helping executives strengthen existing competencies while developing new, future-focused competencies. Related actions may involve facilitating discussions regarding how your senior team believes its business picture will unfold over the next few years, and by helping executives become adept in the techniques of "scenario forecasting" and "decision making under conditions of uncertainty."

- The ninth element is to keep a global focus by identifying international business requirements and the executive competencies needed to support them, by making these requirements part of your discussions in areas such as succession planning and the creation of executive development programs, by benchmarking the activities of international players, and by forming partnerships with schools such as IMD and INSEAD, which can provide a strong international perspective to your executive development efforts.

CHAPTER 10

PLANNING
FOR SUCCESSION

Throughout this book you have been introduced to a series of methodologies and techniques for selecting, assessing, developing, managing, and retaining top-level leadership talent. We now get to the central piece of the puzzle: succession planning. If the executive team is the keystone of your organization's leadership infrastructure, then surely succession planning—the process by which we identify appropriate successors to key leadership positions—is the mortar by which it is secured in place.

Succession planning has had a long-standing reputation as an effective mechanism for managing the transition of organizational leadership. Beginning in the mid-seventies, however, companies began to encounter a turbulent period marked by mergers, acquisitions, changing market conditions, and aggressive competitors who were somehow able to bore through industrial fire walls. As they strove to meet these challenges, many organizations discovered that they had to reinvent themselves, and in the process made extensive changes to their leadership requirements and supporting organizational structures. Much of the organizational transforming that occurred during this time involved continual restructurings, the elimination of middle-management layers, and the radical self-redefinition by many companies of their market positions and business objectives.

Within this context of unpredictable change and fragmented career ladders, organizations became very myopic, focusing on day-to-day fire fighting at the expense of long-term planning. At the same time, given the accelerated pace of change, the traditional model of succession planning, with its emphasis on long-term career paths and predictable replacements, just didn't seem to make a lot of sense.

While succession planning still plays a center-stage role in executive resource planning, many companies appear to be having difficulty adapting this process to today's rapidly changing business environment. A major study of leadership development in fifty-one companies representing eighteen industries conducted by the Saratoga Institute, an organization based in Santa Clara, California, specializing in HR research and consulting and sponsored by the American Management Association, showed that succession planning was the most frequently noted (by approximately 40 percent of respondents) method for identifying high-potential talent.[1] An unaffiliated study undertaken by RHR International, a consulting firm that specializes in executive coaching, showed that half of the 500 HR executive survey respondents reported that their companies were not prepared to replace executives and were relatively ineffective in succession planning.[2]

Only during the last few years have succession planning models begun to be effectively retrofitted to meet the changing conditions of today's workplace. Those companies that have been able to successfully make this adaptation have done so by making a radical shift in how they position, design, and implement their succession planning systems.

EMERGING APPROACHES TO SUCCESSION PLANNING

Table 26 contrasts traditional approaches to succession planning with emerging approaches. Let's take a closer look at each trend.

EXPERIENCE VERSUS ADAPTABILITY TO HIGH-CHANGE ENVIRONMENTS

Downsizing is an example of change that has greatly affected the succession planning process. One impact of repeated downsizings is that they force companies to dramatically reduce internal talent "feeder pools." The elimination of management levels not only makes career paths much more unpredictable, but in many organizations this change has also eliminated certain critical rungs in career ladders that companies have traditionally used as the testing grounds for emerging executive talent. Commenting on this gap, Jeannine Sandstrom of the Dallas-based consulting firm CoachWorks states, "There's a huge gap between middle and upper management, and those companies

TABLE 26	
TRADITIONAL VERSUS EMERGING APPROACHES TO SUCCESSION PLANNING	
Traditional Approaches	Emerging Approaches
A premium is placed on candidates with extensive organizational experience and time-in-grade.	A premium is placed on candidates who demonstrate leadership potential and adaptability to high-change environments.
Succession planning is restricted to top-level management and candidates are pulled exclusively from the next reporting level.	Succession planning extends down to directors and midlevel managers.
Planning assumes a uniform organizational structure.	Planning takes into consideration hybrid organizations composed of merged or acquired companies.
Replacement decisions are influenced by cultural bias.	Replacement decisions take into account multiple cultures.
Planning spans five to ten years, and succession reviews are conducted every one to two years.	Planning spans one to two years, and succession reviews are conducted biannually or quarterly.
Succession plans are owned by the HR department.	Succession plans are owned by the company's senior team.
Planning is "stable state," based on the current organizational structure.	Planning is "dynamic," based both on the current structure and on anticipated business challenges and accompanying structural changes.

that plan to still be in business twenty years down the road need career development, think tanks, mentoring, and cross-platform and cross-functional knowledge."[3] In response to this trend there is a growing emphasis on identifying executives who have the leadership capabilities and potential needed to help organizations quickly adapt to high-change business environments.

TOP-LEVEL VERSUS ALL-ENCOMPASSING
SUCCESSION PLANS

At the same time, we are witnessing an associated devaluation of the premium traditionally placed on seniority and organizational knowledge. Together, these changes mean that today senior managers have to probe deeper into their organizations to search for potential replacements, rather than assuming that successors will always come from the next level of management. Thus the slating of potential backfills for a senior vice president position might include not only high-performing vice presidents, but also one or two high-potential senior directors. Organizations are also beginning to extend replacement planning down to director and middle management levels, as they recognize the need to compensate for holes in bench strength by tracking, retaining, and developing tomorrow's senior leaders at a much earlier point in their leadership careers.[4]

UNIFORM ORGANIZATIONAL PLANNING VERSUS
DEVELOPMENT OF HYBRID MODELS

Organizations that have experienced mergers and acquisitions face the challenge of fusing together a common leadership team from different organizations, each having its own unique needs, culture, executive talent pool, and performance expectations. In fact, a recent Hewitt Associates study of almost 500 organizations around the world found that between 70 and 80 percent of respondents surveyed within each region identified the integration of different organizational cultures as the biggest challenge they faced following a merger or acquisition.[5]

George Klemp and Bernard Cullen are partners in Cambria Consulting, a Boston-based management consulting firm that specializes in building the organizational, work unit, and individual capabilities needed to create and sustain competitive advantage. As Klemp and Cullen explain it, "the need to understand the true operating culture is also important in a merger, when two (or more) different organizational cultures must be combined. For example, a decade after the pharmaceutical companies Ciba (Swiss-French) and Geigy (Swiss-German) merged, salespeople in the combined sales force still thought of themselves as either 'Ciba' or 'Geigy,' even though they were often calling on the same customers. (Today the company is known as Novartis, after a later merger with Sandoz.) The point is that before you can talk about identifying executive competencies to be used in selection or promotion decisions, you have to determine how your different companies will be aligned under a common vision and culture, and whether they are willing to align their resources."[6]

A case in point involves the recent merger between the two very different organizational cultures represented by Mobil and Exxon. In highlighting these differences, a *Wall Street Journal* article stated, "One company uses a stalking tiger in its advertising, while the other uses a whimsical flying horse. In putting together Exxon and Mobil, those differences in image and culture aren't a small detail."[7] The article described Mobil as a company that "always has taken risks," and that is "more open, both to the public and to new ideas." In contrast, Exxon was portrayed as "notoriously tight-lipped and conservative" and "slower to react, a vestige of a culture that took months, or even years, of studies before a decision was made."[8] The question, therefore, naturally arises as to whether these differences in organizational values and culture will translate into very different sets of expectations regarding executive performance.

Setting up a workable succession planning model for such companies takes more than a mail-merge of two separate lists of executive candidates. It requires clear alignment among all executive staff on a variety of important selection and development issues, such as:

- How do we define outstanding leadership and leadership potential?

- To what degree do our different organizations share a common picture of our future growth as a company and the types of leadership competencies we need to begin to develop to meet future challenges?

- What kinds of developmental experiences do we believe to be critical to executive advancement? What are the prerequisite experiences for advancement?

- How will we measure and assess candidates' readiness for promotion?

- How will leadership assessment decisions be made between our respective teams?

- How will candidates be shared or pooled across organizational boundaries?

- To what degree do we believe we can cross-feed executive talent across our organizations? In which organizational units can succession plans be cross-fed? In which units should we maintain separate and discrete succession plans?

- How can we calibrate the respective levels of responsibility and accountability of executives within our different organizations? Does a director, general manager, or vice president within our work function or business unit represent the same level of experience and responsibility as an individual who holds the same executive title in another work function or business unit of our company?

- How will the HR system elements of executive development, assessment, selection, and development be integrated in our respective HR units?

Klemp and Cullen provide the following recommendations for organizations that are attempting to develop an integrated succession planning system after a merger or acquisition:

- Get as clear as possible about the desired business strategy and business plan for the combined culture. For example, is the purpose of the merger to take costs out of the business, or to drive market share?

- Ask the company, "Even without a merger, what were some of the key operational challenges that existed previously? Which of these will continue to need addressing in the future?" (the "business as usual" question).

- If the merger is one where there is a dominant player, ask, "What are the pluses and minuses of the existing way that the senior team operates? What kinds of decisions do they handle effectively, and on what kinds of decisions do they seem to fall on their swords?" (You will need to actually observe how the leadership team interacts. Do not rely solely on self-reports.)

- When the merger is one of equals there is a lot more uncertainty on how these things are going to pan out. In assessing answers you need to look not only at content but also at process. (For example, you might try to find out how much autonomy the functional heads have and will continue to have. To what degree will these business managers function as advisers versus functioning as heads of independent business units?)

- Agree upon the critical business, technical, and behavioral competencies that will be required in the newly merged organization. These requirements should be informed by the business strategy, by an understanding of what competencies will be needed to handle the types of business simulations and challenges to be encountered, and by the kind of organizational culture you are trying to build on or create.

- Identify the top 10 percent of individuals in the company whom the senior team feels will be successful in the converged business culture. Our experience suggests that there will be a handful of strong top contenders. These people are not the issue, however; the issue is the other 90 percent. It is our job to "deconstruct" the other 90 percent through an in-depth assessment and discussion to determine which of these people have the knowledge, skill sets, and business attributes required to be effective. We need to get away from summary evaluations of people and toward detailed discussions of what they've done and accomplished.

- Combine the separate lists of people who pass muster, and slot them against the key position requirements in the merged organization.[9]

CULTURAL BIAS VERSUS ADAPTATION TO MULTIPLE CULTURES

A decade ago when we talked about succession planning it was assumed that the context was a domestic corporation. While expatriate executives were certainly folded into this process, issues of cross-cultural validity seldom entered the discussion. Increasingly, however, succession planning systems must accommodate organizational growth across national boundaries, requiring the integration of multiple cultures. There are subtleties at work in this process, as organizations begin to realize the degree to which their executive selection and planning processes can be blindsided by cultural biases. A group of senior managers can, in the space of an hour, make far-reaching (and entirely inaccurate) decisions regarding the relative promotability of executive candidates from different cultures on the basis of subjective and culturally biased concepts, such as labeling Asian candidates as having "flat personalities" or "lacking presence."[10]

Cross-cultural bias is an issue that should be addressed by any global corporation that intends to evaluate executives from different cultures by use of a uniform and standardized assessment process—such as an assessment center or a 360-degree instrument. The issue of cross-cultural validity can be especially problematic when organizations intend to use these data for the purposes of selection, promotion, or executive succession. This issue has been explored in depth by Michael Hoppe, a senior program and research associate for the Center for Creative Leadership. Hoppe has identified several concerns that HR leaders must address when attempting to apply 360-degree instruments to different cultures, including the following:

- The content of the 360-degree instrument can be culturally biased. Research suggests that certain leadership competencies are differentially valued by cultures.

- Cultures respond differently to the issue of trust, as manifested in the expectation that executives should openly give and receive feedback from one another.
- The way in which we interpret gaps between self- and other ratings on 360-degree profiles is likely to be subject to cultural biases.[11]

While it is outside the scope of this book to provide suggestions for improving the cross-cultural validity of assessment instruments, it would be advisable before blindly attempting to apply such instruments on a global scale to first work with specialists in cross-cultural training to look for ways to adapt evaluation methods to leaders from different cultures.

LONG-TERM PLANNING VERSUS SHORT REVIEW PERIOD

Traditionally, succession plans have attempted to anticipate career transitions over a five- to ten-year period—the period regarded as necessary to prepare an executive for advancement to the next level. In today's high-change and unpredictable environment, HR leaders and senior teams are beginning to contract this time period. Al Parchem, CEO and president of RHR International, notes, "When I got into the business people had five-year plans. Now people talk about two-year plans."[12]

At the same time, the accelerated pace of change has forced organizations to replace the concept of gradual, extended career paths with the assumption that some HIPO candidates will be forced to make significant career jumps with far less preparation than they would have had in the past. Apart from shrinking the time window for career paths, accelerated workplace change has also forced many companies to increase the frequency of their succession plan review process, taking this process from an annual event to a biannual or even quarterly experience.

OWNERSHIP BY HR VERSUS THE SENIOR TEAM

Another feature that distinguishes traditional succession planning from newer approaches is the roles played by the HR department and the senior team. Under traditional models, the succession planning process (like other aspects of the executive resource process) is managed as a backroom event by the HR department. The result is that succession decisions are often formed without sufficient input from the senior staff, causing new executives who are promoted or imported from the outside to lack credibility in the eyes of other

senior managers. Increasingly, companies are beginning to understand that succession plans lose much of their effectiveness if they are
not developed, owned, and supported by a company's top-level management team.

"Stable State" Versus "Dynamic" Planning

One last significant change that is occurring in succession planning is
in the area of organizational modeling. Traditional succession plans
are based on a "stable state" view of the organization, in which the
goal of the planning process is to look for likely replacements in an
organizational context that is assumed to remain relatively
unchanged over a five- to ten-year period. This approach is rapidly
being replaced by succession plans that incorporate a "dynamic"
view of the organization. In this approach we not only look for existing and future replacements for current executive positions, but at the
same time consider organizational changes that we anticipate will
occur over the next two to five years. We then ask ourselves how
these changes will affect both (1) the makeup of key executive positions—roles, responsibilities, spans of control, profit and loss responsibilities, vendor management, account management, technical competency mix; and (2) the degree to which we currently have in place
or could develop appropriate replacements to meet these future
requirements.

To better understand this, let's consider a hypothetical company,
XYZ Corporation, which produces and markets control chips to
first- and second-tier suppliers to the U.S. auto market. XYZ is a relatively small company, with approximately 2,000 employees, half of
whom are based at the headquarters in Auburn Hills, Michigan. The
other half include sales and customer support personnel who are
largely clustered around the company's three satellite offices: Detroit
(East), Chicago (Midwest), and San Francisco (West). Figure 27 on
page 250 shows XYZ's top-line organizational chart along with
selected reports to the senior team.

A traditional approach to succession planning would focus on
identifying likely replacements and backups for each of these positions given the assumption that the current state of the organization
will remain unaltered. Figure 28 on page 251 shows an example of
the succession plan that might be created for XYZ's senior team
given the use of this "stable state" model. (Note that succession planning models are typically color-coded for clarity. The models shown
in this chapter have been adapted to support a black-and-white format.) From this selective representation you can see that in the
current organizational design the vice president of IT reports to the

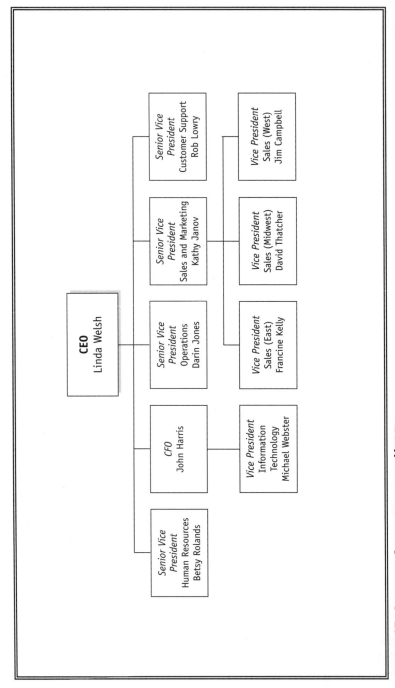

FIGURE 27 CURRENT ORGANIZATIONAL MODEL

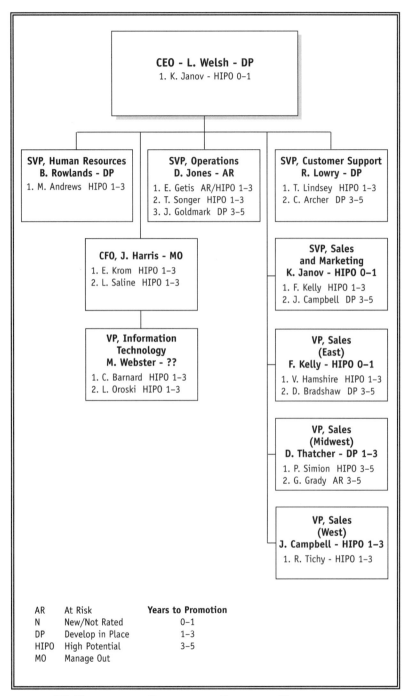

CEO - L. Welsh - DP
1. K. Janov - HIPO 0–1

SVP, Human Resources
B. Rowlands - DP
1. M. Andrews HIPO 1–3

SVP, Operations
D. Jones - AR
1. E. Getis AR/HIPO 1–3
2. T. Songer HIPO 1–3
3. J. Goldmark DP 3–5

SVP, Customer Support
R. Lowry - DP
1. T. Lindsey HIPO 1–3
2. C. Archer DP 3–5

CFO, J. Harris - MO
1. E. Krom HIPO 1–3
2. L. Saline HIPO 1–3

SVP, Sales
and Marketing
K. Janov - HIPO 0–1
1. F. Kelly HIPO 1–3
2. J. Campbell DP 3–5

VP, Information
Technology
M. Webster - ??
1. C. Barnard HIPO 1–3
2. L. Oroski HIPO 1–3

VP, Sales
(East)
F. Kelly - HIPO 0–1
1. V. Hamshire HIPO 1–3
2. D. Bradshaw DP 3–5

VP, Sales
(Midwest)
D. Thatcher - DP 1–3
1. P. Simion HIPO 3–5
2. G. Grady AR 3–5

VP, Sales
(West)
J. Campbell - HIPO 1–3
1. R. Tichy - HIPO 1–3

AR	At Risk	**Years to Promotion**
N	New/Not Rated	0–1
DP	Develop in Place	1–3
HIPO	High Potential	3–5
MO	Manage Out	

FIGURE 28 TRADITIONAL SUCCESSION PLANNING MODEL

company's CFO, with a vice president of sales assigned to each of the three sales territories. The IT function is primarily focused on software design, with network design and administration outsourced to an external provider.

In most cases, successors to XYZ's senior team have been identified from incumbents located in immediate lower levels. Each executive included in this plan has been classified as being (1) at risk—a high probability that he or she might decide to leave the company, (2) managed out (terminated), (3) developed in place, or (4) high potential. In each case we have also noted the estimated time required before the executive is felt to be ready for advancement.

What is wrong with this picture? Simply that the world usually doesn't work this way. The fact is that in an attempt to meet its strategic objective of expanding beyond its auto market and moving into electronics and hardware, XYZ Company is planning to implement a major reorganization over the next three years. The reorganization plan (Figure 29) is to group all sales and sales support into three sales sectors, with each market headed up by a general manager, who will have full profit-and-loss responsibility for his or her respective sector.

Some companies prefer to designate two separate lists of candidates. *Replacements* are those individuals who would serve as the best intermediate substitutes for incumbents, should these incumbents suddenly vacate their jobs due to extended sickness, death, termination, or separation. *Successors* are individuals who are believed to represent the most effective long-term heirs apparent for open positions.

All corporate support functions (HR, Finance, Operations) will continue to be directed by the corporate office. In addition, due to the growth of the IT function, this function will be headed up by a senior vice president who will now have full responsibility for network support and software development. Table 27 on pages 254 and 255 provides a comparative review of the current and anticipated organizational structures.

One could argue that since the anticipated organizational changes will not be occurring for another two to three years, XYZ's current succession plan might be appropriate for determining any expedient replacements that might be required over the next year. While this argument has merit, it neglects the long-term needs of the company. The problem is that XYZ's future reorganization will significantly change the roles, responsibilities, and reporting structure of many of the executive team members. Under the reorganization game plan, each general manager will have many of the responsibilities formerly held by the SVP of Sales, including orchestrating national sales strategies for their markets, identifying sales opportunities, and man-

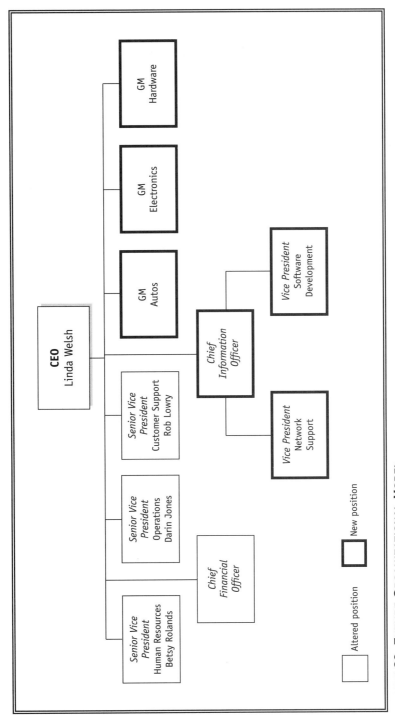

FIGURE 30 FUTURE ORGANIZATIONAL MODEL

CEO
Linda Welsh

Senior Vice President
Human Resources
Betsy Rolands

Senior Vice President
Operations
Darin Jones

Senior Vice President
Customer Support
Rob Lowry

Chief Financial Officer

Chief Information Officer

GM
Autos

GM
Electronics

GM
Hardware

Vice President
Network Support

Vice President
Software Development

Altered position

New position

TABLE 27

ANTICIPATED ORGANIZATIONAL CHANGES FOR XYZ COMPANY, YEAR 2000–YEAR 2003

Year 2000 Organizational Design	Year 2003 Organizational Design
• Sales efforts restricted to a single sales sector: Autos. • Sales efforts orchestrated through a single SVP function.	• Reorganize sales around three discrete sales sectors: Autos, Electronics, Hardware. • Sales efforts distributed under the control of three sector-based general managers. • Electronics and Hardware will be dedicated to a restricted launch in 2003, focused on a market assessment and creation of distribution channels.
• Current staffing level of 2,000. • Half of employees are based in headquarters in Auburn Hills, Michigan. Sales and customer support personnel are largely clustered around the company's three satellite offices: Detroit (East), Chicago (Midwest), and San Francisco (West).	• Projected staffing level of 2,800. • Disproportionate growth in Chicago (50 percent of staff hires will be located here).
• Yearly revenues of $450 million. • Profit margins.	• Projected yearly revenues of $650 million. • Profit margins likely to decrease to 18 to 20 percent to balance increased resource commitments to new sectors.

Year 2000 Organizational Design	Year 2003 Organizational Design
• IT functions under CFO. A large part of network development is currently outsourced.	• IT networking and software development functions are brought completely in-house under the direction of a CIO.
• Customer support is geographically based around the three sales territories.	• Separate customer support start-up teams will be formed in Electronics and Hardware to create the necessary process infrastructure (call desk, complaint management system, quality tracking, and so on). Subteams are expected to be folded back into CS in 2004.

aging profit, loss, volume, and market share. However, in addition to these responsibilities the general managers will be expected to manage the allocation of corporate resources to their sectors, and to develop more effective plans for growing their sectors. The executives who are selected to fill the general manager positions for the Electronics and Hardware sectors will need to know how to direct new product launches, including managing the market assessments for their new sectors, developing business growth plans, evaluating new customer bases, establishing totally new distribution channels, and deciding when and how to shift from initial launch to full rollout. In other words, the requirements for the general manager positions go well beyond sales management accountabilities to include launching and growing new businesses.

These reorganizational changes will dramatically alter our succession lineup for the executive sales team. In our former organizational model, two of the three sales vice presidents, Kelly and Campbell, were rated as high-potential executives who could quickly fill the shoes of their senior vice president, Kathy Janov. However, this assessment is based on the relatively moderate competency leap required to move from the VP to the SVP of Sales position, within the current organizational framework. Under the current structure, the SVP position is responsible for integrating the company's national sales activities for the three geographic territories. In this scenario, demonstrated prior success in expanding volume, increasing market share, and maintaining the profit line for one of the three territories could be considered to be a good predictor of future success in the SVP position.

On the other hand, making the jump from managing an existing sales territory to assuming the responsibilities of a general manager requires candidates to cross an immense competency gap. This is particularly the case for those candidates who will be asked to launch and implement the new Electronics and Hardware sectors. While these extended competency gaps might not require us to reevaluate whether Kelly and Campbell should be considered high-potential performers, it would definitely affect whether they (or Thatcher, the third VP of Sales) were slated as candidates for the open general manager positions. The new job structure would also force us to reexamine the time required to prepare these candidates for these promotions.

A quick scan of the planned reorganization shows two other major changes in executive job responsibilities. The chief IT position has moved from being a vice president position reporting to the CFO to a senior management position (CIO) reporting directly to the CEO. The position now includes discrete responsibilities for both network systems and corporate software development. In addition, the new CIO will also need to be able to develop an upstream plan for meeting the anticipated software and network requirements of the new sales sectors. Can Michael Webster, the current VP of Information Technology, meet this challenge? It is hard to say. What we do know is that the job requirements for this position have now radically changed and Webster's suitability as a successor will need to be reevaluated in terms of the new job requirements.

At the same time, keep in mind that our original succession plan calls for managing out the current CFO, John Harris, over the next three years. Under the planned reorganization, the CFO will no longer have control of the IT function. If Harris's top-rated successor, Eric Krom, is being considered in part because of his expertise in both Finance and IT, the anticipated changes to the CFO position might cause us to reevaluate Eric against his second-rated competitor, Linda Saline. Once again, reorganizational changes have led to changing job requirements, which in turn have forced us to reassess the suitability of successors for predicted openings in the leadership bench.

Before we leave our model, we have to consider the impact of this reorganization on the Customer Support function. Currently this function is geographically based and is devoted entirely to the Auto

Sales sector. As XYZ attempts to grow out two additional sales sectors, this change could have widespread repercussions for the types of executive competencies required of this function. To effectively make the transition, over the next three years the SVP of Customer Support will have to determine:

- The degree to which the Customer Support function established for the auto market can fit the two new markets

- The type of customer complaint tracking and help-desk management systems that will need to be created

- The types of customer support functions that XYZ will need to develop to maintain parity with entrenched competitors in the Electronics and Hardware sectors

- The most appropriate staffing structure needed to support these new sectors

Once these issues have been resolved, the SVP of Customer Support will have to work with the head of XYZ's HR department to determine how the new challenges will affect the job requirements for this senior position and for supporting positions at the VP and director levels.

GUIDELINES FOR SUCCESSION PLANNING

It is difficult to establish a workable, valid succession planning process that will meet the needs of a rapidly changing company. Here are six actions you can take to successfully meet this challenge.

1. *Perform a baseline review of your existing succession planning process.* Even if your company hasn't yet designed a formal succession planning system, there is some method (no matter how chaotic and informal) by which replacement and selection decisions are made in your company. A good starting point for revising or refining this methodology is to conduct interviews with members of your top-level senior team and highly respected junior-level executives to determine their level of satisfaction with your current system. At the same time, there are several performance factors you can use to evaluate the performance of your current succession planning system. These include:

  - *Percentage of holes in your bench.* The number of current executive positions for which no qualified replacement or backup has been designated.
  - *Strength of your talent pool.* The average number of high-potential successors selected for each executive position.

- *Time-to-fill.* The average time, during the last three years, that an executive opening has remained vacant before a qualified successor was located.
- *Internal versus external strength.* The percentage of executive vacancies that have had to be filled by external candidates (with associated costs for searches, sign-on bonuses, and relocation costs) due to the lack of suitable internal candidates.
- *Quality of candidates.* The average performance ratings given to internal or external replacements six or twelve months after being placed in an opening. How well are replacements meeting the requirements for positions? Regardless of the source of the replacement (internal or external), subsequent performance problems should provide a warning flag indicating either that the job requirements for executive positions have not been clearly defined or that an inadequate assessment and selection process is being used to identify candidates for these positions.
- *Executive turnover.* Review both voluntary turnover rates for all executives and those for each executive function, for identified HIPO candidates and for individuals who have recently been hired or advanced into positions. Excessive turnover may indicate that your executives have little faith that the current succession planning system accurately identifies and rewards top performers in the organization. Additional suggestions for implementing an executive retention program can be found in Chapter 14.

2. *Gain senior team alignment on the scope of the succession plan and the methods by which succession decisions will be reached.* One could make a valid argument that the only way to ensure succession planning is to carry it down to the middle management level of the organization. While such an inclusive approach certainly covers the full scope of the executive bench, it could also be incredibly unwieldy, involving the assessment, tracking, and development of hundreds of successor candidates. It could also turn into a paper nightmare, a feature that would cause senior managers to relinquish ownership of the program to the HR department. A more practical option might be to limit the scope of the program to the first two levels of your corporate office and supporting divisions, along with executive positions that are deemed critical by your senior staff. The criticality of a position can be jointly decided by your senior team, based on the relative business impact of losing someone in that position and the difficulty and associated cost of filling that position. As an example, given the high market demand for promising IT execu-

tives, the succession planning process might extend far deeper into the IT sector of the organization than it would in other parts of the company, such as Operations or Finance.

Along with agreement on program scope, senior managers need to have input on the methods by which succession decisions will be made. All too often this is where HR departments become their own worst enemies. They keep their succession planning process cloistered in mystery like an archaic cult that could never by fully understood or appreciated by the uninitiated. The result is that executive teams actively resist the recommendations offered up through HR succession plans, on the grounds that these plans have been formulated in secret. Bringing the succession planning process out of the closet is one of the easiest steps we can take to gain the full support and endorsement of our executive teams. Specifically, senior managers want to know

- How will candidates be selected for succession?
- What qualifies a candidate for succession?
- What roles will the CEO and top-level senior team play in decision making?
- How often will succession plans be reviewed?
- What responsibility will senior managers have in providing input on succession decisions?
- How will disagreements be resolved regarding the suitability of candidates for future positions and the timing of replacements?
- Will successor candidates be informed of their status?
- How will succession planning recommendations be reviewed by the company's governing board?
- What support services (coaching, training, instruction in completion of the succession plans) will HR offer in the process?
- Who will have access to the succession planning data and how will this information be retained within the company?

In responding to these questions, keep in mind that the same guidelines that were laid out in Chapter 6 for the executive team review (ETR)—including planning and facilitating the ETR session, developing a documentation database, and maintaining document control—are also relevant to managing the succession planning process. Nonetheless, treat these two discussions as separate meeting agendas. Your executive team should discuss the selection of successors only after it has reached agreement on the criteria by which high-potential/high-performance leaders will be identified, and has jointly identified these individuals.

3. *Gain alignment on anticipated business and organizational changes and associated changes in leadership requirements.* This step involves articulating the assumptions regarding how your company's business environment is expected to change over the next three to five years, the shape your organization will take during the same period, and how leadership roles will need to adapt in response to these changing conditions. A good method for jump-starting an open dialogue on these topics is through using the three techniques introduced in Chapter 3 (the strategic planning review, scenario forecasting, and business analysis) for predicting anticipated future changes in your company's business environment.

4. *Develop leadership profiles that reflect your evolving organization.* With these future changes in mind, the next step is to develop detailed leadership profiles that reflect the evolving requirements of a given executive position. This process goes beyond a cursory review of a generic job description to delineate job characteristics that are unique to the position in question, while at the same time flagging changes that are likely to transform the scope and requirements of the job over the next three to five years. In the same way that a hunter "leads" a moving target by aiming ahead of the target, succession planning can be aimed in front of the organizational target by identifying and developing competencies that will be essential to future performance.

To get a better idea of how a leadership profile can reflect changing organizational requirements, refer back to Figure 7 in Chapter 3, which shows a business analysis performed for a company's HR function. From this business analysis we can surmise that over the next few years the individual who holds the position of SVP of HR will need to know how to implement international compensation, selection, and employee relations systems; be able to conduct and manage retention studies for improving attrition of high-risk HIPOs (particularly in high-tech areas such as the IT function); and know how to undertake and manage major work redesign efforts, such as the creation of self-directed work teams. By getting senior team members to agree on the most important changing requirements for executive positions, you ensure that replacement and succession decisions are made around the needs of the job, rather than the dominant personal characteristics of the executive incumbent.

5. *Incorporate candidates' input into the selection process.* If selection planning is designed to select out the best candidates for placement and future advancement, then it stands to reason that

self-selection should play an important part. I am continually surprised at the number of companies I encounter that make assumptions regarding their executives' willingness to relocate or take on international assignments, desire for further advancement, career plans (including plans for impending retirement), and willingness to make cross-functional moves. Some employers like to view their executive staff as chess pieces on a playing board, to be moved around as required by the dictates of the company. This kind of attitude is more than just insensitivity to individuals' needs; it is also very bad business. It leads to ill-fitted mismatches of candidates to positions, excessively high turnover rates, and serious morale problems. The simple remedy is for each manager to talk with his or her executive reports and find out more about their career aspirations and the types of tradeoffs they are willing to make to meet career goals before attempting to complete succession planning profiles on those individuals.

6. *Capture all data in a centralized succession planning database.* If you are in a small start-up company, you may be seriously questioning whether you would be better off forgoing the creation of a database in favor of a simple hard-copy system. My recommendation is to design such a database now, and do it from the point of view of what you may conceivably need five years from now. Small companies have a way of quickly growing beyond the catch-all HR systems that are initially designed.

If you do not have any experience in designing databases and your IT department is less than supportive, you might consider purchasing a system from a software consulting firm that specializes in this area. Educational Data Systems is a Dearborn, Michigan–based provider of the Occupational Skills Analysis System (OSAS), a career planning database that has been used by companies to orchestrate their succession planning systems. Bob Schneiders, the company president, explains that his company is a training consulting firm "specializing in workforce preparedness. We do everything from recruitment to outplacement."[13] OSAS is a database system in which a taxonomy of skills is broken down into discrete duties, each of which in turn is broken down into even finer gradients of tasks. According to Schneiders, "companies that use the product are moving away from using titles to describe people and toward key words that describe key functions. In a company that wants to move people up or out, you can describe people by key words. Because the tasks get very detailed, accuracy increases at the detailed level."[14]

As an example of how OSAS can be applied, Schneiders mentions Rockwell Aerospace, which downsized its workforce from 1,700 to 900 employees. To accomplish this the company required an accompanying reduction in its number of job descriptions. Schneiders explains that "they started with software in aerospace vernacular, and had each individual and his or her supervisor read the breakout of skills used for each job and rate their competencies in them on a 1-to-5 scale—1 indicating that the individual is aware of the skill, and 5 indicating sufficient mastery to teach it to others. From this we developed discrepancy profiles, or comparisons of how individuals and their managers viewed their jobs."[15]

International corporations are beginning to understand the benefits of leveraging their best talent across their organizations by using standardized selection criteria, computerized databases, and executive review teams to identify individuals for international assignments. One such company, Colgate-Palmolive, makes use of "a centralized committee that consists of the chief operating officer, the division presidents, the head of global business development, and a human resource representative."[16]

Researchers John A. Quelch, Dean of London Business School, and Helen Bloom say that at Unilever corporation, "HR has a seat on the board's executive committee—the organization that focuses on developing in-house talent and hothousing future leaders in all markets. The result is that 95 percent of Unilever's top 300 managers are homegrown."[17] They advise that in evaluating one's international bench, companies should create a "mobility pyramid" to rate managers in terms of their willingness to be mobile, with the scale ranging from individuals who refuse to budge from their native country, to those willing to move once, to those "glopats" who are continuously on the move around the globe on short and midterm assignments.[18]

Samir Gupte, Senior Director of Human Resources for Choice Hotels International, advises that companies "search their internal databases for candidates who have not only the right technical skills, but also behaviors and life experiences that indicate a propensity toward global and cultural awareness. It makes little sense to select a successful executive who has lived a very insular American lifestyle and has never traveled outside the United States to run a start-up operation in Kenya. No amount of pretraining will prepare that executive for the personal and professional complexities he or she is likely to encounter."[19]

FINAL CAVEATS

Following are a few final suggestions regarding the design and management of your succession planning system.

YOUR CEO MUST DRIVE THE PROCESS

Senior managers sometimes hoard their best talent or are negligent in completing and updating succession planning documentation. I have seen some organizations in which senior managers provide token support to succession planning programs while actively striving to circumvent these programs when it comes time to make important selection or promotional decisions. The only way to avert these problems is through the full involvement and support of your company's CEO. This support takes several forms, including the following:

- Take the time, with the company's chief HR officer, to diligently identify possible candidates for the CEO's own position.
- Make succession planning and the identification of successor candidates and potential replacements a key factor in evaluating the performance of the company's senior managers.
- Personally sponsor and participate in periodic succession planning reviews.

KEEP IT SIMPLE

It is better to create a simple, paper-based succession planning model that you know will be thoroughly completed by all participants than to create a fancy software system or a multiple-page planning document that no one will take the time to complete or review. As a rule of thumb, the summary models for your succession planning process should be no more than three pages in length, color-coded for easier review, and in a graphic format that is immediately interpretable by the reader. Before going far in the design of your succession planning documentation, select a few senior managers who are willing to test it out. Look for aspects of your documentation that are difficult or cumbersome to complete, or areas of ambiguity, such as the definitions that are provided for "promotability" and "potential."

DECIDE WHETHER TO NOTIFY SUCCESSOR
CANDIDATES OF THEIR STATUS

This should be a uniform decision that is carried out in a consistent way across your organization. One argument against notifying candidates who have been designated as "high potential" or "likely successors" is that in so doing you will create harmful competition among all candidates for the same positions. A further argument is that when individuals are notified that they are viewed as rising stars they tend to become complacent, viewing promotion as a sure thing—termed by one succession planning consultant, William Rothwell, the "crown prince phenomenon."[20] The strong counter to this argument is that you gain nothing if you go through the tedious and time-consuming process of identifying HIPOs and successors only to have these individuals leave your company because they see little in the way of advancement opportunities. A reasonable alternative that addresses all of these concerns is to create a development program for high-potential candidates and slated executive successors that is offered on a selected basis to all exceptional performers in your company.

DESIGNATE A SENIOR-LEVEL PROCESS SPONSOR

We know that an effective succession planning process needs the full sponsorship and support of your CEO. Why then do you also need a senior-level sponsor? The answer is that you may not have ready access to your CEO to provide guidance in the design and management of your succession planning program. A senior-level sponsor, one who reports directly to your CEO and who is widely respected by your senior team, can provide an important coaching role by helping you adapt the design of your succession planning program to the changing needs of your company, encouraging you to carefully think through the most effective method of communicating your implementation plan to your executive team, helping you troubleshoot potential problems in your design, and alerting you to sensitive issues that may arise in your team review session.

USE EXECUTIVE COUNCILS TO LINK SUCCESSION PLANS

The succession planning model outlined in Figure 29 deals with the simplest organizational structure of all—a single, unified executive body that provides overall leadership to the entire organization. Those suggestions and guidelines for succession planning are entirely appropriate for a small to midsized company, or for a single division of a large corporation. One might reasonably ask how those methods can be adapted to meet the needs of a large company having several executive talent pools, each of which may be hidden from the view of the others. The answer lies in creating an orchestrating executive council composed of senior HR executives from each division as well as the senior managers who act as process sponsors to those divisions.

Early in the design of the succession planning system these council members should meet to develop a set of recommendations for a companywide succession planning system that can be used to pool talent among their respective divisions. These recommendations tend to fall into two different categories.

The first category comprises recommendations regarding the *design* of the succession planning system.

- How executive competencies will be assessed and measured across divisions.

- The behavioral anchors (see Chapter 4) that will be used to provide greater definition of these competencies.

- The methods that will be used to assess executives against competencies and make succession planning determinations. If one division relies solely on performance appraisal data to make succession decisions while a second uses 360-degree data, it will be difficult to directly compare the performance of candidates across these different work units.

- The specifications for the common succession planning database that will allow executives from different divisions to track the performance and placement of executives. (More specifically, what kind of information will need to be retained and at what level of detail?)

The second category involves issues regarding the *management* of the succession planning system.

- When during the year succession planning data will be gathered and collated within each division.

- How the review process will take place within each division by members of the senior team.

- How the succession planning database will be managed. (Who will have access to these data? Who will be responsible for their periodic updating? Who will be responsible for generating composite reports regarding the implications of these data for corporate performance—assessing the corporation's overall executive bench strength?)

- The review and approval process for moving executive candidates across divisional lines. Each general manager will have a wide degree of latitude for making personnel decisions within his or her division. The objective is to set up guidelines that prevent ill-considered "raiding parties" on executive talent in other divisions.

Often there is initial resistance by divisional senior managers to the idea of developing a companywide talent pool. Such resistance may stem from fear of losing total control over placement and development decisions and the desire to hoard key talent within a division. It is partially for these reasons that CEO sponsorship and support are so critical to the successful implementation of the succession planning process. Without this sponsorship, each divisional "silo" is likely to act in ways that do not support the overall goals of the corporation.

TARGET THE LEADERSHIP NEEDS
OF YOUR ORGANIZATION

Throughout this chapter I have emphasized the importance of using succession planning to identify talented executive successors and replacements. Certainly this should be the central aim and purpose of any succession planning system. A well-designed system can also support other corporate HR goals, such as advancing a company's diversity goals for leadership. Corporate models for such efforts include Dow Chemical, which from 1990 to 1997 experienced a 147 percent increase in the number of senior-level jobs filled by women (108 out of 1,205 positions); Hoechst Celanese Corporation, which has doubled its number of senior-level executives since 1991; and Motorola, which now has women designated as first- or second-choice successors for about 75 of 300 senior-level positions.[21]

Following are several steps your company can take to foster this effort.

- Set firm targets for advancing diversity leadership goals. Hoechst Celanese has set the goal to increase its current percentage of women and minority middle managers (20 percent) and executives (14 percent) to 34 percent of all managers by 2001.[22]

- Tie diversity performance to the bonus goals of senior managers. (Hoechst Celanese's goals constitute 25 percent of its executive bonuses.)[23]

- Pair women and minorities with senior-level mentors.

- Aggressively recruit women and minorities into lower-level management positions.

- Require that women and minority candidates make up part of the slate for succession to senior-level positions. In an article for *Business Week*, reporters Linda Himelstein and Stephanie Anderson Forest explained that of the three successor candidates required for each senior manager position at Motorola, "The first is the manager who would fill the job in an emergency. The second slot is for someone who could be groomed for the job in three to five years. The third spot is dedicated to the woman or minority closest to being qualified for the position."[24]

These examples point out some of the definitive steps that can be taken to ensure that succession planning meets the full range of organizational goals.

COMPARE HIPOS TO EXTERNAL PERFORMERS

It is easy to become so caught up in the bells and whistles of designing a succession planning process that one might not stop to see this process for what it is—a method for looking for the best-of-the-best *internal* executive candidates. In other words, identifying a restrictive HIPO pool of talent does not ensure that these high-potential individuals are, in fact, exemplary performers when measured against world-class standards. For this reason, management consultant John Beeson suggests that some high-performing companies take the extra step of routinely interviewing external candidates, typically for more senior positions.[25] Beeson advises that this type of interview process "allows the company to 'calibrate' the quality of its internal people with world-class talent from other companies and upgrade its talent base where necessary."[26] (For some suggestions regarding how this type of calibration may be performed, review the assessment techniques covered in Chapter 5, along with the structured selection interview process introduced later in Chapter 12.)

CASE IN POINT: THE BOEING COMPANY
Jim Dagnon, Senior Vice President of People

Possibly one of the most massive mergers ever undertaken was the formation of The Boeing Company out of the organizations formerly known as Boeing, McDonald Douglas, and Rockwell. Jim Dagnon, Senior Vice President of People for The Boeing Company, provides the following summary of the challenge his organization faced in building an integrated succession plan for their new organization:

> Each of our separate companies—Boeing, McDonald Douglas, Rockwell—had different pieces, a "space" piece, a "defense" piece, and a "commercial" piece. The result was that after the merger we had to integrate the commercial people, space people, and defense people. So we had a mixture issue and also a concern about how to

get the best people into key jobs. We also had to determine how we could get Phil and Harry [the companies' two presidents] to quickly get to know each other's people. Finally, we had to determine how we were going to implement objective measures, and spend enough time together to be able to evaluate people.

When we merged, the first step was that our two CEOs picked their top teams and sent their HR folks to select the very best people for each job. We did this top-down as a very collaborative process with our senior team. We then constructed a wall chart with magnetic tags. The eleven people who were running Boeing would go to these sites with their VPs and review incumbents and successors, then describe everyone who was in the plan. We indicated the company each person had come from, so you could look at the chart and immediately determine if you were getting a diverse mix.

We then engaged an outside consulting company, PDI [Personnel Decisions, International] from Minnesota. We told them, "We are a new company and we don't know if the skill sets we had are what we need for the new company." They looked at the business challenges and the required competencies. They were also able to determine where we had very different views on people, and in which areas we were long or short on competencies within our bench.

Each executive was run through a two-and-a-half-day assessment center, including role-plays using a business simulation based on a company similar to our own. This fictitious company was a ship manufacturer that (like us) made different products in the areas of defense, space, and commercial. The assessment process included three assessment exercises and psychometric tests. The other output from the assessment was a two-hour interview each manager had with our consultants, so that that manager would be more familiar with the results of the assessment.

We are now running this assessment process top-down through our top 600 people. In addition, we will soon open a $55-million training facility, and personnel will take the development information they received into this training. For twelve days they will be working on areas for development.

Regarding potential roadblocks, keep in mind that instead of a once-a-year practice this is a living document. The room here at headquarters stays intact. We had to work on organizational design ways to ensure that people worked together. After our reorganization we knew that although we had the right organization we might still need some shiftings—situations in which we determined a placement error and would say "so-and-so isn't working out; who do we have to replace this person?" So our succession planning room has become a constant decision-making room. We are in the room once a month. It functions as a think tank for us to see how we tie people together. When we went through the next iteration, to identify those people who were originally on the succession list who were no longer here, we discovered 85 percent of our placements followed our succession plan.[27]

SUMMARY OF KEY POINTS

- There is a renewed corporate interest in succession planning, yet many companies feel that their succession planning processes are inadequate to meet their needs.

- Traditional succession planning, with its emphasis on long-term, stable career paths, is mismatched to the needs of today's organization. Emerging succession planning models differ from traditional models in several respects, including (1) a greater emphasis on evaluating executives' adaptability to high-change work environments, (2) a planning process that extends much deeper into the organization, (3) attempts to adapt succession planning to hybrid (merged/acquired) organizations, and (4) an emphasis on planning for truly global organizations.

- Steps you can take to strengthen your company's succession planning process include (1) performing a baseline review to determine the extent to which your existing succession planning process meets your company's needs, (2) developing leadership profiles that reflect your evolving organization, (3) incorporating candidates' input into the succession planning process, and (4) capturing all data on executives in a centralized succession planning database.

- When attempting to implement a succession plan, consider the following caveats: keep your CEO deeply involved in the process, keep the planning process simple, decide in advance whether successor candidates will be notified of their status, identify a senior-level process sponsor, use an executive council to link corporate and divisional succession plans, and design your succession planning system to meet the larger leadership needs of your organization, such as corporate diversity goals.

CHAPTER 11

UNCOVERING EXCEPTIONAL TALENT

A central characteristic shared by organizations that are able to build superior leadership teams is their ability to acquire outstanding leadership talent. In today's business environment, with its shortage of leadership talent, the ability to uncover superior performers and to attract them to your organization is quite an achievement. Unfortunately, many companies still approach the executive recruiting process in a haphazard and undisciplined manner. A recent study of British companies found that only half of 200 companies surveyed used any formal methods for identifying their top managers. The rest relied either on personal recommendations or (in the case of internal promotions) data from performance appraisals.[1] One executive recruiting consultant places the "mismatch rate" for externally hired managers at 50 percent, and the average cost for an executive mis-hire (including compensation, severance package, and the costs of rehiring, on-boarding, and performance problems accrued by the mis-hire) at twenty-four times the individual's base compensation.[2]

Those companies that are attempting to undertake a formal executive selection and hiring process face formidable challenges. As I outlined in Chapter 1, the current scarcity of executive talent is placing a competitive strain on companies that hope to capture the best talent. As industries become less insular and markets more diffuse, employers are realizing the need to go outside their industries to find world-class leaders. The challenge is in identifying the best executive candidates—often individuals who are not actively seeking employment and who may be hidden within unfamiliar industries. At the same time, the cost for searching is rising rapidly, driven in part by the rise in executive compensation and concurrent increase in search costs.

Finally, there is the challenge of keeping good talent once you have captured him or her. A survey of 5,000 executives by IMCOR, a Stamford, Connecticut–based supplier of interim and project managers, found that 40 percent of respondents have held two jobs in the last ten years, and 30 percent have held three jobs, with 46 percent of respondents indicating that they expect their current or next position to last only one to five years.[3] In discussing the implications of this study, John Thompson, CEO of IMCOR, said, "We will continue to see companies hiring executives for shorter periods of time and relying more heavily on contract professionals who are available on an as-needed basis."[4]

The most effective organizations at recruiting superior talent do so by excelling in three key organizational functions.

- *Marketing* their company in a way that attracts superior talent
- *Analyzing* industries to uncover "hidden" talent
- *Searching* the field to meet targeted job requirements

In this chapter I will introduce some of the cutting-edge practices that world-class organizations are employing within each of these functions.

MARKETING: SELLING THE "SIZZLE" OF YOUR ORGANIZATION

The starting point for attracting a superior leadership team to your organization is to develop what researchers in the *McKinsey Quarterly* study "The War for Talent" have termed "a winning employee value proposition."[5] This means sending a clear and compelling message regarding why a candidate should consider your company an employer of choice. For Microsoft, the compelling value proposition involves convincing job candidates that, *if they are worthy,* they have the opportunity to work for the best—for a company that is quickly exploding into new markets and technologies.

For Southwest Airlines, the value proposition is the opportunity to join a "corporate family" where humor, zany creativity, and entrepreneurship are actively encouraged and supported. Southwest reinforces this message at each stage of its recruiting process, from corporate marketing to final selection. A past employment ad showed a teacher's note attached to a child's picture of a tyrannosaurus, chastising the child for painting outside the lines. The caption to the ad read,

"Brian shows an early aptitude for working with Southwest Airlines." The message to the perspective candidate is clear—if you want to work in a place where creativity is not punished, look no further.[6]

The value proposition your company offers may be the opportunity to work for an organization that encourages balance between work and personal life and makes creative accommodations to lifestyle needs; or the opportunity to enter exciting new markets within a global firm; or being part of a company that is breaking new ground in technology. Whatever value proposition you provide to prospective job candidates, the point is to do more than create a slick corporate marketing message. Uncover the one thing about your company that sets it apart as a work environment where exceptional leaders would want to make a long-term commitment. Having a winning value proposition means that superior job candidates will actively pursue your company as their employer of choice, a factor that easily translates into improved hiring and retention. The McKinsey study found that, "83 percent of top-quintile HR executives say their job offers are rarely turned down compared with 60 percent for mid-quintile executives, while 88 percent of top-quintile executives say they seldom lose top performers to other companies as against 73 percent of mid-quintile executives."[7]

The second major factor in organizational marketing is to develop a compensation package that signals to superior performers that you are willing to pay for exceptional talent. The McKinsey study found that, "To get the people they want, 39 percent of top-quintile companies pay whatever it takes, compared with 26 percent of their mid-quintile counterparts."[8] It is not just pay, but variable pay, that attracts the best performers to a company. A 1998 Robert Half International survey of 150 executives found that 37 percent rated stock options as a "very important" hiring and retention tool, compared with only 23 percent of respondents in a similar 1991 survey.[9] According to Lynn Taylor, Vice President and Director of Research for Robert Half, "Variable compensation, such as stock options and performance-based pay, encourages top performers to remain with a company and help shape its future direction."[10]

As more companies use these kinds of "golden handcuffs" to retain top performers, interested employers will be forced to come up with creative options that counterbalance the financial loss faced by executives in walking away from stock options that have not yet reached their vesting period. For Russ Glicksman, president of the Beam Group, a Philadelphia-based executive search firm, this meant convincing an interested employer, an insurance company, to provide a candidate for a senior marketing position with a special five-year loan. A portion (20 percent) of the loan would be given forgiven for each year the executive remained with the insurance company. Under this agreement, five years of service would completely eliminate the burden of loan repayment.[11] This type of creative deal making is likely to become much more prevalent as companies continue to explore creative, cost-effective packages for luring executive candidates away from competitors.

The final component of organizational marketing involves sending job candidates a clear message about their importance, and about the importance the hiring company attributes to the selection process by getting the CEO directly involved in the recruiting process. Peter Felix, president of the Association of Executive Search Consultants, emphasizes that, "When you are dealing with senior management recruitment, it makes a lot of difference if the top executive gets involved, even for a few minutes, in the recruiting process. If the CEO can meet the candidate and articulate the business strategy, this experience can leave a very strong, positive impression on the candidate."[12]

Bradford and Geoffrey Smart provide several examples of the incredible impact that this personal involvement of the CEO has in strengthening recruitment efforts. "AlliedSignal's Larry Bossidy . . . is personally involved in hiring decisions for the top 150 executives. . . . Bill Gates himself makes calls to talented undergraduates to recruit them to join Microsoft. . . . At William M. Mercer, Inc., managing partner Charles Hartwig has breakfast or lunch with prospective recruits two or three times a week."[13] The bottom-line impact that these actions have on job candidates, especially junior-level managers and professionals, is to reaffirm the importance that the hiring company places on them as a corporate investment.

ANALYZING: DISCOVERING
WHERE THE BEST ARE HIDING

Many companies are beginning to discard the view of executive search as a means to fill immediate openings, in favor of viewing it as a way to continually scour the field for superior talent. Continual search, otherwise known as the presearch, involves exploring the industry for key positions before openings are actually listed.

According to David Lord, president of Executive Search Information Services, a consulting firm that assists companies with their corporate search initiatives, the increased use of presearch by many companies heralds the shift from a tactical to a strategic hiring process. Lord suggests that, "The idea of executive search has switched from 'Gee, we are behind the eight ball and have to go outside,' to 'It is part of our strategy to aggressively go outside and continually bring in new talent that can provide fresh ideas.'"[14] The McKinsey study claims that, "Talent-winners also recruit continuously, rather than simply to fill openings. Thirty-one percent of HR directors at top-quintile companies strongly agree that they are always looking for great talent and bring it in whenever they find it, compared to only 9 percent at mid-quintile companies."[15] *Business Week* writers Jennifer Reingold and Nicole Harris indicate that the trend toward presearch is very lucrative for search firms, "which can get between 40 percent and two-thirds of their normal fee. The number of presearches done by Russell Reynolds Associates, for example, has more than doubled since 1995."[16]

While the implementation of presearch differs from company to company, the most aggressive approach follows the following four-step process.

1. An acquiring company puts together a hit list of key, high-impact leadership positions that it would like to fill as quickly as openings become available, or as new initiatives dictate the need for rapid growth and expansion.

2. The company then makes up a second hit list of potential target organizations that have established exceptional reputations in the functional target areas, and that are believed to house high performers in these areas.

3. Within each targeted company, the employer develops a special list of employee targets, including both incumbent executives and identified high-potential junior-level executives and managers. In the latter case, targeted employees may be informally monitored for years before they are finally solicited with job offers. The idea is to allow them to be developed and properly tested within their host companies before wooing them away.

4. The acquiring company then looks for options (conferences, software bars, Internet chat rooms, third-party contacts) that will put company recruiters and employees informally in touch with executive targets.

An important aspect of presearch is getting to know the field of talent you are exploring. Management consultant John Sullivan claims that every manager "has to become the business equivalent of an NBA talent scout."[17] When it comes to suggestions for meeting potential candidates, Sullivan advises, "You have to hang out in chat rooms on the Net, be a member of the right online mailing lists, go to the right conferences. You have to create 'learning networks' that help you meet great people—the kinds of people that you want working for your company."[18] Some of the other networking suggestions

offered by Sullivan include capturing the names of conference attendees, asking exceptional new hires for their referrals to other job candidates, inviting potential candidates to technical seminars, open
houses, or beer busts, or paying them to work on miniprojects.[19]

Piggybacking on these approaches is a set of techniques that I call
the *spiderweb recruiting approach,* a label that alludes to the innovative methods used by acquiring companies to lure potential candidates to their physical sites and corporate web sites. David Lord
mentions some of the innovative techniques used by companies to
lure potential candidates.

> Management recruiters are starting to identify talent long
> before they will hire people and to begin to develop relation-
> ships with people that they hope will eventually join their
> company. They send high-potential individuals literature on
> their company, and have employees call these candidates from
> time to time as friends. They use recruiter spies in software
> bars to overhear conversations among people who are job-
> hunting, or who voice dissatisfaction with their jobs. They
> also are actively recruiting young professionals through enter-
> tainment and social events."[20]

Go one step beyond the spiderweb approach to recruiting, and
you encounter the use of competitive intelligence as a means of
actively ferreting out potential talent. A recent *Fortune* article echoes
this warning in cautioning that, "some e-recruiters lurk on Internet
newsgroups, where workers gather to discuss everything from database administration to dating. They watch to see who says the
smartest stuff, then make their approach by e-mail. Others use the Net
to track workers around the globe."[21] The same article discusses the
technique known as "flipping" a web site, through which talent spies
can access information not normally provided on company home
pages, such as employee directories, bios, and contact information.[22]

When it comes to applying competitive intelligence to executive
search, one impressive expert is Connie LaDouceur, the principal
of ExecuQuest Corporation, a Baltimore-based provider of
search/research services. ExecuQuest's specialty is uncovering the best
possible candidates in very targeted areas, such as web developers,
operations analysts, and C++ programmers. It does this by providing
clients with organizational charts that identify potential candidates
from companies that are identified as world-class performers in a
given area.

According to LaDouceur, as organizations begin to learn how
they can leverage competitive intelligence, they more actively seek out
the types of services provided by companies such as ExecuQuest.

LaDouceur provides the following example of how competitive intelligence can be used to identify likely prospects for executive hiring.

> The world's largest mutual fund company asked us to take a look at financial services and investment firms that were undergoing change (being acquired or merged) and examine their profit centers, such as equity trading, and the top-level management who ran these functions. We were asked to call these individuals and determine if they were interested in making a move from their companies, and their compensation requirements. Again, the purpose was not for targeted recruiting, which is our primary business, but to determine talent that was considering a career change so our clients could hire opportunistically. We were amazed at how open these people were and the amount of information we were able to gather without having specific positions to discuss.[23]

Competitive intelligence can be applied to other areas of executive resource development, such as the design of staffing structures. LaDouceur provides the following example.

> The HR vice president of one of our clients, a Fortune 200 company, wanted to move from a decentralized to a centralized staffing and recruiting model. To meet this need, we were asked to identify the types of staffing structures used by the best-performing companies. We first identified the five companies that have been cited as "most admired for quality of management development and talent." We then completely broke down their recruiting, staffing, and management development areas, and developed models, templates, sales figures, employee populations, how many people supported the effort, what kinds of budgets they managed, and so on, so our client could compare apples to apples. This research supported our client's decision to centralize staffing and recruitment. We also supplied names and telephone numbers of all employees covered in the study.[24]

Still another potential area of application involves the field of executive compensation. LaDouceur advises, "Companies must be aware of competitive compensation before they lose talent. As an example, one of our clients, a software company in a small town in Vermont, hired us to assess the compensation of two other firms in the area to competitively restructure our client's compensation packages. They are now the preferred employer for IT individuals in that market."[25]

LaDouceur explains that sometimes her company uses a variety of innovative approaches to seek out rare talent.

We were asked by a data services company to identify individuals who could serve as the company's Director of Reuse Technology—a position that involves determining which of their technological systems can stay and which systems need to be upgraded. We started researching companies in the greater New York area, where our client was based, but as we began to call these target companies we found that most of them were just beginning to staff this type of initiative, and in fact no one had yet implemented changes. At one point in our research we discovered an association called OOPSLA—short for "Object Oriented Program and Systems Language Applications." We also discovered a conference this organization was sponsoring, and within the conference a breakout session of six people who were speaking on the subject of Reuse Technology. Three of these people became our candidates. The important point to understand is that no standard research strategy would have included these three companies—Boeing, Fannie Mae, and Brooklyn Union Gas—as holding the candidates we needed, and yet these candidates had the ideal track records.[26]

LaDouceur explains that her company uses a variety of research methods to find the most talented people in the field.

We identify individuals over the phone, using sophisticated research methodologies developed over the years starting at Heidrick and Struggles in the eighties. We use *Fortune, Business Week,* the *Wall Street Journal;* we might also speak with Wall Street analysts, heads of associations, and editors of periodicals. Currently we are looking for a Director of Interactive Marketing, so I have been in touch with Kate Maddox, editor of the Interactive Marketing section of *Ad Age.* We've just identified those people they call the outstanding "digital masters." Along with this I might speak with someone from *Computer World,* or from the e-business firm Scient, and see who they might name, then see which companies are on both lists. We are always looking for the "definitive list" of companies that possess the best people in a given position with the responsibilities our clients seek.[27]

So what do you do if in the process of actively researching your field you come across outstanding executive performers? Human resources consultant John Sullivan advises that because exceptional leaders do not stay available in the job market for very long, it is important to make the selection and hiring process as easy as possible for these types of rare candidates. To do this, Sullivan recommends using what he terms *instant hiring* for "the top 10 percent of the job candidate population—the people that you want to make sure you don't lose to a competitor."[28] Sullivan explains that in the instant-hire process you prequalify for jobs. He notes one company that uses the prequalification process that gives "coupons to great people whom its managers have gotten to know but who aren't ready to make a move. The coupon sends this message: 'The day you want to come work for us, you're hired. You don't have to go through our HR bureaucracy. We will hire you instantly.'"[29]

SEARCHING: SEARCH FIRMS AS THE TRADITIONAL MATCHMAKERS

Even with the use of presearch, spiderweb techniques, and competitive intelligence, there is still a critical role to be played by traditional search firms in the executive recruiting process. Many companies, however, are beginning to critically challenge the efficacy of the traditional search process and to look for ways to increase the value obtained from executive searches. According to the results of the 13th Annual Membership Survey of the International Association of Corporate and Professional Recruitment (IACPR), which surveyed 83 recruitment firms and 81 companies, employers and search firms appear to disagree on the usefulness of external searches. Seventy-one percent of recruiters place the average length for a search at three to four months, while 64 percent of companies claim that a search takes five months or more. Interestingly, both 61 percent of the recruiters and 61 percent of the companies surveyed felt that searches took too long. Companies and search firms disagreed, however, regarding the causes for delays. According to the majority (53 percent) of recruiters, the delays are caused by changes in clients' needs. According to the companies surveyed, the primary problems involve finding qualified candidates (54 percent) and attracting such candidates (46 percent).[30]

According to one HR researcher, Chip McCreary, completion rates for executive searches have fallen from about 90 percent ten years ago to about 80 percent today.[31] A major reason McCreary suggests for this decline is the ethical obligation that search firms have not to recruit from clients or their subsidiaries, with a compounding factor being industrial consolidation. Using the personal computer industry as an example, McCreary suggests that this field, "has evolved from approximately 100 players fifteen years ago to only ten significant players today. If a search firm is barred from raiding even one of these companies, its effectiveness can be negatively impacted."[32]

One of the biggest stumbling blocks employers have in working with search firms is the pricing structure that, because it is based on a percentage of the candidate's overall compensation, may cause search firms to pressure the prospective employer to increase compensation as a means of increasing their own fees. Compounding this problem is the timing of fee payments. McCreary explains that most search firms "charge one-third of their fee up front, one-third after thirty days, and one-third after sixty days. With unacceptable frequency, clients end up paying a firm and having nothing to show for it."[33] In addition to the flat fees are monthly charges, which often "include overhead, research, and administrative costs calculated as a percentage of the [flat] fee. At 10 to 15 percent of the fee per month, these charges can reach $3,000 to $4,000."[34]

So how can you avoid these types of problems? The following seven actions can improve the overall effectiveness of the search firms you employ for executive placement.

ACTION 1: SET CLEAR EXPECTATIONS

Stephen Balough, president of David Powell & Associates, Inc., a Woodside, California–based executive search firm, suggests that in the effort to quickly get started on the search, search firms frequently "miss establishing a clear, up-front explanation of what is required for the position, versus tossing up the first couple of candidates very quickly. One of the things I have been taught is to really push back on clients and help them select, out of everything they've asked for in a candidate, what is really important to them. Having a clear idea of what's expected not only helps you do a better job in the search, it also helps you better sell the position to candidates regarding what the client company is really looking for."[35]

Peter Felix, president of the Association of Executive Search Consultants, supports this position when he suggests that, "There must be a common understanding at the senior levels of the organization about the kinds of people that are needed in the organization and the role that the open position plays in the company. Corporations must know what they are doing and what it is they want to achieve by recruiting externally. This involves understanding the requirements for the job, what it is they want to achieve. A good executive search firm functions as a management consultant by helping the client explain, clarify, and articulate these issues, then by preparing a brief for the client that helps explain this process, and finally by outlining these expectations to the candidate."[36]

ACTION 2: USE CLEAR PERFORMANCE METRICS

David Lord has identified three performance metrics against which he measures the performance of search firms.

- *The time line* is an indicator of ineffectiveness, but also a key for improving the value of the process. Searches have been taking longer and longer throughout the 1990s as talent becomes more scarce, and the cost of not filling a position for several months in today's market is huge. If a lot of time is lost in the beginning of a search, it tells us that there is lack of clarity on the requirements for the position. If time is lost in the middle of a search, it tells us that we may be having problems bringing the right candidate to the table. However, if time is lost toward the end of a search, it is often due to a lack of commitment on the part of the hiring company to make the hire happen.
- *Direct costs* are easy to measure. These are what you pay in search fees and expenses.
- *Yield* represents the number of candidates presented before an offer is made. This number should never be less than two or three, but it should never go over fifteen. A search firm that offers up a large number of candidates indicates that it hasn't accurately assessed its client's needs.[37]

ACTION 3: ESTABLISH PREFERRED-PROVIDER RELATIONSHIPS

Many HR professionals feel that the employer–search firm relationship is changing from that of a distant, helping-hands relationship to one characterized by a collaborative, long-term teaming relationship. Lord suggests that

> There is a long history of companies looking at search firms as body movers, as transactional service providers who bring them bodies. While some of this will continue, a lot of search consultants and companies are hoping to get more out of relationships, marked by the development of preferred-provider programs. This change in relationship involves working with a smaller number of providers to
>
> - Improve the quality of candidates that are recruited by engaging in relationships that better translate company needs into fit of candidate for positions
> - Generate faster searches—the better a consultant knows the company and target population through repeated searches, the faster the search can be completed
> - Control costs by working with smaller groups of providers[38]

PepsiCo has evolved from having each of its divisions separately manage arrangements with executive recruiting firms around the world, to having its headquarters' HR staff coordinate recruiting efforts with a limited number of firms across the company. PepsiCo conducts an annual review in which it provides these recruiting firms with information about the company's global business objectives and related staffing needs. According to Charles Rogers, PepsiCo's Vice President of Staffing and Executive Development, this change is designed to encourage PepsiCo to form long-term partnerships with these selected search firms.[39]

ACTION 4: REMOVE INTERNAL ORGANIZATIONAL OBSTACLES

Lord also suggests that executive search is currently an ineffective process, in part because of deficiencies on the part of employers.

Executive search is successful 60 percent of the time, and most of the ineffective behavior is on the hiring organization's side of the table. I believe that about 80 to 90 percent of the time, search firms are able to present qualified candidates in a timely manner. But 20 to 30 percent of the time, the company can't carry out its commitment because of (1) changing business conditions that alter or eliminate a hiring need, (2) lack of commitment to complete the search, (3) arrogance—the company feels it is paying a high fee to get the search firm to do all of the selling, or (4) inaccessibility of hiring executives. Until we compensate more senior managers on their ability to recruit great talent, this type of behavior will continue.[40]

Felix is another search expert who stresses the need for a well-organized interview process.

Companies should have an effective interviewing process, but one that is as brief as possible. They should ask candidates how they can best organize the interview process, particularly when multiple interviews are involved, to meet the candidates' schedule. They need to ensure that they have proper briefing materials and presentations ready for the candidates, and that meetings are well organized. Resumes, briefing sheets, or videos on candidates that are forwarded to interviewers in advance by the search firm should be reviewed ahead of time. In addition, interviewers should meet together prior to the interview to determine how questions will be organized, so that different interviewers don't end up asking candidates the same questions.[41]

ACTION 5: NEGOTIATE CUSTOMER-FRIENDLY SEARCH FEES

McCreary advises companies to negotiate a flat fee that is "10 to 15 percent less than one-third of compensation arrangements" and then set a fixed monthly fee for expenses. An additional advantage of this arrangement is that the search firm has no personal incentive to increase the candidate's compensation package.[42] The IACPR study indicated that although only 6 percent of responding companies currently make use of a flat-fee arrangement with search firms, 35 percent said that they are moving away from a fee structure based on a percentage of first-year total compensation, with 74 percent of this group adopting a flat fee.[43]

ACTION 6: INVESTIGATE "HANDS-OFF" CONSTRAINTS

Constraints that hamper your search may crop up if the search firm you are considering already represents two or three organizations on your ideal "target companies" list. In such a situation, you may need to consider going with another firm.

ACTION 7: ASK FOR A GUARANTEE

McCreary advises employers to request a fee structure "that includes a one-third, refundable retainer up front, with two-thirds paid upon completion or cancellation. The one-third retainer can be refunded after thirty days if the client isn't satisfied with the results or feels philosophically or ethically incompatible with the search firm."[44] Some companies are extending the concept of a guarantee even further, to require the successful performance of an executive candidate during the first few months on the job. Headhunters are asked to reimburse employers for search fees paid for new hires who "wash out" during this period.

THE IMPACT OF THE INTERNET ON EXECUTIVE SEARCH

The availability of the Internet and research firms like ExecuQuest are changing the value added by search firms from the role of identifying candidates to that of deal broker and negotiator. Steve Balough suggests that the rise of the Internet may shift the advantage away from large search firms to smaller providers. "I don't know if in the future the huge search firm that has the big map on the wall indicating fifty offices across the world, and all the cost that goes with them, will be able to prosper given the access that people now have to the Internet."[45] As a sign of this transition, Balough mentions the entrance into the search scene of Career Central, a company that has started offering executive recruiting over the Net.

Indeed, it seems as if some recruiting firms are beginning to see the handwriting on the wall, even as some online job postings are beginning to invade their territory. In describing the incursion of on-line headhunters into the field of traditional executive recruiting, a *Business Week* article stated, "The online guys are scoring points. Not only are they encroaching onto the old-line recruiters' bread-and-butter business of placing middle managers, they're also poaching their execs. HotJobs, for instance, just recruited Stephen Garrison, ex-CEO of traditionalist Ward Howell."[46] The rapid growth of on-line executive recruiting is reflected in the emergence of a number of Internet ventures by major executive search firms, including LAI Worldwide's LAICompass program, Heidrick & Struggles' Leaderonline program (which specializes in technology profession-als), and Korn/Ferry International's Futurestep program.[47] Another sign of the trend toward online executive recruiting is the increased emphasis that corporate HR departments are placing on the Internet. Motorola has recently used the Net to place ads for over thirty exec-utive positions at the director level and above.[48]

Futurestep is an interesting program because it makes use of online diagnostic assessment tools. When participants register in the system they are asked to take part in a detailed questionnaire that evaluates competencies and career objectives, and to respond to a forty-five-question case study that provides information on their decision-making style. The goal is a more careful matching of candidate to job. Partici-pants are provided with a summary report of findings, as well as a deter-mination of their market value, while corporate clients are provided with a CD containing video previews of candidates and an assessment of can-didates' potential match to jobs by competencies as well as culture fit.[49, 50]

Lord reinforces this position in explaining how advanced infor-mation technology is changing the traditional roles assumed by search firms, "The 'commoditization' of information about individ-ual candidates creates a shift in what real value is in a search firm. In the old days, a lot of value that companies were paying for was the identification of the best candidates. As the identification of people and where they work is spreading so fast, technology is able to bring us tremendous candidate databases. So where is the value of a retained search after that? Those who survive and prosper bring more to the table in helping a company define its needs, assessing those who are apparently qualified, and negotiating the deal that will cause the candidate to move."[51]

Joseph Daniel McCool, editor of *Executive Recruiter News,* the monthly executive search newsletter published by Kennedy Information, LLC, claims that "clients are beginning to see a blurring of lines between high-end executive search firms and other candidate delivery systems, such as the Internet and print advertising. A number of search firms have deliberately decided *not* to get involved in these areas, so we are seeing two schools of thought. One comes from firms that, despite changes in the market, decide to remain in their traditional service sector, while others decide to adjust their service offerings to get the job done for the client."[52]

McCool cites as an example the new hybrid search firm TMP Worldwide, one of the world's biggest yellow-pages advertising and recruitment advertising companies. According to McCool,

> TMP has evolved into an Internet company and now has one of the largest Internet recruitment sites, Monster.com, which recently advertised on the Super Bowl. In 1998, TMP bought Johnson, Smith & Knisely, a New York–based recruiting firm, and Switzerland-based TASA International. Both companies have now been brought into a separate spinout business unit called TASA Worldwide. Through this move, TMP has changed the playing field for the executive search community. TMP Worldwide's philosophy is to provide cradle-to-grave service; that is, they will find the company a summer intern or a CEO. Basically, TMP is trying to become a one-stop shop for staffing. This is putting pressure on other search firms to offer a wider array of search services. Thus if I am an HR manager, I can turn to a search firm to find a CEO over the Internet. In situations in which search firms are owned by large staffing agencies, I can go to the firm and use their relationship with their staffing unit to get ten midlevel account managers if I need them, while also using them for traditional high-end services.[53]

WHERE DO YOU GO TO FIND THE RIGHT PEOPLE?

A different set of challenges faces those companies that need to quickly locate talented executive leaders. Anderson Consulting provides a number of suggestions for strengthening global recruiting efforts, including developing partnerships with international M.B.A. programs, recruiting from such fields as foreign service, and positioning the company's global interests in employment advertising.[54]

When it comes to selecting external search firms as partners for international selection assignments, Chuck Bolton, Vice President of International Human Resources for Boston Scientific Corporation, stresses the need to use both international and local search firms.

In reality there is no such thing as a global search firm. The reality is unlike McDonalds™ where the fries all taste the same no matter where you go; you need to form local partnerships to find the unique people you need for each country. Another problem is the issue of exclusivity. You may want a country manager in China but find that the search firm with which you want to do business is already committed to most of the major companies in China, so you are totally locked out.[55]

Apart from the use of search firms, Bolton recommends conducting "raids" on college campuses for foreign-born business students who can quickly adapt to the role of international executives in their home countries.

We had to complete 300 international searches in three years. We found it increasingly difficult to recruit people locally who could fit into our corporate culture. We began to recruit heavily in M.B.A. programs around the United States, looking for Japanese students who had five to eight years of experience, were ready to graduate, and wanted to go back to Japan. We did this in an aggressive way and were able to get college students who were both adaptable and culturally adept. Another advantage is that they could quickly jump into assignments during the initial stages of new projects. At the same time we used a nonsearch consulting firm that created special hit lists of potential candidates in other firms, and then we had our own HR people cold-call these individuals and discuss our interest in them. This was a very successful and cost-effective technique.[56]

CASE IN POINT: CISCO SYSTEMS
Michael McNeal, Director of Employment

One company that has found an innovative approach to marketing its organization to professionals and executives is Cisco Systems. Cisco's program combines the best aspects of new Internet technology with the very traditional and personable approach of using employee referrals. Cisco's corporate Director of Employment, Michael McNeal, explains that in developing its program, Cisco wanted to take a sales and marketing approach to the recruiting process.

We know that when people come in for a job interview they are usually making a substantial investment in their career. We were looking at our various sources for recruiting that would provide the most cost-effective option yet still provide the highest-quality candidates. We found that we obtained the best results from our employee referral program. So the idea was how to turn this into a two-level distribution channel in which we market our recruiting program to our employees and then have them sell the benefits of the company to interested people.[57]

McNeal says that before building its program Cisco carefully researched the needs of "passive" job seekers.

We tend to target the passive job seeker who is happy in his or her job, who is not the traditional job seeker. To do this we got a focus group together, made up of mostly technical people from other companies, and asked them, "What would it take for you to leave your job?" Their overwhelming response was, "For one of our friends to recommend somewhere else as a great place to work." On the basis of this we decided to create our "Friends" web site. We told our people, "If you know someone who would make a great employee, call them. Or contact our web site, and we will have someone here call them."[58]

Cisco's web site gives interested parties the option of either applying for openings or clicking the "make friends" icon to contact a Cisco employee. McCall says that by developing this approach, Cisco wanted to create a recruiting approach that incorporated technology, while still being very user-friendly.

We know that if you operate in a high-tech environment you encounter what we term "graceless technology"—when you have an automated system where things go into a database in a very depersonalized manner. We wanted to see how we could use technology but at the same time maintain a personal side. We wanted to create a system to build grace into the process, so that when people contacted us they would end up talking to someone about a job without feeling like that person was trying to recruit them. To support this we created a list of do's and don'ts regarding how to be a friend. The way we encouraged employees to sign up was to give out "Friends" T-shirts. We also created a motivational experience by using employees rather than professional models in our marketing campaign, on billboards, and in other advertisements. In addition, if we obtain a hire from one of our employees in our Friends program, the employee gets the bonus. Our goal was to get 8,000 employees for five minutes a day to help us recruit.[59]

The second method by which Cisco attracts prospective job candidates through the Internet is by purchasing advertising space on popular web sites (selected from recommendations by Cisco employees). A special software package developed by Cisco monitors the URLs of site visitors. As McNeal explains it,

> The web offers the opportunity to track our visitors by applications and URLs. I can tell you what a visitor's zip code is, the company they come from, and the time they have spent on the web. Using this information we found out that two-thirds of our visitors came directly from other companies, and that our number one "hit time" was 10:00 A.M. to 2:00 P.M. each day, which told us that our visitors were contacting us directly from their place of work. As a result, we put in a domain name reader that determines if visitors to our sites come from other companies in our field. If they do, our Friends logo pops up. This approach provides a much more targeted approach to employee recruiting.[60]

Over the course of implementing the Friends program, Cisco learned how to adapt its program to the needs of prospective job candidates. Says McNeal,

> We thought the domain-name reader was clever so we put it on our employment page. When a visitor would call, a note would pop up asking, "Are you currently looking for an alternative to your job at . . . ?" When we checked the results, we were surprised to find that as a result of this change people were clicking off after a few seconds. The problem was that they thought, "If they [Cisco] know I am interested in a job, perhaps my company knows." Once we realized this, we removed the note from our employment page.

> Another thing we learned is that visitors would often be stumped by having to create a résumé. When employees transferred interested prospects over to one of our recruiters, the recruiter would ask for an updated résumé. This threw a lot of people, who because they weren't actively looking for work, didn't have updated résumés. To help with this problem, we created "Profiler"—a system that helps people create a résumé in five to eight minutes. The way the system works is you call up a specific job family, such as "human resources" or "programmer." The system then calls up specific questions that force you to differentiate your skills in your field.

> Our Friends program still has a lot of legs—after three years we still get a lot of response on the web. Our employee referral program now averages 50 to 60 percent of our hires, which total 1,500 to 1,600 a quarter. The other two recruiting approaches we have are to directly call people who we see as movers and shakers in the industry, and a college program.[61]

There are a number of bottom-line indicators that suggest that Cisco has created a strong, competitive advantage through its Friends program. According to Barbara Beck, Cisco's top-level HR executive, Cisco has reduced the time-to-fill for all open positions from an average of 113 days three years ago to a current level of 45 days, yet the company's cost per hire is averaging $6,556 versus an industry average of $10,800.[62]

SUMMARY OF KEY POINTS

- We are currently witnessing several important changes in the area of executive recruiting and selection.

- It is important to market your company in a way that conveys a winning value proposition—a reason candidates should view your company as a desirable employer.

- The use of presearch can help you greatly accelerate your hiring process through the prequalification of selected candidates.

- Companies are beginning to make use of competitive intelligence—the long-term tracking of targeted, high-potential candidates—and Internet-based technologies to accelerate the hiring process and capture a much broader pool of candidates.

- As these changes continue, we can anticipate the creation of more long-term, exclusive partnerships between organizations and external search firms, which can readily adapt to these changing requirements.

- A related change will be the blurring of lines that have been historically drawn between executive search services and other staffing services. One-stop shopping may soon become a primary service delivery offering for external search/staffing services.

- To get the most from your external search firm, set clear expectations regarding your job requirements, put metrics in place to identify the best search providers, establish preferred-provider relationships with the best providers, clear away organizational obstacles that can impede the selection process, negotiate customer-friendly search fees, investigate hands-off constraints that can hamper your search, and ask for a guarantee.

CHAPTER 12

SELECTING THE
RIGHT PLAYERS

A few years ago, executive selection was at best a subjective and haphazard process that focused on whether candidates had the prerequisite *leadership qualities* to perform effectively on the job. This "great man/woman" approach was gradually displaced by a selection model that focused on whether candidates had the right *leadership competencies* to make an exceptional contribution to the company.

The starting point for matching leadership competencies to organizational needs is performing a job analysis. According to Valerie Sessa, a researcher at the Center for Creative Leadership and coauthor with Jodi Taylor and Richard Campbell of *Choosing Top-Level Executives: A System for Effective Selection* (Jossey-Bass, in press), the construction of a job analysis is a critical variable in determining the successful placement of an executive. Sessa provides the following conclusions based on research that she and her colleagues conducted on 325 senior executives from 1993 to 1995.

> One of the conclusions we've reached is that it's very important to specify organizational needs and candidates' requirements at the beginning of the process. Most top executives fail at this. Those executives who do a better job in this area are likely to hire an executive who will be successful. One of the reasons senior managers don't specify a job's requirements is a time issue—people want to jump right into the search. Second, they already have in their heads an idea of what they need in a job candidate, but they don't clearly communicate

their requirements to others, nor do they recognize that other people have a different mental picture of what the organization needs and what this job is going to require. In many cases the different parties have a very different picture and little agreement.

Discussing needs and requirements ahead of time enables all stakeholders to form a common picture of their job requirements. Another reason why people fail to specify needs and requirements is that it is a tedious part of the process. It's important, however, not just to specify requirements, but to get people aligned on requirements. Then, throughout the selection process, it is used to paint a picture of what the ideal candidate should look like and can also be used to recruit, orient, and train new candidates and help them see how success will be measured.[1]

These findings are supported by Geoffrey Smart, a Chicago-based industrial psychologist who specializes in selection interview consulting to corporations and private equity investors. According to Smart, it is often very difficult to get CEOs to see the value of constructing a job analysis for their own positions.

Ironically, we often find job descriptions for junior assistants, but a CEO, COO, or president won't take the time to write a job description. To get senior managers to perform this task, we suggest that you start broadly. Look at macroeconomic trends and at what you are trying to achieve in your business—defining where you need this person to excel. We use about forty standard drivers, including strategic thinking, planning and organizing skills, having a collaborative leadership approach, listening skills, general intelligence, and a nice blend of functional skills. . . . Another element involves identifying the two or three things that are key work priorities. For a senior sales and marketing role, this might include driving revenue up, getting mentioned in trade publications, and building up a sales organization to 150 representatives.[2]

The challenge in defining executive job requirements is that sometimes the job experience and competencies that are formally presented are quite different from those that are actually recognized and supported by the hiring organization. George Klemp and Bernard Cullen, partners in Boston-based Cambria Consulting, caution that

You sometimes find a big gap between a company's reported strategy and how it actually gets things done. A financial services company we worked with saw itself as one where the best creative minds were encouraged, and where opportunities for advancement were closely tied to the successful introduction of new products and services. The reality, however, was that those who had the best chance to rise to the top were more expert at working the political influence process with the chairman than at creating the new ideas. Obviously, this is a problem when identifying competencies required for executive success, as it runs the risk of confronting the organization with uncomfortable realities.[3]

THE IMPORTANCE OF FIT

In the last few years executive selection has taken another major turn as companies have begun to recognize the critical roles leaders play in shaping organizational culture. As the next chapter will detail, there is ample research to demonstrate that when new hires act in ways that are highly discrepant from the organizational culture of their hiring company, they are likely to encounter "organ rejection" in the form of resistance and hostility from new peers and team members. As companies begin to understand the difficulties they face in grafting outsiders onto the organization, they are starting to take greater care to ensure a good fit between executive job candidates and the corporate culture they are entering.

According to management consultants Bradford and Geoffrey Smart, "Error-free hiring begins with the hiring manager's rigorous analysis of the job in relation to corporate strategy and the desired organization culture."[4] Richard Hagberg, president of the Hagberg Consulting Group in Foster City, California, claims that, "At the senior level, the executive's fit with the culture is more important than whether a candidate has the prerequisite experience, skills, and expertise to do the job."[5] He suggests that during the final stage of the selection process, the interviewer needs to determine of the candidate, "Can he or she work with the company's cultural values, norms, and style, plus get along with the new boss?"[6] These conclusions are confirmed by Valerie Sessa and associates, who suggest that, "what differentiates selecting successful executives from unsuccessful executives is not track record or technical expertise but fit issues, including fit to the boss, fit to the organizational culture, values, and interpersonal characteristics and style."[7]

Peter Felix, president of the Association of Executive Search Consultants, suggests that

> Today's candidate can walk into a company and size up whether it has a culture conducive to innovation, or one that is highly bureaucratic or entrepreneurial. The culture issue

becomes relevant when you come down to choice. If your candidate is educated and understands the key issues related to the job, he or she will ask questions related to culture, such as "What is the decision-making process here?" "How hierarchical are you?" "To what degree do you support open access to information?" I find that quite often the company may not know how to react to this and may not be able to clearly define its culture to candidates.[8]

In the McKinsey study "The War for Talent," researchers stress the importance of being able to identify the types of individuals that will enhance your organization. "A few companies are good at specifying the qualities likely to translate into success for them. Hewlett-Packard looked for smart engineers who are good team players. The Home Depot wants customer-obsessed, entrepreneurial leaders. Enron seeks independent deal makers with a financial bent."[9]

Stephen Balough, president of David Powell & Associates, explains that assessing person-to-culture fit is an important part of his job as an executive recruiter.

A person who has been with Intel will probably not be a shoe-in for Hewlett-Packard. You have to ask what a person was rewarded for in his or her previous organization. A company may ask us to recruit executives out of large companies who have had global experience to fill the position of Vice President of Marketing Development in assisting with a new global start-up. We have to push back and ask, "Will candidates from a large corporation really work well with a start-up? Do they know how to get the work done, or have they held more of a strategic role in terms of determining the type of work that needs to be done and then depending on others to complete it?"[10]

Bill Birchard, a writer on business and technology, shares the example of EMC, a Hopkinton, Massachusetts–based manufacturer of enterprise storage products. EMC senior managers participated in brainstorming sessions to identify the characteristics of "great EMC employees." As Birchard describes it, "Those sessions led to the EMC Employee Success Profile, a detailed definition of who makes it at EMC. It is built around seven categories: technical competence, goal orientation, a sense of urgency, accountability, external and internal customer responsiveness, cross-functional behavior, and integrity."[11] John Ganley, EMC's Director of Corporate Staffing, insists that over the last few years, "We've held fast to those attributes as the core nuggets of hiring."[12]

An example of what can happen with a culture mismatch is provided by Klemp and Cullen.

The uncertainty is when they are encountering very different challenges from those faced in the past, or are operating in very different business cultures. In the 1980s there was a huge trend for emerging computer companies such as Digital and Prime in Boston's "Route 128" technology corridor to hire IBM marketing people. The problem with this strategy was that most of these hiring attempts were failures, because IBM had a very different culture than that needed for a start-up. A start-up has to work faster and without the same resources. This meant that if you were going to hire people out of IBM, you had to be very selective; just because an individual was successful at IBM didn't mean that he or she would be so in a high-tech start-up. You would have to hire someone from IBM who had also been successful in a start-up.[13]

Felix argues that the idea of culture fit is particularly important when selecting senior-level executives, given their potential influence as organizational change agents.

There must be consensus at the top level of the organization regarding the kind of change agent they need, and the need for change. A good example is British Airlines, which was an operationally driven airline rather than being focused on what their customers wanted. When they went private in the eighties they hired key marketing people and had them report directly to the CEO, because they understood that these people needed to keep from being assimilated into the current culture.[14]

DETERMINING FIT: MATCHING CANDIDATES TO JOBS AND CULTURES

It would be nice if determining fit were an exact science, but the truth is that it is still largely an art form. There are, however, two steps you can take to more carefully determine fit for executive candidates.

IDENTIFY ESSENTIAL CULTURAL NORMS

Organizational cultures are continually changing, in part as a response to external business factors, and in part due to the intentional efforts of a company's leadership. So the underlying question is, "What type of cultural emphasis do you want to support with the types of leaders you bring into your organization?" One method for thinking through this question is to work with your senior team to identify two major cultural norms that strongly shape your organizational culture, and then place these norms on a two-dimensional grid, such as the one shown in Figure 30. To provide context, first deter-

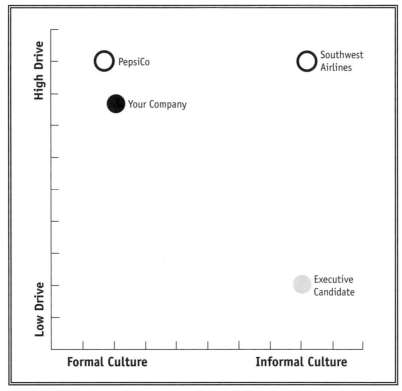

FIGURE 30 DETERMINING THE FIT BETWEEN
LEADERS AND CORPORATE CULTURE

mine where on the grid you would place certain well-known companies, and then triangulate how you would position your own company in relation to these corporate models.

Figure 30 presents the two cultural dimensions of "drive" and
"formality." Drive pertains to the emphasis an organization places on
having executives obtain high-performance results. PepsiCo and
Southwest Airlines come to mind as two clear examples of organizations that have developed high-performance cultures. They differ
greatly, however, along the dimension of formality. PepsiCo is much
more of a "suit" culture, whereas Southwest positions itself as a
highly informal, extended corporate family. Our two-dimensional
grid, although very basic, serves to capture alignment from senior
managers regarding how they would characterize their company, and
where on the grid each interviewer would place different executive
candidates. The objective, of course, is to determine which job candidates represent the best fit with your corporate culture.

Before attempting to assess the cultural fit of an executive candidate, Geoffrey Smart uses the following questions to first help him size up a company's culture.

- What are the strengths of this culture? What is this company going for?

- What are the weaker areas of this culture?

- How do people get things done around here? How are you supposed to offer up ideas? How are you expected to communicate: e-mail, face-to-face meetings, other?

- What kinds of people tend to succeed or fail here?

- Why do good people leave this company? (This question can help you identify what Smart terms a company's "organizational banana peels.")[15]

MATCH LEADERS TO LIFE-CYCLE REQUIREMENTS

Some researchers have suggested that the leadership needs of an organization are tied to that organization's stage of development. According to this concept, illustrated in Figure 31 on page 298, what is required during the start-up phase of a company is a *visionary*—someone who has the strength and energy to carve out of a few selected resources a clear picture of a value-added organization. As the company begins to grow, the entrepreneurial maverick often begins to realize that he or she needs to look for a *builder*—someone with the management skills needed to build the organization. As the company begins to mature, it encounters a number of key decision points: Should it remain focused or begin to diversify? How does it attempt to manage its increased overhead load? What does it do about those competitors nipping at its heels? At this stage, a *pilot* is needed to help the organization navigate through these difficult decision paths. If a company moves into decline and begins to experience a shrinking market, cost controls and resource allocations start to become major issues, requiring a *turnaround expert* who can lead the organization back on track.

Klemp and Bernard Cullen reinforce this concept:

To get a better definition of leadership requirements, we start by looking at the challenges leaders in the organization must face. We find that the challenges imbedded in the situation (turnaround, start-up, growth) and the nature of the business environment (highly competitive, technology-based, pace of change) determine the critical leadership competency requirements. There is therefore no single one-size-fits-all leadership

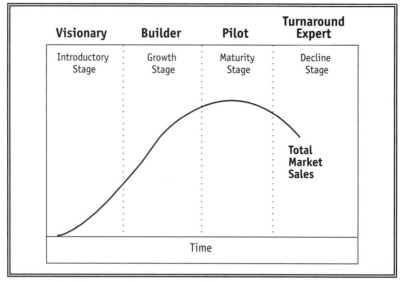

FIGURE 31 MATCHING LEADERSHIP REQUIREMENTS
TO STAGES OF BUSINESS DEVELOPMENT

profile that applies to all companies. For example, an organizational turnaround or renewal demands a willingness to take calculated risks and an entrepreneurial mind-set. In most instances, you won't find a person who can do it all, so we try to determine the most significant business challenges that the executive will face and the leadership capabilities that will support them.[16]

APPLYING THE CONCEPT OF FIT TO CEO SELECTION

According to David Sadtler, a Fellow with the Ashridge Strategic Management Center in London, the assessment of business requirements is a logical first step to the selection of any executive, including a CEO.

In order for any corporate center to add value, it must have the insight to find what its corporate opportunities are and then deliver on them. If a company produces widgets but its manufacturing costs are excessive, the improvement opportunity involves bringing down manufacturing costs. If the people at the corporate center are all from marketing, we would say there is a misfit. In this case, the business requires competencies related to controlling manufacturing costs, and it can't get this from the corporate centers. All of this absolutely must bear upon the selection of a new chief executive, and we believe that this selection process must be done methodically, which it seldom is.[17]

Sadtler adds that in selecting a CEO it is essential to find someone who has a proven track record of successfully tackling the types of business challenges that a company is encountering.

You need candidates who, even if they haven't come from that industry, have at least been in a business that has the same critical success factors as those in the hiring company's business portfolio. For example, the CEO candidates could all have a strong advertising background, yet advertising might not be an important success factor for that company. In this case the likelihood will be that not only will the selected candidates not add value, they will *detract* value, because they won't probe the right problems, nor will they hire the right general managers.[18]

In a 1998 study, The National Association of Corporate Directors (NACD) sponsored a Blue Ribbon Commission on CEO succession. The Commission included twenty key thought leaders in the field of succession planning, including CEOs, academics, consultants, and senior-level HR executives, who met once a month over the course of a year to develop a report recommending best practices in the area of CEO succession. One of the Commission's members is Tom Saporito, SVP with RHR International, a Chicago-based firm of management psychologists who partner with corporate senior managers in assessing and developing individuals, teams, and organizations to help achieve and drive business strategy. According to Saporito, several overall conclusions emerged from the study.

As part of the commission study we had a researcher interview seven senior-level HR leaders, each of whom had fifteen to thirty years of experience in CEO succession. One of the questions we asked was, "What are the qualities of a successful CEO?" We organized the responses around the following five dimensions.

Problem Solving. Supporting competencies include:

- Intellectual resourcefulness
- Sound judgment and keen discernment
- Being strategically focused—someone who has a sense of what should and can unfold in the future

Temperament and Motivation. Supporting competencies include:

- Being emotionally robust
- A strong commitment to personal and business values—someone who establishes performance standards
- Mature use of power (in the position of CEO, the use and abuse of power has much to do with the dominant culture and the level of commitment that people attach to the organization)

Interpersonal Relations and Communication Style. This involves the ability to:

- Communicate effectively
- Manage a variety of internal and external constituencies
- Consistently articulate and adhere to the company vision

Insight into Self and Others. Supporting competencies include:

- Understanding one's own strengths and weaknesses
- The ability to grasp the needs of individuals and the organization to determine how to "move the ball forward"

Leadership Characteristics. A CEO must be someone who:

- Paints an exciting picture of change
- Sets the pace of change and orchestrates it well
- Demonstrates recognition and concern for others
- Clearly defines expectations
- Serves as a trusted example
- Determines the company's value agenda, both on an organizational values level and on an ethical values level
- Develops and enables a talented team

In the next phase of our research, interviewees were presented with four organizational scenarios:

Rapid growth—involving a rapid increase in revenue and market share

Turnaround—involving a company in trouble in need of major restructuring

Merger integration—in which two companies combine their resources

Industry shift—involving a company in an industry undergoing major changes that require a change in culture[19]

A summary of the key leadership factors found to be required for success in each of the four business situations is presented in Table 28.[20]

TABLE 28	
RELATIONSHIP BETWEEN CORPORATE SITUATION AND KEY LEADERSHIP FACTORS	
Corporate Situation	**Key Leadership Factors**
Rapid Growth	• Sees alternatives beyond traditions and habits • Embraces change easily • Effectively communicates clear vision of the future • Willing to surround self with needed talent • Delegates authority; trusts others to get the job done
Turnaround	• Near-term focus with long-term awareness • Stands ground in face of resistance • Clear and concise communicator • Motivates people to think about where the company is going—not where it is coming from • Generates a solid team around a new agenda
Merger Integration	• Able to visualize picture of future organization • Understands the cultures of the two organizations and potential implications of their differences • Recognizes that cultures are more powerful than individuals; willing to work with cultural dynamics • Consensus-building management style
Industry Shift	• Excellent indusrty knowledge • Able to think out of the box • Comfortable with ambiguity • Passion for change • Creates a sense of urgency • Motivates others to change their mind-sets as well as their management practices

It is important to develop action-focused methods for determining the fit of executive candidates. The most frequently used method for doing this involves building into the interview process questions that illuminate the cultural norms candidates operate from when facing tough work challenges. In my case, because I work for a high-change organization, I like to include interview questions that help me obtain a better idea of how well candidates adapt to change. Representative questions might be:

- Tell me about a time when you were attempting to accomplish a difficult project during the middle of an organizationwide change. Describe this change. Did you have to modify the original approach you had taken to this project to account for these changes? How so?

- Let's go through each of the positions you've held during the last ten years. Tell me about your reasons for making each of these job changes. (What I am looking for here is whether an applicant shows a pattern of leaving a job in response to the pressure of adapting to a changing work situation, a new boss, tougher objectives.)

- Tell me about a time in which you took on the role of a change catalyst within your company and you encountered resistance from your peers or work team. How did you overcome this resistance?

While interview questions can help you form a rough idea of job fit, they do not go far enough. Candidates can make up their responses to interview questions or be overeager to tell you what you want to hear. Accordingly, you should consider building into the interview process situations that give you a taste test of a candidate's cultural norms and values. Kevin and Jackie Freiberg, coauthors of *Nuts! Southwest Airlines' Crazy Recipe for Business and Personal Success,* provide an excellent example of how Southwest Airlines tests candidates for the quality of "selfishness." The test involves having candidates take a few minutes to develop a creative presentation about themselves. The Freibergs explain, "As the presentations are delivered, the interviewers don't watch just the speakers; they watch the audience to see which applicants are using this time to work on their own presentations and which are enthusiastically cheering on and supporting their potential co-workers."[21] The point is that, "Unselfish people who will support their teammates are the ones who catch Southwest's eye, not the applicants who are tempted to polish their own presentations while others are speaking."[22]

As you can see from this example, these kinds of tests do not have to take the form of a formal assessment process. They involve the hundreds of small behavioral clues that tell us the type of organizational context in which people are used to working. Some examples:

- If one of your corporate values is employee ownership and equality, watch how executive candidates interact with your support and clerical staff. I have learned a lot about applicants from whether they are rude or abrupt with individuals they consider to be of lesser rank. Earlier this year, during a large-scale interviewing process for the position of Director of Organizational Development, I found out that one applicant had given our secretary a hard time about the company's procedures regarding the reimbursement of travel expenses. Needless to say, he did not make it through the first cut.

- If one of your corporate values is adaptability, consider making minor changes to your published interview schedule, or find out whether applicants are willing to meet with you when you are on the road. A job applicant who becomes testy with small changes during the interview process is not likely to exhibit the flexibility needed to make bigger adjustments.

- If one of your corporate values is teamwork, you might consider inviting the job candidate to a team meeting in which an important work issue is being reviewed or a brainstorming session is being conducted. You can learn a lot from candidates by watching the degree to which they are willing to share "air time" with other meeting participants, draw out others through insightful questions, and establish rapport with others. Another option here is to invite finalists for executive openings to an informal social event, such as an after-hours dinner with key members of the executive team.

In addition to the above suggestions, keep in mind that if you are working through an outside search firm it is also critically important to acquaint your executive recruiter with your company's culture before initiating the search. Joseph Daniel McCool, editor of *Executive Recruiter News,* suggests that HR leaders need to "invite the recruiter to come in on a low-profile basis for a few days, to 'kick the tires' and get a better feel for the company. Recruiters rely on interviews with top management to gauge a company's cultural makeup. From an HR point of view, it is important to introduce as many decision makers to the recruiter as possible, so that the recruiter understands where power resides in the organization. The recruiter is able to learn that, 'the successful candidate will have to get along with John Smith, who can be very disagreeable at times.' The point is that, along with evaluating corporate culture, the recruiter is also assessing the personality scheme in the management ranks. Some personality types just aren't going to match."[23]

As an example of the steps an organization can take to indoctrinate a recruiter into its culture and senior management team, McCool refers to a company that needed a Vice President of Sales and Marketing for a machine shop:

> The company invited the recruiter to come in jeans and sneakers and spend a couple of days on-site to understand the company's culture, which was populated mostly by males, who tended to be rough in their language. The company wanted the recruiter to understand the difference between a CNC machine and a Swiss screw machine, and how candidates' backgrounds would prepare them for the job. This experience gave the recruiter a much better sense of the company's culture.[24]

CONDUCTING THE SELECTION INTERVIEW

Most selection interviews are performed haphazardly, with little thought to using a disciplined or structured approach. Geoffrey Smart argues that "96 percent of managerial interviewers are driving without a license, and 80 percent of professional interviewers are ineffective."[25] Smart makes a sharp distinction between what he terms the typical *informal interview* and the interviewing process that he uses, termed the *past-oriented interview.* He describes the latter as, "used to collect behaviors—using people to give you examples of behaviors they've demonstrated throughout their work life. You can measure the frequency of behaviors—such as, 'Is this something they've done often?'—as well as the recency of behaviors—such as, 'Is this something they've just started doing, or have done since high school?'"[26]

Smart summarizes the essential elements of the past-oriented interview:

> The total interview covers three-and-a-half to four hours, and moves chronologically over the interviewee's life. Essentially we carve a person's life up into five major sections. For each section we ask
>
> 1. Their expectations coming into that job. What did they expect to walk into? Did the job require them to change much?
>
> 2. Their responsibilities in the job.

3. Accomplishments and other high points. Usually we get two accomplishments per section. One of the red flags here is when people can't think of any accomplishments. Talented people can't wait to tell you about their accomplishments.

4. Failures and low points.

5. TORC, which stands for threat of reference check. This means asking candidates, "If we call that former supervisor, what will he or she tell us were your specific strengths and weak areas in that job at that time?" Candidates will often mention three or four weaknesses. A red flag here is noting a continued pattern of interpersonal conflicts.

6. Reasons for leaving. Good responses would be that they had been there and succeeded, had hired talented people underneath them, and were now seeking their next challenge. A bad response might mention overoptimism—getting only 20 percent into a new job and then becoming discouraged and skipping around without getting closure, or having interpersonal conflicts.

At the end of the interview we ask what they are thinking about their future. We find that high-talent people are thinking a lot about their future, while low-talent people think little about it. They might make a comment such as, "I don't know. I just suppose that the next thing will take care of itself."[27]

Klemp and Cullen suggest that a carefully structured interview format can yield significant information about a candidate's fit.

When determining whether a candidate is a good fit with the organization, we essentially mirror the process: We ask the candidate to describe how he or she handled challenges similar to those required in the position. From learning how candidates handled these situations, we can make inferences about their competencies and at the same time get a sense of how they typically operate. For example, you can ask people about a time when they had to take a position in a new organization. Some people may tell you how they pushed their ideas through, relying on their ability to challenge others and force results, while others may tell you how they worked through alliances and built relationships with others to get things done. What helps us is knowing not only *what* results they obtained, but *how* they got results. Two different people may be equally effective, but within very different cultural contexts.[28]

DETERMINING THE COMPOSITION OF INTERVIEWERS AND CANDIDATES

We should consider one last variable in the selection process. In research conducted at the Center for Creative Leadership by Valerie Sessa and associates, it appears that the makeup of both the candidate pool and the selection interviewers can affect the outcome of the executive selection process. Sessa provides the following conclusions.

- Diversity is important in the candidate pool. When atypical candidates were included, the interviewers gave greater consideration to thinking through their rationale for making selection decisions and articulating their selection criteria. When you have someone who is not the typical middle-aged, white male candidate, you are more careful in spelling out your rationale for how and why you make choices— you are more aware of your selection criteria.
- Interviewers who chose an internal candidate actually had more external candidates in their applicant pool. Conversely, those who chose an external candidate had more internal candidates in their applicant pool. While we have no hard data to explain why this is so, we could draw the assumption that having a mixture of internal and external candidates provides some sort of benchmark that makes interviewers more aware of their selection criteria.
- A diverse selection group that includes customers and subordinates—both of which are rarely used in the selection process—is much more likely to be successful. We found that using a group is better than using individuals in hiring a more successful candidate. You can use the group two ways: to forward recommendations to the individual who will make the final decision, or to have the team itself make final decisions. When doing an external search it's much better to have the team make the final decision, versus simply providing recommendations. This incurs less chance of "organ rejection" and a greater buy-in from all involved in the selection process, so there is a stronger desire to make the person successful. Often if you are not part of the selection process you don't understand why the person was chosen. Participating in the selection process gives people access to information on why an individual is a best fit[29]

Possibly one of the most intriguing selection challenges that any company can tackle is how to select executive candidates who will perform well within international assignments. Freddy Cabrera, Senior Director of International Human Resources for PepsiCo, provides the following summary of how his company manages the selection of international vice presidents and general managers.

> At PCI (Pepsi Cola International) we start out by reviewing candidates provided by our three search partners. In addition, I obtain referrals from our employee base as well as from recent hires. In the past we tried to make use of an assessment tool provided by an outside consulting firm that Pepsi has used extensively in the United States. We no longer rely on this tool because we found that there was a low correlation between how executives scored on the assessment and how they actually performed on international assignments. One of the problems here was that the consulting firm had made its assessment decisions on the basis of statistical data from a U.S.-based population.

> Instead of relying on this external assessment, we now make use of multiple interviews. Every executive passes through five to seven interviews. If we want to select a VP for Marketing, the interviewers might include our Senior VP for Marketing, myself, my manager, the senior HR VP for Pepsi International, one other senior VP, and then our German president for Pepsi International.

> In the case of an interview for a position involving one of our presidents for our international business units, these interviewers would be the president of Pepsi International, our CEO of PepsiCo, Roger Enrico, myself, our senior VP of HR, and two or three other senior-level VPs that report to our company president.

Cabrera explains that given their hectic schedules, and the fact that these interviewers are spread out across the globe, each interview is usually conducted independently. All interviewers then forward their interview summaries to Cabrera, who consolidates these separate views together into a composite evaluation of the executive candidate.

Candidates for international executive positions at PCI are evaluated both in terms of their functional competencies and their fit with Pepsi's culture. As Cabrera explains:

For each of our functions we determined what was most important to executive success. As an example, for our franchise organization we sent questionnaires out to our best franchise VPs in the field and asked them to identify the most important competencies required for the success of our franchise directors. Two of the competencies that they identified involved the areas of "interpersonal communications" and "negotiations." From this list we developed the selection interview questions we wanted to use with our candidates, along with an interview guide. We are now in the process of sending these questions back out for validation. For a marketing executive, a representative question might be, "Describe a successful marketing program you managed. What made it successful? What steps did you go through? What obstacles did you have to overcome to implement this program?"

We consider culture fit to be very important when making selection decisions. While we have a lot of data from our contacts and search partners that can help us assess functional competencies, it is in the area of culture fit that many managers can fail. One thing that helps us determine culture fit is that our search firms have worked with us for a long time, and have a solid understanding of the Pepsi culture. In thinking about the defining characteristics of Pepsi's culture, three things stand out. Executive candidates have to have strong initiative, the ability to build and motivate capable teams, and the ability to manage several different things at the same time.

In addition, for international candidates foreign language skills and international experience are also important factors. In a situation in which we can't find someone with the necessary international experience, it is crucial to find someone who can adapt to ambiguity, and who will work well with people from other countries. Executives who tend to see things in black-and-white terms lack the flexibility we are looking for to manage sensitive international assignments. To determine adaptability we might ask questions about how candidates have worked with customers and peers, whether they currently work in a diverse and truly international work setting, and the degree of contact they've had with their company's international team.

Cabrera suggests that at PCI the selection process is well integrated with the process of executive on-boarding.

In my experience the first month on the job is extremely important here at Pepsi. You are being informally evaluated six months into the job, so you can't explain away problems by saying "I'm new."

To prepare new executives, we discuss the on-boarding and evaluation process with them before they are hired. Then, during the first one to three months on the job, these executives are often sent to other countries (not the ones to which they eventually will be assigned)—a situation that we refer to as an operating experience "between brackets." This temporary assignment is the new hires' opportunity to make mistakes and to ask all of the simple questions, in a part of the world in which they won't be evaluated.

At the same time, we try to select countries that will replicate many of the challenges that the executive will eventually have to handle. For example, someone who will eventually be assigned to Brazil may be assigned to Thailand, where he or she will encounter the same packaging and products—something that they will be able to apply in the future.

We prepare an on-boarding program with objectives to follow, with a copy to the executive's in-country guide. During the assignment, the executive is checking the objectives and holding debriefing sessions with his or her future boss—generally the head HR and line person for the country. With very senior people, someone from corporate will be responsible for on-boarding and setting up a schedule for each manager in each country.[30]

SUMMARY OF KEY POINTS

- The starting point for matching leadership competencies to organizational needs is a job analysis, which, ironically, many organizations never perform for executive-level positions.

- An important aspect of the job analysis is to get your senior team aligned on the major job demands related to a position, and on the broader view of what you are trying to achieve for your organization through each executive position.

- Companies are going beyond perfunctory reviews of leadership competencies to ensure that there is a good fit between executive candidates and their strategic requirements and corporate culture.

- The concept of "culture fit" is particularly important when attempting to fill executive positions, given executives' roles as organizational change agents.

- The first step in assessing fit is to identify the cultural norms and values that are an essential, defining part of your work culture and that you want to continue to support.

- A second step involves evaluating leadership requirements in terms of the life-cycle stage (start-up, growth, maturity, decline) of your business.

- You can assess fit not only through targeted interview questions but also by setting up interactions that allow you to see the organizational cultural context in which candidates are used to working.

- An effective selection method is the *past-oriented interview,* which can help you gather relevant examples of the kinds of behaviors and work performance a candidate has demonstrated across his or her work history.

- Research suggests that you can improve the quality of your executive selection process by increasing the diversity of your candidate pool, interviewing both internal and external candidates, and including in the interview committee both potential subordinates and customers.

CHAPTER 13

ON-BOARDING
NEW LEADERS

Throughout this book you have been introduced to a variety of tools for selecting, assessing, and developing an exceptional leadership team. All too often, however, companies spend an incredible amount of time and money on the mechanics of selection and development, yet largely ignore new leaders once they have been brought on board. According to Valerie Sessa, a researcher with the Center for Creative Leadership who has closely studied the success and failure of executive selection methods, the degree of initial support and information that newly hired executives receive is a determining factor in whether or not they will be successful. As Sessa concludes, "One of the things we found is that, once selected, most executives are thrown to the wolves with little support and training. Those who do receive this support are much more successful."[1]

A talent scout for a professional sports team would not consider committing his corporation to a multiyear, multimillion-dollar player acquisition contract only to ignore that new player once he is added to the team, yet somehow we feel that corporate executives constitute a completely different entity. The assumption seems to be that any executive who is worth his or her salt should be able to make an adjustment to a new leadership position without additional coaching or guidance.

This assumption ignores a number of important considerations. The first is that many new executives simply fail to make successful adjustments to their new corporate homes. While we would like to assume that these "dropouts" are restricted to the poorest performers, the truth is that they are often good leaders who simply have had great difficulty in making the critical initial adjustment to a new work environment.

Although one might argue that such adjustment problems are due to competency deficiencies, in fact they constitute initial adjustment difficulties that could be prevented given a little planning and forethought, and the creation of a solid on-boarding plan.

Another often-ignored factor that highlights the importance of on-boarding is that the acclimation process for newly hired executives is far more difficult than ever before. This is partially due to the increased complexity of executives' jobs and the greater number of executives who are being asked to make the adjustment from outside companies and industries.

There is growing recognition among senior managers and HR leaders that an executive's successful adjustment to a new environment involves more than just the transferring of technical skills. It also requires an understanding of the predominant work culture and leadership styles that shape organizational performance. These factors involve subtle influences that cannot be fully explained in a half-day orientation session. Author and consultant Amy Korn suggests that a common cause of adjustment difficulties for newly hired executives "is a poor match between an executive's operating style and the business culture. Here, the importance of screening for culture-critical behaviors and hard-to-develop competencies cannot be overlooked."[2] As an example, Korn cites the cultural dimension of informality, suggesting that if a new recruit "comes from a 'buttoned-down' organization, an environment characterized by a free flow of ideas and constructive conflict might make the new executive feel unduly criticized. Others may begin to mistrust him because he 'plays it so close to the vest.'"[3]

THE PAYOFFS OF ON-BOARDING

While almost every company provides at least a cursory orientation for new work professionals and executives, an on-boarding process goes beyond the standard orientation to encompass a detailed road map for strategically guiding new executives through their job experience during their first six to twelve weeks on the job. It includes those meaningful learning experiences, influential contacts, and informational guideposts that together serve as a learning accelerator for compressing the time normally required by executives to master their new leadership positions. Apart from preventing executive derailment, a good on-boarding process can also help your company *retain* leaders who are performing well within their new jobs. While the subject of executive retention was discussed in Chapter 12, it is important to recognize that the first step to any executive retention strategy is the creation of a solid on-boarding plan.

An on-boarding plan also serves as a method for periodically checking in with new hires to see how they are adjusting to their new work environments and for spotting potential derailment issues before they grow beyond control. By starting new executives off on the right track with their teams, on-boarding plans help new hires build effective work relationships from the their first day on the job. As a final consideration, keep in mind that, at its essence, an on-boarding plan provides a means for accelerating on-the-job learning while eliminating the types of costly and damaging mistakes that normally accrue from traditional hit-or-miss approaches to executive hiring.

When carefully constructed, an on-boarding plan eliminates some of the most frustrating problems that typically plague new executives. Among these are the following:

- Soon after coming on board some newly hired executives experience disappointment and disillusionment in the form of "buyer's remorse." This is most prevalent when new executives feel that the work situation they have inherited does not live up to the promises that were laid out to them during the interview and selection process. Table 29 on page 314 describes six "killer" job discrepancies that can create strong job dissatisfaction issues for incoming executives.

- Costly mistakes sometime occur when new executives act without having complete knowledge of the culture and work systems of their new organization.

- A prolonged and drawn-out adjustment period ensues whenever executives are forced to learn "on the fly" and manage their jobs from the date of hire.

- Frustration forms if new-hires lack a ready, nonthreatening avenue for presenting their concerns and complaints and for quickly resolving adjustment issues before they reach a critical level.

- Job failures may occur as the result of "organ rejection," such as when the current organization and leadership team reject the executive's new ideas and proposed plans of action.

TABLE 29		
SIX "KILLER" JOB DISCREPANCIES THAT CAN LEAD TO BUYER'S REMORSE		
Work Dimension	What Was Promised	What Was Delivered
Autonomy	You will a have high degree of autonomy and will run your own shop.	Micromanagement and second-guessing of decisions; limited authority.
Job Scope	You will have a broad scope of responsibility in your job function.	Restricted scope of responsibility.
Resource Support	You will be given adequate resources and staff.	Limited resources and staff, but no compromising on objective.
Job Challenge	We don't want you to get buried in the "grind work." You've been brought on board to take on exciting new work projects and challenging opportunities.	Short-term tactical problems that are hidden from view during the hiring interview; time invested in clearing out "organizational underbrush" before new projects can be undertaken.
Integrity and Trust	We operate with a high level of professional integrity.	A work environment where "dirty politics" is a common occurrence.
Role Clarity	There will be a clear delineation of job duties and leadership roles. You and the other members of our team will understand the new role you play in our organization.	Job responsibilities become a confused "shell game." High degree of uncertainty regarding the new hire's priorities and accountabilities. May include a tug-of-war with executive's manager, who vacillates between relinquishing responsibility and grabbing back control.

CHARACTERISTICS OF AN EFFECTIVE ON-BOARDING PLAN

All effective on-boarding plans share similar features. Before implementing your plan, check it against the following eight design criteria.

LINE OWNERSHIP

The responsibility for the design and execution of the plan should not be delegated to the HR department. It should be prepared instead by the incoming executive's manager. As a process for getting the new executive accepted by the executive team, the plan should be based in part on input provided by other team members and with oversight review by the company's HR director. For mission-critical positions, the plan is frequently personally crafted by the work function's top-level manager.

INITIAL SAFETY ZONE

The on-boarding period usually covers several weeks and may extend up to three months. This period constitutes a "safety zone" for the new executive, with most job responsibilities and objectives held in abeyance until the on-boarding period is completed. Amy Korn advises that a frequent derailer for newly hired executives is "the rush to put points on the board. . . . Many times, early derailment occurs when a new hire moves too rapidly to make changes and demonstrate an impact."[4] An extended learning process ensures that executives have gathered "critical mass" in navigating the organizational landscape before attempting to undertake drastic changes.

HIRING IN ADVANCE OF REQUIREMENTS

The only way that this extended learning period can work is if a company has evolved beyond crisis management in its executive recruiting function. This means that the recruiting function is able to "swim upstream" to identify, recruit, and hire executives early on, rather than delay hiring and then abruptly throw new hires into the job without adequate preparation. As I stated in Chapter 12, a distinguishing characteristic of companies with reputations of superior executive resource capabilities is that they go one step further and continually scout for executive talent, with the intention of bringing leaders on board well before they are actually required.

AVAILABILITY OF A MENTOR/COACH

On-boarding plans often include intense coaching by a preselected senior-level executive (someone other than the executive's own manager). This individual provides an essential coaching process, consisting of subtle guidance regarding the way decisions are made in the organization, the targeting of influential organizational stakeholders, and advice regarding leadership behaviors that could violate corporate norms. On a day-to-day basis this translates into advising new executives on how to navigate through the executive decision process or providing troubleshooting regarding how to sequence, schedule, and implement actions to obtain desired results. Figure 32 shows an example of the type of visual road map that a coach might provide to a new hire to explain the intricacies of navigating a more restrictive quality-audit process through the corporate decision process.

This coaching function requires a sensitive balancing act on the part of the coach. On the one hand, one of the reasons executive talent is brought in from outside the company is to impart fresh points of view and innovative work methods. On the other hand, new executives need to know when they are about to undertake actions that will invariably be rejected by the organization.

The coach also provides an invaluable check-in service by periodically discussing with the new hire his or her impressions of the new work environment and encouraging him or her to share emerging concerns and adjustment issues. Coaches also provide a "clearinghouse" function by helping new executives interpret and make sense of the wide variety of data that these new hires are taking in from all parts of the organization.

OPPORTUNITIES FOR NETWORKING

The on-boarding process helps new executives build effective influencing networks with peers and support personnel. A simple but necessary starting point for this action is for senior managers and executive coaches to orient new hires to both the formal organizational structure and informal networks—cross-functional teams, organizational committees, interest-based groups, informal luncheons—that serve as influence groups within the organization. A secondary support role that managers and mentors can play is to access executives to these networks and groups.

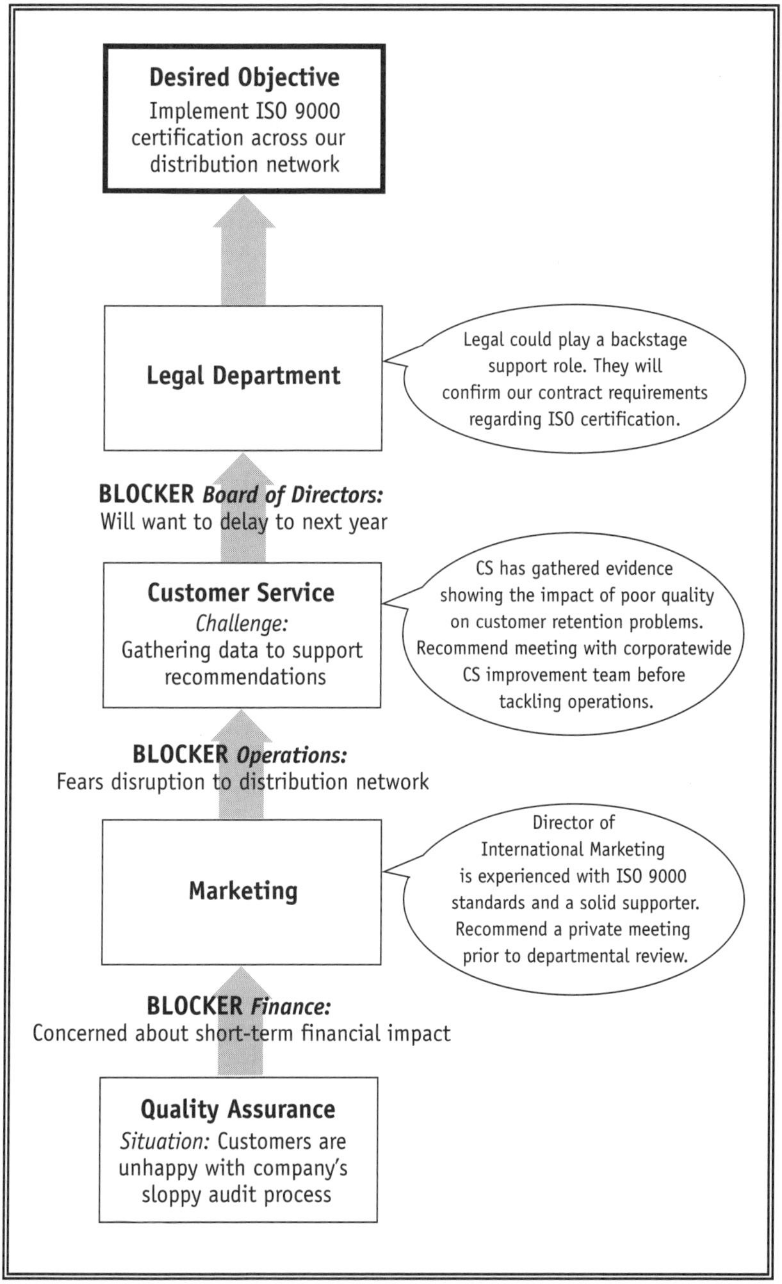

Desired Objective
Implement ISO 9000
certification across our
distribution network

Legal Department

> Legal could play a backstage support role. They will confirm our contract requirements regarding ISO certification.

BLOCKER *Board of Directors:*
Will want to delay to next year

Customer Service
Challenge:
Gathering data to support
recommendations

> CS has gathered evidence showing the impact of poor quality on customer retention problems. Recommend meeting with corporatewide CS improvement team before tackling operations.

BLOCKER *Operations:*
Fears disruption to distribution network

Marketing

> Director of International Marketing is experienced with ISO 9000 standards and a solid supporter. Recommend a private meeting prior to departmental review.

BLOCKER *Finance:*
Concerned about short-term financial impact

Quality Assurance
Situation: Customers are
unhappy with company's
sloppy audit process

FIGURE 32 CREATING AN ORGANIZATIONAL ROAD MAP

ORIENTATION TO ORGANIZATIONAL SYSTEMS AND BUSINESS ENVIRONMENT

Another important element of the on-boarding process involves providing new executives with intensive training on how the company runs its business. This includes an understanding of major markets, product lines, areas for planned expansion, existing and emerging competitors, perceived competitive advantage, and profiles of team members. During the on-boarding period new hires can also be introduced to the new company's proprietary systems and technical tools, such as customer databases, customized financial planning software, and process maps that delineate the company's core business processes.

THOROUGH PLANNING

When compared with the typical orientation process, on-boarding learning experiences are more thoughtfully prepared, including a studied arrangement of the timing and sequencing of activities to produce the best possible leadership learning experience. An example of this would involve the scheduling of field and customer visits, which make up an important part of the on-boarding process. Thus, before scheduling a new executive to visit a major customer account, an on-boarding plan would include a visit to those key sales and field support locations that "own" that particular customer account. One of the major features of the on-boarding process is a formal schedule, such as that shown in Table 30, which orchestrates the timing and sequencing of these diversified learning experiences.

SIGNIFICANT CORPORATE INVESTMENT

An on-boarding process involves a three-way investment on the part of an employer.

- An extended period of noncommitted time dedicated to learning about the new company and corporate culture
- Increased travel and support expenses associated with bringing new executives into contact with customers and field personnel
- Extensive time commitments on the part of other members of the senior team to guide, coach, and educate new executives

ASSESSING PROGRESS: THE CHECK-IN PROCESS

The on-boarding process serves as more than a vehicle for downloading information and organizational context to new executives.

	TABLE 30				
ON-BOARDING PLAN FOR VANESSA GRAVES, VP OF MARKET RESEARCH					
			Week		
On-Boarding Assignment	1	2	3	4	5
Attend corporate finance review	✓				
Meeting with J. Chambers; International	✓				
Accompany H. Franklin on field visits to KJS Stores		✓			
Meetings: S. Johnson, D. Smith (Review 5-year marketing forecast)			✓		
Three-week check-up			✓		
Cincinnati office visit: Shadow marketing team			✓		
Attend Project Review: Arthur Anderson Consulting				✓	
Attend Corporate Leadership Symposium				✓	
Accompany D. Davis on account call					✓
Attend cross-functional project team on customer satisfaction delivery system					✓
Five-week check-up					✓

It also provides a rich opportunity to check in with new hires and find out how they are adjusting to their new jobs. A good person to direct this check-in process is the senior manager who has taken on the role of coach. Some of the questions that often yield important clues about the adjustment process are as follows:

- How does the job measure up to the initial expectations you had formed during the job interview? Were there any miscommunications between what you had thought you were getting into and the job as you see it now?

- What information gaps need to be closed?

- Have you encountered any obstacles that would cause you to recalibrate the preliminary objectives you laid out for yourself?

- How are you adjusting to the relocation? Is there any additional help you need from our HR or relocation office?

- Based on what you know so far, how would you describe the organization's expectations of your job role?

- What have you identified as your primary work priorities?

- Based on what you have learned so far, how would you describe our corporate culture? What do you like about this culture? Given the fact that every new work environment requires some adjustments, what do you think your biggest adjustment challenge will be for this job?

- Are there any meetings or discussions in which you are not currently involved in which you feel you need to take part? Do you need to be included on certain e-mail status updates? Where do you need to be brought into the loop on communications?

WATCH FOR THE STORM CLOUDS

As the mentor checks in with the new executive, he or she should be alert to certain danger signs that typically indicate a new employee may be having difficulty adjusting to his or her new role.

- The individual drags her feet on making a commitment to a relocation. When you hear a string of excuses about why she requires additional time to make the move, a warning bell should go off. Likewise, when the new hire's spouse refuses to work with the company's relocation company, that is an indication they may be resisting the move.

- During the first three months on the job you receive numerous problem calls from peers and associates complaining about the new hire's leadership and communication style. Pay attention to how the individual reacts when you present this feedback. A flexible and adaptable leader will anticipate that a move into a new position or company may require some adjustments to his leadership style, and act accordingly. Blanket denial and angry rebuttals are storm clouds that should put you on alert. Keep in mind that if a new executive is having difficulty during this "honeymoon" period, he is likely to continue to have problems further into the job experience.

- During discussions and meetings, the new hire repeatedly voices concerns about her new job. Aspiring to high scores on some "happiness meter" is not the issue— everyone who engages in a new job faces a certain degree of adjustment difficulty. The true test is when you sense an underlying tone of bitterness and frustration regarding the new work situation. Ongoing negative comparisons between what was promised in the hiring interview and what was delivered (see Table 29) is a strong sign of job dissatisfaction.

- The last warning signal is complete silence. When you encounter a new employee who quickly goes "underground" and distances himself from his manager, a warning bell should immediately go off. Pay particular attention to this warning if you hear that the new executive seems to be complaining to others about his job situation but refrains from openly disclosing adjustment issues to his mentor or manager.

PROVIDING "AIR COVER" FOR NEW EXECUTIVES

There are several support actions you can take to increase the probability that a new hire will be successful in the job transition. The first action is to provide needed support and coaching. Executives who are brought into the organization from the outside sometimes face "organ rejection" from negative or fearful peers or work teams. This scenario is especially common among companies that are embarked on an aggressive changeover of leadership from the outside (see Chapter 2). One way to counter this type of organizational resistance is for senior managers to give visible support to new executives and to let others in the organization know that these incoming leaders have their full confidence. Management consultants Bradford and Geoffrey Smart refer to such actions as "providing air cover for your change agents."[5] Examples include bringing new hires into critical decision-making sessions, giving them authorship roles on important companywide communications, and using staff meetings and cross-functional meetings as vehicles for affirming organizational support for these individuals. Additional steps may include positioning incoming executives as leaders on projects that are directly sponsored by members of the senior team or the CEO.

Wise companies also attempt to team up new executives with senior managers who can function as coaches and troubleshooters in suggesting the most effective pathways for accomplishing tasks. This might involve recommending influential stakeholders who need to be brought into decision-making sessions, helping new executives translate their objectives into words and symbols that are significant to incumbent executives, and identifying organizational "blockers" who will need to be accommodated or neutralized before new initiatives can be engaged.

GETTING ON THE SAME PAGE

One of the most significant variables that influence executives' successful adjustment is whether they are able to start things off on the right foot with their new work team. The way in which a new leader tackles team issues during the first few weeks on the job strongly shapes the nature of the leader-team relationship. This stage setting, while important for all new executives, is especially relevant to those who are stepping into leadership voids created by departing executives. In this situation, the new hire needs to understand the group norms, interpersonal dynamics, and performance expectations that have historically defined his team's operation. For their part, team members want to know who is behind the mask and with what kind of person they are dealing.

One way for new executives and teams to obtain a better understanding of each other is a technique that I call "getting on the same page"—an opportunity for leaders and team members to align their separate views and concerns. This exercise takes about three hours and should be directed by a trained facilitator, preferably someone not affiliated with the executive's department. This technique is similar in many respects to the "new manager assimilation process" used by GE to accelerate the learning of new executives. Following are some suggestions for planning and conducting the meeting session, and directing the follow-up coaching session with the team leader.

PART A: PLANNING FOR THE SESSION

Prior to bringing the executive and team together, the facilitator should meet privately with the executive to confirm the session's objectives. Soon after this planning session, the executive should pro-

---

I know that having a new team leader can sometimes be a little unsettling. You probably have a lot of questions you'd like to ask of me and perhaps a few concerns that you would like to get on the table. At the same time, until now there may not have been a comfortable setting for presenting these questions and concerns. My own personal feeling is that I'd like to get to know each of you better, and I believe that it's important that we take the time to set the stage for the kind of work relationship we'd like to develop. Accordingly, I've asked David, our director of OD, to facilitate an off-site meeting that I'll refer to as "Getting on the Same Page." The meeting will be held on February 16th from 9:00 A.M. till noon in Suite 206 of the Baltimore Conference Center.

Prior to our meeting, I'll be meeting with David to outline the kind of assistance that would be of great help to me as I am acclimating to my new position. During the first part of our three-hour meeting, you will have an opportunity to present any questions and concerns you might have for me to David, who will later provide me with a private debriefing on feedback. Let me assure you that no one will be put on the spot during this meeting. All of your individual comments and concerns will be kept in confidence by David, and only your group feedback will be shared with me. After the debriefing session we will all reconvene to gain closure on the issues and questions we have jointly put on the table.

Please address any questions you might have to me or to David, who can be reached at extension 2296. Thank you in advance for your help and support. I am looking forward to this session and know that we will all benefit from it!

FIGURE 33 SAMPLE CORRESPONDENCE TO ANNOUNCE
THE "GETTING ON THE SAME PAGE" MEETING

vide his or her team with a simple explanation of the intended purpose of this session. Figure 33 provides an example of how this team communication might be worded.

Another planning step involves having the facilitator guide the executive through three questions (see Table 31 on page 324) that address the executive's expectations for his or her team. The answers to these questions are placed on a series of flip charts and held in readiness for the second part of the exercise. These three questions can be summarized as follows:

- *What is important to you as a team leader?* The executive describes his or her performance expectations and leadership

TABLE 31

ISSUES AND TOPICS FOR "GETTING ON THE SAME PAGE"

Exploring the Team's Expectations

Here is what we think we know about you:

Here is what we'd like to know about you:

Here are our initial concerns:

We'd like you to know this about us:

Here are some helpful suggestions:

Questions Addressing the Executive's Expectations

What is important to you as a team leader?

What are you looking for in the way of help and support from your team?

What issues need to be discussed?

values. Representative answers might include: "Say what you mean," "Always communicate honestly with our customers, even if they are not going to like the answer you are giving them," "Challenge me when you think I'm wrong," or "Keep me informed of problems."

- *What are you looking for in the way of help and support from your team?* This question lets team members know where they can be of assistance in supporting their new leader on the job. This might include filling in information gaps, such as the role played by certain work functions. It can also involve providing "here's how we get things done around here" answers—the kinds of answers that can inform the leader of historical factors responsible for shaping a given work system or organizational structure. A leader's answers to this question can also focus on obstacles he or she may be encountering during the relocation. Asking one's team for suggestions regarding the location of good private schools, recommended family physicians, or attractive living communities gives leaders opportunities to reveal a personal side to their teams.

- *What issues need to be discussed?* When addressing this question, the team leader should avoid issues that involve serious performance problems of individual team members. The intent here is not to transform this discussion into an in-depth problem-solving session, but rather to alert the team to work issues that need to be resolved in the earliest stages of the leader-team relationship. The actual exploration of these issues should be postponed to a later date.

PART B: CONDUCTING THE MEETING

During the first part of the meeting the facilitator takes fifteen minutes to restate the meeting purpose and guidelines for discussion. Representative guidelines are: if you have a concern, here is where you should present it; all concerns and questions are valid; and, avoid questions that are merely disguised personal attacks.

After the introduction the facilitator asks the team leader to leave the room for an hour, while the facilitator guides the team through the five key topics listed in the top section of Table 31. Each topic is presented as a header at the top of a flip chart, with team members' responses recorded underneath:

- *Here is what we think we know about you.* Here team members are asked to present what they know personally and professionally about their team leader. This is an important topic, for it often discloses untruths or misrepresentations based on information obtained through the company rumor mill.

- *Here is what we'd like to know about you.* Under this heading members often ask questions that help them form a more complete picture of their new leader, such as: Where did this person come from? Why was he brought on board? What does she think of the company? What is his position on a given project? Does she have any children? What does he like to do in his spare time? I have seen many executives register a great deal of surprise at the interest and energy level that is usually associated with such mundane questions. The fact is, however, that answering these questions helps present the leader as a real, live human being.

- *Here are our initial concerns.* When addressing this statement, team members typically start off with relatively safe questions before venturing into such substantive issues as: Do you anticipate making any major changes in team assignments? Or, Is it likely that we will encounter a second downsizing this year? This question often reveals a team's concerns regarding ways in which the new executive's leadership style might differ from his or her predecessor's. Representative questions might be: Is the new leader more or less accessible than his predecessor? or, Are her performance expectations entirely different from the previous leader's?

- *We'd like you to know this about us.* Answers here point out areas in which the team has taken pride in its accomplishments, and performance areas in which members look for continued recognition and acknowledgment.

- *Here are some helpful suggestions.* As they have interacted with their new team leader during the first few weeks on the job, team members may have noted actions and behaviors that clash with the predominant corporate culture and leadership style. These answers provide a positive context for alerting the team leader to potential problems. Representative answers might include: Be careful of circumventing Brand Management in your decision making, or, You seem to be inaccessible. Try to implement more of an open door policy.

All feedback presented by team members should be listed on the flip charts, with an asterisk placed next to responses that are confirmed by several participants. At the end of the hour the team members are given a twenty-minute break while the facilitator gives the team leader a one-on-one summary of all the questions and feedback members came up with. The purpose of this individual "decompression" period is twofold. First, it gives the facilitator an opportunity to share with the leader any feedback or questions of a sensitive nature, while helping the leader to read between the lines on input that may be difficult to interpret. Second, this private debriefing session gives the team leader time to formulate answers to difficult questions, and to pinpoint issues that will require more time for discussion.

After the break period, the team is called together and invited to listen as the facilitator presents each of the five topic sheets provided by the team. The leader is asked to take five to ten minutes to honestly respond to each set of questions and concerns. In situations in which the leader lacks the needed information to respond, he or she makes a commitment to follow up with the team at a later date. As the final step of this process, the team leader posts the flip charts containing the three questions that he or she had explored prior to the session. A second option is for the meeting facilitator to manage this downloading, with an emphasis on highlighting concerns and issues that were separately noted by the team leader and the team.

PART C: THE FOLLOW-UP COACHING SESSION

This meeting usually generates a lot of thought-provoking discussion between new leaders and their teams. Many new executives take away from such sessions a number of ideas for improving their team relationships but have some confusion regarding where to start. Some executives leave these meetings a bit surprised at the initial impressions they have made on their organization and work team. During the debriefing sessions, facilitators help team leaders sort out their various impressions and interpret the session *content*. At the same time, the facilitators share with executives any pertinent observations regarding the session *process*—for example, the degree to which the session interactions revealed significant aspects of the leader-team relationship. Some of the questions that can be explored during this discussion are as follows:

- Does the new executive have any blind spots; is this individual *unaware* of how her actions and behavior are impacting the performance of her team?

- In what areas do the team leader and team appear to be in alignment? In what areas do they appear to have very different views regarding the needs of their work group?

- What type of personal rapport seems to be developing between the team leader and the team? Would you describe the mood of the meeting as informal and friendly, or cautious and reserved? Were team members comfortable about sharing their feelings or were they unduly concerned about disclosing their concerns?

- How did the new executive respond to the issues that were presented? Was he defensive and hostile or did he remain positive and open-minded throughout the discussion?

- Did any significant patterns emerge in the questions that were presented by the team? For example, did a number of questions center around concerns regarding job security or potential changes in job responsibilities?

- What were the new executive's impressions of this exercise? How did this individual view her role in the discussion?

SECURING THE "FIT" BETWEEN CULTURE AND LEADERSHIP STYLE

In Chapter 12 we reviewed the importance of incorporating into the selection interviewing process questions and background information that can help you look for a good fit between the job candidates and the organizational culture they are entering. The on-boarding process provides the second checkpoint for securing this fit, by exposing executives to those subtle norms, behaviors, and expectations that together comprise "how we get things done around here."

One of the simplest ways to familiarize new executives with an organization's culture is to invite them to participate with their peers in an informal "values-anchoring" session. At this session, the meeting facilitator (usually the company's OD or HR director) encourages participants to openly discuss the types of culture drivers that are listed in Table 32.

Another step you can take to help new hires better understand their new work culture is to make use of informal organizational benchmarks. For example, show them how your company's culture compares with those of such well-known companies as Wal-Mart, PepsiCo, and GE. Each company has certain core-value drivers that serve as basic defining characteristics. PepsiCo is as well known for the aggressive drive of its managers as Southwest Airlines is for its creative playfulness. Take the time to articulate the values that characterize your own organization. One way to clarify this cultural picture is to share stories and examples of corporate executives who have performed well in your organization because of their ability to understand and make use of your company's work culture. You might also include in this discussion examples of business initiatives that have either succeeded or failed miserably as a result of the way in which they were introduced into your organization.

TABLE 32

**CULTURE DRIVERS THAT CHARACTERIZE
AN ORGANIZATION**

1. How do we deal with mistakes here? Do we shoot people, or emphasize learning from our mistakes?

2. How formal or informal are we? Do we thrive on fancy computer-based presentations or is there a strong emphasis on informal information sharing? Do we live on e-mail, or do we favor phone or videoconferencing?

3. How do decisions get made around here? Do we spend extended time in group caucus, or do we rely primarily on one-on-one decision-making sessions?

4. What are we proud of around here? What do we look for in up-and-coming leaders?

5. Do we freely import ideas from the outside or do we build exclusively from the inside under the assumption that no one does it better than we do?

6. Are we cross-functionally team based or are we silo driven (that is, do we focus exclusively on what happens in our respective cultural "silos")?

7. Are we as competitive internally as we are externally? How inwardly focused are we?

8. Do we exchange information freely or on a need-to-know basis? Is it acceptable to contact anyone within the organization to obtain information?

9. How driven are we? Are we the type of organization where the office lights burn late into the night or a company that emphasizes balancing personal life and work? To what degree are executives expected to routinely make lifestyle adjustments (relocation, weekend meetings) for their job?

TABLE 32 (CONT'D)
CULTURE DRIVERS THAT CHARACTERIZE AN ORGANIZATION

10. What are the most important derailers for executives in this organization? One privately held organization is absolutely paranoid about revealing to outsiders any information about their company—its policies, its customers, even the types of generalized information you'd normally expect to find in a company prospectus. One executive who had made a few innocuous comments about the company's plans to a national trade journal was put on notice that any subsequent related actions would result in termination. What are the "hot buttons" that incoming leaders need to know about in your company?

PREPARING EXECUTIVES FOR INTERNATIONAL ASSIGNMENTS

The on-boarding task takes on special significance when it must prepare executive candidates for international assignments. The more realistic the job preview, the better candidates will understand the challenges they are about to encounter and the more prepared they will be for their new roles. Given that family adjustment problems constitute one of the biggest reasons for the failure of international executives, it is also critical for companies to provide spouses and families with a realistic assessment of potential assignments and to gauge their level of support and interest. According to Kay Lillig Cotter, Director of Consulting for Measurement Service for Wilson Learning Corporation:

> With the issue of expatriation, it is often family members who have problems adjusting to the new area. The employee has a job waiting and a built-in network of people with whom to interact, and expectations for the work to be done. The family often has none of this and feels out of place and out of sync.
>
> I think we have a dilemma in the United States related to assessing people for expatriation. We really need to show job relevance in our assessment process. It is hard to justify assessing family members despite what we know about why relocations fail. My recommendation has been to perform the

assessment for the executive first as part of the selection/ placement process. Then, after the job offer is made, assess the family members for developmental purposes. We could help people see what will come easily and what will be challenging by providing realistic simulations of their life overseas and/or by conducting interviews discussing the challenges involved. Accurate preview information would also be helpful.[6]

A design format I have found to be effective is to combine a general cultural and job orientation that helps replicate the work and lifestyle conditions candidates are likely to experience in their host country. I typically find that in an effort to save a few training dollars, companies restrict such training to candidates who have completed and passed the final approval process and made a nonretractable commitment to their new assignment. This type of training approach ignores one of the key payoffs of cross-cultural training, which is that—if provided early enough in the candidate's decision process— such training can provide an effective self-selection process and can alert an employer to any adjustment problems candidates may face in their new assignment. This self-selection process should also extend to the expatriate candidate's family. As Cotter suggests:

> We could assess situations like meeting new people, doing routine activities like grocery shopping, and dealing with situations when you don't speak the language. We could also check for flexibility and versatility to handle new and unexpected situations. After this developmental process, the family should have a chance to decline the assignment if they do not feel comfortable with the challenges they will face.[7]

REPATRIATION: PREPARING THE WAY BACK

When dealing with expatriated executives, the on-boarding process includes not only the initial adjustment to the new job and culture, but also the repatriation back into the host culture and corporate office. One would think that since companies make such substantial investments in their expatriate executives, they would also invest the necessary time to help integrate them back into their organizations upon the completion of their assignment. Unfortunately, this is not always the case. Some companies do not guarantee that their expatriate executives will even have a position at the end of an assignment.[8] Other companies summarily fail to take advantage of the competencies and insights that expats glean from their experiences, when considering HR or business decisions regarding the host country.[9]

Samir Gupte cautions that, "The expected return on investment employed by many companies on their capital investment is about 15 to 20 percent. The same investment analysis should be applied to investing in an expatriate assignment." He adds that planning for an expatriate assignment starts at the beginning of the selection process and requires us to be able to answer the following questions:

- What do we expect the expat to gain from this assignment?

- Knowing what we know now about our organizational objectives and future opportunities, what role do we see this person assuming at the end of a three-year assignment?

- What additional skills, experience, or training do we need to provide during an assignment to help prepare this expat for future assignments?

- What potential pitfalls or showstoppers may come up, and how can we mitigate these problems?[10]

CASE IN POINT: DEPLOYMENT TO SAUDI ARABIA
Robert Barner

Several years ago, while working as the training manager of a Fortune 50 company, I was asked to assist in the development of a cross-cultural orientation and deployment program, to support the deployment of approximately two hundred employees and their spouses/families to two- to three-year assignments in Saudi Arabia. As only a few managers and executives in the internal candidate pool had previously lived and worked in Saudi, our challenge was to give prospective candidates a better idea of the work and lifestyle conditions they would be encountering. The training program we developed contained the following features.

Phase One

Interested candidates were provided with a half-day briefing, highlighting not only the culture and lifestyle of the host country, but also the wide variations in cultural norms that expats were likely to encounter among the three host-site locations (the three cities in question had very different levels of receptivity to Western ideas and norms). At the same time we provided preliminary information on the types of residence and transportation accommodations that would be provided to candidates and their families, as well as the salary, benefit package, and personal travel authorization that candidates would receive as part of their relocation package. We then gave candidates a few days to consider whether they would be interested in progressing to the next stage of the selection process.

Phase Two

A one-day, in-depth briefing was held for candidates and their spouses by a cross-cultural expert who had lived and worked extensively in Saudi Arabia. This was a candid presentation in which the consultant honestly discussed some of the adjustment problems encountered by other expats in the host country. Attendees were given the opportunity to anonymously write down adjustment issues and questions on note cards for review by the speaker. One of our company's senior managers then provided a second briefing detailing stories of other companies that had either made a successful entry into the host country or lost sales and contracts through cross-cultural blunders. Attendees were then divided into breakout teams to discuss the implications of these findings for our own project. Over the next few days we provided a second opportunity for candidates to eliminate themselves from the selection process.

Phase Three

Several days of training and orientation were conducted with the assistance of our outside consultants. Candidates and their families were provided with case-study materials and introduced to several role-play simulations depicting the cultural norms of the host country, as well as problems that could result from a lack of sensitivity to those norms. Candidates were also involved in a second series of role-plays and discussions, with participation by several volunteers from the Royal Saudi Air Force, the primary customer market served by our company. A separate training component outlined the types of work-related challenges candidates might face when directly coordinating efforts with their Saudi counterparts.

Phase Four

Candidates and their families were then teamed up in small groups with families who had previously lived and worked in Saudi Arabia, who shared their own experiences and informally addressed participants' questions and concerns. We intentionally eliminated all HR and senior managers from this discussion to encourage candidates and their families to openly address their concerns. Drawing from these families' experiences and advice from our cross-cultural consultants, we prepared a list of common adjustment challenges and asked candidates and their spouses to rank them in terms of the stress level they felt they would encounter with each adjustment. This exercise was designed to encourage candidates and their spouses to engage in a more complete dialogue regarding what each person identified as his or her most difficult cultural adjustment areas. These difficulties ranged from having to board teenage children outside the country, to being cut off completely from friends and families, to the special constrictions women would face regarding limited work options.

Phase Five

We conducted separate interviews with candidates and their spouses to discuss their expectations of the relocation, their commitment to the assignment, and any special concerns or hesitations they might have.

At a time when the industry norm for failure on this type of expat assignment was averaging 5 percent, this training and orientation approach yielded a 100 percent success rate. Throughout the three-year period that this international team was on assignment, only two employees returned prematurely, and in both cases the reason was due to medical problems.

Over the course of designing this program, and others like it, I have drawn the following conclusions regarding the orientation and selection of expats:

- The biggest mistake is to underestimate the amount of information and training that job candidates and their families require to be able to make a reasonably informed decision about their assignment.

- Simulations can play a critical role in cross-cultural training, especially when they are customized based on previous industry-related experience, and when they closely mirror day-to-day lifestyle adjustment difficulties.

- It is absolutely essential that the training and selection process include both the candidate and his or her spouse.

- Provide several opportunities for candidates to opt out of the assignment, and let them know in advance that this decision will not negatively impact their careers.

- Spreading the training and selection process out over several weeks—as opposed to a consolidated three- to five-day event—allows candidates and their families to carefully think through the relocation decision and to gradually sift through the adjustment demands associated with the assignment.

- Provide opportunities for candidates and their spouses to anonymously share their concerns and fears, and for candidates and their spouses to individually discuss their expectations of the assignment.

- Whenever possible, make use of repatriated executives and their families as mentors and guides for candidates and their families.

- Many companies make significant resource investments to bring the right players on board, only to ignore them during their first few months on the job. One way to improve job performance and executive retention rates is through the use of a formal on-boarding program.

- An on-boarding process goes beyond the standard orientation to guide new executives through their job experience during their first six to twelve weeks on the job.

- A formal on-boarding process indoctrinates new executives in their new corporate culture, accelerates their learning curve on company systems and work processes, and discovers lines of influence within the organization.

- A well-designed on-boarding process provides opportunities for newly hired leaders to voice any adjustment difficulties they may be having, and for senior-level mentors to coach them on the most effective ways of navigating through the decision pathways of their organization. It can prevent "buyer's remorse" on the part of new hires and help new hires avoid costly and damaging mistakes.

- The success of executive on-boarding lies in advance hiring and thorough planning. Senior managers can increase the chances of successful on-boarding by providing new hires with adequate "air cover," assigning them a knowledgeable mentor, and creating a safety zone for them during the first few weeks on the job.

- An on-boarding process provides a rich opportunity to check in with new hires and find out how they are adjusting to their new jobs. A good person to direct this check-in process is the senior manager who has taken on the role of coach.

- The "getting on the same page" meeting helps executives and their teams obtain a better mutual understanding and gain alignment in their separate views and concerns.

- The on-boarding process provides the second checkpoint for securing the fit between the new hire and the organizational culture by exposing executives to the subtle norms, behaviors, and expectations that comprise "how we get things done around here."

- When attempting to prepare executive candidates for international assignments, it is important to develop realistic job previews that can provide candidates with a clear understanding of the challenges they are about to encounter, and that help prepare them for their new roles.

- When dealing with expatriate executives, the on-boarding process should include not only the initial adjustment to the new job and culture, but also a repatriation process that helps the expat make a readjustment back into the host culture and corporate office.

RETAINING
STAR PERFORMERS

S till missing in our overview is one essential element of a good executive resource strategy: how to engage the full effort and commitment of superior performers once they have been selected from the outside or promoted from within. This chapter addresses this subject, with the goal of raising the performance potential of talented leaders and increasing the likelihood of retaining them in our organizations.

Many companies fail to give executive retention adequate consideration, under the faulty assumption that the same factors that first attracted new executives to their organization will be sufficient to keep them from jumping ship. In the study entitled "The War for Talent," involving a survey of 6,000 executives, Elizabeth Chambers and associates found that only 10 percent of respondents reported an ability to retain the large majority of their high performers.[1] When it comes to CEO retention, the challenge may be far greater. In a 1998 study commissioned by the Association of Executive Search Consultants, interviews with 300 corporate leaders—including senior HR directors, line executives, and CEOs—showed that respondents strongly believed that over the next ten years it will become much harder to both attract and retain CEOs.[2] The threefold reason given for this belief included increased pressure from shareholders for short-term results, diminished personal commitment to the company, and fierce competition for the best.[3]

The thing we need to keep in mind is that in today's aggressive market our competitors are always on the prowl for new talent—and they are becoming increasingly adept at ferreting out and soliciting disgruntled employees. You can never fully guard against this type of competitive intrusion—there is always someone out there who can outbid you on salary and perks. What you can do is eliminate those frustration factors that cause executives to consider looking outside their companies in the first place. Also, keep in mind that the payoffs obtained from engaging leadership talent go beyond executive retention. They also translate into improving the overall performance capability of your leadership bench.

There are so many business books in print on the subjects of how to motivate and energize leaders that I doubt you would gain much from having me add to this quagmire of information. What I will do in this chapter is introduce you to four steps for engaging and retaining your best performers.

STEP 1: PERFORM A VULNERABILITY ASSESSMENT

A vulnerability assessment is an evaluation of where and how your company is most vulnerable to the loss of good talent through voluntary terminations. As a basic analogy, think of your company as a fortress under siege by your competitors. Performing a vulnerability assessment is a bit like walking the wall of your fortress to uncover potential areas of vulnerability, before these weaknesses are uncovered and exploited by your competitors.

If you believe that a vulnerability assessment is not needed, that you have a good "gut feeling" for why your best and brightest may be jumping ship, then think again. First of all, the data you have at your disposal for drawing conclusions on this subject are probably incomplete and faulty. Most of the readily available data on retention come from exit interviews, and as we will review, the standard exit interview is inadequate for capturing information on the true causes of executive defections. For now let's simply say that the official reasons that executives put down on paper for leaving are seldom the real reasons that drive them out the door.

A second obstacle to drawing accurate conclusions is presented when the retention data you have available are limited to *aggregate data* on employee terminations. While you may know why the average employee decides to leave your company, you may not know the factors that drive executive turnover by level, function, ethnicity, or gender.

Third, while the data you have at your disposal may give you a snapshot of your organization at a given point in time, you may lack

sufficient longitudinal data to anticipate emerging turnover trends in your organization. Without such information it becomes difficult to determine whether significant work factors—such as dissatisfaction with compensation, lack of development opportunities, or leadership deficiencies within your senior management team—now play a bigger or smaller contributing role in executive defections than they did two years ago.

As a final consideration, keep in mind that in today's fast-paced market, it does not take long for competitive attrition to create cracks in your fortress. Quite often, when other companies sense a retention weakness and the ready availability of fresh leadership talent, they hit with all the subtlety and gentleness of a shark attack. And when they strike, you can believe that they do not go after your midrange performers. They target only the best players within critical work functions—often those who represent the leadership component of a targeted company's core competencies. The strategy at play calls for a competitor to make a double killing—adding to its own leadership bench while crippling that of its competitors. A case in point is Citcorp, which a few years ago experienced the loss of over thirty executives within its global relationship banking group to competitors in an eight-month period.[4] The lesson here is that you do not want to wait until there's blood in the water to be thinking about formulating your retention defense plan. All too often, that luxury is not available.

To overcome these obstacles, the following four actions can help you obtain a more accurate reading on your company's current and future vulnerability to executive job loss.

PERFORM A STRATIFICATION ANALYSIS

A stratification analysis is a technique designed to look beyond your company's overall termination rate to identify those grade levels and functions in which you are experiencing exceptionally high rates of job loss. In so doing, a stratification analysis uncovers job loss patterns that would otherwise be hidden from view.[5] Figure 34 on page 340 shows how a hypothetical company has discovered that its greatest area of vulnerability lies at the director level, with the highest percentage of director-level defections coming from within its IT department. Obviously, this type of analysis can be applied to researching executive job loss by other categories, such as site location, gender and ethnic distribution, and retention/loss ratios for each senior manager (to check for the possibility that ineffective leadership may be a part of the turnover problem).

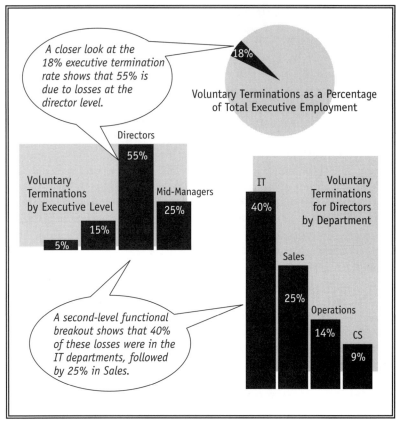

FIGURE 34 ANALYZING TERMINATION PATTERNS

CONDUCT A TREND ANALYSIS

A trend analysis explores patterns of vulnerability as a function of job tenure and/or length of employment. Continuing the example of our hypothetical company, Figure 35 provides a trend analysis for our selected group of corporate directors. You can see that this company is highly vulnerable to director-level defections during the third and fourth years of employment. Leaders who are able to make it over this hump appear to have a good chance of staying on board with the company.

Why three to four years? What happens to executives during this time period? In exploring this question, the HR department might uncover a couple of factors.

- This may be the traditional "make-or-break" time period for directors who hope to achieve the next promotional move to vice

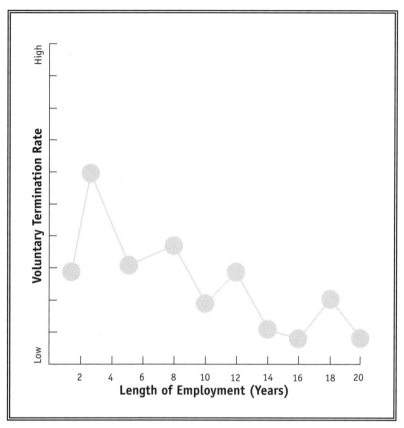

FIGURE 35 TREND ANALYSIS FOR DIRECTOR-LEVEL TERMINATIONS

president. The high level of terminations during this time period may indicate that those directors who are bypassed for promotion are extremely frustrated with the lack of alternative career options.

• Although our hypothetical company may offer a competitive salary and sign-on package to attract new executives, perhaps it fails to provide successive salary adjustments and bonus incentives that are large enough to ward off competitors' offers.

Our representative company could use exit interview data to check on the validity of the first hypothesis and have an outside consulting firm (such as Hay Associates, Hewitt & Associates, or Mercer & Company) provide competitive benchmark data related to the second factor.

CONDUCT A RETROSPECTIVE REVIEW

A different type of trend analysis involves a retrospective review of background data that appear to be correlated with retention or job loss. One professional colleague of mine, who holds a senior HR management position in a federal government agency, performed this type of analysis on executives who had left her agency during the previous three years. In doing so, she discovered that a significant correlation existed between the retention rates for executives and the executive search firms that had originally placed these executives with her agency. Specifically, executive candidates who came from certain search firms were much more likely to stay employed with her agency than were executives who were brought in through other search firms. The same type of comparison showed a much higher retention rate for new hires who had only an undergraduate degree, when compared with those individuals who entered the agency with an M.B.A. In addition, both sets of candidates received the same relative ratings on their annual reviews.

When performing a retrospective study, you need to be careful to rule out mitigating factors in order to avoid drawing unsupported conclusions from your data. In the example of my colleague, some of these factors would be whether all the search firms in question provided candidates for the same executive levels and functions, and whether the search firms were provided with the same degree of detail on position requirements in advance of the search. In the same way, the comparison of retention rates by educational level could have been biased by other factors, such as where these executives received their education, their comparative work history prior to coming on board, and the accuracy of the agency's appraisal system (an inaccurate appraisal process could mean that those executives having an M.B.A. actually outperformed their counterparts and quickly moved on to accept promotional offerings outside the agency). Because of the difficulties involved in evaluating these types of performance interactions, if you are interested in performing a retrospective study I would recommend that you seek assistance from someone from your local university who has a substantial background in research design and statistical analysis.

PERFORM DEFERRED EXIT INTERVIEWS

Earlier I suggested that the standard exit interview is a very unreliable information source for determining the underlying causes of voluntary terminations. There are several reasons for this.

- HR managers are sometimes uncomfortable probing too deeply. As a result, they may limit the interview to a few surface-level, check-in-the-box type questions.

- Exit interviews are frequently conducted during the final week on the job—a period in which the departing executive is frantically attempting to wrap up a number of loose ends before departure.

- Unlike other HR communication competencies—directing annual appraisal reviews, employment selection interviews, or grievance sessions—the exit interview is frequently regarded as a skill that one should be able to pick up through casual observation. Consequently, HR managers seldom receive specialized training in how to effectively conduct exit interviews.

- The exit interview is often positioned relatively low in the HR hierarchy. Thus, while a company's chief HR executive may be brought in to direct the hiring or termination of an executive, the exit interviews of executives who are leaving on good terms with their company are often delegated to junior-level HR specialists.

- Executives are not dummies. They know that at some point a headhunter or prospective employer will be circling back to their former boss to ask about their work. Wanting to keep everything in a positive light, departing executives may be unwilling to expose frustration points. The reason they often give for leaving is to "pursue a better opportunity."[6]

The way to get around these roadblocks is to conduct exit interviews on a delayed basis, three to six months following a departing executive's termination, by a third-party HR consulting firm that specializes in this type of service. The experience will be far less intimidating to interviewees, and the interview data you gather will be far more accurate and detailed than those obtained through the standard interview process. If you decide to pursue this option, I recommend that prior to their departure you obtain approval from employees regarding their willingness to be interviewed at a later time and that you clearly outline the purpose and rationale for the use of this interview format.

STEP 2: REDUCE YOUR RISK LEVEL FOR STAR PERFORMERS

So far we have treated executive terminations as if each executive departure affects our organization in the same way. Obviously, that is not the case. The departure of some executives leaves gaping holes in the leadership bench, while the loss of others is only a footnote in the company newsletter. The challenge is to determine well in advance of an executive's departure the probable impact on your company of his or her loss, and then to take steps to reduce the likelihood that star performers will be lost to your organization.

The first step in this process involves identifying the star performers you want to take steps to retain. Unfortunately, this is where a lot of companies fail to do their homework. One of the conclusions reached in "The War for Talent" was that only 16 percent of respondents felt their companies were able to identify their high performers.[7] One way of meeting this challenge is by applying the potential/ performance matrix you created for your executive bench to target your star performers (see Chapter 6). The four shaded cells of Figure 36 show the eight leaders we have identified through this assessment. The next step in your analysis is to have your senior team place each of these exemplary performers on a two-by-two Risk Assessment Matrix, such as the one shown in the bottom half of Figure 36. Note that the horizontal scale of this matrix measures "probability of loss." This is at best a rough assessment, as few professionals ever openly share their impending plans to jump ship. Nevertheless, your senior team may have available anecdotal information that can help it estimate the relative degree of job dissatisfaction for each executive, as well as the competitiveness of the current job market for leaders in their respective work functions.

You may be a bit confused about the relative placement of these eight performers in our Risk Assessment Matrix. After all, wouldn't we expect to find a one-to-one correlation between assessment of job potential/performance and the impact of the loss of these individuals on their organization? The answer is, not necessarily. While potential and performance are certainly crucial factors for assessing impact, three equally important factors should also be considered.

- *The criticality of the projects and responsibilities currently mentored by these executives.* Thus, even though the executive A. Davies did not receive the highest performance rating, Davies's placement on the matrix is indicative of the fact that the loss of this individual, at this point in time, could trigger significant problems in the company's IT network or key customer accounts. This evaluation factor can, of course, change as projects reach fruition and responsibilities are passed on to other leaders.

- *The executive's visibility to outside customers and the investment community.* Certain corporate leaders may be highly regarded by industry stock analysts and (correctly or incorrectly) favorably associated with the company's recent financial performance. As I suggested earlier, the sudden loss of such leaders can trigger a

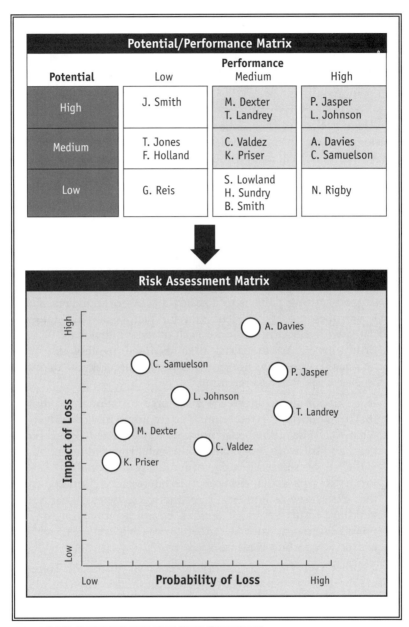

FIGURE 36 DETERMINING THE RISK POTENTIAL
FOR EXECUTIVE JOB LOSS

nasty dive in the company's stock price and should certainly figure into our risk assessment.

- *Whether one or more successors are available in our organization's talent pool who could immediately take over the incumbent's position.* The absence of qualified successors would cause
  us to place an executive higher on our curve.

The corollary to this is the current job market for this type of
position. For example, if a given executive were to defect, how difficult would it be to fill this position from the outside? What type of a
delay factor would we experience? If the current executive is under-
paid relative to current market value, what type of recruiting and
replacement costs would we need to incur? The relative irreplaceabil-
ity of an executive is an important factor that should be figured into
your assessment of risk potential.

Once you have identified those executives whose departures represent a high risk to your organization, you need to work with your
senior staff to develop customized plans for retaining these individuals. A good starting point is to conduct a series of individual interviews with the objective of identifying job factors that are uniquely
associated with job satisfaction for each of these individuals.

Bruce Barge, an industrial organizational psychologist with
Chicago-based Aon Consulting, refers to this process as "taking a
market-based approach to retention."

It is "important to niche the workforce to tailor the things
that are important to retention. One employee market niche is
what I call the *cutting-edge mercenaries,* such as R&D engineers and software programmers. In such firms, pulling an all-
nighter is considered a badge of honor; professionals feel no
loyalty to a particular firm, and are interested in working on
the sexiest new technology. To attract these types of leaders,
you have to market stock options, constant innovation, and
opportunities to work in an innovative environment with
exceptional technical mentors.

Another niche involves *family-oriented professionals.* These
are typically people who got their education first, then started
careers, then started their families. Familiy and work are
equally important to them. They are concerned not just with
the number of hours they spend with their family or at work,
but also in being able to balance trade-offs between one
spouse's career and the other's. They want to be perceived as
taking their careers seriously. In a recent focus group when
I asked these types of people what was important to them
in their jobs, one woman replied, "not talking over me in

meetings." She went on to say that she doesn't want others to assume that "all my brains fell out of my head when I had kids." To retain family-oriented professionals you need to focus on the subtleties. This might include remarks made by top management, or creating a supportive work environment. The interesting thing is that when Pepsi is trying to sell soda, they have a different commercial during Sunday afternoon football than during *Saturday Night Live,* but when HR professionals try to attract people to a company they tend to operate from a one-size-fits-all mentality. Marketing has learned to differentiate according to what different customers value.[8]

Barge also suggests that the connecting link for making this type of employee niche marketing a success will be implementing better HR systems that will enable us to target the varying employment "buying needs" of different employee groups. He contends that, "We have taken a step toward this with cafeteria-style benefits plans which recognize individual differences, but we have not gone far enough in looking at pay plans this way. One executive might be more attracted to stock options, while another might be more focused on base pay."[9]

While there is no standard format for such an interview process, I recommend that it center on the following five key dimensions of job satisfaction.

Work Challenge. High performers (HIPOs) are by nature high achievers. They hate to be locked in a confining box. Executives, in particular, need ample scope of work to hold their interest. To what extent does the current job provide a high level of job challenge to this individual?

Competent Mentorship. HIPOs tend to become very frustrated when they are stuck beneath underachievers. The question here is whether your executives respect and feel that they learn from their managers. If not, keeping high-potential performers might require repositioning them with another executive, or in extreme cases where the impact of poor mentorship is widespread, getting rid of those senior-level executives who offer little in the way of developmental guidance and who constitute a negative retention factor for exceptional subordinates.

Development Opportunities. A number of studies have shown that a major factor in poor executive retention rates is the perceived lack of development opportunities for junior-level executives.[10, 11] Do the executives in your organization feel that the company offers them viable promotional and development paths? What development opportunities would be welcomed by them? Where do they feel the energy and challenge is located in the organization? With what projects would they eventually like to be associated? Have their managers worked with HR to put together a solid development plan?

Power Sharing. The AESC study referenced earlier in this chapter defines power sharing as either: "(1) involvement in major corporate decision making, or (2) autonomy—significant amounts of independence and authority within one's sphere."[12]

According to the 300 corporate leaders who responded to this study, "more than anything else, today's corporate leaders believe that some sort of power sharing is the most effective way to keep valued executives from leaving a corporation."[13] Surprisingly, this factor was rated even higher than compensation as being a key retention factor.

Incentives. The right compensation package can play a key factor in your overall retention strategy. Do your leaders feel that they are being compensated well in relation to their counterparts within the industry? Is your company's incentive compensation process viewed as strongly tied to performance results? Do you have in place incentives specifically designed to retain top performers?

The next step is to develop action plans for increasing the HIPOs' job satisfaction and potential. For an executive whose primary work satisfaction issue is lack of development opportunities, the related action plans might involve

- Participation in a high-potential development program
- Participation in an exclusive executive development program
- Targeted long-term development assignments such as job rotation
- Work sabbaticals to pursue academic studies

For an executive whose primary work satisfaction issue involves difficulty in balancing work and personal life, the associated action plan might include

- Looking for creative options, such as videoconferencing, to limit travel
- Adoption of a flexible work week
- A partial telecommuting arrangement

In many cases, crafting a creative retention plan requires a moderate amount of organizational flexibility along with some out-of-the-box thinking. An example is Santa Clara–based California Eastern Laboratories (CEL), a company that specializes in wireless microwave technology. Despite aggressive recruiting efforts by competitors for CEL's engineers, the company boasts an annual turnover rate of only 10 percent. To achieve this retention rate, CEL provided both a solid employee stock ownership plan and a flexible work schedule. Employees have the option of working eighty hours over nine days, instead of ten, allowing many of them to spend another day at home with their families, while decreasing the aggravation caused by daily commuting. In addition, some managers are provided with laptops and in-home installations of ISDN lines to ease the process of telecommuting.[14] The point is to explore creative options that communicate your organization's willingness to look for innovative options for meeting executives' career and lifestyle needs.

STEP 3: MONITOR THE ACTIVITIES OF INTRUDERS

It is interesting that most companies pride themselves on knowing how to use competitive intelligence to track and anticipate competitors' moves in the marketplace, yet do an abysmal job of applying these same research data to their own vulnerability to losing exemplary executives to those very competitors. In Chapter 13, I pointed out some of the techniques you could use to identify emerging leaders within your competitors' companies. It should come as no surprise that your competitors are probably using these same tactics on you. So what can you do to combat this type of attack? Here are a few suggestions.

- Track defection patterns, noting where departing executives go, and which competitors they sign with.

- Talk to your staff. They probably keep in touch with their peers who have left your company. Openly share your interest in learning about competitors' incentives or perks that may be contributing to these defections.

- Look for areas in need of building new leadership and technical competencies as a prelude to entering new markets. Your competitors will sometimes provide leads on leadership areas that are targeted for raiding through information they share at college recruiting fairs, in management speeches, or in conversations with vendors, outside consultants, and/or trade associations.

STEP 4: EXPLORE OPTIONS FOR SECURING RETENTION

Once you have isolated the work factors that appear to be most highly correlated with retention and turnover, the next thing to do is to systematically set out to change them. This may require adopting different strategies for different retention target groups.

For Roger Marach, CFO of Speedfam International, this means providing employees with attractive financial incentives. Marach states that, "We offer attractive stock options, but to exercise them all, you have to have been here five years. As for our pay scheme, we want to be in the 50th percentile for base salary, but 75th for total compensation, exclusive of options."[15] Speedfam's strategy seems to be working, as its annual employee turnover rate is only 2 percent.[16]

For New York–based professional services firm Ernst & Young LLP, this meant taking steps to retain women in all levels of the company. One of the bottom-line business drivers for reducing the higher turnover rate among women was increased customer dissatisfaction, as clients stressed the importance of establishing continuity of service.[17] To counteract this problem, Ernst & Young has undertaken several change initiatives, including

- Providing flexible work arrangements to everyone in the company
- Providing employees with a database listing other employees who have successfully implemented different types of flexible work arrangements, so that interested individuals can identify success models for the use of flexible work arrangements
- Providing, as part of the database, a ten-step road map detailing how to apply for a flexible work arrangement process
- Establishing an annual award that is presented to the employee who has contributed the most to the development of women at their company[18]

THE INCENTIVE QUESTION

We are rapidly finding ourselves drawn into a talent war that is greatly inflating the cost of attracting and holding top-level executives. In part this is showing up in the rampant inflation of CEOs' and other senior executives' salaries. Another emerging trend is the growing use of *retention bonuses,* or *completion bonuses,* to secure executive retention during times of transition, such as mergers and acquisitions. A retention bonus is always contingent upon an executive's commitment to remain in position for a predesignated period of time, although companies vary regarding whether such bonuses are tied to explicit performance targets. It is estimated by some compensation experts that during a major corporate reshuffling, 10 to 20 percent of corporate staff may be given retention bonuses.[19] According to Hay Consulting Group, retention bonuses typically average twelve to eighteen months' salary for a senior executive and twelve to twenty-four months' salary for a CEO.[20]

Perhaps the most pervasive compensation trend we are seeing is the growing corporate reliance on the use of stock options as a retention tool—for all levels of the organization. A 1998 Robert Half International survey of 150 executives within the largest 1,000 U.S. corporations found that 37 percent of respondents rated stock options as very important "in attracting and retaining American workers at all levels of a company." By comparison, a similar survey conducted in 1991 found that only 23 percent of respondents had rated stock options as being very important.[21] As we move up the corporate ladder to the CEO, options play an even more critical role in retention strategies. According to executive recruiter consultant Pearl Meyer & Partners, stock options now make up 54 percent of CEO pay, with average grants worth about $5 million.[22]

The problem, of course, is that the value of stock options is a function not only of corporate performance but also of wide swings in the stock market. The bull market we've experienced over the last few years has allowed even many ineffective executives to passively watch their boats rise with the economic tide. Similarly, in a sudden downturn, options quickly lose their value as a retention incentive.

To get around this problem, many companies have implemented the practice of repricing options. In this approach, the value of options is recomputed at a price that is lower than their current stock value—and one that's more attractive to the holders of these options. Consider the case of Mirage Resorts, which, when faced with a strong downturn in its stock in late 1998, subsequently granted its CEO and seven other executives a significant repricing of their options from previous levels. Four months later Mirage's rival, Circus Circus, followed suit with a repricing agreement for six of its senior managers.[23] While there are no available studies on the number of companies that have repriced options, some compensation analysts place that figure at 10 percent of publicly held companies.[24]

There is questionable support for the belief that the repricing of options strengthens their effectiveness as a retention tool. In addition, repricing could actually increase turnover if executives were to decide to execute their options and leave. To avoid this problem, San Francisco–based compensation consultants WestWard Pay Strategies recommend that companies require a "blackout period" before repriced options can be exercised.[25] A second problem with repricing is that it tends to be viewed as an inequitable process, with shareholders and lower-level executive options holders taking the brunt of stock downturns, while senior-level executives are pulled out of the pain zone. Perhaps the most serious argument for not using repricing is that it diminishes the effectiveness of using options as a method for rewarding executives and CEOs for superior corporate performance. After all, if a CEO or executive officer's stock option package retains or increases value despite poor corporate performance, where is the incentive for building shareholder value?

To address these shortcomings, many companies are implementing the following remedial strategies.

Mandatory Stock Ownership. Many organizations now require their CEOs and senior-level executives to own stock, based on the rationale that even if options are repriced CEOs stand to lose a lot if they allow the value of their stock portfolios to decline. A growing trend appears to be to tie the level of required stock ownership to the level of stock options that an executive is awarded. A recent *Business Week* article references a study by KPMG Peat Marwick, in which "53 percent of large-cap companies have adopted formal CEO guidelines, with the median target holdings equal to four times salary."[26]

Premium-Priced Options. These plans award stock options at a fixed price, which is frequently 25 to 100 percent above the current market price, under the expectation that these options stand to gain a high degree of value given moderate, steady increases (2 to 7 percent) in the company's stock value over a ten-year period.[27] The good news with premium-priced options is that they are at least somewhat linked to growth in stock value. The bad news is that they don't evaluate corporate performance in terms of competitors' performance.[28] Once again, when the tide rises, all boats are lifted.

Indexed Stock Option Grants. By contrast, the value of indexed options is made contingent upon a company's ability to outperform selected competitors, or the overall market. It is quite possible that indexed options may play a more predominant role in executive compensation in the years ahead. According to the same *Business Week* article, "on March 31 [1998] the Council of Institutional Investors, a group representing over 100 pension funds with assets totaling over 1 trillion dollars, called for companies to 'index' option grants."[29]

Deferred Non-Stock Compensation Plans. Another approach being employed by some companies is to attempt to avoid altogether some of the drawbacks associated with stock options, by designing non-stock–based deferred compensation plans. One such alternative is the LeaderShare™ program created by Kansas City, Missouri–based compensation and change consultant Thomas McCoy. Unlike stock options, the value of which fluctuates as a function of both company performance and market shifts, LeaderShare is based on the idea of awarding executives *deferred compensation units,* which can grow in value if the executive and the company meet agreed-upon performance objectives, regardless of the company's changing market value.[30] According to McCoy, this is how the program works:

> Cash equivalents called *deferred compensation units* (DCUs) are awarded for short-term (annual) performance. The value of these cash equivalents can appreciate based on the increase in the long-term value of the organization. This creates a dynamic tension between achieving short-term results and long-term outcomes—no short-term results, no DCUs to appreciate. Make decisions that sacrifice long-term value for short-term gains, and the DCUs you receive fail to appreciate. [The LeaderShare plan] represents an emerging trend to link long-term, deferred compensation to the profitable growth of the organization rather than to stock value. The plan design represents a fundamental assumption that it is the executive's responsibility to add value to the company and, in doing so, create real, long-term value to the stockholders and all stakeholders.

Another additional advantage of a plan such as LeaderShare is that it can be used by privately held companies, which lack the use of stock options as an executive incentive.[31]

CASE IN POINT: ERNST & YOUNG
Deborah K. Holmes, Director of Office of Retention

One company that has done an excellent job of integrating the dual objectives of increasing executive retention and supporting corporate diversity goals is Ernst & Young. While Ernst & Young has been active on a number of innovative fronts in the fields of executive development, diversity, and retention, perhaps its most notable achievements are in the area of adopting programs targeted toward the retention of women professionals, which includes the following initiatives:

• The Women's Plan (Partners Leadership Alliance & Network), which each year matches twenty-five promising female partners who are identified by E&Y's management committee to both a committee member mentor and an external coach.

• A computerized database, through which both men and women employees are able to explore career options that support flexible work arrangements (FWAs). Employees can access the Lotus Notes network on their laptops and receive candid descriptions of over 500 E&Y professionals who are currently participating in flexible work hours or other flex time arrangements such as telecommuting or part-time employment. The database also serves as a contact list, through which employees can find out the pros and cons of becoming involved in a flexible work hours arrangement from employees who are already making use of such arrangements. Moreover, the database helps to overcome the potential fear factor sometimes associated with requesting flextime arrangements, by providing numerous success stories that outline the successful implementation of flextime arrangements.

- The annual Ernst & Young Women's Leadership Conference, which provides a forum in which the company's top women executives can discuss issues pertaining to work performance and career development, and learn from the experiences of women who hold senior-level positions in the company.

A central figure in all of these successes has been Deborah K. Holmes, National Director of Ernst & Young's Office for Retention. According to Holmes, three major business drivers have been responsible for getting E&Y more strongly focused on the areas of diversity and retention.

> The clearest driver was that for the past fifteen years Ernst & Young had been recruiting about 50 percent women, but fewer than 10 percent of our partners were women. This suggested to us that we had a great opportunity to do a better job in the retention of women. The second factor involved a change in our recruiting model. Traditionally we had recruited our consultants directly off campus, with the result that we experienced a heavy loss as people attempted to squeeze through the funnel and move up the ladder. Over time, we've seen that our clients have increasingly demanded more experienced people and greater consistency in the management of projects—they didn't want to continually see new faces coming through the door. Again, this emphasizes the need for better retention. The third factor was that we've become a much more global firm, requiring people who can function within a variety of work climates. Together, these three factors pointed to the need for having a different business model—one geared toward building a more experienced staff, with much greater retention.

Holmes explains that before launching her diversity and retention initiatives she took several steps to obtain senior management and employee buy-in.

> When I joined E&Y I knew that we needed to break out into different directions and I had an idea of what we needed to do, but I didn't want to force these initiatives on others in the company. One of the conditions of my employment was that I would have the latitude to try some programs out on a relatively small scale. So, I launched five prototypes in our business, each of which focused on an initiative

that dealt with a different issue related to retention. Each prototype involved a cross-functional, multilevel steering committee (both men and women were involved) that then formed subteams to implement each initiative. Four of these prototypes were undertaken within our Tax and Assurance Advisory Business Services Group (AABS), and one within our Consulting group. We have eighty-seven offices, and each corporate office has a lot of freedom to experiment with programs such as these.

As examples of these prototypes, Holmes cites E&Y's *external networking* prototype, which is designed to provide female employees with networking opportunities outside of their organization.

There is ample evidence to suggest that Ernst & Young has developed a very successful corporate model for enhancing both retention and employees' quality of work. In the company's largest business unit, AABS, where four of five retention prototypes have been implemented, women's turnover at the senior management level is down more than 7 percent. Moreover, according to Holmes, two-thirds of the 550 participants in the flexible work arrangements program indicated that, had these arrangements not been available, they would have either not joined or (for those already on board) not remained with the company. By reducing turnover, which costs 150 percent of an employee's salary, E&Y has realized significant gains, amounting to over $9.3 million in savings to the company over a two-year period. Ernst & Young's innovative policies and programs directed toward diversity and retention were one of the reasons why E&Y made the top 100 list for both *Working Mother* magazine's "best companies for working mothers" (1998) and *Fortune* magazine's "best companies to work for in America" (1999).

Holmes attributes the success of her company's retention programs to several factors. As she explains it:

> The most important factor has been that we have addressed a business issue that everyone in our field feels strongly about in his or her gut. Retention is a major business challenge today, and everyone at · Ernst & Young knows that keeping the best people is critical to our success. I also feel that the support of our very popular chairman has been a big factor. The approach of relying on line people to develop the solutions has also been critical in obtaining buy-in from our employees and managers. Finally, I really think that the people at Ernst & Young are extraordinarily smart and nice, and I think that this has made an incredible difference in obtaining strong support for these programs.[32]

- Companies usually fall short when it comes to putting in place a solid retention strategy for their executives.

- Companies willing to take steps to retain executives are able to keep at bay those competitors who are always on the lookout for exceptional talent.

- Steps for retaining star performers include: (1) performing a vulnerability assessment to determine which leadership segments are most susceptible to high levels of voluntary turnover, (2) taking steps to reduce your risk level for loosing star performers by eliminating the most obvious job dissatisfiers, (3) monitoring the activities of intruders, including defection rates and intrusive incursions into your leadership group, and (4) exploring options for securing retention, including accommodations to executives' lifestyle needs and competitive incentive plans.

- A vulnerability assessment is an evaluation of where and how your company is most vulnerable to the loss of good talent, and those factors that are responsible for these losses.

- Without a vulnerability assessment, we must rely on incomplete data, in the form of standard exit interviews, aggregate (unsorted) data, and the lack of sufficient longitudinal data to anticipate emerging turnover trends.

- Three methods for performing a vulnerability analysis include: (1) using a stratification analysis to identify the grade levels and functions in which you are experiencing exceptionally high rates of job loss, (2) using a trend analysis to explore patterns of vulnerability as a function of job tenure and/or length of employment, and (3) performing a retrospective review of background data that appear to be correlated with retention or job loss.

- The reasons standard interviews are ineffective include the facts that HR managers are sometimes uncomfortable probing for the underlying reasons for voluntary termination, that little training is provided to HR professionals who conduct these interviews, and that departing executives are often unwilling to expose difficulties or concerns that may present them in a bad light to headhunters and hiring managers.

- The way to avoid these difficulties is through the use of deferred exit interviews, which are often performed by independent third-party interviewers several weeks after an executive has left the company.

- The five key dimensions of job satisfaction that can influence retention rates are the degree of work challenge provided to executives, the availability of competent mentors, the use of substantive development opportunities, the use of power sharing, and the availability of competitive financial incentives.

- It is important to monitor the activities of intruders—those companies that would enjoy having access to your executive talent pool. To do this, consider tracking defection patterns, talking candidly to your staff about work factors that may be fueling job dissatisfaction, and looking for competitors who tip their hand through information they share about marketing and staffing strategies at college recruiting fairs, in management speeches, or in conversations with vendors.

- The competitive market for executive talent is showing up in much larger sign-on packages and the growing use of retention bonuses and stock options at lower levels in the organization.

- One difficulty in the use of stock options is that the value of options can rise or fall as a function of market growth or decline, somewhat independent of a company's financial performance.

- The increasingly common practice of repricing options creates several problems, including detaching executive job performance from incentive structures and creating a strong perception of inequity between top executives and stockholders and lower-level employees.

- To circumvent these problems, some companies are beginning to experiment with deferred compensation incentive programs that are not tied to a company's stock value.

ENDNOTES

CHAPTER 1

1. Kadlec, Daniel. "Betting on a CEO." *Time* (Nov. 16, 1998): 131.

2. Scism, Leslie, and Patrick McGeehan. "A Resignation at Citigroup Adds to Doubts." *Wall Street Journal* (Nov. 3, 1998): C1.

3. Kadlec, "Betting on a CEO."

4. Davidson, Paul. "Borland Says Microsoft Raided: Lawsuit Charges That by Hiring Key Employees, Giant Undermines Rival." *USA Today* (May 8, 1997): 06B.

5. "Borland Sues Microsoft, Alleging Raid on Top Ranks." *Financial Post Daily* (May 8, 1997): 7.

6. "Wal-Mart Sues On-Line Bookseller." *Washington Post* (Oct. 17, 1998): G3.

7. Wysocki, Bernard, Jr. "Why an Acquisition: Often It's the People." *Wall Street Journal* (Oct. 6, 1997): A1.

8. Ibid.

9. Byrne, John A. "The Corporation of the Future: Cisco Is a Good Model. It Reads the Market Well, Responds Quickly, and It Knows How to Harness High Tech." *Business Week* (Aug. 31, 1998): 102.

10. Henry, Shannon. "Adding Up AppNet Building by Acquisition, Ken Bajaj's E-Commerce Roll-Up Looks to a 1999 IPO." *Washington Post* (Nov. 9, 1998): 5–6.

11. Clark, Don. "Scient Ology: Web Consultant Lands Talent, Dollars." *Wall Street Journal* (Oct. 29, 1998): B6.

12. Chambers, Elizabeth G., Mark Foulon, Helen Handfield-Jones, Steven M. Hankin, and Edward G. Michaels III. "The War for Talent." *McKinsey Quarterly*, no. 3 (1998): 44–57.

13. Latour, Almar. "The Hunt Is On." *Wall Street Journal, Europe* (Jan. 27, 1997): 14.

14. Ibid.

15. Personal interview with Arnoud De Meyer, Associate Dean, Executive Education, INSEAD (June 2, 1999).

16. Bolt, James F. "Tailor Executive Development to Strategy." *Harvard Business Review* reprint (Nov.–Dec. 1985): 1–10.

17. Ibid.

18. Ibid., 5.

CHAPTER 2

1. "Between a Dream and a Nightmare: On the Integration of the Human Resource Management and Strategic Business Planning Processes." *Human Resource Management* 24, no. 4 (1985): 429.

2. Pickering, John W., and Robert E. Matson. "Why Executive Development Programs (Alone) Won't Work." *Training & Development* (May 1992): 91–85.

3. Chambers, Elizabeth G., Mark Foulon, Helen Handfield-Jones, Steven M. Hankin, and Edward G. Michaels III, "The War for Talent." *McKinsey Quarterly,* no. 3 (1998): 44–57.

4. Ulrich, Dave. *Human Resource Champions.* Boston: Harvard Business School Press, 1997.

5. Personal interview with Al Vicere (May 29, 1999).

6. Ibid.

7. See Brady, G. F., and D. L. Helmich. *Executive Succession.* Paramus, N.J.: Prentice Hall, 1984.

8. Helmich, D. L. "Organizational Growth and Succession Patterns." *Academy of Management Journal,* no. 17 (1974): 771–775.

9. Pfeffer, J. *Power in Organizations.* Marshfield, Mass.: Pitman, 1981.

10. Gupta, A. K. "Executive Selection: A Strategic Perspective." *Human Resource Planning* 15, no. 1 (1992): 47–61.

11. Lubove, Seth. "The Odd Couple." *Forbes* (Sept. 7, 1998): 52–53.

12. Rosenbush, Steve. "AT&T Boss Cables the Future." *USA Today* (Nov. 2, 1998): B1.

13. Helyar, John, and Joann S. Lublin. "More U.S. Firms Are Choosing Portable CEOs." *Wall Street Journal, Asia* (Jan. 27, 1998): 8.

14. Ibid.

15. *Executive Advantage.* New York: Association of Executive Search Consultants, July 1998: 29.

16. Byrne, John A. "The Corporation of the Future: Cisco Is a Good Model. It Reads the Market Well, Responds Quickly, and It Knows How to Harness High Tech." *Business Week* (Aug. 31, 1998): 102.

17. Smart, Bradford D., and Geoffrey H. Smart. "Topgrading the Organization." *Directors & Boards* (Mar. 22, 1997): 22.

18. Pearson, Andrall E. "Muscle-Build the Organization." *Harvard Business Review* reprint #87408 (July–Aug. 1987).

CHAPTER 3

1. Personal interview with Al Vicere (May 29, 1999).

2. Ulrich, Dave. *Human Resource Champions,* 59–60. Boston: Harvard Business School Press, 1997.

3. Ibid., 60.

4. Ibid., 60.

5. Ashley, William C., and James L. Morrison. *Anticipatory Management: 10 Power Tools for Achieving Excellence into the 21st Century.* Leesburg, Va.: Issue Action Publications, 1995.

6. Albrecht, Karl. *The Northbound Train.* New York: AMACOM, 1994.

7. Schwartz, Peter. *The Art of the Long View.* New York: Doubleday Currency, 1991.

8. Golden, Eve. "Nothing Succeeds Like Succession." *Across the Board* (June 1, 1998): 36–41.

CHAPTER 4

1. Chambers, Elizabeth G., Mark Foulon, Helen Handfield-Jones, Steven M. Hankin, and Edward G. Michaels III. "The War for Talent." *McKinsey Quarterly,* no. 3 (1998): 44–57.

2. The Advisory Board Company. *Forced Outside: Leadership Talent Sourcing and Retention,* 12. Washington, D.C.: Corporate Leadership Council, 1998.

3. Ibid.

4. Carroll, Anna, and McCrackin, Judith. "The Competent Use of Competency-Based Strategies for Selection & Development." *Performance Improvement Quarterly* 11, no. 3 (1991): 45–63.

5. Mirabile, Richard J. "Everything You Wanted to Know About Competency Modeling." *Training & Development* (Aug. 1997): 73–77.

6. Lombardo, Michael M., and Robert W. Eichinger. *For Your Improvement: A Development & Coaching Guide.* Lombardo and Eichinger (1996): Introduction.

7. Ibid.

8. Smith, Martin, E. "The Search for Executive Skills." *Training & Development* (Sept. 1992): 88–95.

9. Chowanec, Gregory, and Charles Newstrom. "The Strategic Management of International Human Resources." *RHR International, Business Quarterly* 56, no. 1 (1991): 65–70.

10. Quelch, John A., and Helen Bloom. "Ten Steps to a Global Human Resource Strategy." *Strategy & Business,* no. 14 (1st Quarter 1999): 18–29.

11. Patrick, Joseph A., and Lisa Russell-Robles. "Challenges in the Education of the Contemporary U.S. International Manager." *International Executive* (May–June 1992): 251–261.

12. Personal interview with Kay Lillig Cotter, Ph.D., Director of Consulting for Measurement Services, Wilson Learning Corporation (Feb. 3, 1999).

13. Marquardt, Michael J. *The Global Advantage: How World-Class Organizations Improve Performance Through Globalization,* 111. Houston, Tex.: Gulf Publishing, 1999.

14. Woodall, Jean, and Dianna Winstanley. *Management Development: Strategy and Practice,* 249. Malden, Mass.: Blackwell Business, 1998.

15. Patrick and Russell-Robles, "Challenges in the Education of the Contemporary International Manager."

16. Ibid.

17. Geber, Beverly. "The Care and Breeding of Global Managers." *Training Magazine* (July 1992): 32–37.

18. Personal interview with Samir Gupte, Senior Director of Human Resources, Choice Hotels International (Mar. 20, 1999).

19. McCall, Morgan W. *High Flyers: Developing the Next Generation of Leaders,* 127. Boston: Harvard Business School Press, 1998.

20. Lobel, S. A. "Global Leadership Competencies: Managing to a Different Drumbeat." *Human Resource Management* 29 (1991): 39–47.

21. Black, J. S., M. Mendenhall, and G. Obbou. "Toward a Comprehensive Model of International Adjustment: An Integration of Multiple Theoretical Perspectives." *Academy of Management Review* 16 (1991): 291–317.

22. Marquardt, *The Global Advantage,* 90–91.

23. Personal interview with Chuck Bolton, Vice President of International Human Resources, Boston Scientific Corporation (Feb. 10, 1999).

CHAPTER 5

1. Bracken, David W. "Straight Talk About Multi-Rater Feedback." *Training & Development* (Sept. 1994): 44–51.

2. Craig T. Chappelow. "360-Degree Feedback." In *The Center for Creative Leadership Handbook of Leadership Development,*

29–65. Cynthia McCauley, Russ S. Moxley, and Ellen Van Velsor (eds.). San Francisco: Jossey-Bass, 1998.

3. Bracken, "Straight Talk About Multi-Rater Feedback."

4. Wilson, Jane L. "360 Appraisals." *Training & Development* (June 1997): 44–45.

5. Ibid.

6. Van Velsor, Ellen, Jean Brittain Leslie, and John W. Fleenor. *Choosing 360°: A Guide to Evaluating Multi-Rater Feedback Instruments for Management Development.* Greensboro, N.C.: Center for Creative Leadership, 1997.

7. Turnage, J. J., and P. M. Muchinsky. "A Comparison of the Predictive Validity of Assessment Center Evaluations Versus Traditional Measures in Forecasting Supervisory Job Performance: Interpretive Implications of Criterion Distortion for the Assessment Center." *Journal of Applied Psychology* 69 (1984): 595–602.

8. Personal interview with Kay Lillig Cotter, Ph.D., Director of Consulting for Measurement Services, Wilson Learning Corporation (Feb. 3, 1999).

9. Personal interview with Joe Sefcik, president of Employment Technologies Corporation (Feb. 13, 1999).

10. Ibid.

11. Ibid.

12. Robertons, I., P. Iles, L. Gratton, and D. Sharpley. "The Impact of Personnel Selection and Assessment Methods on Candidates." *Human Relations* 44, no. 9 (1991): 963–981.

13. Gaugler, R. B., D. B. Rosenthal, G. C. Thornton, and C. Bentsons. "Meta-Analysis of Assessment Center Validity." *Journal of Applied Psychology* 72 (1987): 493–511.

14. Personal interview with Kay Lillig Cotter (Feb. 3, 1999).

15. Personal interview with Dan Stolle, director of Tellabs (Feb.15, 1999).

CHAPTER 6

1. Charan, Ram, and Geoffrey Colvin. "Why CEOs Fail." *Fortune* (June 21, 1999): 69–78.

2. The Advisory Board Company. *The Role of 360° Feedback in the Performance Appraisal Process.* Washington, D.C.: Corporate Leadership Council, 1995.

3. Lombardo, Michael M., and Robert W. Eichinger. "High Potentials as High Learners." *Human Resource Management Journal* (Winter 1997).

4. Ibid.

5. McCall, Morgan W. *High Flyers: Developing the Next Generation of Leaders.* Boston: Harvard Business School Press, 1998.

6. Personal interview with Tom Westall, president of Westall & Associates (Apr. 19, 1999).

CHAPTER 7

1. Personal interview with Tom Saporito, senior vice president of RHR International and member of the National Association of Corporate Directors (February 10, 1999).

2. Taft, Bradford H. "Planning and Implementing Successful Workforce Retentions." *The Right Communiqué* 2, no. 3 (3rd Quarter 1998): 4–6.

CHAPTER 8

1. Marquardt, Michael J. *Action Learning in Action,* 64–73. Palo Alto, Calif.: Davies-Black, 1999.

2. Personal interview with Michael J. Marquardt, Ed.D., Professor with George Washington University's Global Human Resources Development (Feb. 12, 1999).

3. Ibid.

4. Schank, Roger. *Virtual Learning: A Revolutionary Approach to Building a Highly Skilled Workforce,* 30–31. New York: McGraw-Hill, 1997.

5. Ibid., 35.

6. Ibid.

7. Personal interviews with George Winnick, managing director; James Allen, director, Client Engagement Group; and Bridget Doyle, Best Practices Consultant for Strategic Management Group, Philadelphia (Feb. 15, 1999).

8. Ibid.

9. Ibid.

10. Ibid.

11. Ibid.

12. Ibid.

13. Ibid.

14. McCauley, Cynthia, Russ S. Moxley, Ellen Van Velsor (eds.). *The Center for Creative Leadership Handbook of Leadership Development,* 321–323. San Francisco: Jossey-Bass, 1998.

15. Liedman, Julie. "Teach Your Leaders Well." *Human Resource Executive* (Oct. 19, 1998): A4.

16. Ibid.

17. Strazewski, Len. "Staying Current Through Consortiums." *Human Resource Executive* (Oct. 19, 1998): A10–A16.

18. Personal interview with Arnoud De Meyer, Associate Dean, Executive Education, INSEAD (June 2, 1999).

19. Ibid.

20. Ibid.

21. Ibid.

22. Ibid.

23. Personal interview with David Butler, Associate Dean, Executive Education, School of Hotel Administration, Cornell University (June 12, 1999).

24. Ibid.

25. Personal interview with Arnoud De Meyer (June 2, 1999).

26. Personal interview with Alison Peirce, Program Director for Wharton Direct (Feb. 5, 1999).

27. Ibid.

28. Ibid.

29. Donoho, Ron. "The New MBA." *Training Magazine* (Oct. 1998): DL4–DL9.

30. Bradshaw, Della. "The Mounties Always Get Their MBAs." *Financial Times* (Feb. 15, 1999): 8.

31. Personal interview with Youssef Bissada, professor of entrepreneurship, INSEAD, and owner of Bissada Management Simulations (June 28, 1999).

32. Ibid.

33. Ibid.

34. Personal interview with Curt Mason, Vice President of Sales and Marketing for Henninger Media Services, Arlington, Va. (Feb. 11, 1999).

35. Ibid.

CHAPTER 9

1. Vicere, Albert A., and Robert M. Fulmer. *Leadership by Design,* 93. Boston: Harvard Business School Press, 1996.

2. Ibid., 83.

3. Personal interview with Bruce Barge, industrial organizational psychologist with Aon Consulting, Chicago (Feb. 10, 1999).

4. Ibid.

5. Ibid.

6. McCall, Morgan W., Mike M. Lombardo, and A. M. Morrison. *The Lessons of Experience: How Successful Executives Develop on the Job.* Lexington, Mass.: Lexington Books, 1988.

7. Personal interview with Arnoud De Meyer, Associate Dean, Executive Education, INSEAD (June 2, 1999).

8. Personal interview with Michael J. Marquardt, Ed.D., professor with George Washington University's Global Human Resources Development (Feb. 12, 1999).

9. Ohlott, Patricia J. "Job Assignments." In *The Center for Creative Leadership Handbook of Leadership Development,* 131–134. Cynthia McCauley, Russ S. Moxley, and Ellen Van Velsor (eds.). San Francisco: Jossey-Bass, 1998.

10. Ibid., 143.

11. McCall, Morgan W. *High Flyers: Developing the Next Generation of Leaders,* 87. Boston: Harvard Business School Press, 1998.

12. Chambers, Elizabeth G., Mark Foulon, Helen Handfield-Jones, Steven M. Hankin, and Edward G. Michaels III. "The War for Talent." *McKinsey Quarterly,* no. 3 (1998): 44–57.

13. Ibid.

14. Himelstein, Linda, and Stephanie Anderson Forest. "Breaking Through." *Business Week* (Feb. 17, 1997): *Business Week* Internet archives http://bwarchive.businessweek.com.

15. Chambers et al., "The War for Talent."

16. See: Lombardo, Michael M., and Cynthia McCauley. *The Dynamics of Management Derailment: Technical Report No. 34.* Greensboro, N.C.: Center for Creative Leadership, 1988; McCall, Morgan W., and Michael M. Lombardo. "What Makes a Top Executive?" *Psychology Today* (Feb. 1983): 26–31; Ramos, John. "Why Executives Derail." *Across the Board* (Nov.–Dec. 1994): 16–22.

17. Van Velsor, Ellen, and Jean Brittian Leslie. "Why Executives Derail: Perspectives Across Time and Cultures." *Academy of Management Executive* 9, no. 4 (Nov. 1995): 62–72.

18. McCall, *High Flyers,* 35–52.

19. Ibid., 137.

20. Personal interview with Craig Chappelow, product manager for the Center for Creative Leadership, Greensboro, N.C. (Feb. 7, 1999).

21. Ibid.

22. Ibid.

23. Van Velsor and Leslie, "Why Executives Derail."

24. Ibid.

25. Ibid.

26. Spreitzer, Gretchen M., Morgan W. McCall, and Joan D. Mahoney. "Early Identification of International Executive Potential." *Journal of Applied Psychology* 82, no. 1 (1997): 6–29.

27. Ibid.

28. McCall, *High Flyers*, 47.

29. Kaplan, Robert E., Wilfred H. Drath, and Joan R. Kofodimos. *High Hurdles: The Challenge of Executive Self-Development: Technical Report No. 25*. Greensboro, N.C.: Center for Creative Leadership, 1985.

30. Personal interview with Sara King, Program Director for the Center for Creative Leadership, Greensboro, N.C. (Feb. 25, 1999).

31. Ibid.

32. *Chief Executives in the New Europe: Challenges, Shortages, and an Agenda for Change*, 4–5. New York: Association of Executive Search Consultants, 1998.

33. Ibid.

34. Personal interview with James Pulcrano, Dean of Executive Education for IMD, Lausanne, Switzerland (June 7, 1999).

35. Personal interview with Arnoud De Meyer (June 2, 1999).

36. Personal interview with Sara King (Feb. 25, 1999).

37. Interview with Linda Krom, Director of Executive Development for GTE Services Corporation (Feb. 1999).

CHAPTER 10

1. Saratoga Institute. *Leadership Development: Programs and Practices, Future Directions, Examples and Models*. New York: AMACOM, 1998.

2. Golden, Eve. "Nothing Succeeds Like Succession." *Across the Board,* Dow Jones Publications Library (June 1998): 36.

3. Ibid.

4. Beeson, John. "Succession Planning: Building the Management Corps." *Business Horizons* 41, no. 5 (Sept.–Oct. 1998): 61–67.

5. Arthur, Jodi Spiegel. "Facts and Figures" (column). *Human Resources Executive* (June 4, 1999): 74.

6. Personal interviews with George Klemp and Bernard Cullen, partners in Cambria Consulting, Boston (Feb. 1, 1999).

7. Liesman, Steve, and Allanna Sullivan. "Tight-Lipped Exxon, Outspoken Mobil Face Major Image, Cultural Differences." *Wall Street Journal* (Dec. 2, 1998): A3.

8. Ibid.

9. Personal interviews with Klemp and Cullen (Feb. 1, 1999).

10. Wood, Robert, and Tim Payne. *Competence-Based Recruitment and Selection,* 101. West Sussex, England: Wiley, 1998.

11. Hoppe, Michael H. "Cross-Cultural Issues in Leadership Development." In *The Center for Creative Leadership Handbook of Leadership Development,* 336–378. Cynthia D. McCauley, Russ S. Moxley, and Ellen Van Velsor (eds.). San Francisco: Jossey-Bass, 1998.

12. Golden, "Nothing Succeeds Like Succession."

13. Personal interview with Bob Schneiders, president of Educational Data Systems, Dearborn, Michigan (Feb. 1999).

14. Ibid.

15. Ibid.

16. Marquardt, Michael J. *The Global Advantage: How World-Class Organizations Improve Performance Through Globalization,* 108. Houston, Tex.: Gulf Publishing, 1999.

17. Quelch, John A., and Helen Bloom. "Ten Steps to a Global Human Resource Strategy." *Strategy & Business,* no. 14 (1st Quarter 1999): 18–29.

18. Ibid.

19. Personal interview with Samir Gupte, Senior Director of Human Resources, Choice Hotels International (Mar. 20, 1999).

20. Rothwell, William. *Effective Succession Planning,* 122. New York: AMACOM, 1994.

21. Himelstein, Linda, and Stephanie Anderson Forest. "Breaking Through." *Business Week* (Feb. 17, 1997): *Business Week* Internet archives http://bwarchive.businessweek.com.

22. Ibid.

23. Ibid.

24. Ibid.

25. Beeson, John. "Succession Planning: Building the Management Corps." *Business Horizons* 41, no. 5 (Sept.–Oct. 1998): 61–67.

26. Ibid.

27. Personal interview with Jim Dagnon, Senior Vice President of People, The Boeing Company (Feb. 1999).

CHAPTER 11

1. Arkin, Anat. "A Suitable Old Boy?" *People Management London* 4, no. 9 (Apr. 30, 1998): 28–30.

2. Smart, Bradford D. *Topgrading: How Leading Companies Win by Hiring, Coaching, and Keeping the Best People*, 46–47. Paramus, N.J.: Prentice Hall, 1999.

3. McShulskis, Elaine. "Executives Optimistic and Flexible." *HRMagazine* (Mar. 1998): 25–26.

4. Ibid.

5. Chambers, Elizabeth G., Mark Foulon, Helen Handfield-Jones, Steven M. Hankin, and Edward G. Michaels III. "The War for Talent." *McKinsey Quarterly*, no. 3 (1998): 44–57.

6. Freiberg, Kevin, and Jackie Freiberg. *Nuts! Southwest Airlines' Crazy Recipe for Business and Personal Success*, 70–71. Austin, Tex.: Bard Press, 1996.

7. Chambers et al., "The War for Talent."

8. Ibid.

9. Spiegel, Jodi. "Options Anyone?" *Human Resource Executive* (Sept. 1998): 72.

10. Ibid.

11. Spiegel, Jodi. "Job Lure." *Human Resource Executive* (Sept. 1998): 72.

12. Personal interview with Peter Felix, president of the Association of Executive Search Consultants (May 31, 1999).

13. Smart, Bradford D., and Geoffrey H. Smart. "Topgrading the Organization." *Directors & Boards* (Mar. 22, 1997): 22.

14. Personal interview with David Lord, president of Executive Search Information Services (Jan. 22, 1999).

15. Chambers et al., "The War for Talent."

16. Reingold, Jennifer, and Nicole Harris. "Headhunters: Casting for a Different Set of Characters." *Business Week* (Dec. 8, 1997): Business Week Internet archives http://bwarchive.businessweek.com.

17. Imperato, Gina. "How to Hire the Next Michael Jordan." *Fast Company* (Dec. 1998): 212. www.fastcompany.com/online/20/jordan.html.

18. Ibid.

19. Ibid.

20. Personal interview with David Lord (Jan. 22, 1999).

21. Useem, Jerry. "For Sale Online: You." *Fortune* (July 5, 1999): 67–78.

22. Ibid.

23. Personal interview with Connie LaDouceur, principal with ExecuQuest, Baltimore, Md. (Jan. 25, 1999).

24. Ibid.

25. Ibid.

26. Ibid.

27. Ibid.

28. Imperato, "How to Hire the Next Michael Jordan."

29. Ibid.

30. International Association of Corporate and Professional Recruitment (IACPR). *13th Annual Membership Survey* (Sept. 1998).

31. McCreary, Chip. "Get the Most out of Search Firms." *Workforce* (Aug. 1997): 28–30.

32. Ibid.

33. Ibid.

34. Ibid.

35. Personal interview with Steve Balough, president of David Powell & Associates, Inc., Woodside, Calif. (Jan. 23, 1999).

36. Personal interview with Peter Felix (May 31, 1999).

37. Personal interview with David Lord (Jan. 22, 1999).

38. Ibid.

39. McIlvaine, Andrew R. "World Premiere." *Human Resource Executive* (Oct. 19, 1998): 1–20.

40. Personal interview with David Lord (Jan. 22, 1999).

41. Personal interview with Peter Felix (May 31, 1999).

42. McCreary, "Get the Most Out of Search Firms."

43. IACPR, *13th Annual Membership Survey.*

44. McCreary, "Get the Most Out of Search Firms."

45. Personal interview with Steve Balough (Jan. 23, 1999).

46. McNatt, Robert (ed.). "Upfront: 'Invasion of the Cyber Headhunters.'" *Business Week* (Feb. 15, 1999): 6.

47. Reingold, Jennifer. "Headhunting 2000: Upstarts, the Net, and Fussier Clients Are Altering the Rules." *Business Week* (Mar. 17, 1999): 74+.

48. Useem, "For Sale Online: You."

49. Reingold, "Headhunting 2000."

50. "Go to the Headhunters." *Kiplinger's Personal Finance Magazine* (Mar. 1999): 70.

51. Personal interview with David Lord (Jan. 22, 1999).

52. Personal interview with Joseph Daniel McCool, editor of *Executive Recruiter News,* a Kennedy Information, LLC, publication (Feb. 12, 1999).

53. Ibid.

54. Marquardt, Michael. *The Global Advantage: How World-Class Organizations Improve Performance Through Globalization,* 97. Houston, Tex.: Gulf Publishing, 1999.

55. Personal interview with Chuck Bolton, Vice President of International Human Resources, Boston Scientific Corporation (Feb. 10, 1999).

56. Ibid.

57. Personal interview with Michael McNeal, Director of Employment for Cisco Systems (Feb. 16, 1999).

58. Ibid.

59. Ibid.

60. Ibid.

61. Ibid.

62. Useem, "For Sale Online: You."

CHAPTER 12

1. Personal interview with Valerie I. Sessa (February 3, 1999). An in-depth review of this research will be found in: Sessa, Valerie I., Jodi Taylor, and Richard Campbell. *Choosing Top-Level Executives: A System for Effective Selection.* San Francisco: Jossey-Bass (forthcoming).

2. Personal interview with Geoffrey H. Smart, author, researcher, and psychologist, in Chicago (Feb. 3, 1999).

3. Personal interviews with George Klemp and Bernard Cullen, partners in Cambria Consulting, Boston (Feb. 1, 1999).

4. Smart, "Topgrading the Organization."

5. Spiegel, Jodi. "Job Lure." *Human Resource Executive* (Sept. 1998): 72.

6. Ibid.

7. Sessa, Valerie I., Robert Kaiser, Jodi K. Taylor, and Richard J. Campbell. *Executive Selection: A Research Report on What Works and What Doesn't Work.* Greensboro, N.C.: Center for Creative Leadership, 1998.

8. Personal Interview with Peter Felix, president of the Association of Executive Search Consultants (May 31, 1999).

9. Chambers, Elizabeth G., Mark Foulon, Helen Handfield-Jones, Steven M. Hankin, and Edward G. Michaels III. "The War for Talent." *McKinsey Quarterly,* no. 3 (1998): 44–57.

10. Personal interview with Steve Balough, president of David Powell & Associates, Inc., Woodside, Calif. (Jan. 23, 1999).

11. Broden, Fredrik. "Hire Great People Fast." *Fast Company* (Aug.–Sept. 1997): 132–135.

12. Ibid.

13. Personal interviews with George Klemp and Bernie Cullen (Feb. 1, 1999).

14. Personal interview with Peter Felix (May 31, 1999).

15. Personal interview with Geoffrey Smart (Feb. 3, 1999).

16. Personal interviews with George Klemp and Bernie Cullen (Feb. 1, 1999).

17. Personal interview with David Sadtler, Fellow with the Ashridge Strategic Management Center, London (May 31, 1999).

18. Ibid.

19. Personal interview with Tom Saporito, senior vice president of RHR International and member of the National Association of Corporate Directors (February 10, 1999).

20. Ibid.

21. Freiberg, Kevin, and Jackie Freiberg, *Nuts! Suthwest Airlines' Crazy Recipe for Business and Personal Success,* 66. Austin, Tex.: Bard Press, 1996.

22. Ibid.

23. Personal interview with Joseph Daniel McCool (Feb. 12, 1999).

24. Ibid.

25. Personal interview with Geoffrey Smart (Feb. 3, 1999).

26. Ibid.

27. Ibid.

28. Personal interviews with George Klemp and Bernie Cullen (Feb. 1, 1999).

29. Personal interview with Valerie I. Sessa (Feb. 3, 1999).

30. Personal interview with Freddy Cabrera, Senior Director of International Human Resources, PepsiCo (May 15, 1999).

CHAPTER 13

1. Personal interview with Valerie I. Sessa (Feb. 3, 1999). An in-depth review of this research will be found in: Sessa, Valerie I., Jodi Taylor, and Richard Campbell. *Choosing Top-Level Executives: A System for Effective Selection.* San Francisco: Jossey-Bass (forthcoming).

2. Korn, Amy Newman. "Gotcha!" *Across the Board* (Sept. 1998): 30.

3. Ibid.

4. Ibid.

5. Smart, Bradford D., and Geoffrey H. Smart. "Topgrading the Organization." *Directors & Boards* (Mar. 22, 1997): 22.

6. Personal interview with Kay Lillig Cotter, Ph.D., Director of Consulting for Measurement Services, Wilson Learning Corporation (Feb. 3, 1999).

7. Ibid.

8. Peak, M. H. "Darned Expensive to Take for Granted." *Management Review* (Jan. 1997): 89.

9. Gates, S. *Managing Expatriates Return: A Research Report.* New York: The Conference Board, 1996.

10. Personal interview with Samir Gupte, Senior Director of Human Resources, Choice Hotels International (Mar. 20, 1999).

CHAPTER 14

1. Chambers, Elizabeth G., Mark Foulon, Helen Handfield-Jones, Steven M. Hankin, and Edward G. Michaels III. "The War for Talent." *McKinsey Quarterly,* no. 3 (1998): 44–57.

2. *Executive Advantage,* Association of Executive Search Consultants (July 1998).

3. Ibid.

4. Goldblat, Jennifer. "Citicorp Suffering Defections from Its Capital Market Staff." *American Banker* (Oct. 10, 1996).

5. For an excellent review of how stratification analysis can help you target in on retention problems, I recommend The Advisory Board Company. *Forced Outside: Leadership Talent Sourcing and Retention.* Washington, D.C.: Corporate Leadership Council, 1998.

6. Pounds, Marcia. "Better Not Dismiss Exit Interviews: Reasons Given for Leaving Can Help Firms Retain Others." *The Record* (May 17, 1999).

7. Chambers et al., "The War for Talent."

8. Personal interview with Bruce Barge, industrial organizational psychologist with Aon Consulting, Chicago (Feb. 10, 1999).

9. Ibid.

10. Retention Management, Saratoga Institute (New York: American Management Association, 1997).

11. *Executive Advantage,* 1998.

12. Ibid.

13. Ibid.

14. Ettore, Barbara. "Keeping the Cream." *HR Focus* 74, no. 5 (May 1997): 1–4.

15. Gray, Carol Lippert. "Holding Your Own." *Financial Executive* (Sept.–Oct. 1998): 14–22.

16. Ibid.

17. Sunoo, Brenda Paik. "Initiatives for Women Boost Retention." *Workforce* (Nov. 1998): 97–100.

18. Ibid.

19. Lawson, Mark. "Firms Pay Up to Keep the Big Guns." *Australian Financial Review* (Apr. 3, 1998): 3.

20. Ibid.

21. Arthur, Jodi Spigel. "Options Anyone?" *Human Resource Executive* (Sept. 1998): 72.

22. Strauss, Gary. "Retaining Skilled Leaders Hinders Tying Pay to Results." *USA Today* (Apr. 22, 1999): B1–2.

23. Ibid.

24. Ibid.

25. Lublin, Joann, and Tamar Hausman. "Repriced Options: The Gift That Retains?" *Wall Street Journal* (Nov. 3, 1998): B20.

26. Reingold, Jennifer, Richard A. Melcher, and Gary McWilliams. "Executive Pay: Stock Options Plus a Bull Market Made a Mockery of Many Attempts to Link Pay to Performance." *Business Week* (Apr. 20, 1998): 2.

27. Rappaport, Alfred. "New Thinking on How to Link Executive Pay with Performance." *Harvard Business Review* (Mar.–Apr. 1999): 91–101.

28. Ibid.

29. Reingold et al., "Executive Pay."

30. Stafford, Diane. "Deferred Compensation Units: A New Lure for Top Executives." *Kansas City Star* (Apr. 18, 1999).

31. Personal interview with Thomas McCoy (May 27, 1999).

32. Personal interview with Deborah Holmes, Director, Office of Retention, Ernst & Young (June 18, 1999).